De-/signing the Urban.

Techno-genesis and the urban image

Delft School of Design Series on Architecture and Urbanism

De-/signing the Urban.

Techno-genesis and the urban image

Editors Patrick Healy and Gerhard Bruyns

With contributions by **Brent Batstra, Henriette Bier and Douglas Spencer, M. Christine Boyer, Gregory Bracken, Gerhard Bruyns, Isabelle Doucet, Arie Graafland, Karsten Harries, Deborah Hauptmann, Patrick Healy, Tahl Kaminer, Viktor Kittlausz, Agustina Martire, Javier Peinado Pontón, Camilo Pinilla, Camila Pinzon Cortes, Stephen Read, Jeroen van Schaick, Lara Schrijver, Ceren Sezer, Qiang Sheng, Heidi Sohn, Łukasz Stanek, Alta Steenkamp, Alexander Vollebregt**

010 Publishers **Rotterdam 2006**

Introduction: Technogenesis and the Inventive City

Patrick Healy

The immediate context of this essay is a series of questions which have come to the fore in different areas of research, many of which have been gathered by Bernard Stiegler in his work on *Technics and Time*, and one of which can be put as follows: what is the direction of research in a time of technological innovation, where the demands of the technological place innovation before invention?[1]

For Stiegler a guiding question is, whether we can predict or orient the evolution of technics, or, stated otherwise: what power do we have over power? One of the specific characteristics of modern technicity is that it opens up a new kind of systemics of the technical. This also shifts the relationship of *episteme* and *techne*, which may also be read as the relation of science, knowledge and image.

The key difficulties with such convergences of science and image can already be found in problems emerging in Renaissance science, where the forerunner of encyclopedism had already been constructed, as has been noted by Frances Yates, in the memory theatre of Giulio Delmino Camillo's *Idea del Teatro*, actually built by Camillo, as a place where all knowledge was to be contained.[2] Camillo's efforts were subject to a stinging attack by Alessandro Citolini in his work *Tipocosmia*, published in Venice, 1561. Citolini raised the question as to how, in a greatly expanded universe, such a collection could be anything other than the repetitive gathering of what already is in the mind?[3]

In a garden near the city of Venice, the setting for the conversations in *Tipocosmia*, several gentlemen begin with an agreed task; they decide in seven days to order the world and put it in a book. This initiates a paratactic orgy, as they have undertaken to list everything. One participant insists that numbers too must be included, and as Hilary Gatti in her work on *Giordano Bruno and Renaissance Science* notes, they end up in self-referentiality, or what is today called a closed loop in which the mind is fed back with things it already knows.[4]

A problem starts when listing numbers, and is further aggravated with a moment of delirious cartography, when they want to list all the place names in the world and the universe. One starts off in alphabetic order, offering a mental scheme at least, but is interrupted and asked to follow the place names in their true order as they are on the map; they agree to this and begin in Piedmont. But with thirty pages of place names they only get as far as Capodistria, at which stage they agree, 'enough', and desist from their toponymic mania.[5]

Another feature of such systematicness is that technics becomes a series of commands, especially within the cybernetic model. If there is a plannifying and programmed character in new technics, how does one account for disequilibrium and risk? Doesn't the means/ends distinction of a technical process expose itself necessarily to risk, since the end of what is made is always open to

1 Bernard Stiegler, **Technics and Time, 1, The Fault of Epimetheus,** translated by Bernard Beardsworth and George Collins (Standford, California: Standford University Press, 1998). The French original was published in 1994.

2 For this see: F. Yates, **The Art of Memory** (Chicago, 1966) pp.135-62.

3 A discussion of this work can be found in L. Bolzoni, **La stanza della memoria: Modelli letterari e iconografici nell etá della stampa** (Turin, 1995) pp. 257-259.

4 Hilary Gatti, **Giordano Bruno and Renaissance Science** (Cornell University Press, paperback 2002) pp. 171-204.

5 Gatti, **op. cit.**, p.182; for details and translation of Citolini at page 310 from **Tipocosmia**.

uses outside the process of making, especially when such technics enter social and cultural systems? What way the anthropological can proceed if the subject is grounded in technology, is the question raised in the work of Leroi-Gourhan.[6] Bernard Stiegler reads the project of Leroi-Gourhan in light of the problem of technogenesis, which is how he understands the necessity of technics qua the science of technical evolution, and maintains that these are the terms in which Marx creates a critique of the traditional point of view on technical evolution:

> A critical history of technology would show how little any of the inventions of the eighteenth century are the work of a single individual. Yet such a book does not exist. Darwin has directed attention to the history of natural technology, that is the formation of the organs of plants and animals which serve as the instruments of production for sustaining their life. Does not the history of the productive organs of man in society deserve equal attention ... Technology reveals the active relation of man to nature, the direct process of the production of his life, and thereby it also lays bare the process of the production of the social relations of his life, and of the mental conceptions that flow from these relations.[7]

The manner in which Leroi-Gourhan universalises technics, and then situates it as moments of ethnic concretisation, offers a theory of material culture that adverts to a universalist enterprise with concomitant local manifestation. Research in the technical sciences provides a new basis for global coherence, and also steers the direction of research. This can be elaborated in more detail. It raises the thorny problem of how a history of techniques can be included in a general history. As will be argued later, Heidegger is set against such an historical and anthropological project. In its simplest outline it can be seen at work in the notion of a technical system that is required in which there is a stabilisation of the technical concretised by a particular technology.

For the study of the urban this is best exemplified in the work of Walter Benjamin in the Arcades Project, where again Benjamin uses the ordering of the alphabet to bring the fragments of his research into a kaleidoscopic mirroring of the process of innovation and technological change which is literally incarnated in his object of study, namely the formation of arcades and the display of luxury goods, which result from industrial commodification. It is the fetish character of the commodity to which Benjamin attributes a magico-religious excess. Various technical inventions of modes of visualisation, panoramas, daguerreotypes, photography, shifts in the understanding of the commodity as having its value in display, the innovation of glass and iron, all culminate in a projective phantasmagoria in which capital materialises and creates the new physiognomy of the city. Benjamin tracks how the technical, social and cultural systems come together, and what the nature of their projective contingency entails.[8]

Benjamin's study however did not raise the question of what the limits of the system would be; in some sense his entire enterprise also became an explanatory discourse on the relation of cinema and space, which gave his own period in which he was writing the work, from the late 1920's to the beginning of the 40's, its surreal character. His research is a montage, and itself a filmic re-constellation of all the various processes of the interdependence of technical means of reproduction and social and cultural configurations. It is perhaps this interdependence which marked the following period of planetary projection, not as a phantasmagoria, but as instrumental rationality. One can speak of an epoch as being governed by a hegemonic phantasm which may even include simple conceptual items.

What needed elaboration is the way in which the logic of the system could be decided, or what is the logic of innovation. In Benjamin that point is raised in his consideration of fashion, where time itself is challenged by motion, and the instant of fashion dooms it to immediate disappearance. Mobility of techniques can overcome the time of human existence, and leave only the flickering of images as substance. The extent of transfers through different but interrelated systems, economy, technics, social and cultural, remains mysterious.

It can even be that, as Marx maintained, there is no inventor; what results from the advent of luxury commodities in the market as a result of industrial means of production, bypasses empirical analysis. It is in a sense how the abstraction of commodification concretises itself as essence and phenomenon. Francesco Coniglione has understood this well, that theoretical science needs to abandon empirical data, from which it begins, in order to build ideal models for physical systems free from disturbing particulars. Otherwise there could be no grasping of essential structure. This is a critical difference between descriptive and theoretical science: it is only through scientific theory that the 'truth' of what is happening is grasped. Coniglione remarks that Marx was to borrow this concept of theoretical science and tried to apply it to his construction of economic science, in explicit reaction to empiricism. It is the process of idealisation which characterises the way fundamental concepts transcend actual data and the image of nature. It is this which also gives the theoretical character to modern science, and is also implicit in its use of apparatuses. Cassirer had argued persuasively that the fundamental theoretical laws of physics throughout speak of cases that are never given in experience nor can be given in it; for in the formula of the law the real object of perception is replaced by its ideal limit. The insight gained through them never issues from consideration of the real alone, but from the possible conditions and circumstances; it includes not only the actual, but also the 'virtual'.

Cassirer has already identified for modern science that what is at issue for physical concepts is not their ability to reflect but their logical value, in obeying the general requirements of scientific knowledge, that is the a priori need for clarity, non-contradiction and lack of ambiguity. Coniglione suggests that it is with Cassirer this becomes an awareness of the multiplicity of conceptual images, in individual sciences and different sciences, which leads to problems of

6 Two of the main works of André Leroi-Gourhan are considered, his **L'homme et matière** (Paris: Albin Michel, 1943); and his work of 1945, **Milieu et techniques** (Paris: Albin Michel, 1945). Leroi-Gourhan's **Gesture and Speech** is available from Cambridge, Mass, MIT Press, 1993.

7 This citation can be found in Karl Marx, **Capital** (London: Penguin, 1976), 493, n4; quoted by Stiegler in **Technics and Time**, p.26.

8 Walter Benjamin, **The Arcades Project** (Harvard: Belknap Press, 2000), **passim**.

incommensurability, variance in notions of meaning, the incompleteness of verification, the important function of falsification, and the influence of the philosophical perspective in deciding between empirical theories.[9]

How the conjugation of economy and science takes place as investment or speculation in the creation of the technosciences, may depend more on this theoretical feature of abstraction, than on any specific program. The effort to make these concurrent for example in what has been referred to as 'a knowledge economy' then involves state politics. Innovation requires necessarily that projects are in development, because as Stiegler points out, these cascading convergences are needed to stabilise the system, and no one of them should be viewed in terms of a priority. Thus aesthetic values can motor the economy, the requirements of science, the availability of capital for new kinds of work, or indeed, speculation. There is no space for economic and scientific progress to function separately. Inter-disciplinarity recognises the fact of these criss-crossed domains, which is then the shape of research and development. Gille concludes by stating: 'in all domains, in the economic as well as the military domains, the future must be organised'.[10]

It is in this relation to the future that the studies of Gille and Leroi-Gourhan focus on technical ensembles in respect to anthropogenesis linking it directly to technogenesis, and perforce an evolutionary schema is treated as open-ended and indeterminate. Leroi-Gourhan speaks of a technical universality; in one sense he will perform what was accomplished in classificatory zoology with the *phylum* in the 18th century, except that in the ethnic relation of the living and the non-living the lines of material possibility in the external milieu, he reduces the multiplicity to where the paths of invention narrow. Technicity, as Stiegler argues, is emblazoned in this project into a zootechnological determinism, in that the lines are not free variables. One can follow a logic of progression: the technological lines, or lineages, are analogous to Darwin's zoological lineages, where evolution occurs. This however contains the caveat that the technical object, inert matter, is viewed zoologically and as a relation of human to milieu. However, matter is not passive. The organisation of matter cannot be simply its form:

> [T]he tendency does not simply derive from an organizing force -the human-, it does not belong to a forming intention that would precede the frequentation of matter, and it does not come under the sway of some wilful mastery: the tendency operates down through time, by selecting forms in a relation of the human living being to the matter it organizes and by which it organizes itself, where none of the terms of the relation hold the secret over the other.[11]

A major objection is raised within the work of Leroi-Gourhan itself; there is something enigmatic about the human, capable of being non-human, also depending on the non-living through the prosthetic, of tool or technics, which takes place in constant crossing-over within groups and among cultures and peoples. Within a long cluster of historical and other analyses the concept of tendency is used by Leroi-Gourhan to show how the interior milieu gains a foothold in the external milieu, which is how morphogenesis is explained, and which also shows that the tendencies once established as materialisation cease to be tendencies.

What is at work is the constant selection of the best possible solutions, and this is the notion of technical convergence: features of material culture can be explained then as normal, in the way one speaks of it being normal for gastropods to have twisting shells. Not only is there the gaining of a foothold in the external milieu, but this process of tendency and convergence as solution, or problem solving, brings technical knowledge into a strong evolutionary understanding.

The actual tendencies are continuous and for the most part gradual. With the acceleration and speed of technics, this limiting and balancing of milieu may no longer be possible. It would be necessary to argue that the theory of evolution itself evolves, and what the human will be cannot be cast in terms of continuous species distinction and historical precedent. What would occur is a leap in which the compromise of the double milieu is anticipated and directed by the intelligent agent, through a logic of combination and design. This view of efficient causality is precisely what Heidegger dislodges from the answer to the question of the technological; and the auto-referentiality of the technical functions as loop in the sense of a limit, which the human becomes.

It is here that Stiegler identifies the veritable collapse of technocratic euphoria. It is also here that the 'state of emergency' is proclaimed. That the politics of the state of emergency and the limit of the techno-calculative domain of the scientific should coincide, from its long origins in the Baconian project of the control over nature, through experiment and knowledge, in Empire conducted as war, should be no surprise. For Stiegler, there is a glut that comes with the full elaboration of the technical, which he himself describes as a dramatised presentation:

> Countless problems are being engendered by the expansion of technical equipment: ever-increasing risks consequent upon the increase in traffic and improvement in performance speeds; the installation of a 'general state of emergency' caused not only by machines that circulate bodies but by data-transport networks; the growing paucity of 'messages', illiteracy, isolation, the distancing of people from one another, the extenuation of identity, the destruction of territorial boundaries; unemployment – robots seeming designed no longer to free humanity from work but to consign it either to poverty or stress; threats surrounding choices and anticipations, owing to the delegation of decision-making procedures machines that are on the one hand necessary since humanity is not fast enough to control the process of informational change (as is the case for electronic stock-market network), but on the other hand

9 Francesco Coniglione, 'Between Abstraction and Idealization', in: **Poznañ Studies in the Philosophy of Science and the Humanities** (Amsterdam, New York: Rodopi, 2004) pp. 59-110.
10 The references are from Stiegler, and refer to Bernard Gille's work in **Histoire des Techniques** (Paris: Gallimard, 1978).
11 Stiegler, **op. cit.**, p.49.

> also frightening since the decision making is combined with machines for destruction (for example in the case of polemological networks for the guidance of 'conventional' or non-'conventional' missiles, amounting to an imminent possibility of massive destruction); and just as preoccupying, the delegation of knowledge, which not only modifies radically the modes of transmission of this knowledge but seems to threaten these forms with nothing less than sheer disappearance.[12]

He is not referring here only to pocket calculators and diminishing arithmetical skills, or spelling checks, but sees the problem as extended to data-banks, in the way the media operates on collective behaviour, or the way the system is parasitized by 'forms of terrorism of vulgar propaganda', how the local can be made dependent on the *diktat* issued by an unruly world opinion. It is hardly necessary to draw attention to the exploitation of natural resources, or the way in which the question of ecology becomes a mundane given. But of all the striking technical developments, it is genetic manipulation which has given rise to the most disarming discourse.

It could be that the threat of the destruction of humanity is no worse that the threat of the fabrication of humanity. Genetic manipulation has been proposed as a new 'humanity', where the individual human body can by copyrighted, there is vast traffic in human organs, and the specific memory of the body is directly threatened. One might call Stiegler's scenario an outline of fear at the time of a Second Creation; the fear being that the technological as resource is joined to the human as resource and can dispose of any originary notion of nature, while at the same time the technological remains saturated with the traditional aim of empirical science: to know and control. Stiegler sketches rapidly the problems which occur when the euphoria of the technical is for a moment muted, and one sees the claims and achievements in a colder light.

The ferocity of his account brings one to a series of startling aporia. The question that still emerges is: is it the case that technics develops for itself, and that anthropocentrism is simply a disappearing case, even if developed and nurtured in historical and societal conditions? Taking Leroi-Gouhran's position in view, anthropology is technology. It is no longer the case that technics should be confined to tools, instruments and machines. Almost everything social is a skill, but technics refers to something produced from something. However broadly one acknowledges such skill, in professions, in dancing, spectacle, nothing in the skill is seen as essential for the human. Today, and Stiegler follows Habermas in this, the technical allies skill and science, where rationality is confined to usefulness, that is the usefulness of capital as purposive-rational action.[13]

In what sense is that usefulness useful for humanity? Do not these questions remain entrapped in a particular instrumental-pragmatic view, which actually masks the answer to the question of the 'what is', of 'what is technology'? How did that question become conjugated with the question, 'what is man'? In that question one might ask how the 'who' and the 'what' is held together. It is not the questioning which is noteworthy, not to the what is, as essence, but a matrix of questioning, with the interrogative markers; but every noun could be marked with an interrogative, every word, even if only as intonation, which marks the being that is in question which questions: who, how, what, and why?

Must one speak of the end of humanity in the time of technics? The problematic can be put in a way which grants to the ends of technology, and the ends of the human, a new teleology where the technical ends are co-incident with the human, and in a new materialism, the end, or goal, is only coincident with its own activity as science and image.

A crucial text which lies behind much of the arguments in Stiegler, is Heidegger's 'The Question concerning Technology'. This is a revised version of one of the four lectures delivered by Heidegger to the Bremen Club in December 1949 under the general title 'Insight into What Is'; and the title of these four lectures was: 'The Thing', 'The Enframing', 'The Danger', 'The Turning'. David Farrell Krell suggests that 'The Enframing' was read to the Bavarian Academy of Fine Arts completely revised as 'The Question concerning Technology' (November 18th 1953).[14] Heidegger's text is directed to the raising of the question to technology. In questioning we build a way, and the way is one of thinking, which will, Heidegger suggests, prepare a free relationship to technology that is a way which will allow the technological to be experienced in its bounds. What is then pervasive?

There are two errors which can de-route the question: one, to think that technology is the equivalent to the essence of technology, and secondly, that we can minimise how we are everywhere 'unfree and chained to technology' by thinking of it as something neutral, which makes us utterly blind to its essence. The non-equivalence of essence and technology is no different than realising when we seek the essence of tree, that what is pervasive for every tree, 'is not itself a tree that can be encountered among all the other trees'.

If it were the traditional question of essence, that which answers to the question 'what it is', then two statements would give the answer for technology: one, technology is a means to an end, and two, technology is a human activity. The two answers provide the instrumental and anthropological definition of technology. The instrumental definition still holds even in the complexity of modern technology, and is the conception of technology which conditions every attempt to bring man into a right relation with technology.

Technology also becomes manipulated as a means. Something in this will to mastery, manipulation, is the pervasive. This is correct, but as Heidegger insists, not, therefore, true. It constitutes a fixing of the thing and not an uncovering, where alone the true can flourish, and the essence be revealed. We can seek the true by way of the correct, in this question, by asking what is the instrumental itself, within what do such things as means and ends belong? Here Heidegger

12 Stiegler, **op. cit.**, p.86.

13 For this see: J. Habermas, 'Technology and Science as Ideology'; in: J. Habermas, **Towards A Rational Society** (Cambridge: Polity, 1987).

14 Martin Heidegger, **Basic Writings**, ed. David Farrell Krell (London: Routledge, re-print, 2000)pp.308-9; the translation can be found at pp. 311-341, and I have followed the text closely throughout what follows.

reverts to Aristotle: to what means and ends belong is clearly causality, wherever ends are pursued and means employed. Where instrumentality reigns, there rules causality.

Traditionally philosophy has given four causes: the *causa materialis*, the material cause, or the matter out of which something is made, for example, the silver out of which a silver chalice is made; the *causa fomalis*, that is the shape or form into which the material enters; the *causa finalis*, the end, for which the required chalice is determined as to its form and matter, e.g. a sacrificial rite, and fourth, the *causa efficiens*, which in this case is the silversmith who brings about the effect that is the finished chalice.

What technology is, when represented as a means, can be disclosed when we trace instrumentality back to this fourfold causality. However, Heidegger raises the question, what if causality is itself veiled in darkness in respect to what it is? Why are there only four causes, and in the above example, what does cause really mean? How is it that the causal character of the four causes is determined, in that they belong together like this?

If we do not approach these questions, then Heidegger contends that the accepted definition of technology, the first answer given to the 'what is?' of 'what is technology? ', as a question is obscure and groundless. Within the current situation it is the case that we have been accustomed for a long time to equate cause as that which effects or brings something about. There are results and effects. It is the efficient cause which sets the standard for causality. It is understood as *causa*, from the Latin verb *cadere*, to fall, and that which means something that brings about something as a result in such and such a way.

In the Greek term *aition*, Heidegger argues the notion of something to which something is indebted, *das, was ein anderes verschuldet*. This is to say that the four causes are not in this sense anything to do with bringing about and effecting. They are the ways, all belonging to each other, of being responsible for something else. The fourfold of this intricating responsibility, as a play of the four ways, lies before us as occasion. Silver is that out of which the silver chalice is made. As this matter, *hyle*, it is co-responsible for the chalice; the chalice is indebted to it, i.e. owes thanks to the silver for that of which it consists. It is also indebted to the *eidos*, its appearance in the aspect of chalice. Bounds are given to the thing in circumscribing, that is *telos*, misinterpreted in the words, 'aim' and 'purpose', rather here it is the responsibility for what as matter and as aspect are co-responsible for the vessel, the silver chalice.

The silversmith is not then a *causa efficiens*; he rather considers and gathers the three ways, which considering is a bringing into appearance, by the pondering of the 'that' and the 'how' of their coming into appearance and into play for the production of the sacrificial vessel. How without lapsing into indebtedness as morality, or in terms of effects can we understand such co-responsibility?

Heidegger proposes that in thinking what the Greeks understood in what is lying before us and lying ready (*hypokeisthai*), this characterises something presencing as present; 'the four ways of being responsible bring something into appearance'. How, then, does this bringing into presence, this essence of causality as 'to occasion', the playing in unison of the four ways of occasioning, occur? Heidegger finds the answer to this in a sentence of Plato's *Symposium* (205b): 'he gar toi ek tou me ontos eis to on ionti hotoioun aitia pasa esti poiesis'; which he translates in his own way as 'every occasion which passes beyond the non-present and goes forward into presencing is *poiesis*, bringing-forth'. *Poiesis* is therefore bringing-forth, that is, *her-vor-bringen*, which Heidegger hyphenates to capture the sense of *poiesis* in the Greek.

For the Greeks this bringing-forth refers to handicrafts, artistic and poetical bringing into appearance and concrete imagery. It is also *physis*, nature, the bringing of something from out of itself. The bringing forth in nature has the irruption belonging to bringing forth, but from itself, the bursting of a blossom into bloom. What the artist brings forth is an irruption belonging in another, *en alloi*, and not *en heautoi* as in *physis*, that is, in the craftsman or the artist. The question now arises as to what is the bringing-forth, in which the fourfold way of occasioning plays? It brings what is concealed into unconcealment. It is a coming and resting freely in what we call revealing, *das entbergen*, for which the Greeks have the word *aletheia*, uncovering, and this has been translated as *veritas* in Latin, which gives us 'truth', that is a correctness of representation, as usually understood.

Behind this crucial argument lie long years of Heidegger's thinking of the Greek understanding of 'nature', the term that for him belongs to the disaster, mostly Ciceronian, of the translation of Greek concepts into Latin, in this case *physis* into *natura*, and thus the English here, 'nature'. Part of this disaster was already prepared in Plato, where the *physis* is understood as the material world. In his *Introduction to Metaphysics*, Heidegger speaks of *physis* as the process that irrupts, arises, emergent from what is hidden, where the hidden is made to stand. This arising takes place in conflict, part of which is how through language one can hear what language has to say. Heidegger states this clearly in the *Introduction to Metaphysics*, that words and language are not wrapping paper for the commerce of those who write and speak: 'it is in words and language that things first come into being and are'. By using language as representation and descriptive, a system of signs, it functions like tools and instruments, and it is in this interpellation of the everyday, assertion gives a definite character to things and this is taken as everyday communication. There is a seeking to know certain relations between objects and ourselves. It is logic which orders such an operation. This is what is meant by the *adequatio*, a measuring up to that about which the determination and statement is made, and is what is generally meant by the truth of statements. The function of discourse is to make manifest what is being talked about. Logos, or the interpretation of *logos* as logic, makes manifest what is being talked about.

Much of our conceptual language, it can be argued, is a language of clarity, or daylight. It is here that already Heidegger in *Being and Time* argues we have wandered from the path of the Greek understanding of truth. For Heidegger *logos* is to be seen as *apophansis*, a showing of itself, which if it is to be true is an un-covering, *aletheuein*, which means not a moment of logic and judgment, but rather a taking of entities out of their hidden-ness and letting them be seen in their unhiddenness; and Heidegger wonders whether it is accidental that in one of the fragments of Heraclitus – the oldest fragments of philosophical doctrine in which the logos is explicitly handled – the phenomenon of truth in the sense of uncoveredness as we have set it forth shows through? To the logos belongs unhidden-ness, *a-letheia*. To translate this word as 'truth', and above all, to define this expression conceptually, in theoretical ways, is to cover up the meaning of what the Greeks made self-evidently basic for the terminological use of *aletheia* as a pre-philosophical way of understanding it. Logic abstracts from the real and creates the general features of the discourse of the everyday. Common sense then is the product of this abstraction and generalisation.

This is the domain in which the question of technology belongs, and if one enquires into what technology actually is, represented as means, then we arrive at revealing. 'The possibility of all productive manufacturing lies in revealing'. Technology is a way of revealing, i.e. of *aletheia*, truth. Technology is therefore no mere means, it is where truth happens.

Heidegger again returns to his fundamental arguments, to think through language, and to ask the simple question once more: what does the word technology mean? He draws attention again to the Greek. The word stems from *technikon*, and means that which belong to *techne*. Firstly, it should be noted that *techne* is not only the name for skills and activities of the craftsman, but also for the arts of the mind and the fine arts. It belongs to *poiesis*, to bringing-forth. Secondly, and more significantly, from the earliest times until Plato the word is linked with *episteme*, that is knowledge, taken as being at home in something, understanding and being expert in it.

This is the knowing that opens things up, as such an opening up it is revealing. In a passage of Aristotle, from the *Nichomachean Ethics* (Bk VI, chapters 3 and 4), a text which Heidegger comments on extensively in his lectures on Plato's *Sophist*, he draws the significance of *techne* and its relation to *episteme* in the following way, and also in respect to how *techne* and *episteme* reveal. *Techne* is a mode of *aletheuein*. It reveals whatever does not bring itself forth and does not yet lie here before us, whatever can look and turn out now one way or another. Whoever builds a house or a ship or forges a sacrificial chalice reveals what is to be brought forth. According to the terms of the four modes of occasioning. This revealing gathers together in advance the aspect and the matter of ship or house, with a view to the finished thing envisaged as completed, and from this gathering determines the manner of its construction.

It is this which is crucial for Heidegger, in his account of *techne*: that it does not lie in making and manipulating, nor in the using of means, but rather in revealing, and it is as revealing and not as manufacturing, that *techne* is a bringing-forth.

In two moves Heidegger disposes of two accounts of technology: one, that it is historically tied to the Industrial Revolution, from the end of the eighteenth century, and secondly, that there is a difference in modern technology to the account he is offering of *techne* from his interpretation of Greek thinking. Towards the first he dismisses the objection that what has been so characterised can be applied to modern machine-powered technologies, and that it does not take into account the way modern technology is based on modern physics as an exact science.

The latter claim in the second part of the objection can be true, but for Heidegger it is merely an historiological establishing of facts and says nothing about that in which this mutual relationship is grounded. The decisive question remains: of what essence is modern technology that it thinks of putting exact science to use? Only by granting the character of revealing can one come to an understanding of modern technology. What does it reveal? It reveals that what holds in modern technology is not a bringing forth in the sense of *poiesis*, but that the revealing which rules is a *herausfordern*, that is a challenging, and it challenges nature to the demand of extracting energy that can be extracted and stored as such.

There is a new setting-in-order which 'sets upon nature'. This setting upon is a challenging, where the field that the peasant once cultivated the setting-in-order meant to take care and maintain; the work of the peasant does not challenge the soil of the field, in sowing grain seed is placed in the keeping of the forces of growth and the peasant watches over its increase.

This setting up turns agriculture into the mechanised food industry, earth as mineral and fossil fuel resource, uranium to yield atomic energy. The setting forth, in direct contrast to bringing-forth, is an expediting. It expedites in two ways: one, it unlocks and exposes, and two, it drives for maximum yield at minimum expense. Thus the characteristics of this technology and its spaces, are ones of unlocking, transforming what is unlocked, storing the transformation, distributing what is stored, and what is distributed is switched about and around ever anew.

This revealing does not come to an end, it continues, but not in some vague and indeterminate way, rather, the revealing as challenging requires constant regulating which must be secured, thus the interlocking of these diverse paths, are revealed in modern technology, through two chief characteristics, and which hold sway in every domain, namely, regulation and security. There is in this an unconcealment that is peculiar. Everything is put literally on hold, on hold as a standing-reserve, or *Bestand*; it expresses this word, an inclusive rubric, it is there no longer as a *Gegen-stand*, even as typing this text, it is connected directly to this *Bestand*, for here the machine has no autonomy, unlike the craftsman's tools, the machine, has its standing only on the basis of the ordering of the orderable.

The very technology of information proceeds apace even as the hegemonic phantasm of the epoch is named Information Age. Google does not claim directly to produce information, but merely to create algorithms for ordering data. In this phantasy view of neutrality, agency is said to belong to the searcher, who is then responsible for the matching of values within the information. The inner aim of this amassing is to create computer algorithms for all possible information. This repeats the essential view once uttered by Heisenberg, that everything is measurable, or in this case everything is data. The cosmopolitan programme is expressed in one aim, to make information universal and useful. In this is buried all the questions of whether a monopolistic control of knowledge will occur, and the claim of availability which is geared for more enterprise, and innovation, whilst refusing the issue of what happens to knowledge in the public sphere.

The terms that are revealed in modern technology occur as setting-upon, ordering, standing reserve, and they accumulate and obtrude in a dry, monotonous, and therefore oppressive way. Modern technology as a revealing that orders is, Heidegger insists, no mere human doing. This difficult part of Heidegger's arguments can be presented only summarily. Man is challenged too; the challenge also brings him to the objectlessness which the standing-reserve calls for. Man does not control unconcealment, into which at any time the actual shows itself or withdraws. Something is addressed to man. There is now a challenge set upon man, which gathers into ordering, and asks for the ordering of the actual as *Bestand*, standing-reserve. The challenging claim that challenges man with a view to ordering self-revealing as standing reserve is named by Heidegger as *Gestell*, enframing.

What Heidegger allows for in the strangeness of this term is first indicated in its departure from idiomatic meaning, and his linking it to the process of unfolding such as occurs in a mountain range, the gathering which unfolds. Here in *Gestell* man gathers the setting upon that sets upon him, what challenges him to reveal the actual mode of ordering as standing reserve. This involves his claim that enframing means the revealing that holds sway in modern technology and that is in essence nothing technological.

A merely instrumental anthropological definition of technology is untenable. In the *Ge-Stell*, the sense of another *stellen* is also preserved, that of *her-* and *darstellen*, a producing and presenting that allows *poiesis*, lets what presences come into unconcealment. After all nature is set up in a way by physics that it is asked to exhibit itself as a coherence of forces calculable in advance, and its experiments are set up for the purpose of asking whether and how nature reports itself when set up in this way.

But, for Heidegger even this does not get to the way in which technology in the modern sets up. It belongs to the coming to presence which always conceals itself. The essence of modern technology lies in enframing and thus it requires the illusion of employing exact physical science. However, we have yet again to ask: what is enframing? It is not technological, nor is it of the order of the machine; 'it is the way in which the actual reveals itself as standing reserve'. This neither happens exclusively nor definitely through man. We necessarily always ask the question too late, as to technology. Why Heidegger refuses the historical is that this destining of enframing already belongs within the destiny of the technological which is mysterious. Part of this contains the illusion that because the essence of modern technology is enframing, it must employ exact physical science. Thus the deceptive appearance arises that modern technology is exact physical science. What is put forward in the revealing that is enframing is that the actual becomes everywhere, including the human, a standing reserve. Something is sent on the way, and this is what as destiny determined the essence of history. Heidegger deploys etymological connection for the sending that gathers, *versammelnde Schicken*, and destining, *Geschick*, and history, *Geschichte*, to operate this claim.

Enframing is also an ordaining of destining. It is in belonging to that realm of what is destined that the free occurs. It is to this which he must listen, but not necessarily obey. Again Heidegger shares in this understanding a view that is close to that of Adorno and Marcuse. In this observation there is an awareness of the dominion of *Gestell*. The mastering of nature has led to human self-subjugation. Sampson has argued that:

> Horkeim and Adorno – in the *Dialectic of Enlightenment* – see the subject seeking to govern the object (nature) and in this very process being swallowed up and destroyed. The identity between subject and object eventually destroys the subject itself. The dialectic presents the process whereby what begins affirmatively as conquest, administration, and technical control of nature ends up creating just its opposite – namely, self-understanding from the viewpoint of technical control. The result is a technocratic consciousness or instrumentalised rationality in which the core of domination is both contained and concealed.[15]

Freedom stands in closest and most intimate relation to truth, that is the occurrence of revealing. This occurrence is the event of truth. Revealing comes out of the free, and goes into the free and brings into the free. Freedom is 'that which conceals in a way that opens to light, in whose clearing shimmers the veil that hides the occurrence of truth, and lets the veil appears as what veils'. Here again Heidegger mobilises a metaphor which comes from the notion of revealing etymologically, the parting of the veils. What starts the revealing in destining is freedom.

Technology is the inevitable and unalterable course, the 'fate', of our age. But in experiencing enframing as destining, we are already in a free space, where we are neither obliged to push on blindly with technology, nor rebel against it and curse it as the work of the devil. For Heidegger, it is quite to the contrary: 'when we once open ourselves expressly to the essence of technology we find ourselves taken into a freeing claim'.[16] However it is here that the danger lies; on one side man, underway in this destining, may only coincide in his being with the promulgation of

15 E. Sampson, **Justice and the Critique of Pure Psychology** (New York and London: Plenum, 1984), p. 64.

16 Heidegger, 'The Question concerning Technology'; in: Krell, **Basic Writings**, p. 331. See note 14.

what is revealed in this ordering, and be blocked from a more primal admittance to the essence of what is unconcealed, and to its unconcealment. Placed between these possibilities, man is endangered by destining. There is always the danger of misconstruing and misinterpreting, even God, for representational thinking can sink to the level of a cause, of a *causa efficiens*, an intelligent designer. Similarly with viewing nature as a calculable complex of the effects of forces, and the same danger that in the midst of the correct the true will withdraw.

But this danger is attended by further illusions. Man comes in this to be a standing reserve, whilst exalting himself as Master of the Universe. This engenders a final illusion, that man only encounters himself everywhere. This is a failure to hear what is spoken to man in the claim of enframing, and a failure to know how he exists, what his essence is in this realm, and thus realise that he can never encounter only himself.

This enframing drives out the mode of revealing as *poiesis*, which lets what presences come forth into appearance. The real threat is not that of lethal weapon and techno-science, but that a man could be denied, because of the rule of enframing, to enter into a more original revealing and hence to experience 'the call of a more primal truth'. In the enframing is the danger in the highest sense.

It is here that Heidegger reaches another consideration, drawing on the world of poetry, from Hölderlin's poem *Patmos*:

> But where the danger is, grows
> The saving power also.

The saving grows because technology makes the demand on us to think the essence. To think the essence no longer as the genus which answers the question of 'what'? The question now is to be answered by the way in which, what is asked about is said to hold, how it sways, develops, decays. It is in the unfolding of what endures that one knows the way of something.

It is in the granting of the propriative event that the destining endures. In this sense it is an event to the open. To this granting is what man essentially belongs, and it is in the very danger of enframing that threatens man in his very freedom that he is thrust, where he discovers this indestructible belongingness. Within the essential unfolding of technology is the possible rise of the saving power.

The essence of technology is therefore ambiguous. This ambiguity points to the mystery of all revealing, that is of truth. For Heidegger in the here-and-now and in little things the saving is cultivated, by always keeping one's eyes on the extreme danger. Saving power must be seen as a higher essence than what is endangered, even if kindred to it. This indicates the answer to the question of power over power. For Heidegger the word *techne* once also belonged to poetry and he wonders if in art, *techne* might foster the growth of the saving power. The confrontation with technology must take place in a realm that is akin to its essence and different from it, and such a realm is art which is mindful of the constellation of truth which is being questioned.

Thus questioning, we bear witness to the crisis, that in our sheer preoccupation with technology we do not yet experience the essential unfolding of technology, that in our sheer aesthetic mindedness we no longer guard and preserve the essential unfolding of art. Yet the more questioningly we ponder the essence of technology, the more mysterious the essence of art becomes. The closer we come to the danger, the more brightly do the ways into the saving power begin to shine and the more questioning we become. For questioning is the piety of thought.[17]

One can recapitulate Heidegger's account in the following way: a question is raised, the answer given requires another question, that is how the definition of means and end relates to a traditional philosophical account of causality; this version of causes is put in question, and a recourse to a re-thinking of what is understood in the Greek term *aition* leads to Heidegger defining *techne* and the technological in its ways of being, which he then contrasts with modern technology. This turns on the distinction between bringing-forth, and setting-upon, or, setting forth. A characteristic move of Heidegger is to reverse the understanding of the relation of what is forwarded in the claims of science: the relation of technology to physics, in which the project of science is shown as already enmeshed in a calculation and projection which demands that nature yields arguments in a precise direction.
In an unpublished paper delivered to the Delft School of Design Tuesday seminar group, Brendan O'Byrne marks this as the real rupture with the traditional cosmological argument, where one finds a complete holistic ordering of everything from the gods through to unformed matter, in that sense a continual passage from *kosmos* to *logos*. The basic distinction which informed this cosmology was that of the mortal and the immortals, that *physis* was the self-emerging emergence, cognate with being, and in Aristotle clearly was that everything is subject to change and the principle of change. It is also possible to say that necessity was of central significance. There were fundamentally two forms of motion: sub-lunar and celestial, and it is this which Newton reduces to one, and which presupposes abstract space. Heidegger had outlined this in detail in his discussion of 'What is a Thing?', where he shows that the Newtonian axiom makes the distinction obsolete. The ancient view that *kosmos* was not in space, but rather a place, is dislodged. The concept of nature changes, and is no longer the inner principle out of which the notion of the body follows. It is the collapse of such a principle that ultimately marks the modern. Beings are phenomena, that is the aspect of something that presences. Time is an indifferent series of infinite nows, *to nun*, the now of the instant. In this account the *kosmos* is neither created nor destroyed; it is forever presencing in accordance with its governing principles, which are under-

17 Heidegger, 'The Question concerning Technology', pp. 340-341. See note 14.

pinned by the prime mover (physical), and the *nous noetikos* (metaphysical). The *aitiai* are the eidetic, the huletic, the kinetic and the telic. Heidegger, in considering these *aitiai*, will change the account of the answer to the traditional *ti estin*, 'what is it?', or *to ti einai*, the 'what it is?', to the way and being of what is pervasive in the revealing as revealing of entities.

What is of particular interest is that Heidegger is prepared in other works to consider the shift in the modern as belonging to a particular time, the destruction of the Aristotelian worldview through Newtonian physics, and place the characteristics of the modern project of science and the perfectibility of the world in an historical setting, and in his writing on the question to technology to literally dismiss the historical and replace it with a much more highly impersonal view of a destining of being, of something which is sent to man, in which he questions as a danger.

This shifts profoundly the emphasis he had given almost 20 years earlier in his consideration of the world-picture, *Die Zeit des Weltbildes*, where he argues that there are two faces of representation in which the ontological foundation of modernity can be seen, that man becomes a subject, and that the world becomes an image. There the world becomes image because it is given to the subject in representation. The epoch of representations is inseparably the world of technics and science. What is clear however is that Heidegger's questioning has eliminated completely any positivist demand, and also has refused the notion of a communicative action which is other than the technical, as Habermas tries to establish in his 'Technics and Science as Ideology'. For Heidegger technics is resolutely the history of being itself. This is what is sent as the challenge to man. In a real sense man and nature must lose the qualities with which metaphysics has endowed them. The technical is also the overcoming of man. In that sense this overcoming is the 'end' of humanity. It marks the revolutionary caesura in the multi-directionality of many of Heidegger's texts, in which different directions have been read.

A critical difference in how Heidegger understands that relation is found in the move towards enframing in his argument, and can be taken as the point where Heidegger and Deleuze have a decisive and radical difference. The difference belongs to the way in which Heidegger construes the fold. The example again is that of the folding and unfolding of mountains, which in Heidegger is the mountain chain itself: 'that which primordially unfolds into mountain ranges and pervades them in their folded contiguity is the gathering that we call *Gebirg* (mountain chain). That original gathering from which unfold the ways in which we have feelings of one kind or another we name *Gemut* (disposition)'. Deleuze risks the concept of image again and reverses its Platonic ideality: *eidos* is matter. It requires that the notion of the fold be differentiated more concretely, the difference does not reside in a previous undifferentiated, but to a difference which endlessly folds and unfolds.

Deleuze grants this relation of science and image to a particular historical constellation, the period called the Baroque, where the criterion or operative concept is the fold, and where the fold has unlimited freedom. The fold is also the smallest unit of matter. The model for the science of matter is origami. There is no longer a proportional dividing of parts into parts, but of an infinity made up of smaller and smaller folds. The organic is made up of endogenous folds, and the inorganic of exogenous folds, always determined by the surrounding environment. Thus the external and internal milieu are constantly being in-formed, and per-formed. This dynamic of plastic forces is the image-matter in its becoming. Between the organic and the inorganic there exists a difference of vector, and there is no longer question of essence, rather the movement of traits and operative functions.[18]

Deleuze aligns the aim of Baroque physics with the traits of the Baroque, and takes its goal as curvilinear, and he notes that for Leibniz the curvature prolonged according to the fluidity of matter, the elasticity of bodies and the motivating spirit of mechanism. In view of that, one can understand the material traits more closely, in the specific architectural sense, as descriptive features: the horizontal widening of the floor, the flattening of the pediment, the low curved stairs rushing into space, the handling of masses as aggregates, the avoidance of the perpendicular, the elimination of jagged edges, the spongy cavernous quality of spaces that are spilling over, verticality put in motion by renewed turbulence, and the spinning in space which does not favour tangents and the rectilinear.[19]

What is in play is an infinite division of matter. Matter divides endlessly like vortices in a maelstrom. Deleuze could have added, that much of this is prepared in the work of Leonardo da Vinci, and in the philosophy of Bruno. It is also the movements of traits and operative functions which discharge the question of the human in terms of origin; it not only discharges but makes it utterly redundant. In operating this constellation Deleuze must abandon the human in art, and stress the inhuman. The subject too is an image among others, and Deleuze contents himself with a radical empiricist activity of taxonomy, classifying images and signs. There is a ceaseless performative contradiction in the position, which posits the irreducibility of experience to perception. There is a universe of image-movement, which is not unlike Cassirer's abstractions. The prosthesis of seeing replaces human perception; in the cinema of matter the very complexity of variability of angles, the constant introduction of framed and unframed zones, speaks of universal variation and objective perception. This chaosmos chimes with Vertov's idea of the kino-eye, in which every type of montage and juxtaposition is possible, irrespective of what point of the universe, or what temporal order, even to the point of violating all the conventions of film itself.[20]

In this account of image-movement as de-centred, Deleuze expatiates on the chaotic and double nature of the system of reference for images. In the first, the images act and re-act on each other

18 For a discussion of this in Deleuze, see: Todd May, 'Gilles Deleuze, Difference, and Science', in: **Continental Philosophy of Science**, ed. Gary Gutting (Blackwell, 2005) pp. 239-258.

19 This discussion is guided by a reading of Deleuze in his work **Le Pli**.

20 For this see: Paola Marrati, **Gilles Deleuze, cinéma et philosophie** (Paris: PUF, 2003).

in every direction. In the second aspect all the images vary for one, a specialised image, which varies its direction and is capable of selecting the received movement and the movement to be executed. The thing and its perception are the same image. The only difference is the system in which they come into rapport. Thus, the initial perception is immediate, complete and diffuse.

This is where Deleuze also eliminates phenomenology, because awareness here is only the swell and surge of a function of the needs of life. By forming itself from a natural into an objective perception, awareness completes itself in being less fine, in its tracing of the continuity of movement, but this is adequate to the exigency called living. There is no privilege for either perception or experience. Perception is not just a sense organ for knowledge; one cannot ignore as philosophers frequently have, its sensorial-motoric aspect, and the aspect which is directed ineluctably towards action. Philosophy must open up to what is non-human to go beyond the human condition, or otherwise we remain badly analysed mixtures.

Perception is nothing more than the dark screen, light reflected by a living image. The brain is an image, an interval between the action and a reaction. The brain is an image among others in a plane of immanence which consists only of matter and light. If one really observes the first level of subjectivity it is merely a selecting, a centre of indetermination and a dark screen, the perceiving image is nothing more than its selecting. However it doesn't just extract, it incurves the universe around it, it gives the world an horizon, and in that sense perception is always senso-motoric and pragmatic. It does not have its beginning or end in pure knowledge. To be mistaken about perception is to be mistaken about knowledge and its limits. This process of incurving, is the second aspect of perception, and belongs not to image-movement, but to image-action.

In that sense the event of novelty, what comes from states of affairs, has no causality in the sense of the traditional four causes either. Deleuze gives an account of a way of becoming, an event. For Deleuze even the bodily is regarded as problems, intensities, simulacra; and any concept of causality of the body is deprived of inner direction or systematic unity. With increasing complexity the demand for precision is less and less operable. What subsists in the event is an image reality, because there is no opposition between the real and the image, even the concept of image here is take as effectuating, as it is no longer situated in the ontology of what Merleau-Ponty describes as the 'great object'. Without cosmological anchoring, in the sense of a theological principle of creation *ex nihilo*, there is only an account of free valences, which may be taken as pervasive features of events, which our perceptual world registers according to its living needs. However, in the virtual philosophy of Deleuze, the ceaseless work of concept formation is itself a universe of interleaving, rather than *adequatio* between perception and signification. This is a world without history, without genesis, but with forces.

A further difference with Heidegger is that in the thought of Deleuze, the question of the being of the world as disclosed by the being that is there which questions, is not at issue; instead, Deleuze concerns himself with the effectuation of a universe, or, of several. Jean-Luc Nancy has drawn attention to the descriptive, *ekphrastic*, in Deleuze's view of naming. That is, the drawing up of a picture which one can show, the sudden irruption of the event, resonates as manifestation.[21] This is a philosophy of passage, not of ground or territory. Deleuze provides a philosophy of continuous creation, which at each moment singularly composes and re-composes, traversing the chaos, and not explaining or interpreting it. Problems then, arise as multiplicative, in movement, becoming and difference. In co-ordinating these latter differences, the difference which makes a difference, 'transcendental' empiricism operates. Instead of the question of the one and the many, there is the multiplier, because movement in becoming other than itself is a qualitative change, it is through a genetic constitution of the given that a theory of the actual can be supplied. Actualisation brings things into conflict with one another, and these conflicts may only be grasped by a form of methodic intuition. The dominant transcendental illusion against which Deleuze stakes his philosophy of passage, is the illusion which results in a preoccupation with extended magnitudes in space at the expense of intensities in time. Deleuze, one may say, privileges continua over discrete manifolds, and processes over things, and one can further add, problems over solutions, learning over culture, encounters over recognition, tendencies over results. New tendencies have the reality of the virtual which exists in order to be actualised. A virtual x is something which, without being or resembling x, has nonetheless the efficacy – *virtus* – of producing x. In distinction to the virtual, the possible has no reality, whereas the virtual without being actual is real. For the virtual to exist is to be differentiated. From this Deleuze draws out further consequences, namely that it is intensity, which despite its self-concealing nature, constitutes the diversity of the sensible. This is to say that for Deleuze, the manifold is given by intensity, which is that which our senses ought to sense but cannot. This is the 'excess' in our feeling, perception and senses, and the same excess, of what is not given to experience, requires in the Platonic interpretation of *aesthesis*, the idea, that lies at the basis of the doctrine of forms, where they are understood as knowable *Gestalt*, in which the mind gathers patterns of the real, which is supra-sensible.

In Deleuze's account he acknowledges the primacy of the *sentiendum*, the sensed, but also acknowledges that differentiation does not alone determine the process of actualisation, that it is also a generator of problems, and that virtualities equally generate disjunctions as much as they actualise tendencies, which were contained in the original unity and compossibility.

In matter at the lowest degree of difference there is dilation and contraction, and in that sense the concept of absolute degree zero is a category error, since even at the smallest conceivable molecular level, there is always movement, and further that, at degrees of extreme simplification,

21 I have discussed this in more detail in: **Images of Knowledge, An Introduction to Contemporary Science** (Amsterdam: SUN, 2005).

one often finds asymmetry and chaos. What one may say then, is that we can in fact only speak of a generalised vibration, vibrating matter and energy; difference is nothing but a difference of degree, and everything is event.
How in fact the *ekphrasis* takes place is through the indexing of proper names, in the sense that for Deleuze for the concept there is a becoming and process, or a becoming-proper-names for the concept, so 'plateau', 'plane of consistency', 'rhizome', 'refrain', 'fold'. Things subsist and insist as event. An effect can have a life of its own, it can be a structure, or source of potential energy, and of consequences; it can be both transcendental and an infinitive capable of various actualisations. The event is both produced in and presupposed by the event. This is the manifestation of the singular, the example given being that a season, a winter, a summer, an hour, a date, have perfect individuality, which lacks nothing, although it is not that of a thing or a subject. It is as event, and singular in the sense it is only a relation of movement and rest between molecules and particles, a power of affecting or being affected, a becoming on a plane of consistency.
It may still be possible to ask how nevertheless, for Heidegger and Deleuze an account of the open, or, becoming can be given? In this there is a specific unknowing, which belongs to the non-philosophical understanding of philosophy, or, the end of philosophy, the end of which Heidegger spoke required in thinking after the accomplishment of metaphysics as nihilism. In this sense the post-humanist situation is the abandoning of the 'world-picture'. For Deleuze that will require a turn to the radicalising of the senses, creating a new trust and faith in the senses, because the seeking in the indeterminacy of the possibility of sensation is also the search for sensation as the conditions of the possibility of thought.
If thinkers are concerned with an emancipatory enquiry which requires the ridding of transcendental illusions, for Deleuze this requires a logic of sense and event, which is not a logic of predication and proposition, but rather a conception of philosophy as a logic of multiplicity. In one sense the ridding of 'transcendental illusions' is a ridding oneself of bad images, such as the 'ideal city'. The work of the concept creates its figures, of 'friendship', which is the disposition towards wisdom itself, a friendliness to wisdom, as the definition of philosophy, where the unknown and the unknowing constitute the dialogic exchange, through discourse, concept figures, that involves the open precisely in the sense of the unknown, where the unknowing is not a 'lack' of knowledge, but is at first a refusal to be determined by fixed qualities, where the conversion of conversation turns to the open, and that is the event which cannot be calculated, numbered, which remains necessarily *inachevé*. Individuality is achieved in these various relations of differential rhythms and affective intensities, is in that sense defined by relations of rest and movement, of swiftness and slowness, and it is this power of affecting and being affected that constitutes individuality; it is here that the image gives an 'interior' to matter, makes it individual. This also

defines for Deleuze a body without organs. Here the invention is what literally comes into being. Such an account goes against the compulsion of novelty as an insistence of technics. For Deleuze that is simply the consequence of a fatal misunderstanding of immanence.

In Heidegger radical finitude forecloses the endless possibilities mediated by the way that everything is shown as being a resource, which is nothing less than the culmination of metaphysics, and so the end of philosophy. It is there that the thinking of the open and the event occur.

Acknowledgments
I would like to thank all participants at the DSD Tuesday seminar, and Professor Arie Graafland.

The Urban Understanding

Arie Graafland

Introduction The cultural dimension in urban planning and design is getting more and more important to the assessment of our spatial problematic. Increasingly more emphasis is placed on the complexity of space, while the notion of hierarchical structures is disappearing. Instead, we are confronted with ideas about networks, streams of information, knots, and a space that is no longer to be controlled or planned. Economics, politics, and social sciences are all currently seeking terminology to describe this process. Even within the fields of urbanism and planning, the vocabulary is undergoing a shift; this shift is visible in, for example, the definition of the Dutch Randstad (consisting of the four big cities Amsterdam, Utrecht, The Hague and Rotterdam). Years ago, the Dutch sociologist de Swaan already pointed out that metropolitan areas such as the Randstad and the Rhine-Ruhr area in Germany are principally *conceptual* constructions of planners.[1] He especially appreciated urban culture, specifically as exemplified in the city of Amsterdam. The terminology used by de Swaan extended not only to formal statistics such as number of inhabitants and density per square kilometer, but also dealt with issues such as functional connective tissue surrounding an urban center. In this sense, he considered the Randstad as a metropolis or mega-city, and one of the most eminent ones in Europe.

The question I want to address here is about these assessments in urbanism: how do we understand the notion of 'city', 'mega-city', and 'urban culture'. How can we reach a critical assessment of contemporary urban culture, urban planning and urban policy? Is 'critical' today even the right category to use in our discourse? I will deal with these questions in addressing two recently published books on the urban development in Switzerland, both coming from ETH Zurich. The first one, *Switzerland, an Urban Portrait* explicitly refers to the critical perspective of Henri Lefebvre, and the second one, *Urban Scape Swizerland*, is more of a 'conventional' study on the same urban landscape – the question being whether the 'critical' study gives us a better and more insightful picture of what is going on in this country. In doing so, I will also briefly relate to de Swaan's notion of the Dutch Randstad, a notion that more recently has been debated as one of the central issues in Dutch urbanism, where the term 'Randstad' has been upgraded to 'Delta-Metropolis', developing it into a political issue for Dutch urbanism.

Reflexive Modernization: Out of Control For his theoretical foundation, Christian Schmid has written an extensive introduction to Henri Lefebvre, in my opinion one of the most important French Marxists of the late seventies. In Schmid's *Urban Portrait,* a link is made between architectural practices and Marxist theory.[2] Over a period of sixty years, Lefebvre wrote about a wide range of themes – from literature, language, history, philosophy and Marxism to rural and urban sociology, space, time, the everyday, and the modern world.[3] In this context it is impossible to really deal with his writings extensively. Suffice it to say that Lefebvre's *Pro-*

1 Abram de Swaan; **Perron Nederland**, (Amsterdam: Meulenhof, 1991) p. 23.
2 Christian Schmid; 'Networks, Borders, Differences: Towards a Theory of the Urban' in **Switzerland, an Urban Portrait**, and Introduction, (Basle, Boston, Berlin: Birkhäuser, 2006) p. 164ff. Also See Christian Schmid; **Stadt, Raum und Gesellschaft, Henri Lefebvre und die Theorie der Produktion des Raumes** (Stuttgart: Franz Steiner Verlag, 2005).
3 Eleonore Kofman and Elizabeth Lebas; translation and commentary on Henri Lefebvre; **Writing on Cities** (Oxford: Blackwell, 1996) p. 6.

duction of Space published in 1974, and translated into English in 1991, caused a controversy in France at the time. The book shifted away from the categories of political economy where concepts of the political, the economic, and ideological as employed by Althusser and Castells, were the dominant factors explaining the urban. Lefebvre, in contrast, moved in the direction of a spatio-temporal understanding of the everyday life. Schmid, in his introduction, very briefly explains how to understand Lefebvre's categories of *perceived*, *conceived*, and *lived space*. Space, for Lefebvre, does not exist prior to the 'things' that occupy and fill it. Space is, indeed, produced, offering three dialectically related processes, three different aspects of space. On the one hand, Schmid explains the triad of spatial practice: representation of space, and spaces of representation. On the other hand, are the concepts of perceived, conceived, and lived space. This double helix emphasizes the dual approach – phenomenological and linguistic at the same time.

Although I can only briefly mention these concepts in this essay, in my opinion they offer valuable insights, and a contribution to a wider discussion. To be able to relate to notions of lived space, I will make an association with the ideas of a critical theory, and especially thinking as a *reflexive* enterprise. The term 'critical' can only be used for theory, not for mapping in architecture and urbanism. 'Critical' is a term mostly associated with the Frankfurt School of Adorno and Horkheimer. 'Critical' was, in fact, the alternative term for 'Scientific Marxism'. Their position is well known; criticizing both Stalinist Marxism, fascism, and capitalist production, addressing questions of the culture industries, art and philosophy. Contrary to, for instance, Bruno Latour, I think that a lot of their work is still relevant; it might be outdated, but the direction of their thoughts is still useful. Quite a few of the contemporary authors like Julia Kristeva, Michel Foucault, and even Gilles Deleuze were influenced by Marxist thinking. Kristeva and Foucault have eventually chosen another way; Deleuze has always been an outsider, coming from directions earlier taken by Spinoza, Bergson, and Nietzsche, being more difficult to associate with Marxism. The idea of *reflexivity*, in contrast, comes from Scott Lash, who addresses questions of 'reflexive modernization' in a second modernity.[4] Reflexivity involves both the ordering through reflection of social processes, and on the other hand, those same social processes slipping out of control and escaping the logic of that ordering. Reflexivity consists of a moment of self-ordering, and a moment of 'ambivalence' or 'contingency'.

Lash stresses this moment of contingency, ambivalence, out of control-ness in second modernity. The theory of reflexive modernization, in contrast to positivist and high modernist ideas of social engineering, asks what sort of self, what sort of institutions are possible in an age of *chronic* contingency, of *chronic* ambivalence. Both the social philosophy of experience, and the theory of judgement, use the notion 'reflective'. In the first modernity, the subject is in principle epistemic; in the second and reflexive modernity, there is a shift to an experiencing and judging subject. Phenomenology uses 'reflective attitude', the latter uses 'reflective judgement'. Lash stresses the connections with the idea of reflexive modernization, where in the latter reflexivity descends, as it were, from the realm of thought into the activities of everyday life. In his book he connects 'reflective' with 'reflexive', bringing the more philosophical considerations intentionally into contemporary debates. The sociological theory of reflexivity is primarily about the moment of contingency, of experimentation, with seemingly little to separate it from contemporary ideas of deconstruction and difference, he writes. Difference is always about ontological difference; it is to engage with ontology through encountering a thing.

We find a similar observation in Elizabeth Grosz. Addressing Deleuze, Grosz constructs a 'checkered, even mongrel, philosophical history', of the same active thing that culminates in what she calls a self-consciously evolutionary orientation: the inauguration of philosophical pragmatism that meanders from Darwin, through Nietzsche, to the work of Charles Sanders Peirce, William James, Henri Bergson, and eventually, through various lines of descent, into the diverging positions of Richard Rorty, on the one hand, and Gilles Deleuze on the other.[5] These are all pragmatist philosophers who put the questions of action, practice, and movement at the center of ontology. What they share in common is the 'thing' as question, as provocation, as incitement or enigma, she writes; the 'thing' that also generates invention, the assessment of means and ends, and in that way, enables practice. To my mind, Henri Lefebvre's work is related to these contemporary thinkers.

Urbanization Eleonore Kofman and Elisabeth Lebas, the translators and editors of some of Lefebvre's major texts, draw our attention to Nietzsche's influence, whom he sought to conjoin with Marx. The emphasis on the body, sexuality, violence and the tragic, and the production of differential space and plural times, have a direct resonance in Nietzschean thought, they write. Schmid uses Lefebvre's theory to explain the fact that we experience today the complete urbanization of society; the whole world is caught up in a process of urbanization. This process is linked to industrialization; the industrial revolution initiated a long sustained migration from the country into cities that caused urban areas to spread. Industrialization in this way provides the conditions and means for urbanization, and vice versa. The urban fabric is reshaping and colonizing rural areas at the same time as they are transforming, and partly destroying historical cities. An important effect is that it has far reaching implications for daily life. Lefebvre borrows a metaphor from atomic physics to explain the process of urbanization – implosion and explosion. A tremendous concentration of people, activities, wealth, goods, objects, instruments, means,

4 Scott Lash; **Another Modernity, A Different Rationality** (Oxford: Blackwell, 1999) p. 138**ff.**

5 Elizabeth Grosz; **Architecture from the Outside** (Cambridge, Mass.: MIT Press, 2001) p. 168.

and thought of urban reality, and at the same time an explosion of disjoint fragments, peripheries, suburbs and satellite towns. A process that has been described for the United States, for instance, by Edward Soja in his notion of 'exopolis', the metropolis turns inside out, and outside in at the same time. The city is the site of mediation between the global and the private, its form is *centrality*, a site of meeting, encounter and interaction. Both in the economical sense of Saskia Sassen, and Soja's site of difference in his *Thirdspace*[6], of differences colliding with one another.

Difference is a social category, being one of the fundamental categories Schmid is distinguishing in the *Urban Portrait*. He makes a threefold distinction: *networks*, *borders* and *differences*. Networks are of course not distributed homogeneously in space; it is full of holes and gaps, knots and nodes. Urban regions are crisscrossed by many borders that cut territories off from the flow of network interaction. It is a common term in many urban theories. Urbanization is a process that transcends borders and cannot be stopped by administrative and politically defined territorial borders. Urbanization is related to the dissolving of external borders when city walls, ramparts and moats all lost their meaning. Difference is a social category; it is the possibility to choose one's way of life, so well formulated in for instance *Soft City*.[7] The way these differences interlock is crucial. They can create new forms of urban life, but they can as well get locked into seemingly insurmountable social conflicts. Examples are manifold, but do not seem to be present in Switzerland.

The *Urban Portrait* gives us a brief history of the territory, and is certainly an interesting part of the complete project, but in the end it has little to do with Lefebvre's interest in daily life. The so called 'drills' (random probes into the urban field) might have been important here, but we do not find these in the books either. The distinction into five urbanization types: metropolitan regions, networks of cities, quiet zones, alpine resorts, and alpine fallow land which causes urban spaces to drift apart in everyday, economic, and social terms will need a much more developed program to investigate what is going on here in Lefebvrian terms. The pronounced political issue in this specific place is about the Federalist state which, according to the book, distorts our view of the urban realities in Switzerland. The political situation prevents the recognition of the suggested potential that lies in these differences. 'Difference' here is seemingly without any conflict. *The Brief History of the Territory* is informative but certainly not enough to live up to a contemporary notion of Lefebvre's lived space.

Apparently, the hand of the architects and urbanists in mapping techniques is a strong one. Lefebvre's philosophy is disappearing into urban mapping techniques. In the Deleuzian terminology, the project is more of a 'tracing' than of a 'mapping'; it does not really show the potential of differences. Is it really that different from the other book on Switzerland?

The High Lands and the Low Lands in Urban Planning; Switzerland and the Netherlands Town and country might be among the myths of our present day society, Angelus Eisinger writes in his Introduction to *Urban Scape Switzerland*.[8] Referring to Roland Barthes, he suggests that these common notions serve as communications systems, conveying knowledge diffusely, and establishing causalities in a simplified form. They might shed some light on the topic, but they conceal more than they actually make clear. With these notions, the scope of the book is formulated, regionally and functionally. Switzerland is a tightly-knit network, a multicore conurbation located at the heart of Europe.

Yet, describing this collage of urban, suburban and rural elements with our notions of town and countryside is becoming increasingly difficult. The tendency to consume space is rising, not least because housing construction still primarily means erecting single family and two family houses in densely settled areas. Already in his introduction, Eisinger states that the comparative developments with, for instance, the Dutch Randstad are quite small. The bigger Swiss towns are generally only half the size of Dutch cities that form the Randstad. Nevertheless, the traditional image of a country of peasants and pretty villages that still plays an important role in the way the Swiss see themselves is fading away more and more. The Swiss farmers make up less than 5 percent of the country's employed persons. Today 2,200 of the total of 2,850 communes still come under the idea of rural parishes, but calculations show that three quarters of their inhabitants now live close to urban regions. These communes are not rural Arcadias, neither are the cities the highly concentrated urban centers we know from for instance the German Rhein-Ruhrgebiet. Just as in the Netherlands, farming villages have been thrown into a state of limbo from which they have been unable to escape.

During the period 1950-1998, farmlands diminished by 20 percent. At the same time, the number of farms and labourers was reduced by more than 65 percent. The rise in productivity was enormous – much more was done with ever smaller lots of farmland. And similarly in the Netherlands, the rural has become an idealization of the past, Eisinger writes. With ever more cars on the roads and ever denser networks, the areas between the urban settlements are filling up. The Swiss Federal Statistical Office concludes that the country has become more urban over the past decades, both in the growth of agglomerations and in the formation of metropolitan areas. The older concepts are transformed into an 'aggregate state'. In Switzerland about 70 percent of the population lives in agglomerations. The question of course is about this new urban quality. What

6 Edward Soja; **Thirdspace: Journeys to Los Angeles and other Real- and-Imagined Places** (Oxford: Blackwell, 1996).

7 Jonathan Raban; **Soft City** (London: Hamish Hamilton, 1974).

8 Angelus Eisinger and Michel Schneider (eds); **Urban Scape Switzerland: Topology and Regional Development in Switzerland, Investigations and Case Studies** (Basle Boston Berlin, Birkhäuser, Switzerland: Avenir Suisse, 2003) p. 8 **ff.**

exactly are we talking about? *Urban Scape Switzerland* defines itself as an archaeology that lays bare the scars of a complex modernization process.

A recent Dutch study on the effects on green areas caused by increase/stabilization of the population, economic growth, a strong or weak collective sector, and technological innovation, results in four possible scenarios: Regional Communities, Strong Europe, Transatlantic Market and Global Economy.[9] Problematic, however is the fact that these scenarios can only generate static possible future developments, certainly no policy instruments for acting and very little for our understanding of our contemporary society in a state of flux. Conceptually the four scenarios are related to Max Weber's '*Idealtypus*', the 'ideal types' he introduced early on in his writing, a logical aid for his '*Verstehende Soziologie*', a fictive conceptual extreme in sociology. We cannot find them in our daily world; they are descriptions coming from our empirical observations. They are static concepts unable to grasp the fleeting qualities of our contemporary world. The dynamics in our present society are too complex to grasp in models based on ideal types.

As the Swiss landscape underwent transformations, the settlement models ended up in the waste paper basket. Like in the Netherlands, many development plans misjudged the situation, or came too late to have any influence. In a discussion reproduced in *Urban Scape Switzerland*, Franz Marty states that transport links have had a more critical impact on development in rural areas than all the legislation and spatial plans put together in Switzerland. Certainly the case is no longer a version of (urban) 'form follows function', but of urban form following car infrastructure. Public transport can no longer compete with private car transportation.

In the Netherlands, the average Vinex (*Vierde Nota over de Ruimtelijke Ordening, Extra* 1990) location has 30 to 35 houses, with virtually no density, that is to say, the density you will need for public transportation. In both countries, the higher income groups have the opportunity to live their dream of a single family house, preferably in the Swiss countryside or Dutch Vinex location. The Dutch white paper *Vinex* not only meant a policy change in reorganizing the different public and private parties involved in the development process of urban areas (municipalities had to learn to be more entrepreneurial), but also a change in environmental issues. Car traffic had to be restricted, too. Vinex locations were planned at the level of urban areas (*Stadsgewesten*) with better and shorter travel opportunities between work and housing. One of the issues was more and better housing for middle and higher income groups. Development of existing urban areas had high priority; the notion of a 'compact city' should not suffer from the newly built projects. Proximity to the urban centers, accessibility by public transport, coherence between housing, workplace and recreation, and the subsequent protection of green areas were, and are, important issues. In Switzerland, higher income groups also cater to the needs of the Communes. Higher income groups are ideal for their fiscal policies. Like Switzerland, the Netherlands does not have large cities – comfortable mass transportation is under constant pressure, with profitability difficulties. More than a million people are necessary for a metro net to be profitable; trams can be feasible with half this amount. Mass transportation depends on infrastructure and densities in residential areas.

In the Netherlands public transport has suffered from retrenchments due to expanding costs of the HSL (high speed train) and Betuwelijn which went over their budgets considerably. The Betuwelijn initially was projected as a public-private enterprise, but at the moment it is a hot issue on the political agenda; neither private investors, nor the Rotterdam Port Authority is interested anymore in its exploitation. Pro Rail, part of the Dutch national train system, is the only one that remains involved. New plans for more advanced and faster rail systems have, so far, never made it through the political arena. The so-called *Zuiderzeelijn*, a rail network connecting Amsterdam and Groningen, was recently cancelled, despite the government's promises to the north of the country to construct the line. The proposals for new magnetic tracks are not only expensive, but will also pose too strong a competition for the existing rail network which has to be expanded and renewed.

First, Second, and Third Nature Contemporary urban theory is trying to come to terms with these recent developments, both in the United States and in Europe. There is no such thing as a semantic field that could cover all the empirical observations, Eisinger already related to that phenomenon. Questions about center and periphery, town and country, miss the point, especially now that globalization of market activities has turned towns and cities into purely commercial locations. Part of globalization is our network of microelectronics and communications technology, which might change local interests in a very short time span, even changing our notions about nature and society. 'Communication', as a commonly used term, has changed its meaning. Digitalization as part of globalization has changed our outlook on the world. Most of this communication travels at high speeds, and I believe the 'means' are not to be separated from 'contents', especially not in design practices like architecture and urbanism. Cyberspace in particular, forces human beings to re-conceptualize their spatial situation inasmuch as they experience their positions in cyberspace only as simulations in some 'virtual life' form, Timothy Luke argues.[10] His argument is that we might need another reasoning to capture these

9 Leo Pols, Femke Daalhuizen, Arno Segeren, and Cees van der Veeken; **Waar de landbouw verdwijnt, Het Nederlandse Cultuurlandschap in beweging** (The Hague: Ruimtelijk Planbureau, 2005) p. 50**ff**. See for the raise in productivity: **Ruimte maken, ruimte delen. Vijfde Nota over de Ruimtelijke Ordening 2000/2020.** Publication from the Ministerie van Volkshuisvesting, Ruimtelijke Ordening en Milieubeheer (The Hague: Rijksplanologische Dienst, 2001) p. 71. See also **Van A naar Beter, Nationaal Verkeers- en Vervoerplan 2001-2020**, Kabinetsstandpunt Deel A, Ministerie van Verkeer en Waterstaat (The Hague, 2001) p. 16**ff.**
10 Timothy W. Luke; 'Simulated Sovereignty, Telematic Territoriality: the Political Economy of Cyberspace' in **Spaces of Culture**, Mike Featherstone & Scott Lash editors (London:

digital worlds. The epistemological foundations of conventional reasoning in terms of political realism, as we find them in notions about city and countryside, are grounded in the modernist laws of second nature. In taking up the notions of 'first' and 'second' nature, Luke defines the 'third nature' as the informational cybersphere/telesphere. Digitalization shifts human agency and structure from a question of manufactured matter to a mere register of informational bits. Human presence gets located in the interplay of the two modes of nature's influence. 'First nature' gains its identity from the varied terrains forming the bioscape/ecoscape/geoscape of *terrestriality*, Luke writes.

Earth, mountains, water and sky provide the basic elements mapped in physical geographies of, in this case, the Swiss biosphere that in turn influence human life with natural forces. Terrestriality – no longer like in the Greek polis or early city – directly correlates to second nature. The process of urbanization has dissolved the city walls, moats and ramparts, just as Schmid is referring to in this process described in the *Urban Portrait*. 'Second nature' finds expression in the technoscape/socioscape/ethnoscape or *territoriality*. The physical environment of first nature, as well as the artificial environment of the anthropogenic domain of the second nature of technospheres, is supplemented by digital environments of a new third nature, according to Luke.[11] 'Third nature' almost by definition has no fixed location in first nature; these environments are spread out over the globe in digital networks. In a way, this dissemination was similar to Schmid's notion of the dialectics of networks and borders. The actions of people, cities, economies, etc. constitute the space and time of the technosphere. The problem I have with Luke's distinctions is that it rests too much on theorizing the process of digitalization. In addition, Lefebvre's lived space no longer seems to have a fundamental role to fulfill. A much wider problem, however, is the 'over determination' of the digital, causing a lack of attention to the social aspects of the problem.

Spatial Developments What we can learn from the discussion, is that spatial developments in different areas only vaguely correspond to political divisions, both in Switzerland with its many Communes, and in the Netherlands where for instance the Randstad as 'city' has no election system or representational governance. Political divisions in the Netherlands also slowed down the development process of new areas. Reorganization of area borders among the different cities involved in the orchestration and development of the housing production in these new locations, has been an important factor for delayed development in the larger areas.[12] The decisive question for *Urban Scape Switzerland*, on the other hand, was how to react to the discrepancy at the political and legal levels. Quite a lot of the common terminology of the Swiss authorities is still in modernistic functional terminology. What is called the 'functional greater

Zurich region' consists of 3.5 million inhabitants and 1.5 million jobs. The catchment area starts in the Basle region, extends far into central Switzerland, and includes the area around Lake Constance on the Austrian and German sides of the border. This functional region, Eisinger writes, contrasts with the pronouncedly heterogeneous political arena, which is dissected by a great number of local, communal, cantonal and national boundaries. In other words, the spatial structure of 'first nature' is crying out for material and 'immaterial' infrastructures as he calls them; that is to say, the infrastructures of second and third nature. But due to a 'lack' of competence and insufficient coordination in the communication between the local and various regional authorities, this 'supply' is hindered. The national level apparently no longer provides an adequate basis for political action. New developments are initiated at the level of major regions like the Zurich region.

The same situation is happening in the Dutch Randstad. Of course, Switzerland has much bigger problems in the sense of accessibility; its position in Europe is marginal in that sense. The location of the Netherlands is optimal in comparison to Switzerland. The Netherlands with its two mainports of Schiphol/Amsterdam and the Rotterdam Port are much better connected to global transport. Yet determinations of an optimal scale of a region is impossible to say; in order to be ideal in scale, we have gone from an economy of scale to an economy of scope. The territorial size of an agglomeration is hardly related to its competitiveness – quite a lot has to do with the scope of the companies, infrastructure, and tax systems. At present, no statistically defined metropolitan area, and certainly no Swiss agglomeration, has the critical mass which would allow it to survive at an international level. But of course this threshold might be crossed in the near future, Eisinger argues.

Urban Scape Switzerland detects what is called The Leman Metropolis, the interlinked urban agglomeration of Geneva (including the French communities that surround it), Lausanne, Vervey-Montreux, and Yverdon. Bassand, Poschet and Wust's conclusion is that the emergence of a new type of society based on information technology is crucial for the process of metropolization. Switzerland cannot escape this tendency to metropolization, but as the authors write, it is occurring here in a very specific, very Swiss way. The country is seeing the rise of five 'metropolises' or metropolitan areas, each itself very idiosyncratic: Zurich, Basle, Bern, Sotto Ceneri, and the Leman Metropolis.[13] In the Netherlands we see the same discussion: can we see the Randstad as urban configuration, as a metropolis? A couple of years ago, we organized an international conference, published in *Cities in Transition* (2001) dealing with these issues.[14]

Sage, 1999) p. 28**ff.**
11 **ibid.**, p. 28.
12 Margit Jóкövi, Claudia Boon and Friedel Filius; **Woningproductie ten tijde van Vinex, een verkenning.** Ruimtelijk Planbureau (The Hague: NAi Publishers, 2006) p. 28.
13 Eisinger and Schneider; **op. cit.**, p. 148.
14 Arie Graafland; Introduction to **Cities in Transition** (Rotterdam: 010 Publishers, 2001) pp. 19-35.

Briefly, the issue at stake was not just information technology, but also the cultural context within which it takes place, as I suggested with the notion of 'third nature'. Information in and of itself has no meaning; it is rather what is done with it that is relevant. This distinction becomes a qualitative, not just quantitative, question, as is apparent in the Randstad debate. The Randstad will grow out into a Deltametropolis, one of the major urban areas in Europe. Road infrastructure is seen as the ordering principle, sustaining a network economy. In the Netherlands, the question of 'city' has been asked with reference to this concept of Rand*stad*. In comparison to similar questions in Paris: do the five outlying towns belong to the city of Paris or not? The answer is 'yes' when the criteria are length of journey and accessibility. According to Sudjic, who made extensive studies of the urban conglomeration of Paris, it is incorrect:

> to see the five Parisian new towns as distinct entities in their own right. Rather, they are essential parts of the city itself. They could not exist without the network of motorways, airports, and above all metro lines that constitute Paris just as much as the picturesque crust of masonry buildings of Haussmann and his predecessors. It is not just that you can get from one part of Marne-la-Vallée to another by train that counts. The fact that you can get to the shopping malls of Les Halles in less than twenty minutes, and on to the other new towns on the far side of the city without changing platforms, had transformed the mental map of the city that Parisians carry in their heads.[15]

In the opinion of Sudjic, the Dutch claims for the existence of the Randstad megalopolis – the ring of cities that takes in Amsterdam, Utrecht, The Hague and Rotterdam – amount to a deliberate political statement, an attempt to turn what would otherwise be regarded as a nation of extremely modest size into a very large city. If it actually existed, Randstad would be vast. More than eight million people live amidst its baroque steeples, prefabricated concrete housing estates and bulb fields. But as he notes, large numbers of people living in close proximity do not in themselves constitute a city, an analysis that led the Dutch urbanist Niek de Boer to conclude that the Randstad does not exist.[16] If we look at the maps, as he suggests, any comparison of the Randstad with the metropolises of London and Paris seems outlandish. The latter two cities are compact agglomerations, whereas the Randstad is a rather arbitrarily delimited set of cities, towns, villages, and farmlands. Moreover, in the latter case, it would be irresponsible to include all the activities that take place in the area and add them all up together as if the Randstad functioned as a single urban entity. The Randstad definitely does not perform as a metropolis of more than eight million inhabitants. It simply does not have the metropolitan quality of a Paris or London. Niek de Boer's analysis is much more tempered; if the Randstad is a metropolis, it should operate on the level of importance it claims by virtue of its population level and its being situated in the center of Europe. Since it does not function at this level in cultural, economic or jurisdictive aspects, it should not be considered a metropolis.

But other perspectives are also possible, the 'metropolitan qualities' could also be seen in Rem Koolhaas' perspective as adhering to old identities of traditional city centers, blocking the view of his new *generic* regions with their complete lack of tradition. I do believe the same is true for Switzerland; there is no 'metropolis' in Switzerland but rather like in the Netherlands, a *process of urbanization* producing centrality and generic fields at the same time. During an interview in 2002, published in *Urban Scape Switzerland*, Jacques Herzog announces the project he just launched at the ETH Studio Basel: the *Urban Portrait*. Herzog is keeping his critical attitude to notions of metropolization. His earlier study, *Basel – A City in the Process of Becoming?* still has the question mark. His position in the discussion comes close to that of Niek de Boer: that of traditional centrality, a city comes to life through the people who live and work there. The big question to Herzog is to ask how can a city generate an attractive living environment? 'The more complex and concentrated urban phenomena appear at a specific location, the more we can speak of the kind of city we all dream of'.[17] Although Basle is 'becoming' in the Deleuzian terminology, it is still behind Zurich which itself is still a village in comparison to, for instance, Munich. The main difference is that Basle does not have the same inner dynamics as Zurich. But when you cross the borders, you immediately encounter an 'exotic world, the other'.

MVRDV and Abstract Image Production MVRDV's input in *Urban Scape Switzerland* is a selection of topics that might have relevant consequences for Switzerland's urban planning.[18] Already in their opening remarks, they set themselves apart from what they call 'serious scientific and/or empirical work', with the aim to show 'totally different "Switzerlands"'. They mostly draw their figures from the Swiss Federal Statistical Office, and a couple of web sites. The issues they discuss are settlement, agriculture, forests, water, tourism, energy, and transport infrastructure. Their aim is to formulate a few 'what-if questions' regarding the urban development of Switzerland. These formulations could generate a number of different scenarios like 'super sprawl', and if the main transit axes were intensified, the result would be a highly accessible country. The modeling exercises are extreme extrapolations resulting in 'highway cities', 'urban nodes', 'border cities', and a 'super Zurich' of 8.7 million people concentrating virtually all of the country's inhabitants. The same procedures are followed for other categories; in other words, they produce their late modernistic and in architectural circles well known 'Data Scapes'.

Their line of thinking is comparable with the recent Dutch study I just characterized as Weberian *Idealtypus*, static concepts unable to grasp the fleeting qualities of our contemporary transitory

15 Deyan Sudjic; **The 100 Mile City** (San Diego/New York/London: A Harvest Original, 1992).
16 Niek de Boer; **De Randstad bestaat niet** (Rotterdam: NAi Publishers, 1996).
17 Jacques Herzog; in **Urban Scape Switzerland, op. cit.,** p. 162.
18 MVRDV; in **Urban Scape Switzerland, op. cit.,** p. 214.

world. It is the 'what if' question that is paramount in both cases. In the first case, it is about static concepts; in the case of MVRDV, it is about static images. Their way of working is the opposite of an existing analysis of Zurich Limmattal, under the title of *Learning from the Limmattal*, an almost phenomenological survey of the different aspects of this area.[19] The scenarios that MVRDV are describing are those of a 'splendid isolation', a 'fragmenting Switzerland', a 'dissolving Switzerland', and a 'specialized Switzerland', which are followed by project proposals. One of them, 'The Swiss Cross', discusses an improved traffic infrastructure that would enable urban regions such as Basle, Bern, and Zurich to compete better with other European regions. New high-speed train-links would link the urban centers more effectively. Redesigning the north-south highway would also improve accessibility. The proposals aim to intensify the usage of the transit system and encourage the formation of destinations. They envisage the emergence of a European central access strip, which extends the urban belts of Basle and Milan. Included is a Super Zurich, Europe's central metropolis with 2.5 million inhabitants. Other options are a Park City, using the mountainous topography. More and more options are laid out, Scenic Highways, Energy City, and a Matter City as Europe's Ski City where we could ski all year round in the streets while cars would be restricted to tunnels below.

Their designs carry with them all the reminiscences of Super Studio and Archigram, but always in the dominant image production of a late modernistic abstract geometry going back to the Dutch urban planning as in the General Expansion Plan (Algemeen Uitbreiding Plan, 1934) for Amsterdam by the Public Works Department of van Eesteren and van Lohuizen. As in the AUP, the images of Switzerland's possible developments are deceptive. The geometry is only there to designate the ground; the drawings in both cases are an illustration of a *possible* future image. Realization is not implied; possible developments are up for discussion. MVRDV does not seem to be interested in digital or blob-architectures. Their built architectural projects are of a different order. Only the planning research they do is digital. It would be a mistake to see their digital geometries as tectonic – the two worlds are separate. Digital architectures question the authority of place and space: dematerialization and non-location are the issues. MVRDV's planning strategies are on the level of digital machines; they begin to question the authority of vested interests in the planning bureaucracy. However, the temptation to go beyond abstraction in false concreteness is always

19 Michael Koch, Martin Schröder, Maresa Schumacher, Christian Schubarth; **Learning from the Limmattal**, pp. 238-269.
20 Jacques Herzog; in the Introduction to **Switzerland, An Urban Portrait, op. cit.,** pp.136-137.

there, also in MVRDV. Their Scenic Highways in *Urban Scape Switzerland* might look futuristic, but those who followed the construction of the Viaduct de Millau in France will have other ideas. The solar power panels and the Matter City fall however in the trap of the entertainment industries. Superstudio is the determining factor here, not van Eesteren.

Conclusion In the end, the thesis of the *Urban Portrait* is not convincing. In my opinion, the possible critical impact of a Lefebvrian perspective has not found its way into the book. Schmid's introduction is rather clear, but it does not translate into the ETH project. Jacques Herzog in the end, is critical about the research practices of his colleagues. Koolhaas' work at Harvard, Rossi, or Venturi in Philadelphia, they all were important at the time, but they are kind of boring right now. A strong need is present for something else to follow it, something that takes up the subject of difference again, Jacques Herzog says. For Herzog, what we need is intimate, slow-paced work on the city.[20] That might be true, but it was not that easy, even impossible, to get that kind of slow paced work that will generate these 'differences' in the book. The 'instrument' they used to achieve this, was the 'at random' probes or 'drills' into the urban field. These might have shown us a much better developed picture of social 'difference'. Yet Marcel Meili states that maybe ninety percent of what they have found by 'drilling' into the material has not appeared in the book at all. Moreover, many architecture books are ill-suited as instruments for a new understanding of the city, Jacques Herzog adds. By leaving out all these 'stories' that might result from the 'drills', the intimacy they have been looking for was very hard to grasp with their urban maps, or even photographs. Jonathan Raban's *Soft City* at the time was certainly better equipped to do that, but the problem with urban stories, as in Italo Calvino's *The Invisible Cities* or *Soft City*, is that they do not relate very well to the mapping techniques as used in architecture books. *Urban Scape Switzerland* in the end gives us the better picture, it combines an 'at the moment' phenomenological perspective with a more 'traditional' descriptive and analytical urban analysis. MVRDV's contribution is an exception here, but at least it is an exception that will provoke discussion between architects and planners.

[**1**]

[**2**]

1-2 Viaduct de Millau, France.
3 What could Switzerland become? Scenarios and project proposals, Urban Scape Switzerland. Source: MVRDV.

3]

The world-as-film: The evolution from the world-as-picture to the world-as-multimedia

Heidi Sohn

Abstract This article is an edited version of a lecture paper I presented at the DSD in November 2004. In it, I explored the possibilities of developing alternative mapping techniques, which could adapt in a more appropriate way to the increasing complexity of the urban environment. The point of departure for this examination is based on the forthcoming article 'Twisted Webs: cinematographic representations of contemporary Mexico City', in which I argued that the film *Amores Perros* (1999) once devoid of its narrative, presents a quite odd diagrammatic representational structure, one that may be approached as analogous to the city itself. Furthermore, the heterogeneity of this diagram in contrast to more conventional forms of 'mapping' (of film and the city) seems to point to a shift in the way cities and the urban experience are represented; from a fixed, static form of mapping, to a much more dynamic and systemic 'structure' that implies a variety of 'movements'.

This new character of mapping calls into question such notions as 'the world-as-picture', and the progression of *technè*, since it is through these concepts that we may begin to understand the transformations that are playing themselves out upon the urban dimension, and hence 'taking-place' upon material reality. For this purpose I elaborate on the work of Samuel Weber, who argues for the emergence of what he terms 'mass-mediauras'. I borrow from his work, in particular his readings of Heidegger's notions of *technè*, and the world-as-picture, on the one hand, and on the other of Benjamin's elucidations on the loss of aura to advocate that the contemporary complexity of the urban environment indeed requires the exploration of alternatives to the more conventional representational techniques.

Introduction *Twisted Webs: cinematographic representations of contemporary Mexico City* is the title of a forthcoming article that elaborates on the contemporary situation of Mexican cinema, focusing on the apparently dominating role that the urban, as its central thematic, has in it.[1] The mentioned article looks into the impact of political ideology – or the lack thereof – on the characteristics of Mexican filmmaking, and on the thematic of Mexican cinema throughout the twentieth century. One of the central arguments in the mentioned article is that in the genealogy of Mexican cinema there is a waning of the thematic of the rural, and its social connotation, that runs parallel to the decline of the authority of political ideologies, and the rise of a different type of logic, an economic one – that in turn has produced a change in the ruling ideology. Until the 1950s, Mexican cinema was entirely dominated by the discourse of the state (the political), which tended to elevate the notion of '*the rural*' over '*the urban*'. Due to a series of historical, political, social and economic developments during the following decades, the dominance of State – or political – ideology experiences a significant loss of influence. Hence, the weakened power of the State to influence ideological discourses, and the emergence of a new

1 Sohn, Heidi; 'Twisted Webs: cinematographic representations of contemporary Mexico City', in Jaimes, Hector (ed.), **History and Politics in Latin American Film** (North Carolina: The University of South Carolina and Duke University Press, forthcoming).

dominating ideology may be traced along the thematic shifts of Mexican films. Furthermore, the article argues that during approximately three decades, from the mid-1950s till the mid-1980s, the curve of Mexican cinema steadily declined in the quality and quantity of produced films, reaching rock bottom, almost disappearing entirely from the international scene. Paradoxically, this waning also signified the only threshold that a particular stream of Mexican cinema and filmmaking, once liberated from the ideological constraints they had been subjected to due to a strong current of nationalistic views, would encounter to reposition itself in the international scene.

In the mid-1980s, in particular during the thirteen months between August 1984 and September 1985, the confluence of two highly specific occurrences triggered a significant phenomenon, which placed Mexico City – or rather its representations – in the global spotlight. On the one hand, the publication of the August 1984 issue of The National Geographic Magazine, titled *Mexico City: An Alarming Giant*, devoted a large section of this number to the increasingly chaotic urban situation of Mexico City, which according to the author was becoming an uncontrollable megalopolis, dominated by uncertain and unpredictable forces.[2] The NG article on Mexico City was followed by another section dedicated to what was there (and possibly also 'then') labeled as an emerging phenomenon of urban gigantism.[3] In it, Mexico City reappears, and is represented as the first, and most notorious, of a series of megalopolises, which at the time were first noticed to be sprouting all over the developing world. The undertone of both these articles, as well as the accompanying photographic material, contributed to the perception of alarm and immanent danger there was in the emergence of these 'third-world' urban giants.

Less than thirteen months later, on September 19th, 1985, Mexico City became again the center of international attention. The earthquake that shook the city, the worst in the city's history, not only produced havoc and large-scale physical destruction; it also placed Mexico City as the main object of international media coverage. The first reactions in the hours and days that followed the earthquake, especially in newspaper headlines and television broadcast 'specials' were tainted with post-apocalyptic undertones, suggesting that Mexico City had been entirely devastated and reduced to rubble and debris. Without entering a discussion in relation to which of these images and discourses were factual, and which were being distorted (both, exaggerated and downplayed), nor trying to engage here in the hidden or overt motives behind the strategies of different media, the fact remains that the confluence of both these occurrences unleashed an unprecedented tidal wave of representations of a city either in ruins, or enmeshed in the chaotic situation of explosive urban growth.

The uncanny and eerie quality of a large amount of these representations, in particular photographs, set off a complex shift in the aesthetic sensibility through which the city was perceived, both locally and internationally. In short,

these occurrences unleashed a process through which Mexico City (re)encountered a mutated meaning of itself and thus (de)formed an identity based on the characteristics of these representations as a point of reference in the process of configuration.
In this, the collection of images, which originate from – but also return to – the city, once reconciled through the media [in a marriage between images (photojournalism, television video and film) and their accompanying texts], arguably fulfill an important function in the formation of individual and collective perceptions, understandings and knowledge of the city. In other words, through the photo- and cinematographic operations and techniques, the city is formed, informed, transformed, deformed and eventually conformed by the manipulation of imagery as a highly subjective phenomenon, which is nevertheless presented as a more or less 'faithful' representation of reality; of truth.
'Twisted Webs' approaches these issues through an analysis of the relatively recent and highly controversial Mexican film *Amores Perros* by Mexican director Alejandro González Iñárritu.[4] Drawing from the main conceptual idea behind the forthcoming article – namely that representations of contemporary Mexico City's experience of reality are centered around the conundrum of 'twisted webs', the article argues that this experience can be represented schematically; once emptied of its narrative contents, it can be diagrammatically rendered, traced or delineated: a set of animated meshes conformed by tangled (narrative) and 'spatial' relational triangulations, which account as much for the complexity of the film, as they do for the complexity of the city. The architectonics of the film, if one may adapt this Kantian term to this type of representational object, reveal a complex formation that resembles a landscape of protuberances, flattened or evened out surfaces, open fields, cycles, lines-of-flight, vectors and trajectories, as well as the configuration of afterimages that produce phenomena comparable to 'plateaus' that when taken into an interpretative level can be inserted into a reading of the city as comparable to the diagrammatic structure of the film. In this sense, then, the underlying scheme in this film becomes a semi-unconscious representation of the forces that shape the experience of the city, and which as such, cannot be divorced from the discussion that links representations to their object. Arguably, the city plays a secondary role in this film, but it is precisely through the interstices (intervals) between the scenes, that the city takes on a life of its own. In this, as Deleuze's points in Cinema I, it is essential to comprehend not only the structure of this film, but also how the structure of the film influences and shapes the way the city is perceived.[5] And as the medium, which utilizes the frame and the interval as one of its essential elements, film becomes crucial in this discourse.
The interval, the 'in-between' frames and images, also accounts for another central issue: the

2 Bart McDowell (ass. ed.), Stephanie Maze (photographs); 'Mexico City: An Alarming Giant'; in **National Geographic**, August 1984, Vol. 166, No. 2, pp.138-177.
3 Robert Fox; 'The World's Urban Explosion', in **National Geographic**, August 1984, Vol. 166, No. 2, pp. 178-185.
4 **Amores Perros** [trans. Love's a Bitch] (1999) dir. Alejandro González Iñárritu, Script by Guillermo Arriaga, Mexico City: Mexico. It is noteworthy that **Amores Perros** is González Iñárritu's début as a film director.
5 Gilles Deleuze; **Cinema I: the Movement-Image** (Minnesota: University of Minnesota Press, 2003).

temporal element. The interval allows for positioning but also, and simultaneously, infers a kind of temporality, and hence of movement. In this, and similarly to film, the experience of the megalopolis is given by an overriding perception of movement, acceleration and speed, by the vertiginous experience of forces, desires and affects, which as practices, shape space and set it into 'motion'.

The representation of the experience of urban life implies the necessary involvement of movement; particular 'forces', which precede and determine motion and action, are therefore at hand. In short, life is animated, and needs to be represented through a combination of both static and dynamic processes.

The contemporary condition of the urban, as an increasingly growing complex systemic formation, calls out for an intense search for comprehensible, yet adaptive, instruments of mapping.

In this, and as I will elaborate at the end of my paper, Fredric Jameson's proposal to develop new forms of representations that suit and adapt better to an increasingly depthless and superficial 'reality', is key to the questions of mapping urban complexity. As such, mapping is indispensable in the organization of a universe of representations and representational artefacts, the institutions of representation and the institutions that we seek to represent, as well as the institutions of knowledge. Film, photography and cartography provide the efficient presentation of visual information, on the one hand, and on the other, the availability of sophisticated techniques of 'montage' and editing allow for a mediation between different aspects of cities, from their materiality, to their abstractions.

Technè, place and the construction of 'reality' through representation Before embarking upon the exploration of alternative forms of mappings it becomes paramount to mention that this search is a consequence of – and departs from – the so-called 'crisis of representation'. This crisis, as would be expected, unleashes similar predicaments in virtually all fields, especially those that are dependent on the image in all its variants for the production and dissemination of 'knowledge'.

Although the crisis of representation may be approached through various directions, the lead that interests us in this context is the one that springs from the post-structuralist corner, and which reaches its climax in deconstructive thought. The work of Derrida, Lacoue-Labarthe, Deleuze and Guattari, to name only a few, reflects a continuing and long-standing effort to delimit the authority of representational thought by exploring its consequences in areas that have been particularly resistant to such questionings: 'history', 'politics' and 'ethics'.[6]

To briefly explain the operation through which the world is 'constructed' through representations, I will introduce the work of Samuel Weber, in particular two lecture-essays dealing with the work of Martin Heidegger and Walter Benjamin, collected under the title *Mass Mediauras*.[7] According to him, the work of Martin Heidegger, despite remaining relatively unexplored in North

American poststructuralist theory, offers interesting alternatives in the rethinking of history, sociality and politics, while simultaneously addressing an additional question: that of 'place'. According to Weber, Heidegger's work 'emerges as a privileged place from which the question of place itself is put into play,' stating that 'the name that Heidegger assigns to this play, in which the question of determination joins that of institutionalization, is *technics*.'[8] The association of *technics* (understood as a form of *technè*, and not properly as 'technology') with both the political and knowledge (episteme) in Heidegger's essay 'Die Frage nach der Technik'[9] is not only related to what Lacoue-Labarthe identifies as a pivotal element in Heideggerian thinking[10] but also to the fact that the type of knowledge which it produces is a quite particular one. The knowledge of *technè*, or *technics*, is thus not addressed at manufacturing or producing particular things per se, but rather at the 'unlocking of beings as such'. Hence, *technics* may be understood as a form of *poiesis* (as the distinct object, or end of a creative act or *praxis*), which in tandem is closely related to *art*.[11] Furthermore, the notions of *technics* are associated to other operations, such as the processes through which objects and things, beings and phenomena acquire their position, their place, and hence result in a sort of system of classification that relies on the 'fixing' of certain objects in relation to an observing or perceiving subject. This 'place-making' ability of *technics* relates – in a problematized form – to the second level of analysis in Heidegger's essay, namely the distinctions he draws firstly, between *technè* and *physis* as two distinct forms of *poiesis*, and secondly, between a 'pre-modern' form of *technè* (understood as a skill, a craft), and the more contemporary understanding of *technè* as a forerunner of modern technology. Both these distinctions are held against the idea of 'nature', since it is against nature, or upon nature, that *technè* 'takes place'. Although the first distinction is relevant in Weber's interpretation of Heidegger's notions of *technè* in that it explains the phenomenon of 'outbreak' (*Aufbruch*) and 'opening-up', what I would like to elaborate on in this context is the second distinction, namely that of the differences between traditional and modern *technics*. Heidegger does not explicitly go into this intratechnical distinction;[12] he however does offer the example of pre-industrial agriculture as a form of 'pre-modern' or traditional *technè*. In this form of cultivation, *technics* cooperates to further what Weber calls spontaneous 'openings', but which depend on external intervention to present themselves – or 'come-forth' – fully.[13] In a pre-modern praxis of *technè* the peasant works or tills the ground (*bestellen*) while retaining the idea that this work requires an amount of care (*Pflege*). As Weber says, this type of cultivation 'does not challenge nature, does not goad and drive it forth

6 Samuel Weber; **Mass Mediauras: Form, Technics, Media** (Stanford, California: Stanford University Press, 1996) p. 59.

7 The titles of these lectures (published as part of the book **Mass Mediauras: Form, Technics, Media**) which concern us in this article are 'Unsettling the Setup: Remarks on Heidegger's "Questing after Technics"', pp. 55-75; and 'Mass Mediauras, or: Art, Aura and Media in the work of Walter Benjamin. The 1992 Mari Kuttna Lecture on Film', pp. 76-107.

8 **op. cit.**, 6 (Weber), p. 59.

9 Martin Heidegger; **Die Frage nach der Technik**, **Vortraege und Aufsaetze** (Pfullingen: Guenther Neske, 1967).

10 Philippe Lacoue-Labarthe; **Heidegger: Art and Politics** (Oxford: Basil Blackwell, 1990) p. 53.

11 **op. cit.**, 6 (Weber), p. 60.

12 **ibid.**, p. 67.

13 **ibid.**, p. 68.

and thus transform it into a mere source of 'energy, which as such can be extracted and stored.'[14]

In the industrialized era, however, nature ceases to be cultivated, in the sense of being plowed, tilled and cared for (*bestellt*). Instead, industrialization relates to nature in that it 'places' it (*gestellt*). This nevertheless carries a threatening, obscure undertone of cornering, entrapping, or maneuvering nature 'into a place from which there is no escape.'[15] This all too familiar phenomenon of natural exploitation is intimately related to the praxis of 'placing', of assigning place, and hence of determining an 'unnatural' order to nature itself. In other words, 'nature is *placed on order*.'[16]

The spontaneous order of places that characterizes nature in regard to traditional *technics*, is shattered and replaced by a different kind of order: the placing-of-orders that tends to dislocate and level all pre-established orders of places. Traditionally a way of bringing-forth, *technics* has now become a driving- or goading-forth: exploiting, extracting, expelling, inciting. This 'un-securing' evidences and is marked by both a movement and a change of direction. This means that instead of being brought 'up-front', *technics* – in its progression – is transformed into a demanding, exacting and outward-bound *poiesis*.

But rather than being a simple 'continuation' (in the sense of its going-on, its progression) the transition from traditional to modern *technics* is accompanied by an increased drive to control, to regulate and secure the orders of place. This drive, something Weber describes as an 'obsession with securing, with placing into safety', paradoxically, derives from – and responds to – the unchanged 'un-securing' in which *technics* as such continues to take part. Or how the movement of un-securing evokes as response its diametrical opposite, 'the frantic effort to establish control and security.' *Technics* takes its place as that which assembles the disparate in a fixed and stable order.[17]

Nevertheless, there is an inherent dysfunction in the former sentence, that evidences the shift that 'place', or rather the understandings we have of it, has undergone since the Aristotelian view that sees place as an immanent, stable and contained concept, as 'the inner-most motionless boundary of what contains'.[18] Modern *technics* forces this deep, motionless boundary out, driving it away from its motionless state. 'It begins to move', as Weber states. This is not foreign to the going-on of *technics*, in its un-securing, 'un-sheltering', and displacing capacities. What makes modern *technics* different from older, more traditional forms is that the principle of 'containment' has lost its function as a prerequisite of order. Place as 'container' breaks up, and hence discloses the problematic consequences of an ordering that can no longer be taken as a given.[19]

Weber goes as far as to suggest that in the breaking up of the container of place, what emerges is not a confused state of place, or even a de-centered or displaced order, but rather a *Gestell*: an apparatus, a 'skeleton', a frame, that collects, assembles and displays the new, predetermined orders, and which simultaneously shows a predisposition of this apparatus to place (or assign a place) as well as to stake out a place. In this, there is a strange combination of movement and stagnancy present, one that problematizes and complexifies the meaning and signification of the very act of 'placing-order'.

At this point the notions of emplacement may be brought up to explain this operation of collecting and assembling into a 'skeleton' (*Gestell*) in which everything, from human beings to inert objects, are cornered and set in place. Places must continually be established, orders constantly placed. As emplacement, the progression of modern *technics* thus displays a markedly ambivalent character: it arrests, brings to a halt, by setting in place; but this placement itself gives way to other settings, to the incessant re-placing of orders through which new places are set up and upset. On the other hand, if we approach emplacement as more than a static 'status quo', as a dynamic process, it becomes evident that it holds the potency to simultaneously open-up and close-down specific orders. This possibility reflects a fundamental issue in Heidegger's concept of the progression of *technics* and its relationship to an objectifying, representational thought and the subjectivism and voluntarism of modern metaphysics: 'the fact that man becomes a subject and the world an object is a consequence of the institutionalizing of *technics*, not vice-versa.'[20] In other words, Heidegger seems to assert that once the 'matrix of representational thinking' – the subject-object relationship – becomes institutionalized by the emplacement of modern *technics* (and in this sense also of modern technology), the progression or continuation of *technics* will undermine the objectivity upon which that matrix depends. Moreover, representational thinking determines reality as its foundation, and hence treats objects as quantifiable data, as accountable information. In tandem, and regardless of whether this occurs in economic practice or in modern art, objects are stripped of their objectivity (or de-objectified), hence becoming subject to the calculations of a subjective will, which struggles to realize its representations in an effort to place itself in a secure place. The paradox in this, is that there are no safe places, since emplacement remains subject to the movement of un-securing that it seeks to escape or ignore. It is precisely in this paradox that the 'danger' of modern *technics* emerges, namely in that in its progressions, in its continuation, in its 'going-on', it not only dislocates and displaces the emplacement that aims at the attaining of a problematic order, but also wipes out its own heterogeneity. The progressions of *technics*;

> set in place, but the fixity of such place-setting turns into a placing of orders that can never stop. The more technics seeks to place the subject into safety, the less safe its places become. The more it seeks to place orders, the less orderly are its emplacements. The more representational thinking and active strive to present their subject matter, the less the subject matters, the more it idealizes itself as pure will.[21]

14 ibid., p. 68. [Here, Weber directly quotes from Heidegger's **Die Frage nach der Technik**, p. 14.]
15 ibid., p. 68.
16 ibid., p. 68. (original italics).
17 ibid., pp. 69-70.
18 ibid., p. 70. [Here, Weber quotes directly from: Aristotle, (1984) Jonathan Barnes (ed.) **Physics, The Complete Works of Aristotle: The Revisited Oxford Translation**. Princeton: Princeton University Press [IV, 4, 212a].
19 ibid., p. 71.
20 ibid., p. 73 [Here Weber quotes from Heidegger's **Holzwege**, 1963, p. 268].
21 ibid., p. 74.

From the 'world-as-picture', to the 'world-as-film' The aforementioned crisis of representation is thus a problem that ramifies into many directions, touching upon not only the questions of place and *technics*, of its relations, and hence of the geo-political and the social implications, but which also involves multiple dimensions: 'reality' and the material world included. Reality seems increasingly 'polluted' by an apparatus of imagery that produces, reproduces and disseminates a massive amount of 'pictures' of it, which at some point erase the direct or indirect link they allegedly hold to its referents, thus generating a simulation of the world. The question in this regard is related to the processes that may be taken to be responsible for this condition. Regardless of what is often believed, representation rarely depicts 'reality' as such. Instead, representations often represent other representations 'in a chain of signifiers that circulate from one medium to another all the while believing, or letting us believe, that there is a direct referent.'[22]

This reminds us that a system of representation is not just a technique (or science), but also an ideology that allows for a rationale to be developed that would make the representation seem natural and thus invisible as such. If seen closely, this point is related to the subject, and also to the notions of world-view and world-as-picture. These may be transposed into the understanding that the city, as man's construction of the world, falls more or less generally under the same premises that follow Heidegger's concepts. Heidegger's essay 'The Age of the World-Picture'[23] becomes a crucial issue in this context, since in it he elaborates on the notion of world-as-picture (*Weltbild*), differentiating – but simultaneously relating it – to the notion of worldview (*Weltanschauung*). The former is what characterizes modernity since the Renaissance in that instead of substituting one worldview for another, this age (*Neuzeit*) attempts to conquer – or grasp – the world as an image. In short, it tries to determine the world as having the structure of a picture. As an image, the 'reading' of the world-picture involves various processes. Firstly, the heterogeneity (difference) of beings is accepted only in so far as it can be objectified and represented, grasped and *named*. In the process of naming, a double movement is implied, which simultaneously sets things in front, and brings them towards oneself.[24] In addition, this dual movement is subordinated to the overriding aim of 'putting things into place', of 'classifying', 'categorizing', or 'ordering'. The place of the subject is hence confirmed, which because of its power to represent, becomes the 'reference point of beings as such'.[25] When this place is secured, and when the movement of presenting (placing before, *vorstellen*) encompasses the totality of beings as such, the world itself takes the form of a picture, whose final aim is to establish and confirm the centrality of man as the being capable of depiction: 'once the world has become an image, the human position grasps itself as a Weltanschauung.'[26] Weber states in this regard, that the age (or time) of the world-picture may be considered to be that of the presentation, of the 'Vorstellung.'[27]

In very brief terms, Heidegger attributes two structural characteristics to the world-as-picture: First, its pretensions to universality and totality (or what he names 'planetary ambitions'), and secondly, its tendency to be schematic or systematic: 'where the world becomes a picture, the system becomes predominant, and not only in thinking.'[28] This evidences two related issues. On the one hand, the systematicity of the world-as-picture (as a *system*) reunites several dissimilar elements, while on the other, it establishes a representational *structure* within which these elements are inserted, and to which they have to conform. This structure is not merely a static structure; as has been said earlier, it implies a dual movement: a highly ambivalent oscillation of bringing-forth and setting-before, which aims at securing the foundation of the subject at and as the center of things.[29]

The system, then, is highly dynamic, something that goes in hand with a tendency of things to move with greater velocity, and acceleration. Hence, and taking into account that the growing predominance of speed determines movement, and hence also undermines the basis of traditional spatial relations, the question to be addressed is how pictures can contribute to this race for speed and acceleration, and more if this race is driven by the agenda of securing the place of the human subject.

Heidegger's interpretation of the subject-securing function of the world-picture is related to what might be called the kinetic, or cinematic structure of pictures.[30]

Furthermore, the premise and the interpretation that the world – and in tandem the city – is read under similar rules by which pictures, images or graphs are deciphered, that is: subject to a structure and to the kinetic, necessarily leads to the work of Walter Benjamin, 'The Work of Art in the Time of its Technical Reproducibility' (more widely known as 'The Work of Art in the Age of Mechanical Reproduction').[31] Here, a comparison between Heidegger's 'The Time of the World-Picture' and Benjamin's essay shows that, beside being joined by a certain pictoriality (*Bildlichkeit*) in thematic and language, both center and originate from a fissure, or rather shift, in Western culture, which gradually emerges as the epicenter of the modern period.

For Heidegger, this shift can be traced back to Descartes, and from here that we receive the so-called 'Cartesian anxiety'. This point will be associated further on in this text to the reading that Jameson makes of Heidegger's notions of world-picture, in particular in relation to the position of the subject.

22 Diana Agrest; 'Postscript: Representation as Articulation between Theory and Practice', in Stan Allen, **Practice: Architecture, Technique and Representation** (The Netherlands: G+B Arts International, 2000) pp. 163-178.
23 Martin Heidegger; **Die Zeit des Weltbildes, Holzwege** (Frankfurt am Main: Klostermann, 1963) In English: 'The Age of the World Picture' in **The Question Concerning Technology and Other Essays** (New York: Harper and Row, 1977), pp. 133-4.
24 **op. cit.,** 6 (Weber), p. 78.
25 **op. cit.,** 23 (Heidegger, **Holzwege**), p. 81.
26 **ibid.,** p. 86.
27 **op. cit.,** 6 (Weber), p.79.
28 **op. cit.,** 23 (Heidegger, **Holzwege**), p. 93.
29 **op. cit.,** 6 (Weber), p. 80.
30 **ibid.,** p. 81.
31 Walter Benjamin; 'The Work of Art in the Age of Mechanical Reproduction', in **Illuminations** (New York: Shocken Books, 1968).

In Benjamin, however, this shift can be concretely pinpointed to the mid-nineteenth century, where, together with – or perhaps due to a phenomenon of – urbanization, the increasing mechanization of reproductive techniques, the traditional distinction between production and reproduction begins to blur, and break down. It is in this blurring division between production and reproduction, between the original and its copies, that the so-called 'aura' of art-works is progressively eliminated.

But perhaps more importantly, this division, and the decline of the aura, permits '… the reproduction to meet the beholder or listener in their particular situation', and hence to actualize 'that which is reproduced'.[32]

Hence, it appears, Benjamin is implying a dual process: the changes in the forms of production and reproduction – namely technology – propel humanity into a historical crisis: that of representation, which, nevertheless, simultaneously represents the promise of renewal for society. Furthermore, the crisis, and the promise of renewal '… are intimately connected with the contemporary mass movements. Their most powerful agent is film.'[33]

In this context, and drawing from the previous quotes, I will briefly analyze three main points in order to investigate whether in Benjamin's account one could prognosticate the emergence of something comparable to an aura emanating, or enveloping the more contemporary notions of mass-media. These points are 'the beholder', 'the receiver', or 'the listener', mass-movements and the medium of film.

Firstly, what Benjamin refers to as 'the beholder' or 'listener' (in German *dem Aufnehmenden*) implies both that the action of beholding is at once receiving and recording, producing and reproducing, and further, that instead of a single subject, the beholder, the produced and the reproduced is a 'mass'.

In short, and very simplistically, the receiver as a mass is a matrix from which all traditional behavior toward works of art issues today in a new form. Quantity has been transmuted into quality.[34]

Here, it is the mass understood in its qualitative, and not quantitative character: as massive or mass-like, and the implications of the massive character of the mode of reproduction that appear to be especially intriguing for Benjamin.

Mass as in dispersion (*Zerstreuung*) refers not only to the diversion or distraction typical of a mass, but also of its physical dispersion, of mobilization. In this sense, dispersion implies a kind of movement, and this brings me to the second point of analysis: the idea of 'mass-movement'.

Benjamin's approach to the 'mass-movements' probably may be implying more than the obsolete idea of mass as an inert, heavy collective, typical of the 1930s. Rather, or in addition to this latter reading, the mass could be interpreted as a dynamic element, which is the result of a detachment (or movement) that absolves – or more correctly, dissolves – the aura. For aura relates to mass not just as uniqueness does to multiplicity, but also in spatial terms, as a fixed location does to one that is caught up in an incessant and complex movement. Again, very simplistically, movement as in dispersion, together with the massiveness of this mobilization, and the massive character of production and reproduction, can be taken as the core of the problem of the decay of the aura of the artwork.

But despite of its progressive decay and dilapidation, the aura never fully disappears. In fact, and as Weber argues, it seems to always return with a vengeance in those forms of representation that are most hostile to it: film, and in more contemporary terms also video, and television. The aura, as the appearance or apparition of an irreducible separation, is always constituted in a process of self-detachment: a process of detachment from the self, and as a demarcation of a self.[35] The aura would then be something like an enabling limit. The aura, understood as the emanation of an object, once it removes itself from the object, is a frame falling away from a picture. In its fall, in its decay, it becomes light.

Benjamin was obviously fascinated by the techniques of film production, as a process of recording, of reproductive inscription, of *aufnehmen*. The mediation of an apparatus in the process of recording – a camera – as an instrument of re-inscription, 'takes up' the given and does three very strange things to it: it apprehends it, arrests what seems to be its spontaneous or intrinsic movement and submits it to a series of operations that have nothing to do with its 'natural' inclinations; secondly, it opens the way for those elements to be dislocated and relocated, broken down into elements and recombined into ensembles that have little to do with their initial state; and thirdly, the finished product is placed into circulation, accompanied by the semblance of what has been radically undermined.[36]

But is this process enough to dissolve the aura for good? This points towards something that Benjamin already seemed to prognosticate: the loss of the aura of the artwork is never a total loss; it's not a total disappearance. Rather, it is an uncanny mutation of the aura, which occurs and perhaps even begins within at the specific – and operative – process of filmmaking: the torn-up, fragmented images which in a latter process of re-composition 'find their way together in accordance to new laws.'[37] This operative process of re-configuration (montage and editing) recalls the practice of surgeons during invasive operations, on the one hand, and on the other, it points towards the understanding of *technics* as the knowledge upon which things are ordered and organized, thus receiving and inhabiting a specific place. The *poiesis* that accompanies this understanding, and which is also related to art, permits the aura in its mutated form to take on a completely new character: that of mass-media, or in Weber's terms 'mass mediaura'.[38]

This concept is relevant in the context not only of how we have come to perceive the world, and the urban, but also of how we represent it, and thus of how we establish a system that eventually will assign its place to it; of how the aura of mass-media provides the world-as-picture with a wider option of retaining – although in a mutated form – its aura.

32 ibid., p. 221.
33 ibid., p. 221.
34 op. cit., 6 (Weber) p. 89.
35 ibid., p. 87.
36 ibid., p. 90.
37 ibid., p. 91.
38 ibid., pp. 105-107.

Technology (understood now as a form of production and reproduction, rather than as Heidegger's form of 'knowledge acquisition') has changed the way we come to 'see' the world, it has modified our 'reading' of it as a picture, and transformed it into a recording of it in its changed form: the world-as-film. In tandem, and considering the contemporary state of affairs in relation to new technologies and the knowledge these convey, it may well be possible that we are moving towards the understanding that 'sees' and renders the world-as-multimedia.

The City as Multimedia According to Wolf Schneider, in his book *Ueberall ist Babylon: Die Stadt als Schicksal des Menschen*[39] the city is the world man has constructed for himself. This idea of 'construction' seems to point towards what Jameson has interpreted as Heidegger's world-as-picture, namely that of the notion of 'representation' as a way of constructing the object in a specific way.

The privileged example of an object in representation is perspective, both in painting and later in the related ideological analysis of film theory. Perspective clearly reconstructs the object as a phenomenon (in Kant's sense), as an object perceptible and conceptualizable to us. As Jameson states: 'The object in perspective is not merely a figment, an idea for me, a projection or a product of my own subjectivity. It merely offers a certain construction of the real among other conceivable ones.'[40] In the context of a construction of the object by representation, the self that seems to automatically accompany the cogito and the focus of the represented object must also be grasped as a construction.

Jameson's critique to Heidegger's model as a 'purely formal account of the emergence of the subject'[41] departs from the fact that Heidegger sees the construction of the object of representation as perceptible only in so far as perception can 'take place': it is this structural or formal place, and not any kind of substance or essence, which is the subject.

This critique of representation denounces perspective as being ideological in and of itself, without intervention of the subject. But this is also the sense in which, in Heidegger's narrative, the object may be said to produce the subject. Here, Heidegger's connection to Descartes as the point of emergence of modernity becomes clear: the purpose of this construction is the construction of certainty, something that in Cartesian terms can only be achieved by way of a preliminary construction of doubt. Certainty can only be achieved by a systematic dispelling of doubt, which one must produce in advance and control.

Unfortunately, and as is increasingly becoming clear, certainty in this Cartesian sense is extremely elusive and quite impossible to achieve. The search for historical and other types of certainty has confronted us with the fact that human constructions, and here I refer specifically to the construct of the city in all its variants, have remained sites of doubt, and not of places of certainty. The historical evidence we have in and about them is inherently unstable. Their vastness both in scale and complexity, their mutability, the historical erasure to which they are subject, confront to the daunting obstacle of 'reading' sense and certainty into them, and making sense of all the representations that have been made of them. And while there certainly are genre distinctions between oral histories, written documents, quantitative data, maps, and photographs about and of cities, each is subject to the same Cartesian anxiety that the knowing subject may not be adequately representing the reality of the urban condition, or that (as in Kant) the knowing subject is simply debarred from knowing the 'thing-in itself' of that reality.

Jameson approached the topic of the 'illegibility' of the modern metropolis arguing that cities evidence most clearly the emergence of a new condition. History is effaced by the 'depthlessness' that characterizes a core condition of the world space of multinational capital: the ultimate source of exploitation and alienation. In this, metropolis is the signature location of modern indeterminacy. As Marshal Berman puts it: 'The city has become not merely a theater, but itself a production, a media presentation whose audience is the whole world.'[42]

At this point, I forcefully need to make a short detour and bring forth the concepts of the 'world-as-picture' once more.

In his *Tractacus*, Wittgenstein asserts that: 'Pictorial form is the possibility that things are related to one another in the same way as the elements of a picture. That is how a picture is attached to reality; it reaches right out to it. It is laid against reality like a measure.'[43] This quote, although very much in synchronicity with Heidegger's views, shows that the discourse of representation is essentially pictorial, photographic, as is history, the past, memory and so on. As historical artefacts, and as containers of both past and present, cities converge with their representations through a phenomenology of indexical linkages. To recognize artefacts from the past as part of our world is to draw a set of index lines from the institutions of representation to the institutions we seek to represent.

But what confronts us nowadays is not so much the barrier to reality imposed by the Cartesian anxiety, but rather the sheer complexity of the mapping problem. Even before Kevin Lynch, and as an answer to the Cartesian anxiety as exposed by Bernstein and Rorty, Jameson foresaw an 'as yet unimaginable new mode of representing [the world of multinational capital], in which we may again begin to grasp our positioning as individual and collective subjects and regain the capacity to act and struggle, something which is at present neutralized by our spatial and social confusion.'[44] The confusion to which Jameson is referring in this quote is analogous to the tangled perceptions of urban space and time, and the difficulty of mapping these 'perceptions'.

39 Wolf Schneider; **Ueberall ist Babylon: Die Stadt als Schicksal des Menschen, von Ur bis Utopia** (Germany: Droemer Knaur, 1968) p. 7.

40 Fredric Jameson; **Postmodernism, or the Cultural Logic of Late Capitalism** (Durham: Duke University Press, 1991) p. 52.

41 Fredric Jameson; 'Postmodernism, or the Cultural Logic of Late Capitalism', in **New Left Review** (July – August 1984) pp. 59-92.

42 Marshall Berman; **All That Is Solid Melts Into Air: The Experience of Modernity** (New York: Simon and Schuster, 1988) p. 288.

43 Ludwig Wittgenstein; **Tractacus Logico-Philosophicus**. D.F. Pears and B. F. McGuinness, trans. (London, 1974) 2.151 – 2.1512, p. 9.

His plea for new modes of representation highlights the necessary development of tools of 'cognitive mapping' in order to visualize a particular intersection: 'the coordination of existential data [the empirical position of the subject], with unlived, abstract conceptions of the geographic totality.'[45]

Here, multimedia mappings may be considered a viable alternative to Jameson's probe.

However, before elaborating on just how to merge maps and multimedia into a methodological experiment that allows us to pursue some empirical and interpretative strategies to gain knowledge of the city, it is necessary to 'delineate' the two key elements of this fusion: maps, as artefacts, and mapping as practice, on the one hand, and on the other multimedia.

Firstly, the questions of maps and mapping: Despite the fact that maps are essentially ambivalent – that is, that while the mappability of historical evidence of cities oscillates between the certainty of what inheres in their location, this specific evidence always raises consciousness of alternatives that were not identified or mapped, and that they have been associated as instruments of political, ideological and social power and control – maps are simultaneously keys to access 'certain' knowledge (space-time phenomenology). Mapping is a powerful metaphor of the historical knowledge, and as such, it is a concrete tool for affirming the presence of the historical condition of the present. Maps allow for the mediation between the local and the global, or said in other words, between the domestic and the foreign, fostering the establishment of new knowledge communities.

Secondly, multimedia – understood as a technique of representation, but also as a form of taking-up, of recording, of '*Aufnehmen*' – shows how the world-picture and the city-image have become dispersed, while retaining something of an aura: Samuel Weber's 'mass-mediaura', and hence remaining susceptible to critical inquiry. Furthermore, this understanding of multimedia as dispersed and fragmented is approachable through the analogy of 'reading the newspaper': the reader moves freely between fragmentary articles, images, photographs and

44 **op. cit.,** 40 (Jameson), p. 54.

45 **ibid.,** p. 52.

46 Michel de Certeau; **The Practice of Everyday Life** (Los Angeles: University of California Press, 1988) See also: Pierre Bordieu; **The Logic of Practice** (Stanford: Stanford University Press, 1990).

47 Prasenijt Duara; **Rescuing History from the Nation, Narratives from Modern China** (Chicago: University of Chicago Press, 1997) p. 72.

48 Bruno Latour (2001). In a lecture Bruno Latour held in Rotterdam in 2001, he countered the ideas of Bentham's panopticon and Foucault's analysis of this concept in **Surveiller et Punir** [Discipline and Punish, Penguin, London, 1991] with another Greek term: the 'oligopticon'. In contrast to the notions of panopticon, an oligopticon implies 'seeing a little, very well, but just a little bit.' Latour argues that cities are not made according to a panoptic idea of a complete visual space, but rather 'thready characters of the whole being built in a city, so that you never have actually a whole which is not connected to a small place where very little information is actually gathered.'

captions, film-clips, etc. This is a practice, which has been liberated from a linear narrative. Its experience is somewhat comparable to surfing a web site, or exploring an interactive CD, or DVD, practices that are becoming increasingly commonplace.

Multimedia mappings, or rather a methodology that supports such mappings, depends on a 'theory of practice', much in the sense of Michel de Certeau and Bourdieu.[46] And in their pursuit of other forms of enquiry, the categories or classifications to which subjects and objects need to be subjected to respond to a systemic mode of selection. There will always be the open-ended and subjective. Multimedia mappings open the possibility to include in one single 'here-and-now' a vast collection, and selection of representations in static and dynamic terms: the trace, the drawing, the animation; the photograph, the film; the text, manuscripts and documents, as well as any other historical artefact, including narrative and narratology, can easily be included in a multimedia map.

The 'system' of a multimedia mapping reminds one of a 'space-time' panopticon, which departs from Bentham's notions, and the disciplinary function that Foucault criticized, by creating what Duara calls a 'dispersion' of narratives.[47] Moreover, and to mention only a few other possibilities of the type of information, and the broad approaches that may be included into a multimediatic 'map', Bruno Latour's concept of 'oligopticon'[48] is a relevant example. Lastly, but no less importantly, Benjamin's concept of counter-representations, or apperceptions, may be inserted into the concept of a multimedia map. Benjamin claimed that architecture, for instance, is perceived in a state of constant distraction, and hence is never fully grasped. The medium of film, in its mediatic character is able to incorporate the object of architecture into a frame, where the city and its architectures are received and recorded by the subject.

The process of multimediatic mapping provides for a substitute to what Benjamin proclaimed as 'healers' – magician and surgeon, painter and cameraman – translating its functions and characteristics to contemporary times. The work of art in the time of 'digital reproduction', a concept which is possibly more adequate and in tune with the present 'world', allows to bring forth the 'world-as-picture'. But in addition to this, and through a series of operative processes, multimedia mappings permit us to enter the 'world-as-picture', bring it closer to us, while simultaneously bringing ourselves closer to it, and mediate these to-and-fro movements in much the same way that film did in Benjamin's times.

Like an insect eye with thousands of independent points of view, a multimedia mapping resembles a labyrinth, just like the city.

Art, Beauty, and the Mystery of Form

Karsten Harries

Part one In his Epilogue to 'The Origin of the Work of Art', Heidegger claims that the truth of Hegel's pronouncement that art in its highest sense has come to an end has not yet been decided. For the time being 'the judgment remains in force.' But for that very reason the question is necessary whether the truth the judgment declares is final and conclusive and what follows if it is.[1] That question is not answered by the fact that most of the art that people care about today, as measured, e.g., by sales of reproductions of works of art or by the art hanging in people's homes, or by what people come to see in our galleries and museums, is art created after Hegel lectured on the death of art. For what do people care about when they care about art? They may be looking for something more soothing or beautiful than their everyday surroundings; or they want to be amused or entertained; or they want to be provoked, challenged, even shocked, at any rate experience something more interesting than their daily routines have to offer; or they want to keep up with the latest development in the art-world. But what does any of this have to do with what Hegel took to be art's 'highest task':

> Fine art ... achieves its highest task when it has taken its place in the same sphere with religion and philosophy, and has become simply a mode of revealing to consciousness and bringing to utterance the Divine Nature, the deepest interests of humanity, and the most comprehensive truths of the mind. It is in works of art that nations have deposited the profoundest intuitions and ideas of their hearts, and fine art is frequently the key – with many nations there is no other – to the understanding of their wisdom and their religion.[2]

On this Hegel and Heidegger agree: in its essence art is tied to the sacred. And for both that means further that the distinction between art and great art must be drawn in terms of art's relationship to truth. But does the establishment of truth today still require art? Hegel answered this question with a decisive no. He would have granted Heidegger that 'The history of the nature of Western art corresponds to the change of the nature of truth', granted him also that this change 'is no more intelligible in terms of beauty taken for itself than it is in terms of experience',[3] but he would have challenged Heidegger's understanding of truth. Hegel would have us understand history as the progress of truth and freedom. For him and his many followers there is no reason to follow Nietzsche and Heidegger in understanding modernity as the age of nihilism. To do so would be to fail to recognize that science can rise beyond the understanding that is a presupposition of our science of nature: today we no longer need art to tell us what most profoundly matters. We have our reason, which today must take the place of both art and religion and give voice to 'the deepest interests of humanity, and the most comprehensive truths of the mind'. 'For, on the one hand, science, in the shape of the subservient understanding, submits to be used for finite purposes, and as an accidental means, and in that case is not self-determined, but determined by alien objects and relations, but, on the other hand, science liberates itself from this service to rise

1 Martin Heidegger, 'The Origin of the Work of Art', **Poetry, Language, Thought**, trans. and intro. Albert Hofstadter (New York: Harper and Row, 1971) p. 80.
2 Georg Wilhelm Friedrich Hegel, **Introductory Lectures on Aesthetics**, trans. Bernard Bosanquet, ed. and intro. Michael Inwood (Harmondsworth: Penguin, 1993) p. 9.
3 Heidegger, 'The Origin of the Work of Art', p. 81.

in free independence to the attainment of truth, in which medium, free from all interference, it fulfills itself in conformity with its proper aims.'[4]
But does a Science that refuses to allow itself to be determined by what Hegel here calls 'alien objects' remain scientific? Must the attempt by 'Science' to liberate itself from such service not lose itself in the clouds, as Aristophanes suspected? Must it not lead to thought losing touch with that earth which remains the source of all meaning? Like Schopenhauer or Nietzsche, Heidegger insists that reason is unable to 'fulfill itself' as Hegel had confidently proclaimed, that the dream of such fulfillment is vain and can only lead to self-alienation. What Hegel understands as progress, Heidegger thus understands as an obscuring of the earth and with it of the mysterious advent of truth in beautiful form.[5] Heidegger would thus recall us to the way form can join beauty and truth concealed by both modern science and aesthetics:

> The beautiful does lie in form, but only because the forma once took its light from Being as the *'isness'* of what is. Being at that time made its advent as '*eidos*'. The idea fits itself into the *morphe*. The *sunolon*, the unitary whole of *morphe* and *hule*, namely the *ergon*, is in the manner of *energeia*. This mode of presence becomes the *actualitas* of the *ens actu*. The *actualitas* becomes *realitas*. Reality becomes objectivity. Objectivity becomes experience. In the way in which, for the world determined by the West, that which is, is as the real, there is concealed a peculiar confluence of beauty and truth.[6]

'The Origin of the Work of Art' would thus return us to that mysterious power of form concealed in complementary fashion by both, an understanding of reality as the totality of objects and of artworks as occasions for aesthetic experience. What most fundamentally distinguishes Hegel and Heidegger here is their different understanding of reason, reality, and their relationship. Hegel takes reason and reality to be essentially commensurable. That leaves no room for Heideggerian mystery. All that deserves to be called real is there for us to comprehend. That also goes for whatever forms we may discover. And is not part of our modern understanding of reality such conviction that reality does not in principle transcend our understanding? As T. J. Clark suggests, modernism turns on the impossibility of transcendence.[7] Such impossibility denies form that ontological illumination Heidegger invokes.
Important here is Hegel's insistence that reality not be reduced to those 'alien objects' that concern the natural sciences: reason may not stop with nature so understood. While Descartes thus put humanity on the right track when he promised a method that would render us the masters and possessors of nature, reason can and must rise higher if human beings are to truly take charge of their destiny and become truly autonomous. Reason must take the place of religion. The marginalization of art is part of that progress.
Only a certain circle and grade of truth is capable of being represented in the

medium of art. Such truth must have in its own nature the capacity to go forth into sensuous form and be adequate to itself therein, if it is to be a genuinely artistic content, as is the case with the gods of Greece. There is, however, a deeper form of truth, in which it is no longer so closely akin and so friendly to sense as to be adequately embraced and expressed by that medium. Of such a kind is the Christian conception of truth; and more especially the spirit of our modern world, or, to come closer, of our religion and our intellectual culture, reveals itself as beyond the stage at which art is the highest mode assumed by man's consciousness of the absolute.[8]

Hegel here ties the marginalization of art, not to the rise of science and the objectification of nature it presupposes, but to 'the Christian conception of truth, and more especially the spirit of our modern world', which he takes to have come closer to understanding the 'proper aims' of reason than the scientific conception. It is our religion, transformed now into the modernist faith in the power of reason to lead humanity to what it most deeply desires, that demands the marginalization of art. Is such faith justified? Is reason able to give our life its proper form? I shall have to return to these questions. But regardless of what position we take here, we can agree that any insistence on a profound relationship between art and the sacred is in tension with the dominant tenor of today's intellectual, religious, and artistic life.

The history of Western art can thus be written as a history of the progressive emancipation of art from everything foreign to its essence. The first part of such a history might discuss the emancipation of art from religion; the second the emancipation of art from representation; the third the emancipation of art from the demand for all external meaning and content. That history is also a story of the progressive loss of that light beautiful form owes to Being, according to Heidegger. A remark made by Frank Stella in a discussion, broadcast in 1964 as 'New Nihilism or New Art?' testifies to that loss: Stella wanted to create works that would allow one just to look at them, works that would convince by their absorbing presence. Not meant to refer beyond itself, to be approached as either symbol or allegory, the work of art here is not supposed to say something. It can therefore be neither true nor false. But it is precisely this, here explicitly renounced, quality of pointing beyond itself that is inseparable from all sacred art. As suggested by the broadcast's title, such a conception of art would seem to entail the divorce of art from the sacred. What matters now is that by the absorbing strength of its form the art-object provide an occasion for an experience that we appreciate because it is what it is. Should we be troubled by such substitution of the artwork's absorbing presence for the sacred? That will depend on what we take to matter about art, indeed about anything, will be bound up with the concrete way in which we exist in the world. What sense can we still make of that light that according to Heideger the beautiful once took from Being? What does it matter?

4 Hegel, **Introductory Lectures**, p. 9.
5 Heidegger, 'The Origin of the Work of Art,' p. 81.
6 **ibid.**
7 See T. J. Clark, 'Farewell to an Idea': **Episodes from a History of Modernism** (New Haven and London: Yale University Press, 1999).
8 Hegel, **Introductory Lectures**, pp. 11-12.

Part two But does this supposed exclusion of the sacred from art do justice to the evolution of modern art? Can we not say with just as much reason that modern art has taken over and reoccupied the place of the sacred? How else are we to understand Michael Fried's celebration of paintings by Kenneth Noland and Jules Olitski or sculptures by David Smith as transporting us by their presentness into a state of grace? To be sure, time does not stand still in aesthetic experience. What Fried calls 'presentness' is no more than an elusive idea that may haunt painters, but inevitably withdraws when they try to seize it. All art can do is gesture towards such a standing still. Fried hints at this when he retreats from the indicative to the subjunctive: 'It is this continuous and entire presentness, amounting, as it were, to the perpetual creation of itself, that one experiences as a kind of instantaneousness: as though, if only one were infinitely more acute, a single infinitely brief instant would be long enough to see everything...'[9] 'If only one were infinitely more acute.' This corresponds to Stella's wishful pronouncement that if a painting 'were lean enough, we would be able just to look at it.'[10] But of course, it will never be lean enough, we will never be granted a completely innocent perception. The dream of creating an art object self-sufficient and dense enough to absorb all of our attention, full enough to allow us to experience it in a way unclouded by meanings, by words, by absence, remains a dream. No art object can ever have the required plenitude and density. Meanings will always get in our way. The idea of presentness is itself such a meaning. The modernist works praised by Fried do not so much grant presentness as they signify it. Signifying presentness they mean a secularized grace.

Even the most minimal art, I pointed out, is not simply present, but gestures towards an ideal meaning. Precisely because it does, it calls for the interpreting word. That passionate interest so many brought to minimal art cannot be divorced from an interest in its meaning.
What does such presence matter? Is what is merely present not essentially meaningless? One answer to such questions is provided by Kasimir Malevich, whose decision in 1914 to place a black square on a white background and to present it as a painting constitutes one of the decisive acts in the history of modern painting. In explanation Malevich points out that he chose the square as the most abstract form and black and white as the most abstract colors. 'Abstract' here means not only non-representational. It means free of all associations, feelings, emotions, interests that tie us to the world. The square is chosen because it has no physiognomy, because it is in this sense uninteresting and because of this more purely present. Interest stands in the way of presence.

The question returns: why this fascination with presence? Why this attempt to get away from meaning? In his answer Malevich appeals to the conflict between human demands for meaning and the silence of the world. Again and again this conflict has led human beings to veil this silence with words, with the words of poets, with the words of philosophers, but especially with the words of religion. Today, Malevich suggests, these words have shown themselves for what they are, human creations born of wishful thinking and, once recognized as such, unable to sustain us. The disintegration of the old value system has left us an oppressive silence. But that silence only remains oppressive as long as we demand meaning of the world. Malevich dreams of an existence no longer burdened by the demand for meaning. He knows that to pursue this dream, we have to take our leave from the familiar world. We must learn to let things be, to encounter forms without asking anything of them, without trying to wrest meaning from them. Yet we are so used to our world, so used to questions, to expecting answers, that we need to be transported by art into a stranger and cooler environment, into the white world of Suprematism. The white square is to grant us an unprecedented freedom and a similarly unprecedented clarity of vision.

The simple white square is a limit of modern art that Malevich thinks, but does not try to mark with a particular work. His black on white compositions already represent a further step: the silence has been broken. Geometrical shapes announce their presence. And precisely the black square and the black circle have so little meaning in the usual sense, they announce their presence more forcefully than do the more familiar things of the world, which, because we know where to place them are easily overlooked and taken for granted. Because these things have a meaning, in this sense speak to us, their simple presence is obscured. Silence and presence belong together. But Kant was right to insist that all art speaks to us of an intention and thus has a meaning. This art, too, strikes us as not just being, but as meant just to be. Malevich's Black on White, and the same is true of much recent art, is a theatrical gesture that refers us beyond itself, to the artist's intention, and perhaps this intention speaks to us more strongly in the case of Malevich's suprematist compositions than in much more traditional, say representational art. What is the meaning intended by Malevich? Malevich's self-interpretation provides us with an answer: his art is to silence all meaning, all words; it gestures towards whiteness, towards the void. His suprematist compositions are icons that seek to establish zero as the holy. In a way that recalls Schopenhauer, they offer an illustration of what Nietzsche wrote in *The Genealogy of Morals*: 'man would rather will nothingness than not will'. [11]

Part three If those committed to aesthetic autonomy must welcome the divorce of art and religion, so must those convinced that their religion does not permit a too intimate link between the beautiful and the sacred. Protestantism can thus be said to have purified religion by distancing itself from art. Thus it was in terms of its greater inwardness and spirituality that Hegel understood the superiority of Christianity over Greek religion. Essentially the same position is

9 Michael Fried, 'Art and Objecthood', **Minimal Art: A Critical Anthology**, ed. Gregory Battcock (New York: E. P. Dutton, 1968) p. 146.
10 Bruce Glaser, 'Questions to Stella and Judd', **Minimal Art: A Critical Anthology**, ed. Gregory Battcock (New York: Dutton, 1968) p. 158.
11 Friedrich Nietzsche, **On the Genealogy of Morals**, III, 28, trans. Walter Kaufmann and R. J. Hollingdale, **On the Genealogy of Morals/ Ecce Homo** (New York: Vintage, 1967) p. 163.

defended today by the philosopher Louis Dupré:

> ... religion became caught in its own aesthetic images. The Greek gods, at least as we know them through Homer and Hesiod, were conceived as human ideals. The more perfect they grew, the more they lost their meaning as religious symbols, that is, as finite appearances which reveal an infinite transcendence. Ultimately their perfect containment within finite forms, their aesthetic potential, killed the Greek gods. Their very conception demanded an aesthetic treatment, long before poets and sculptors made them into actual works of art. Once they received it, they turned into sculpture and literature, and died to religion altogether.[12]

From the very beginning Christianity thus has struggled to keep its proper distance from the beautiful forms of art. Dupré grants that art loses much when it loses its connection with religion, but presumably not something that really belongs to it, and thus he, too, insists that once religion and art have come to be differentiated, it is essential that the difference between the two be preserved. On this view, it is not a degeneration of art that lets it sever its ties to religion. Both parties should welcome the divorce. If it is the very dynamism of religious transcendence that lets religion leave art behind, that same distance allows art to seize beautiful form as what is truly its own.

'Religious transcendence': just what is being transcended here? Temporal reality? Reason? Especially when we add the attribute 'infinite' to 'transcendence' we run the risk of emptying it and also God of all meaning until in the end mysticism and atheism come to coincide. But must transcendence be thought in opposition to temporal reality, to sensuousness? The link of transcendence to both eternity and disembodied spirit invites questioning. Is this link essential to Christianity? Is it even compatible with it? This much seems certain: to the extent that spirit is privileged at the expense of sensuousness, eternity at the expense of time, it will be impossible for human beings to arrive at a full self-affirmation.

Characteristic of modernity is a splintering of the life-world into increasingly autonomous spheres: a splintering that means inevitably also the disintegration of individuals. Phrases such as 'war is war', 'business is business', 'art for art's sake' belong together.[13] One aspect of such splintering is insistence on the autonomy of art. The expression 'aesthetic distance' is telling. And is not religious life today marked by a similar distance? It, too, would seem to have separated itself from the whole of life, a separation that may well seem demanded by the separation of church and state.

And yet, as Dupré also emphasizes in *The Other Dimension*, 'it is equally obvious that religion cannot survive as a particular aspect of life.' He thus links the importance of the sacred to its 'unique power of integration'.[14] Heidegger would have us link that power to the Greek *logos* or to what in the passage cited above he calls the light of Being.

But does this not suggest that to the extent that art sets itself up as an autonomous sphere, it has to be attacked by any genuinely religious person? This implies a more general claim: so understood, religion is incompatible with a way of life that scatters life into autonomous provinces, even, or perhaps especially, when one of these claims the title 'religion'. Given a commitment to an integrated way of life, one may well want to call the modern insistence on the autonomy of art false – false in the sense of doing violence to what life should be. Art for art's sake is linked to the individual's inability or unwillingness to affirm him- or herself in her entirety.

Does this then argue for the kind of understanding of art and religion Hegel and Heidegger associated with the Greeks, where we may also think of archaic religion? Must Christianity not distance itself from all such views? Should we not look to the form-giving spirit for the demanded integration, not to the sensuous? There is no need here to rehearse the history of Christian iconoclasm. That the marriage of art and Christian faith should have been an uneasy one from the very beginning is to be expected, given Christianity's emphasis on the spirit, on the one invisible God, who suffered no other gods.

And yet: this God incarnated Himself and thus closed the gap between spirit and body. Must we understand the Incarnation with Asterius of Amasia as a humiliation to which God submitted 'of his own free will and for our sake'?[15] Should we not understand it rather as a mysterious necessity, demanded by both body and soul, sensuousness and spirit? And if so, should we not join those who appealed to the Incarnation to defend art, it, too, an incarnation of spirit in matter, a becoming visible of logos in beautiful form? But Christianity is the religion of the God who died on the cross. After that death, we should not expect God to show himself here on earth: he needs to be reborn within us, in the spirit. Modern Christianity thus has difficulty accepting the Incarnation, which confronts us with the paradox that Mary should be God's mother, daughter, and bride, just as it has difficulty granting more than an aesthetic significance to art. Thus many Christians today relegate the Incarnation, like art in its highest sense, and like so much of the religion they inherited, to a past whose remnants have their proper place in some museum. Christianity has become the religion of the no longer visible, the dead God, the religion of a spiritual and increasingly empty transcendence.

We have inherited such suspicion of religious art. If we are no longer iconoclasts, this is because we have difficulty taking the religious function of art seriously. But must we not agree with Hegel that 'thought and reflection have' indeed 'taken their flight above fine art'?

Part four Dupré suggests that, the more perfect the images of the Greek gods grew as aesthetic objects, the more they lost 'their meaning as religious symbols, that is, as finite appearances which reveal an infinite transcendence'. I agree that the understanding of the work of art

12 Louis Dupré, **The Other Dimension. A Search for the Meaning of Religious Attitudes** (Garden City: Doubleday, 1972) pp. 169-170.

13 See Hermann Broch, 'Der Zerfall der Werte', **Essays,** vol. II, **Erkennen und Handeln** (Zurich: Rhein, 1955) p. 42.

14 Dupré, **The Other Dimension**, p. 18.

15 Arnold Hauser, **The Social History of Art**, trans. Stanley Godman, vol. 1 (New York: Vintage, n. d.) p. 138.

as a beautifully formed aesthetic object threatens a loss of the aura of the sacred. I agree also that human beings finally find meaning only in what transcends their freedom. Freedom needs to be tied to responsibility if it is not to degenerate into increasingly arbitrary and pointless spontaneity. Such responsibility in turn presupposes an ability to respond to something that transcends freedom and yet has sufficient claim on us to bind freedom. But I cannot think such transcendence in opposition to world and time. A God who does not descend into the sensible cannot bind freedom. The Enlightenment sought in reason the necessary bond. But not only has God died; Hegel's confidence that reason can 'rise in free independence to the attainment of truth, in which medium, free from all interference, it fulfills itself in conformity with its proper aims' has met with a similar fate. Responsibility demands a different sort of transcendence, where the very word 'transcendence' may blur what matters: I here call 'transcendent' what eludes the grasp of our concepts and words. In that sense we transcend ourselves precisely as embodied, temporal beings, where, as Nietzsche recognized, the body should not be placed in opposition to soul. With Nietzsche's Zarathustra I would rather say that the self, which Zarathustra calls both 'body' and 'a great reason', transcends the spirit, our 'little reason'.[16] Heidegger's 'earth' points in the same direction.

Self-transcendence may and indeed must also be understood in a very different sense, as is suggested by these words by Meister Eckhart: 'Yesterday as I sat yonder I said something that sounds incredible: "Jerusalem is as near to my soul as this place is." Indeed a point a thousand miles beyond Jerusalem is as near to my soul as my body is, and I am as sure of this as I am of being human, and it is easy to understand for learned priests. My soul is as young as the day it was created; yes, and much younger. I tell you, I should be ashamed if it were not younger tomorrow than it is today.'[17] 'Youth' here means proximity to the origin, where origin is thought as the infinite abyss of the godhead that lies within us. While I recognize the possibility and seductive power of such a return to this origin, I also fear its anarchic potential: the abyss of the infinite that opens up here within the self swallows whatever might distinguish God, the core of the soul, freedom, and nothing. God, once he has become so infinite, so indefinite, threatens to evaporate altogether. Such an empty transcendence cannot provide human beings with a measure and thus leads to a new experience of freedom. But freedom that acknowledges no measure must degenerate into caprice.

We therefore need to distinguish a material from a formal transcendence. In the first case what is transcended is precisely that linguistic or conceptual space in which things must find their place if they are to be understood and comprehended. 'Material transcendence' points in the same direction as the Kantian 'thing-in-itself', which is present to us only as appearance, and as Heidegger's 'earth'. What invites talk of a thing in itself is the fact that, even if constituted by our language or concepts and as such appearance, what thus appears is not created by our understanding, but given. Inseparable from our experience of what Heidegger calls the thingliness of things is a sense of this gift, an awareness that our understanding is finite, and that means also that the reach of our words is limited. Nothing real can ever be fully translated into words. Like Kant's 'aesthetic idea', it is 'inexponible'.[18] More than our ordinary experience of things, the experience of the beautiful reveals the rift between thing and word, between reality and language, earth and world, a rift that can only be closed at the price of reality. Speaking that refuses to recognize this rift must degenerate into idle talk. Any philosophy that would take the place of religion is subject to such degeneration.

Language opens human beings to reality. Yet language conceals even as it reveals. Where this essential concealment is forgotten, language cannot but replace reality with a false, merely linguistic reality – and that holds also for religious reality. This, to be sure, is challenged by Hegel's conviction that 'Science' is able to liberate itself from its subservience to the given and rise 'in free independence to the attainment of truth', fulfilling itself in conformity with its proper aims. Such liberation Hegel would have us understand as the fulfillment of the Christian promise. But those who are unable to make sense of such a homecoming, will want to insist that we cannot dispense with art, especially with art that does not rely just on words.

To be sure, human being is essentially a dwelling in language. But it is important not to let the house of language become a prison. Art, I have suggested, can, but as so much art today demonstrates, need not be, a way of opening the windows of that house. That goes also for poetry, which should not be understood as a speaking that is privileged in that it offers particularly effective descriptions of things, but rather as speaking that re-presents the essence of language in such a way that that essence becomes conspicuous and with it the rift between language and reality that is essential to language.[19]

In this sense material transcendence or Heidegger's earth are a necessary, but not sufficient condition for what may be called 'sacred transcendence'.[20] What they lack is precisely that 'unique power of integration' Dupré rightly takes to be a defining attribute of the sacred. Sacred transcendence is material transcendence experienced as possessing an integrating power. This is how Heidegger understands the Greek temple's world establishing: 'In setting up the work the holy is opened up as holy and god is invoked into the openness of his presence. Praise belongs to dedication as doing honor to the dignity and splendor of the god. Dignity and splendor are not prop-

16 Friedrich Nietzsche, **Zarathustra**, **Erster Teil**, 'Von den Verächtern des Leibes', **Kritische Studienausgabe**, vol. 4, p.139; trans. Walter Kaufmann, **The Portable Nietzsche** (Harmondsworth: Penguin Books, 1976) p.146.

17 **Meister Ekarts Predigten**, ed. and trans. Josef Quint, 3 vols. (Stuttgart: Kohlhammer, 1936-1976), 'Adolescens, tibi dico: surge!' 2 : 305. **Meister Eckhart**, trans. Raymond B. Blakney (New York: Harper, 1957) p. 134. Translation changed.

18 Immanuel Kant, **Critique of Judgment**, par. 49, A190/B193; ; trans. J. H. Bernard (New York: Harper, 1951) p. 157.

19 Karsten Harries, 'Poetry as Response. Heidegger's Step Beyond Aestheticism', **Midwest Studies in Philosophy**, vol. 16, **Philosophy and the Arts** (Notre Dame: Notre Dame Press, 1991) pp. 73–88.

20 See Louis Dupré, 'The Sacred as a Particular Category of Transcendence', **Transcendent Selfhood. The Loss and Rediscovery of the Inner Life** (New York: Seabury Press, 1976) pp. 19–22.

erties beside and behind which the god, too, stands as something distinct, but it is rather in the dignity, in the splendor, that the god is present. In the reflected glory of this splendor there glows, i.e. there lightens itself what we called world' (p. 44). Splendor is understood here as the presence of the divine.

Heidegger links the world establishing of what he calls 'great art' to an openness to what I have called material transcendence: setting up a world, the work is said to set forth the earth. Much art today struggles to keep human beings open to this elusive dimension. The recent fascination with the abject participates in this struggle. But 'great art', as Heidegger understands it, demands more: the holy needs to be 'opened up as holy', 'the god needs to be invoked into the openness of his presence', if the work of art is to possess the integrative power needed to establish a world in Heidegger's sense. Heidegger's word for that power is splendor. – But what is such talk of the holy and god to us moderns?

Part five I have distinguished material from sacred transcendence in terms of what Dupré calls the latter's 'unique power of integration'. Heidegger points in the same direction when he grants that 'The beautiful does lie in form', but warns us that such an understanding of beauty will mislead us should we forget that this is so 'only because the forma once took its light from Being as the isness of what is.' But if that is accepted, must we not associate something like sacred transcendence, not just with the establishment of a world, but with what Heidegger calls the thingliness of the thing? We fail to do justice to that thingliness when we approach it just in terms of Heidegger's 'earth'. What such an approach misses is what philosophy inadequately grasps when it understands the thingliness of the thing as what gathers a throng of sensations into a whole. We have 'long been accustomed to understate the nature of the thing' by representing it 'as an unknown x to which perceptible properties are attached. From this point of view, everything that already belongs to the gathering nature of this thing does, of course, appear as something afterwards read into it.'[21] What is here called the 'gathering nature of this thing' demands more careful consideration. How is it linked to beauty? To form?

Any successful naming of the essence of things presupposes that these must already have touched human beings more immediately. To find the right words we have to experience how some thing or things belong together, have to respond to some gathering or integrating power. Think of perceiving a family resemblance. We often perceive such a resemblance without being in possession of the concept that would explain it. The perception of how a work of art fits together is not so very different. Plato thus understands beauty as a descent of the idea into the visible. In the visible we experience the idea's gathering power. Baumgarten might have spoken of a clear, but confused perception of perfection, Kant of an aesthetic judgment. Following the poet Hölderlin, Heidegger often speaks a different language: the gods themselves have to let us speak.[22] To name a god is to find a word for the ground of such a belonging-together of things. Heidegger therefore calls the divinities 'the beckoning messengers of the godhead'.[23] Once again following Hölderlin, he will also speak of angels. Artists and poets respond to their message and make it public. Such ability to hear binds the imagination. But every attempt to thus name the gods and to make public what remains incomprehensible in order to give human beings the measures they need to come together as a community does violence to what surpasses comprehension. Again and again we are in danger of replacing gods with golden calves.

What is such talk of gods and angels to us today? Would we not have been better served, had Heidegger listened more to Kant than to Hölderlin? Are we not talking here about the productive imagination as the ultimate ground of empirical concepts, where the German Einbildungskraft points to the gathering together of some manifold that Heidegger connects with the word 'logos'? As Kant recognized, we cannot look for the ground of such gathering in either the subject or the object. It surpasses our understanding and it is therefore not surprising that we should grope for it with inadequate symbols.[24] But if such a shift in language would move the discussion into more familiar territory, by appearing to locate the power of integration in the subject, it also threatens to obscure what Kant recognized: that the ground of such integration transcends subject and object and must be sought in the supersensible to which theory has no access. Heidegger's self-consciously poetic use of words underscores the elusiveness of the measure-granting ground of human dwelling.

'Mortals dwell in that they await the divinities as divinities. In hope they hold up to the divinities what is unhoped for. They wait for intimations of their coming and do not mistake the signs of their absence. They do not make their gods for themselves and do not worship idols. In the very depth of misfortune they wait for the weal that has been withdrawn.'[25] But if we can only await the divinities and if they are yet necessary for an authentic dwelling, must such a dwelling not elude us, hoped for perhaps, but something that cannot be willed. Heidegger asks us to dwell in the knowledge of the absence of the godhead's messengers, to resist the temptation to dance around some golden calf, warns us not to substitute idols for angels, measures we have made up for measures gained by interpreting the messages of the godhead's messengers.

But if Heidegger rejects idolatry, how, in the absence of divinities, is our modern dwelling to find measure and direction? His suggestion that we wait for what has been withdrawn hardly allows for the content necessary for authentic dwelling, renders the idea of such a dwelling utopian. This much, however, has become clear: Heidegger opposes to our modern way of life a mode of existence that once gave human beings measure and ground in what we can call sacred order. Heidegger, too, would seem to dream of Greece and its gods. Or of that Catholic faith he lost and yet never quite left behind, otherwise how could he have said: 'Only a god can still save

21 Martin Heidegger, 'Building, Dwelling, Thinking', **Poetry, Language, Thought**, trans. and intro. Albert Hofstadter (New York: Harper and Row, 1971) p. 153.
22 Martin Heidegger, 'Hölderlin und das Wesen der Dichtung', **Erläuterungen zu Hölderlins Dichtung, Gesamtausgabe,** vol. 4 (Frankfurt am Main: Klostermann, 1981) p. 45.
23 Heidegger, 'Building, Dwelling, Thinking', p. 150.
24 Immanuel Kant, **Critique of Judgment**, 'Introduction' and pars. 49, 57, and 59.
25 Heidegger, 'Building, Dwelling, Thinking', p. 150.

us.'[26] Why does he speak in the singular of ein Gott, rather than in the plural of gods? Key here is Heidegger's understanding of authenticity, which calls for self-integration. This is why the authentic life cannot finally be satisfied with a plurality of gods. As long as human beings hear only their voices, while God remains absent, dead, or mute, there is no escape from fragmentation and dispersal. Without God there can be no measure of the human being in its entirety. For Heidegger, too, purity of heart is to will one thing. This the gods deny. To will one thing is possible only in response to the claim made on us by one God. Only such a God can become the theme of an all embracing world, in which persons and things find their proper places, and thus allow for an interpretation of the totality of things as a cosmos.

Despite the terminology, we should not overlook how much separates such a view from the tradition. On the traditional view God created the human being in His image. This makes human being dependent on God. On the view outlined here human being in the world receives its measure in an ideal image of itself. To establish such an image and thus to give human being its measure is the task of art.

But how can human beings experience God as their measure, if they are given measures only through human work? Heidegger suggests that it is art that establishes God as God. But if God is to provide human existence with its integrating center, God must be more than just a poetic or an artistic fiction. Such fictions must be created in response to a power that issues from within, but also beyond human being and gather human being-in-the-world into a meaningful whole. Heidegger's understanding of art as an establishment of the world and of God as the hidden center or theme that gives world its form are thus not really different. Without this center we have worlds, but no world.

26 'Nur noch ein Gott kann uns retten', **Der Spiegel**, 31 May 1976, pp. 209. Trans. Lisa Harries, 'Der Spiegel Interview with Martin Heidegger', **Martin Heidegger and National Socialism: Questions and Answers**, ed. Günther Neske and Emil Kettering (New York: Paragon, 1990) p. 57.

The Form of the City

Stephen Read

The substance of 'the urban' The presumed 'shift' to 'the urban' as a universal condition, a shift Lefebvre signalled at the end of the 60s,[1] was also a shift, in his analysis, *away* from categories such as the political, the economic, the industrial or the social, understood as sufficient producers of an urban condition and frames for explaining the city, and a shift *towards* an analysis which was framed *spatio-temporally* and which submerged these other categories in a radical relationality.[2] Lefebvre was signalling that the instruments of the analysis of the urban were failing, as the urban itself began to assert a forceful autonomy in being the agent of its own dynamism and change. The city we knew had begun a relentless and accelerating drift in directions given by attractors set by no human hand and framed within no contemporary explanatory diagram. The human artefact *par excellence* had broken free of the moorings that had been constructed for it and was charting its own course; a course that was drawing an ever denser creeping web of urbanisation over the globe's surface, and was changing profoundly the conditions of contemporary life. This change was being driven, apparently, all the while by the energies *of* that life – in a 'groundless ground of lived/living concatenation, conglomeration and visceral cross-reference'.[3]

The urban world seemed suddenly to change in substance; away from being a ponderous construction built towards the social end of the overdetermined poles of society and nature,[4] it had become something pulsing, alive, polyrhythmical, contingently eventful, and inexorably spreading and thickening. The 'black box' Lefebvre referred to turned out in the end to be both more forceful *and* more real, *and* more alien and autonomous, than even he had imagined. It has forced us to reconsider our constructions of a bounded 'social' and revise our presumptions of the constitutions of urban societies and cities. All of a sudden, and concomitantly with massive regularisations and compressions induced at regional and global scales by institutional systematisations, connectivities and mobilities, we were being confronted with the limits of presuppositions that had been around so long we had forgotten they were creatures of our own making. The city had become other than unambiguously 'social construction', more than unambiguously 'artefact', product of our civic and technical deliberations and wills – and closer to a 'force of nature'. It had become a field of forces and intensities with its own dynamical behaviour; a site of autonomous creation and no longer simply architecture, product of humanly creative action. The urban had 'become "objective", that is creation and creator, meaning and goal'.[5]

To approach the urban as 'objective', as 'autonomous creation' and as 'force of nature', is to approach the constitution of the world differently. We have been forced to understand that the

1 Henri Lefebvre; **The Urban Revolution**, trans. Robert Bononno (Minneapolis: University of Minnesota Press, 2003).
2 See: Gregory J. Seigworth & Michael E. Gardiner, 'Rethinking everyday life', in: **Cultural Studies**, vol. 18 (2004): no. 2/3, pp. 139-159.
3 **ibid.**, p. 141.
4 The 'constitutional settlement' of Latour. See: Bruno Latour, **We Have Never Been Modern**, trans. Catherine Porter (Cambridge Mass: Harvard University Press, 1993).
5 Lefebvre (2003), p. 28. The layers of 'the rural' and 'the industrial' have turned out to lack the power, even as 'floating signifiers', over urbanisation processes that Lefebvre granted them at the

city, in its dynamic order, is linked to universals which are more concrete and self-propelling and *real*, less transcendental and differentiated from the material of the world, and less inclined to follow or reflect the orders *we* use to make sense of these things.[6] To approach the urban in this way – as a *genesis* of form in a field of 'events'[7] rather than as some representative or reflective form consequent on 'the social', 'the economic' or some other such framing – is to say that we no longer subsume this term within some social or other 'structure' whose levels and connections are guaranteed as if its integration belonged to 'the order of things'. It is to say that the condition of the urban is *of* the world and its material relationality, and working on its own terms, rather than being an issue of either 'structures' or 'representations' – though the urban no doubt, as a dynamic, *carries* representations. But it is also to suggest the possibility that the urban has *always* been of this 'objective' generative order, and that the urban may be less about one way of life, one mode of social organisation over another, and more about the way an urban phenomenon and an urban society emerges everywhere, and everywhere autonomously, out of the ways life intersects with situation in the very 'moment' or 'event' of its becoming. It is to say that a monadology of everyday life could belong to an imbricated *urban* ecology – each 'event' and 'moment' a new 'whole' in an erupting and particular becoming out of an extensive urban space. And the process of 'moments' and their succession becomes in this framing *intrinsically open* as the 'multiplicity' of 'moments' expands inexorably.[8]

'The urban' becomes located therefore in the 'concrete abstraction' of situation in a live and erupting urban surface, rather than with the universals of our categories. We begin to see the possibility of linking the moment of *sociality* directly with material and urban situations and to understand that the urban is fundamental to the constitution, and to an everyday *emergence* of an urban social, in its everyday presences, co-presences and visibilities.

A produced space-time of the city In spite of the volume of words spoken about space and time as a *product* of the processes of the city, it seems still that there is a lack of understanding of the real implications of this notion. The idea of the 'production' of space or of space-time has been used as a slogan, or, a rallying call against positivistic models of the city and its functioning. But the idea has then been too often, and without further thought, put to work to support another ideological position; that of the primacy of the human subject and his or her direct (though sometimes unwitting) involvement in a production of a *social* space of the city. The perhaps too quick assumption is that the alternative to a positivist, universalising, functional-spatial model will necessarily affirm the human-centred (and rather *socially* positivist and functionalist) predilections of the objectors. The human subject is elevated to primacy as universalising (and active) principle, in place of a functional-spatial process and we are not necessarily closer to understanding a space or space-time produced in, or, by the city and its processes.

Urban space and time is misunderstood, I argue, precisely because we have not considered *the urban* to be a producer in its own right of its own spaces and times – and the logic of the urban to be its own self-integration as a dynamic and process. This is not to deny the fact of the city's social inhabitation by humans, nor to deny the importance of the perspective of the human subject in defining urban 'matters of concern'[9] – it is simply to say that the perspective of the human is not necessarily privileged in defining 'how things work' – and especially that it is not the only one implicated in integrating the urban world into a form for us. There are large implications for the matter of our being and of our 'being urban' and 'being social' – even for our 'being human' – in this last statement; I take seriously both Latour's re-enrolling of objects (including the object of the city) into our collective of 'objects that judge', of 'beings' with 'agency',[10] and DeLanda's insistence that generative bodies (and agency) exist at all scales and consist of all substances.[11]

An urban space may, I propose therefore, be implicated in setting up fields of presence and encounter which powerfully *form* our understanding and expectations of what it means to be a social being in place – and may have integrative and formational effects on everyday, situated sociality. This space may also be a producer of the variety and specificity of urban place – which may become socially formed and variably intelligible by virtue of the fact that it is indexed to this integrative space. These claims cannot all be elaborated and defended in one paper:[12] They are likely in any event to be claims that can only be demonstrated as being plausible, as a foundation for an everyday social reality – for a situated and embodied being 'before social being', a social 'knowledge before knowledge' – and this demonstration is the subject of on-going research involving the mapping of everyday lives and spatial societies and economies in the Spacelab laboratory. I will attempt here simply to elaborate some of the characteristics of a hybrid urban-social space as well as some of the practical effects of this space and its relevance for urban form and design.

time of writing and from his particular ideological position in the 1960s.

6 See: Bruno Latour; **We Have Never Been Modern**, trans. Catherine Porter (Cambridge Mass: Harvard University Press, 1993).

7 'Events' are from A.N. Whitehead, **Process and Reality** (New York: Macmillan, 1979). Lefebvre's own 'monadology' involves 'moments'. See: Henri Lefebvre, **Critique of Everyday Life: volume II**, trans. John Moore (London: Verso, 2002).

8 This is a rather Whiteheadian reading of moments and time though it appears to also be implicit in Lefebvre. See Charles Hartshorne on 'Whitehead's novel intuition' in: George L. Kline, ed., **Alfred North Whitehead: Essays on his Philosophy** (Englewood Cliffs: Englewood Cliffs N.J, 1963).

9 See: Bruno Latour (2004), 'Why has critique run out of steam?: From matters of fact to matters of concern', in: **Critical Enquiry** 30,2 (Winter 2004) pp. 225-248.

10 See: Bruno Latour; **We Have Never Been Modern**, trans. Catherine Porter (Cambridge Mass: Harvard University Press, 1993).

11 See: Manuel DeLanda; **Intensive Science and Virtual Philosophy** (London: Continuum, 2002).

12 Two books are proposed; the first dealing with urban form and design, the second with movement, form, technology and society.

Ostensible versus performative spaces If we consider a social – consisting of spaces of everyday sociality, encounter and visibility – to be *produced* within processes of relationality in an urban space, they must first of course be *performed*. We have to, in contrast to an *ostensible* social given by classical social theory, provide a *performative* definition.[13] The classical definition had certain characteristics, according to Strum & Latour:[14] it assumed the possibility in principle of detecting the 'typical properties of what holds a society together' and held that these principals are given in an *ostensible social*; it held that social actors are part of a 'society', which is given and already present and which constrains or enables their actions.

A performative definition however would allow that the social bond can have *extra-social*, that is heterogeneous, properties; and that actors and agents *perform* society and in so doing define what the social is. A 'spatial-performative' social theory would 'follow the actors'.[15] Seen in this way the social is constructed, formed and transformed *through* the multiple performances that define it. That is to say that the social, understood as a multiplicity of networks, has an important discursive component – but also that we have to be able to acknowledge the actions and 'agency', the forming and transforming power, of objects. A theory of performed networks – of actor-networks – draws on the work by Foucault in concentrating on micro-technologies as well as the social and discursive aspects of assemblages in social-urban space.

Foucault calls the Panopticon, for instance, a 'technology',[16] and, 'Foucault's discourse analysis is concerned not exclusively with language, but with a wide range of different materials. Indeed, it is *precisely* about how those materials (people, architecture, etc.) perform themselves to generate a series of effects'.[17] The social becomes simultaneously spatial and hybrid in this conception; it is a gathering into form, a *morpho*genesis,[18] that consists of discursive and non-discursive, human and non-human elements, which come together as more or less coherent, more or less fleeting or long-lasting assemblages. Society is held together through this gathering[19] which happens also, I am arguing, in a variable urban *situation* of potential and actual presence, connection, visibility and co-presence. This urban situation may *itself* facilitate, form and coordinate this gathering in space-time. This is a matter of form and the gathering of assemblages of people and things in dynamic fields and has nothing to do with the categorical orderings of planning's functional and demographic places and zones. Categories and spatial boundings of similars are not the issue here; what we are talking about are dynamic *gatherings* of heterogeneous elements into situation or place.[20]

A truly *network* space of society implies therefore a different topology of the social: 'modern societies cannot be described without recognizing them as having a fibrous, capillary character that is never captured by the notions of layers, territories, spheres, structures, or systems'.[21] This new topology recasts issues of far versus close, small scale versus large scale, and inside versus outside – and these questions come to be framed more in terms of a monad-like 'containment' of the whole in the parts, than in terms of simple relations of elements with attributes at a distance. The global will be found *in* the local; the 'far' or the 'large scaled' becomes gathered to and *contained in* the 'near' or the 'small scaled' – by way of pathways that must be imagined, constructed, regulated and maintained – in order to be realised. Far to close relationships and scale in both social and physical space become thought of not in terms of metric distance and micro-macro distinctions but in terms of associations supported by networks: 'A network is never *bigger* than another one, it is simply *longer* and *more intensely* connected'.[22] And: 'A network is all boundary without inside and outside. The only question one may ask is whether or not a connection is established between two elements.'

A crucial point which actor-network theory makes is that, without the inclusion of objects, which according to Latour give back to the social its 'missing mass',[23] social theory gets polarised between micro and macro, agency and structure, constructivism and objectivism. The separation of the social and the material produces a separation of action and structure; on the one hand we get human agency and on the other a thing-like, social structure.[24] The theory of the actor-network concerns itself with *hybrid* order, showing how what is horizontally and vertically differentiated becomes reintegrated in a stable and consistent way in situation. It is a theory of gathering – of 'drawing things together'.[25]

Space types Annemarie Mol and John Law present an explicit recognition of the fluidity and ambivalence of the social and have introduced the concept of a 'fluid' space as a complement

13 The main line of argument in this section follows Niels Albertsen and Bülent Diken, 'What is the Social?' (draft), published by the Department of Sociology, Lancaster University at: http://www.comp.lancs.ac.uk/sociology/soc033bd.html
14 Strum S.S. & Bruno Latour, 'Redefining the Social Link: From Baboons to Humans', in: **Social Science Information** 26(4) (1987) pp. 783-802.
15 Bruno Latour; 'On Interobjectivity', in: **Mind, Culture & Activity**, 3 (4), (1996) pp. 228-45.
16 See: Michel Foucault; **Discipline and Punish** (London: Penguin, 1991) pp. 195-230.
17 See: John Law; **Organizing Modernity** (Oxford; Blackwell, 1994) p. 25.
18 See: Stephen Read; 'Questions of form', Paper presented at the 5th Space Syntax Symposium, Delft University of Technology, June 2005 (Amsterdam: Techne Press, 2005).
19 See: Latour (1996) p. 238.
20 See: Edward Casey, 'How to get from space to place in a fairly short stretch of time', in: Feld S. & K.H. Basso (eds), **Senses of Place** (Santa Fé: School of American Research Press, 1996). See also: Bruno Latour (1996b) 'On actor-network theory. A few clarifications'. **Soziale Welt** (47) pp. 369-81.
21 See: Latour (1996b) p. 370.
22 See: Latour (1996b) p. 371.
23 See: Bruno Latour; 'Where are the missing masses?: Sociology of a few mundane artifacts', in: Wiebe Bijker and John Law (eds), **Shaping Technology – Building Society; Studies in Sociotechnical Change** (Cambridge Mass: MIT Press, 1992).
24 See: Latour (1996).
25 Bruno Latour; 'Drawing Things Together', in: Lynch, Michael & Woolgar, Steve (eds) **Representations in Scientific Practice** (Cambridge Mass: MIT Press, 1990) pp. 19-68.

to a 'network' space. The social, according to them, doesn't exist as a single spatial type. Rather, it performs several *kinds of space* in which different 'operations' take place. They propose: first, that there are *regions* in which objects are clustered together and boundaries are drawn around each cluster; second, there are *networks* in which distance is a function of the relations between the elements and difference a matter of relational variety. These are the two topologies with which social theory is already familiar. They propose also however another kind of space, a *fluid*, where neither boundaries nor relations mark the difference between one place and another. In these spaces boundaries may come and go, allow leakage or disappear altogether, while relations transform themselves without fracture.[26]

Drawing on Mol's and Law's work, John Urry argues that 'much of what happens in a "society" is influenced by flows or fluids',[27] and that social theory should pay attention to flows 'within but especially beyond the territory of each society. ... Moreover, not only people are mobile but so too are many "objects", as a consequence of diverse global networks and fluid-like flows'.[28] The mobility of humans and nonhumans must, according to Urry, become part of a society performed.

Rob Shields[29] summarises the characteristics of social flows as follows: first, they are spatial, temporal, and 'beyond merely being processes'. They have a content, and are material. Second, they have rhythms, and intensities – 'tones' one may almost say. Third, they have intentionality built into their vectoral directions, rather than origins or end-points, causes or purposes. They are relational, without being positional or being structures. Fourth, they have viscosity, and speed-related capacities for accommodating and producing shapes and geometries. Urry adds a fifth point; that flows are channelled within what he calls territorial 'scapes' or networks, which also organise in relational terms, and a sixth; that they facilitate diffusion of relations of domination/subordination and the exercise of power through their intersections, so that, seventh; a result of flows and the 'scapes' through which they are channelled, are new forms of social power relations and inequality. Landscapes of flows generate new opportunities, new desires, and at the same time new social risks.[30]

The truth is we may find many forms of spatial fluidity once we begin to look at space dynamically. The 'fluidity' of Mol's and Law's space also amounts to a recognition of the schematic nature of our known spaces and the way these schemas abstract real world spatial relations and *fix* links and boundaries, as well as causes and effects. We all too easily take space to be a singular and universalising given, and can all too easily overlook the schematic and static natures of the spaces we talk and think in, not to mention the fact that forms we find in the world, which we use these schemas to outline and articulate, are the effects of much more dynamic, complex, fine-grained, interdependent, and contingently constructed and maintained relations. We could argue therefore for a *development* of different schemas of (especially dynamic) space – recognising their reductive and conceptual natures (as well as the necessity of our working with schemas when it comes to spatial matters) – to a point where we can begin to visualise and imagine some of the fluidities of these spaces and especially to see how spatial articulation – here we should start to perhaps use the word 'formation' – may begin to be produced in dynamic network-fluid relations *without* recourse to bordering or outlining.

From spaces to scapes and spatial productivity When we consider the urban *productivity* of flows today it becomes more and more evident that the city is not simply a form which spreads out from within; growing from the inside, as if it were spreading at its edges and enclosing territory and colonising the landscape. Rather it emerges as local eruptions – and as 'thickenings' of pre-existent vectors in a dynamically constituted outside-less connective surface whose scope usually exceeds by orders of magnitude the limits of the thing we in the past (and still too often today) hold as being the city. As paths and trails pre-exist the first city as an object in the landscape,[31] so also the 'object' city today exists in the first instance as thickenings of the wispy traces of stuff passing through – and this thickening, like any concrescence, is a work of translation and of alchemy; of the transformation of one kind of substance and energy into another.

The emergence of the city is therefore, we would argue, one of the eruption of fixed identifiable stuff out of a fluid and relatively non-differentiable, but 'already there' substrate. Jane Jacobs' obsidian traders tracing pathways over the Anatolian plateau,[32] are antecedent to the city, and exist as the virtual to the object-city's actual. We can today, when the fact begins to force itself on us, see the city again for what it is – for something emergent and radically open, out of processes which integrate it with what appears to us to be its outside, and with a dynamic forceful continuity that gathers to its movements and flows a heterogeneous mass. The city can at last again be

26 Annemarie Mol & John Law; 'Regions, Networks and Fluids: Anaemia and Social Topology', in: **Social Studies of Science**, Vol 24 (4), (1994) pp. 641-72.
27 John Urry; 'The Concept of Society and the Future of Sociology'. Paper presented at the conference **The Future of Sociology**, Aalborg University, October (1997) p. 3.
28 Urry (1997) p. 8.
29 Rob Shields, 'Flow', in: **Space and Culture**, vol 1,(1997) pp. 1-8.
30 Urry (1997) pp. 6, 8-9.
31 See Stephen Read; 'A brief history of flights to the periphery and other movement matters' in: Read & Pinilla (eds), **Visualising the Invisible** (Amsterdam: Techne Press, 2006a).
32 Jane Jacobs; **The Economy of Cities** (New York: Vintage Books, 1970). The proposal I am making is a speculation built on a speculation, whose veracity, I would argue, is to be determined in its productivity as a model for thinking, rather than in its literal applicability to every settlement form in every historical circumstance. There may have been other types of settlement in the course of history – villages perhaps, towns even, of variable size – conforming to the conventional model which would see 'community' as providing the 'glue' for social aggregation and settlement forming. My argument is that settlement as a product of and as an expression of 'social aggregation' is an inadequate model for understanding **cities** – and this fact becomes all the more clear as cities distribute themselves everywhere and begin to constitute our whole world.

seen as something constructed within dynamics which take place very substantially beyond what we take to be its borders, and which *becomes* in its own right according to its own and not our laws. In this view the city is 'machinic' in the sense Deleuze and Guattari use the term, where the dynamics of the 'organic' are conceived 'not in terms of organs, organisms and species, and their functions, but in terms of affective relationships between heterogeneous bodies … A "body" can be anything – an animal, a body of sounds, a mind or an idea, a social body or collective … This means that evolution speaks in fact of an involution, that is the dissolution of forms and the indeterminacy of functions, as well as the freeing of times and speeds.'[33] I would go further here to say that this involution is something like a progressive generative folding, of the order of a fractal 'space-filling', in an implosion of imaginable worlds or bodies at ever finer scales (from the global, to the metropolitan, to the municipal, to the neighbourhood) – a sort of 'layered cake' assembly of the city collapsed into finely pleated places as we zoom in from the ultimate scale of the global. This ultimate scale has always been given – today only more forcefully and insistently so – by the *global* limits of connective and communicative networks and infrastructures.[34]

It becomes questionable whether the city could ever have been 'organic' in Mumford's sense. Today there can be no doubt the city and its parts are *points of articulation* and of translation between different extensive layers of the multi-scaled, multi-worlded, urban 'cake' in its scaled and timed circuits – their processes constrained and ordered by the networks and infrastructures which constitute and relay them and the 'vertical' processes of 'translation' between them. The space I will propose presumes firstly therefore, as Jane Jacobs has already more or less done, that a 'virtual' first city pre-existed its actualisation on the Neolithic Anatolian plain, and that this 'virtuality' consisted in the long-distance trading routes that criss-crossed the sub-continent before the processes of urban actualisation began drawing in other finer-scaled processes and circuits down to the most local.

An idea that cities emerge, or just *happen* at the level at which we encounter them – as opposed to one which considers them to be our civilised construction and *reflection* of our bodies and societies – begins also to acknowledge the difficulty of inventing life forms or social forms out of nothing, and to take seriously the contingency involved in any creation. The possibility would first, I propose, have had to be *seen* to exist, in at least a rudimentary form, before it could have occurred to our proto-urban ancestors that *polis* or *civitas* may have been an interesting possibility for social existence. Developed social forms may be therefore a creative addition to – a building upon – a matrix of encounter that is in the first place *urban*. What I am trying to begin to build here is therefore a speculative story of *social* becoming at the same time as it is one of urban becoming. [see figure 1]

Centres in mobilisations Individual stories of caravans and their masters, of ship fleets and their captains and crews, are largely lost, along with the details of their achievements and hardships and failures. What *do* remain are the trails they wore, the strings of provisioning posts and trading stops and ports they established. Today we see little of the details of the complex overlapping arrangements and agreements which underwrite exchanges in commodities, finance and other formal and informal, legitimate and illegitimate business, not to mention the countless movements and exchanges made for reasons of personal attachment or gain. What we do see, and what does remain, is the more systematised flight and train schedules, the seasons and the calendars – and the routes which draw together into one movement all the individual stories lost in every way except as another pair of lights in the moving stream on the freeway, another passenger in the queue at the check-in, another pedestrian in the moving tide on the pavement of the shopping street – or another sequence of pulses in the terabytes of data transmitted down optical cables.[35]

Before the city as we know it, before the city as a setting for individualisable stories and the times and spaces of institutions and people, comes a collective mobilisation of material, data and populations. The city is mobile mass, masses and messages that dissolves the forms of everyday appearance – to gather them together again according to *another* logic of a convergence of multiples in the space of the urban. The city is given, it is *there*, as a pulse, a rhythm particular in every place, shifting and sorting us by way of its 'freeing of times and speeds' into an articulation of times and speeds in a flat connective frame subject to its own dynamic logics. These flat movements of anonymous materials and populations are the virtual, antecedent to a location or place that is a *relay*, a passing on of matter and pulses and rhythms that inform and transform each place in their passing.

This flat, virtual or antecedent centrality finds its most visible expression today in the freeway network – an evenly distributed net of pure movement *producing* as well as regulating its own dynamic integrative coherence – its own *time*. Flying over the urban landscape at night, this virtual 'engine'[36] of the city is perfectly visible, perfectly concrete, but prior to anything we would call an urban place in its developed actuality. The visibility and intensity of this tracery at this scale points also to a mode of growth of cities. The movements of people, goods, money and

33 See: Keith Ansell-Pierson; **Viroid Life** (London: Routledge, 1997).
34 The model presented here begins to become suggestive as regards the idea of 'omnicausal' systems (when the whole determines the behaviour of its parts) as opposed to those which are 'particausal'. See: G.E. Mikhailovsky, 'Biological time, its organisation, hierarchy and presentation by complex values', in: A.P. Levich (ed.) **On The Way To Understanding The Time Phenomenon: The Constructions Of Time In Natural Science (Part I)** (London: World Scientific Publishing, 1993). There is a potentially rich line of investigation here which goes into the purported 'negentropic' properties of omnicausal systems.
35 See the movie 'Koyaanisqatsi' (1983), directed by Godfrey Reggio.
36 This engine is again not that of a system – of a technocratic movement-connective machine – but as part of a 'machine' effecting translation and transformation, and the actualisation of urban virtuality or potential. This 'engine' produces at the moment of its encounter with another 'concrete virtualities', creating a 'thickness' of present time – somewhat in the spirit of Mikhailovsky (1993). This is a point which will be developed elsewhere. See for a first step:

information at this metropolitan scale were in previous times, outside the city as it was then commonly (but mistakenly) understood. Today, there is no question any more about it; this scale of movement exists *inside* the life of the *metropolitan* city as we now think of it. In fact what has happened is that a new layer of movement, a newly dominant *stratification* of connection and infrastructure and the centralities and times it produces and regulates has imposed itself '*over*' what already existed, changing – by processes of translation through the layers of the 'cake' – every local reality 'under' it.

There are multiple virtual centralities existing at different scales and in different modes in the city at the same time – each configured by connective webs gathering movements into flat mobilisations. Technical (and informational and in general *connective*) infrastructures *stratify* these mobilisations into layers of different speeds and *produced* times. Time enters this realm of pure intensity as speed or vibration or rhythm. The impulse of these distributed networks is to distribute, but they distribute *themselves* as well as the material they are distributing; as they seek to cover the surface they are involved in integrating. A metropolitan freeway network will seek to cover and integrate the metropolitan surface, an urban boulevard network will seek to cover and integrate a functional urban surface, and a global telecommunications network will seek to cover and integrate a global surface. In the same way as a soap bubble economises by distributing tensions and energy evenly over its surface, these infrastructures tend, other things being equal, to distribute evenly over the surface available to them.[37] These infrastructures and the integrations they effect establish and *define* the surfaces they integrate, in the process revealing certain possible realities and suppressing others. They are also *built*, are costly, and are never ideologically neutral in that they will always tend to construct reality in the shape of the perspectives and interests they reveal, and render invisible other perspectives and interests.

Urban place, as relay point on multiple stratified movement nets, becomes a place of recombination and of translation – of the conversion of matter or energy of one sort into another. The urban we know, in its architectural, actualised form, emerges at the point where flat virtual centralities overlap, allowing globalised, metropolitanised, urbanised lives and other processes to adhere, to inhere, to become entrained and situated, in points of layered and mutually supportive and dependant connectivity. This is the point where multifarious centralities come together: it is not a coming together in one scale, one speed, one time and one space; rather the coming together is of a variety of times and spaces in a process of combination that creates the rich, complex, and active individuated compound out of multiple purer spaces and times. There is a *concrescence*, an alchemy, a real generative moment, which takes place in these overlaps between virtual centralities, activating situated condition, catalysing individuation; *actualising* the centralities we recognise as such in real urban places.

Locus or place is also the point at which the individual and his or her stories comes back into focus, and the actualisation of urban place is also its becoming as setting for embedded stories of individual everyday lives. The 'non-place',[38] the 'concretely preindividuated' simplistically accessible places we more often than not make today, cannot *hold* real lives and stories. It lacks the 'thickness' of the space-time layering of situation, in a *fabric* of multiple scaled and flat webs. Place requires layering and overlap in which speeds can collapse and ground themselves. The collapse of the layers generates friction and difference, providing the depth and 'stickiness' necessary to support the imbroglio of the everyday. [see figure 1]

The city as a technology of visibility and emplacement It is clear today that the urban has overflowed the limits of the traditional urban centre. It is even more clear that the instrument by which this overflow has been effected, is in the first instance the infrastructures of movement and communication that have spread themselves over the surfaces of the metropolis, the megacity region, the global region and the world. It is clear once one begins to think about it that the city has always overflowed its limits, and that this overflow is the engine of the city's being in the first place.[39]

The spatial schema outlined here serves as an instrument for making urban processes visible and for identifying the often hidden 'urban' in 'urban phenomena'. It is against this space that movements, patterns, formations and transformations are identified and mapped in our research. Underlying this spatial model, is the presumption that both our experience of specific urban places and the nature of the urban object itself are founded in the movements and connections we and others make through it. These movements then compound and generate *another* body with its own generative power, where we encounter other people and things, and are *formed* in interfaces structured in movement. Our preconceptions of what the urban is though have remained static while the urban itself has shifted and adjusted itself to new layerings of infrastructure and connection and the new dominant movements within those infrastructures. If the city of our preconceptions is no longer precisely the city we inhabit, it is because we associate the forms we see with similar forms produced by a city of the past. We may discount real and global relations and dynamics of our lives today because the local is the universal we reference our lives to.[40] And the global and metropolitan become embroiled, and available to us, *in* the local, which is

Gerhard Bruyns & Stephen Read; 'The Urban Machine' in: Read & Pinilla (eds), **Visualising the Invisible** (Amsterdam, Techne Press, 2006).

37 This assertion needs some qualification of course because at certain moments in history all roads **did** lead to Rome or London or Paris or wherever. Nevertheless today in the time of Negri and Hardt's **Empire** (2000), it seems that this statement is becoming more, rather than, less true.

38 See: Marc Augé; **Non-places: Introduction to an Anthropology of Supermodernity** (London: Verso, 1995).

39 See: Stephen Read (2006a).

stabilised and more or less constant in its form by virtue of its more or less dense layering. The grids of the new dominant scales are layered *over* grids of the past which *still* inform the ways the new scales come down to earth and ground themselves in the local.

A profound shift in the scales of dominant movements may manifest itself on the ground therefore in ways which reflect a continuity with the past at the level of *form* – while at the same time manifesting profound changes in *content*. As far as today's urban is concerned, the global and metropolitan scales overlay and infect everything that looks local.[41] Beyond this, telecommunications, instantaneity, and media in general impact the image of our evolving city.[42] But the invisibility *as a form* of a core that coordinates – that choreographs and draws multiple worlds together in movement, and that makes the everyday practices of our realities stable, or relatively so – means precisely that we are *not* determined by profound changes in the technological means of our lives. We absorb these changes into practical patternings as what James Gibson calls 'affordances'[43] – alternative possibilities that open within the 'optical array' of our immediately local lives – and we do not necessarily succumb as automatons (though those least empowered may be forced into even less empowered situations) to the global machine. [see figure 2]

We have always placed ourselves and understood our place in the world through the ways we have moved in it – whether that movement was bodily through 'real' movement channels or through telecommunications channels, and today we begin to see the urban itself as a technology – consisting of a dense layering of 'skins' of mobility and communications infrastructure; extending our 'reach' into the world and effecting an ever more implicated exchange between global and local, whose resolution *is* the local. Much contemporary thinking on the issue of connectivity focuses on the so-called 'virtual' networks of the world wide web, telecommunications and data-communications networks, including those of global financial transactions, mobile telephones, the distribution of information through broadcast and printed media and the pervasive reach of promotion and advertising. These networks need to be seen as part of, and as grounding themselves in, a re-spatialised urban ecology which includes the more traditional communications channels of bodily mobility, and the mobility of all the brute physical stuff traversing our landscapes.

Urban ground It is into an *already* mobile and fluid and communicative place that the effects of the new flows of data and information come back down to earth. It is into bodily experience and lived time, already extended and transformed by mobility technologies and the older communications channels that we now take for granted, that all this other newer stuff becomes submerged and embedded and grounded. There is an integral, indestructible (in spite of rather shallow claims to the contrary) continuity between the 'virtual' and 'physical' urban worlds. There is a continuity, over and above all the so-called 'revolutions' in mobility and communicability, of a phenomenal, information-rich and legible urban world as an accretion of layers of communication, that in their layered density *form* a ground that simply said, *does not even exist* as a 'pure-locational' thing or surface apart from them. The lower scaled grids fulfil a vital role in this layering, founding the conditions and experience we understand as 'place'. This is so even while the quality of that experience is transformed, and explains why, with the breakdown of a particular structuring of the urban fabric in the last century, we have come to experience our new urban world as 'placeless'.[44]

We need to understand our global and metropolitan cities as an *effect* of all this layering of communication and mobility, and as a consequence of an accumulative and evolutionary process of extension, through distributed physical, informational and electronic spaces – and the technological systematisation of this extension – rather than being either on the one hand architecture, or on the other, simple systems of nodes in global networks.

Expanding, overlapping and systematising networks of communications and flow, set up a different class of ecology; one which does not depend in the classical way on relations and exchanges over static boundaries, but on the ways that horizontal strata of relations and flow intersect and interact with each other. The urban world becomes a layering of flat distributed communicative strata, producing depth and mass in the interval and at the intersection *between* strata. The globalised, metropolitanised city we recognise in place is what emerges out of this interval of intersection, and the productive creative work of alchemy that takes place there. Social reality cannot be distinct from these grids and the way we engage with them. Social reality is necessarily produced, inflected and actualised in their intersections, and in the way they constrain and enable, the way they open relations as well as effecting 'stabilisation' in levels of material infrastructure that provide some of the 'missing mass' of our societies. At the same time these grids, in their 'stratifications and tangles',[45] draw together affects and effects into highly specific urban moments of integrated hybridity – those 'concretely abstract' places I mentioned earlier. We produce a *horizontal* and spatial society at this level,[46] a society remade in every moment around forms of encounter that are in the first place mobile and urban.

How can one conceive the production of the urban body today – something with mass and substance that in our contemporary state of urbanisation we can no longer simply understand as

40 See: Bruyns and Read (2006).
41 The PhD work of Gerhard Bruyns for example.
42 The PhD work of Marta Mendonça for example.
43 J.J. Gibson; **The Ecological Approach to Visual Perception** (Hillsdale NJ: LEA Publishers, 1986).
44 See: Read (2006a).
45 See: Henri Lefebvre (1991), **The Production of Space**, Blackwell, Oxford, p. 402.
46 See: John Urry (2000), **Sociology beyond Societies**, Routledge, London.

pure artefact, constructed of a transparent mentality and in proportions which reflect our own? – something we can no longer either understand as a system of dematerialised relations that function in a graph space of pure abstraction? What is the nature of an *urban* society or of a *social* city in a world of increasing connectivity and mobility? The ideas outlined in this paper aim to set up a framework to start thinking about the way we can begin as a practical matter addressing the problem of a social urban form today and for the future.

A methodological implication We seem to become trapped in an untenable position in our research by certain methodological presuppositions about the categories of the 'real' and the 'imagined' that can no longer be claimed to be helpful in furthering that research or serving the cause of 'methodological' rigour. The problem revolves around the question of objectivity, and a far too narrow view, I believe, on the part of some, of what constitutes a *scientific* objectivity.

The matter becomes critical when the object of study is the city – whose reality is clearly something which is difficult to consider apart from the way it works between and draws together issues of 'objectivity' and 'subjectivity' in a dynamic implicated *functionality*. Much current urban research done on the basis of a methodological empiricism opens itself to criticism by the distance of its methods and results from anything approaching a corporeal urban experience. There is, meanwhile, a pressing need to approach the *reality* of the experience of the city. This need is felt clearly when it comes to matters of value, quality, and power – but exists also, I believe, when it comes to matters of a hard-nosed and objective 'how things work' – given that matters of functionality must on the face of it follow those of experience to at least some degree. It is clear that the way the city *works* is also something that owes a great deal to the *imaginaries* of the people who use it.

There is I believe a simple misunderstanding, and some entrenched and for the most part hidden and unexamined presuppositions founded on this misunderstanding, at the root of this dilemma.

Some current methodological presumptions – and this could apply equally in 'modernist' *and* 'post-modernist' research – see 'subjective' and 'objective' as constituting polar opposites, consigning 'imaginaries' to an idealist and '*subjectively' multiple* realm of the representational, while granting 'reality' to an '*objectively' singular* realm of the real. The underlying assumption here – as I say, seldom examined but underlying much everyday research thinking – is, simply put, that perspectives may be multiple but that reality is in the end singular. The point I want to argue is not that our world is subjectively relative, and that this is what keeps it open and available for different perspectives – in other words that multiplicity is a factor of *interpretation* – but rather that multiple worlds may be entirely objective and *real*, and put together as part of a construction (*not* a social construction) of realities. Further – that what we think of as our subjectivity is a co-construction as part of the same process of world-construction and the orchestration or coordination of those worlds.

The matter of the coexistence of different experiential and functional worlds in one urban landscape is therefore not one of real and imagined, or objective and subjective – but of (always provisional) constructions of worlds at multiple real levels. And we find we may objectively map these world-constructions as part of our research. Worlds may be crafted in multiple ways – but very often we find, in the city, to the production of similar patterns. When one of these ways of crafting is the researcher's we feel we are getting somewhere with our research – but it is a matter of a harmonisation or coordination of practices and processes, including *scientific* practices, relating to situated events, not to the final discovery of some kind of universal truth or formula. These practices and processes take place in space and time; one practice or process clicks, or at least appears to click, into sync with another; *forms* coordinate, and – bingo – something becomes intelligible and we have a result.[47]

But the realities we construct, and that our urban processes construct, profoundly constrain any further realities we may understand as being possible to construct. This Heideggerian point demonstrates the insidiousness, even the danger, of a singular dominant reality – we cannot even *see* any more the fact that other realities may be perfectly possible. Our *subjectivities* and imaginaries become very substantially constructed and constrained *in* the networks of 'made visible' or 'known' things and processes – and this channelling of our presumptions and preconceptions within a given constructed network of reality makes us quite literally blind to alternative networks which may follow other process and practice pathways. The whole of the world becomes constituted in a certain network of relations (and remember even objects are constituted in relations) and the gaps in – the alternative relations occupying the in-between of – that network space become invisible.

This is the substantial constructive effect of our technologies – and both knowledges and cities in this sense can be thought of as technologies: they construct realities that come to appear 'natural'. They *naturalise* the pathways of thinking and doing they enable – which of course can be either a good *or* a bad thing. One could imagine how environments of comfortable familiarity, or stimulating edginess, as well as oppressive places inhabited by 'docile bodies', could all be naturalised patterns. The object of our research is also therefore to deal with hidden or suppressed

47 The argument, in its broad outline, is taken from Mol and Law. See: Annemarie Mol; **The Body Multiple** (Durham UP: Duke UP, 2002); John Law, **After Method** (London: Routledge, 2004).

realities – empiricism is not simply about dealing with what 'exists'; it becomes about dealing with both immanent and suppressed realities, and with both real and virtual-as-real objects, in order always to expand the scope of what is visible and available to our thinking processes.

What I am arguing really is that there is something objective about subjectivity – at the same time as there is something flimsy and contingently constructed about the objective. Our city is a technology that sits in the middle of all this – and can perhaps even help us in fact to unravel the muddle in our thinking. I have argued that the city is itself a machine that achieves a certain coordination between worlds – effecting interferences and interdependencies between those worlds – which have both subjective and objective characters – and establishing 'urban-social' forms, in their 'interfaces'. What we in our research try to engage is an urban relationalism that never descends to relativism – the reality of the urban world *also* demands that it coordinates multiple realities, and we come to the apt little catch-phrase of Annemarie Mol which captures something of the shape of what it is we are dealing with. Reality according to her is 'more than one and less than many'. It's a motto we use to keep our eyes on the balls, as we attempt to juggle the complex realities of our urban worlds in a forward-looking empiricism.

The substance of 'the urban'.
Source: taken from the PhD work of Gerhard Bruyns, 2006.

The Way Things Work: City Maps and Diagrams

M. Christine Boyer

In this discussion of city maps and diagrams, I begin with Michel Foucault's 1967 lecture 'Of "Other" Spaces' and his confusing definition of heterotopic space – they are mysterious spaces that can not be fully known, contest places that belong to the invisible. So this paper tries to look at the 'mysteriousness' and 'invisibilities' of representational space. It does so by re-reading Foucault across Bruno Latour's questioning of image wars and matters of concern.

Of 'Other' Spaces Michel Foucault's 1967 lecture 'Of "Other" Spaces' and what it tells us about the fundamentally ambiguous role of architecture and the city in the shaping of modernity, must simultaneously be read against his general understanding that a society's imagination is linked to how it organizes space. In addition, it must be read against his 'archaeological metaphor' specifying that different planes of space correspond to different ways knowledge is organized and power articulated at different periods of time. Power operates only when it is part of a chain, never localizable in space, relayed across networks from point to point.

In this lecture, Foucault describes three different moments in a general history of space, moments that overlap and are often coterminous. During the Middle Ages, space was conceptualized as emplacement with a clear demarcation between order and disorder; it was a closed space that governed knowledge and what was considered to be true. Galileo ushered in the conception of an infinitely open space; replacing localization with extension. A point became a location on a trajectory that was moving, and time became a central focus. This of course challenged religious and political authority depending on a closed site to control the truth; it opened on an infinite number of perspectives and different points of view. By the 19th century, time or history was something to dread with its inevitable cycles, accumulation of the past, surplus of dead moments, and a world cooling down. Finally, a modern conceptualization turned space into a series of sites, a set of relations that juxtaposed unlikely things, placing side by side contradictory sites. This space was describable in trees, networks, matrices and series. Keeping open the possibility of new spatial arrangements it disrupted a concept of contiguous space, or ordinary everyday notions of place.

If we stop right here, there are three questions Foucault has raised: first, what is the difference between Renaissance space, or, a map, and Modern space, or, a network; second, how does a network differ from everyday space and ordinary time; and third, how is this 'other' space of heterotopia related to power, knowledge and discourse?[1]

This last question is the easiest to answer for 'the theory of discursive practices', and how a subject is constructed as an effect through and within discourse or a discursive apparatus was a central component of Foucault's writings. Turning back to Foucault's lecture, moreover, we find that between utopias where society forms ideal perfected images of itself and that have no real space and heterotopias, counter-spaces, or scenes where otherwise disconnected elements co-exist, he

1 Dehaene and De Cauter explain through Michel Foucault's dispositif a term they think is close to emplacement or 'a notion which provides a spatial equivalent for the language-based and sequential logic, a constellation in which a set of relationships is encoded, inscribed' (p. 19). See 'The Rise of Heterotopia', EAAE Colloquium, KU Leuven, Belgium, May 2005.

erects a third space, the mirror. As Foucault describes this mirror, it is a virtual space, or no place, although I see my image reflected in it, there where I am not, and my gaze in this mirror is directed back at myself. Thus I turn from this reflected image of myself to reconstitute myself where I am in the likeness I perceive in the mirror.

This 'other' space – open both ways to utopic and heterotopic space – is all about subjectivity and the technologies of the self. Subjectivity is imaginary – a fantasy construction or idealization – it is ambivalent, never complete, always open, and absolutely contingent on time and space. Moreover it is always constructed in discourse and it operates across difference or fictitious relationships. Consequently something is always left outside in the process of consolidating these perceptions into an image. In other words perception of this mirror image is fabricated against the 'other' which it excludes or leaves outside.[2]

Thus it can be argued that Foucault's 'other' space is all about subject formation, and not about physical material reality – it is the space of the docile body that disciplinary techniques control with their normative discourses, institutions, spatial apparatus, and architectural forms. We need to remember that Foucault was neither a geographer, nor a map-maker but a diagrammer and a creator of visual tableaux.

His most dramatic tableau is taken from Jeremy Bentham's Panopticon prison of the 18th century. It is his heterotopia of heterotopias. As an apparatus of imaginary surveillance it instills a normative model of a docile body with minimum effort. The guard located in a cylindrical kiosk in the centre, looks out towards the perimeter of the structure where 192 prisoner cells are arranged on its perimeter four stories high. Light from the kiosk filters into each cell, so that prisoners can be seen at all hours of the day, but they can not see into the darkness of the kiosk. At night reflectors are imagined to be set up on the exterior reflecting light into each cell. Hence a prisoner never knows if the guard is present or not – yet surveillance is assumed to be constant and thus the prisoner assumes normal behaviour all of the time. Consequently the heterotopic space of the prison is a visual apparatus and a machine to produce docile behaviour.[3]

This image of the Panopticon prison expresses the effects of power, how a strategy operates across a series of points that are linked together, hence Foucault's use of the series, the tree, the grid as his spatial diagrams. These disciplinarian diagrams, or abstract machines of normalization, are linked to other technologies operating across other spatial assembles: in schools, factories, hospitals, or barracks, wherever multiplicities are gathered together into productive assemblies. This is how bodies are distributed in space, placed in a series, ordered in time, turned into productive objects and how knowledge flows across these forces of normalization and integration; how an archive is assembled out of all that can be said, described, put into statements and words.

Let us return to the mirror in Foucault's account, for it is a place of devilish doubling. It is necessarily a space of comparison between the virtual image in the mirror and the image of the self, comparison between an image of utopia and dystopia, the past and the present, the outline over-there and the details up-close. Hence the in-between becomes a place of haunting, of a shadowy silhouette in which something is missing or repressed, the ghost of another reality.[4] In this mirror we are dealing with images: a scene, or representation that mediates access to something else, a process of constant comparison. And we are focused on images, moreover, that do not stay constant but keep shifting across time and along series in space. This process of comparison, Foucault defines as the process of normalization and thus he conjures up the coexistence of different modes of existence, different temporalities and spatialities outside the spaces of normalization which exist alongside of them and at the same time – these constitute counter-discourses and 'other' spaces. The danger is to take the image or representation as a norm, as a convention and destroy, cover-over or eliminate all other images. Foucault's concern was how to keep these other images and counter-discourses open to reinterpretation, inclusion, and uncertainty.

Image Wars Can we take this understanding of how diagrams or abstract machines operate across spatial forms and language and shift to focus on the mirrors of architecture and the elimination of 'other' spaces that do not fit the construction that architects perceive is correct or the norm? In other words, architects are looking at mirror reflections of the city which they seek to destroy, replace, or improve – a constant comparison and substitution of one representation for another they assume to be better.

Michel Foucault's discourse concerned the image of man, his life, work and language that dominated the disciplinary diagrams and archives of knowledge formed in the 19th and the first half of the 20th century. But a shift in the forces of information technology and new man-machine assemblages of the second half of the 20th and early 21st centuries have displaced – not necessarily done away with but transformed – the image of man and the disciplinary diagrams so carefully constructed, bringing the space of the network, the grid, the diagram into sharper focus. On one hand there are images of the city that architects as physicians and diagnosticians can understand, with their concerns about the management of populations as life emerged as an object of disciplinary power or bio-techniques, and on the other hand there are images which architects as info-technicians can not visualize strongly or can grasp only in the dimmest of outlines.

Perhaps as Bruno Latour has outlined, this shift in image is only a tactic of iconoclasts in a constant battle of 'image wars'. Architects have always been good iconoclasts – destroying images or defacing them as touchstones of their critical prowess or artistic creativity – even though such displacements may not usher in a new diagram of knowledge and power. As soon as an image is

2 Stuart Hall, 'Introduction: Who Needs Identity?', **Questions of Cultural Identity,** pp. 1 -17.

3 Michel Foucault, **Discipline and Punish.** As Foucault's work evolved, moreover, subjectivity is re-conceptualized – as it moved from places of enclosure to a displaced, decentred position in the network of heterotopias. There is no stable core of the self, or stages of development that remain universal no matter where or when. The self is constructed over fragmented, multiple, and varying discourses, practices, positions, and historical times.

4 Harry D. Harootunian, 'Ghostly Comparisons: Anderson's Telescope', **Diacritics** (Winter, 1999) pp. 135 -149.

smashed into bits, there always follows an attempt to sweep them up as if something else was unwittingly destroyed for which apologies must be offered and atonements made – the acts of erasure and substitution, of defacing and refacing, Latour argues, appear as if coeval. Thus attempts to get rid of images only result in the proliferation of new images – one fabricated construction cascading after another.[5]

Latour describes different types of image-breakers – those who fear that living with past images is dangerous and want to purify the present by getting rid of these threatening images. Another type of iconoclast attempts to freeze-frame an image, extract it out of the cascading flow so that the image becomes static and its powers destroyed. Others are not against images per se, but only against images their opponents cling to so forcefully. Revolutionaries are this type of iconoclast, destroying images their predecessors held sacred. Then there are innocent vandals who destroy out of ignorance. Architecture, Latour assumes, is filled with this type destroying the old in order to build anew on a tabula rasa.[6]

Death to the Image of the City Recently considerable energy has gone into destroying the image we hold of the city. We are constantly being told that the end of the city has occurred, it ceases to exist or has become a fictive entity.[7] We have – or so we are told – a 'crisis of perception, the loss of a beloved image' no longer reflected in Foucault's mirror.[8] And hence in this altered way of seeing we lack an urban strategy, and need a new conceptual apparatus because traditional ways of looking at the city lead to dead ends. Rem Koolhaas ends his essay on 'The Generic City' which also ends the big book of *S,M,L,XL*, by offering us a cinematic scene as a galvanizing conclusion to the entire dilemma of the contemporary city:

> Imagine a Hollywood movie about the Bible (he writes). A city somewhere in the Holy Land. Market scene: from left and right extras cloaked in colourful rags, furs, silken robes walk into the frame yelling, gesticulating, rolling their eyes, starting fights, laughing, scratching their beards, hairpieces dripping with glue, thronging toward the centre of the image waving sticks, fists, overturning stalls, trampling animals... Now switch off the sound – silence, a welcome relief – and reverse the film. The now mute but still visibly agitated men and women stumble backward; the viewer no longer registers only humans but begins to note spaces between them. The centre empties; the last shadows evacuate the rectangle of the picture frame, ... Silence is now reinforced by emptiness:... Relief ...it's over. That is the story of the city. The city is no longer. We can leave the theatre now [9]

We can also consider a witty essay written by Mark Wigley entitled 'Resisting the City' as exemplary of the iconoclastic position of contemporary architectural critics.[10] His opener is meant to be provocative:

> We don't go to cities. Cities come to us, stream towards us. The limit of the city is not the limit of some physical terrain but the limit of its packaging…To go to Manhattan is only to go to the hard copy… to all the images that you know so well, to swim in the source of the flow.[11]

In other words cities are experienced in terms of images, and these shaped in terms of our expectations gathered from the flow of information in photographs, the cinema, magazines and books. Thus Wigley believes the architect as an organizer of city space, marginalized, even irrelevant. Moreover this is not new, for long ago the architect was replaced by the typographer, as Victor Hugo explained as far back as when this (the printed book) killed that (the cathedral or book of stone). But now there is added marginalization caused by the non-place age of electronics. Wigley's main comment is about discourse, the talking of architects being greater than their image-making abilities – he thinks for example of architectural juries, magazine articles, the writing of books – so much out pouring of words.

Yet architects, he continues, seem both unaware of this long-term decline and so frightened of losing their imaginary place as the pre-eminent image-maker of city form, that they become addicted to the production of images they continue to make. These are only emergency calls, for cities exceed any architect's capacity to draw or describe them. All of their efforts are merely working against the city by taming its wildness, ordering its unruly form, perfecting and beauti-

5 Bruno Latour, 'What is Iconoclash? Or is There a World Beyond the Image Wars?' in Bruno Latour and Peter Weibel (eds) **Iconoclash: Beyond the Image Wars in Science, Religion, and Art** (Cambridge MA: The MIT Press, 2002) pp. 14-37.

6 Beyond the Image Wars: Are we looking in the wrong spot, armed with the wrong critical weaponry of discourse analysis, heterotopias, power/knowledge when the problem lies elsewhere. What are the new threats we have to face, and are we armed with critical tools to address them? Bruno Latour suggests that we need to renew empiricism, we need a new set of critical tools in order to get closer to states of affairs: to become realists, not of facts but of matters of concern. Latour claims he sees 'the merging of matters of fact into highly complex, historically situated, richly divers matters of concern.' What assemblies have to be gathered together, what to hold matters of concern firmly in place, concerns that are fragilely constructed, that need care and concern? Bruno Latour, 'Why Has Critique Run out of Steam: From Matters of Fact to Matters of Concern.' **Critical Inquiry** 30, 2 (Winter, 2004) pp. 225-248. Latour utilizes the ambiguous word 'constructivism' wanting to deploy its hidden promises that he associates with a list of words such as: 'history, solidity, multiplicity, uncertainty, heterogeneity, risk taking, fragility, etc.' and wanting as well to relate this word to the heterogeneous associations that produced it, that kept it upright. Bruno Latour, 'The promises of constructivism' (2002) to appear in Don Idhe (ed.), **Chasing Technoscience: Matrix of Materiality** (Indiana Series for the Philosophy of Technology): pp. 1-11. http:www.Ensmp.fr/~latour/articles/087.html But there are problems associated with the metaphor of a man who constructs a house: it assumes not only that there is material, and a process, but someone is the master-builder, and yet any architect will tell you there are so many constraints that surround any construction, many things, agents, other actants with which they have to share the action, and over which they have no control. As for materials, they too add their own independent weight.

7 Ulrich König, 'On Grafting, Cloning, and Swallowing Pills: Scapes as a Future Model of the City', **Daidalos** 72 (1999) pp. 18-27.

8 Ulrich König, 'On Grafting, Cloning, and Swallowing Pills: Scapes as a Future Model of the City', **Daidalos** 72 (1999) p. 18.

9 Rem Koolhaas and Bruce Mau, et al.: **S,M,L,XL: Office of Metropolitan Architects, Rem Koolhaas and Bruce Mau**, edited by Jennifer Sigler (Rotterdam: 010 Publishers, 1995) p. 1264.

10 Mark Wigley, 'Resisting the City', **TransUrbanism** (Rotterdam: V2_Publishing, 2002) pp. 103-129.

11 **ibid.,** p. 103.

fying its façade.[12] So Wigley concludes:

> It (the discipline of architecture) can only survive with a sense of permanent crisis, governed by nostalgia for a status it never had, endlessly repeating the same story while slowly changing the images.[13]

This is what Bruno Latour would call 'a conspiracy theory of gullibility' trademarked 'Made in Criticalland'.[14]

Why is Wigley so intent on smashing images to bits: be it the image of the architect, the discipline as an image maker, or the image of the city? Why are architects who search for an image of the city given the gloss of a naive believer, steeped in nostalgia, seeking stability and comfort in worn-out fetishes and icons of imaginary cities and the discipline of architecture compared to a religion demanding its litany be repeated over and over? Is there a politics of representation at stake?[15] In England iconoclasm was an important part of the Protestant Reformation – the Puritans turned from the practice of using images as an aid to memory (worshipping images) to memorizing texts; they substituted on the walls of the church and in books of prayer words for visual images.[16] They did not stop there – for words can be dangerous idols as well – so they sought to attack all 'set forms' of liturgy and other rituals. As Foucault taught, words are mental constructs just as visual images are, and as mirrored reflections involve distorted perceptions, false hypotheses, scepticism and doubts.

It is interesting to note that Wigley uses no images in his texts, and chooses to talk about texts that city planners wrote in the 1960s that were both anti-visual and anti-architectural if one cares to read them. In other words he too fears looking at images, how they are deployed across a grid of power/knowledge because images are to be resisted! Stripped of all illusion, so we can see more clearly, what are we expected to do with the broken images of the city that lie smashed at our feet? Jean Baudrillard has written: '(i)t is no longer we who think the object, but the object who thinks us.' Meaning that an image imposes its presence on the viewer – but it is no longer an image that attracts, but numbs, for it does not illicit a compelling desire.[17]

What is it contemporary architects or architectural critics fear in the image of the city they see reflected in Foucault's mirror?[18] Is it fear of finding themselves on the side of disciplinary control and normative order and thus not being, as they might desire, on the side of the insurrections of subjugated knowledge that derive their power from all that is different from what surrounds them?[19]

Just when it is needed the most, at the moment of its apotheosis, the image of the city no longer attracts: there is no adequate terminology to discuss the essential phenomena and no conceptual framework to guide the discourse that will redefine and revitalize the operational procedures of urbanism. This is Koolhaas' complaint and it has gathered force with each repetition: '(a) maelstrom of modernization is destroying everywhere the existing conditions … and everywhere creating a complete new urban substance.' The problem is drastic – a plot for a tragedy – because the urbanist hides under 'a cloud of unknowing' which puts a lie to the assumption that 'globalization equals global knowledge'.

It is another technology – the computer – that has disrupted space and time, brought the assembly and the series up close. This creates the need to develop a new set of critical tools and a new set of engaged conceptions. If modern architects visualized the field of the city as a closed system, now it is the open-ended multiplicity of the network and the chaotic growth and universal expansion of cities and mega-cities around the world that need an image and new understanding. This requires the architect to become experimental by playing with different 'models', combining different approaches to urban diagnostics. Mapping and diagramming are exploratory techniques deployed to examine the complexity of the city while keeping all options open-ended in order to avoid fixing the image into concrete forms and imposing semantic closure. They are two ways of creating fictional realities to compensate for city images and an urban discourse we no longer desire.

Of Maps and Mappings Now we can return to the other questions that Foucault's lecture 'Of "Other" Spaces' raised: the difference between Renaissance space or a map and Modern space or a network, and implicitly how a network differs from everyday space and ordinary time.

During the Renaissance linear perspective and mathematics began to rule the figuration of the city – and images of the ideal city appear. Ruled by the principles of linear perspective based on

12 Mark Wigley, 'Resisting the City', p. 118.

13 Mark Wigley, 'Resisting the City', p. 120.

14 Bruno Latour, 'Why Has Critique Run out of Steam: From Matters of Fact to Matters of Concern.' **Critical Inquiry** 30,2 (Winter, 2004) pp. 225-248.

15 Peter Weibel, 'An end to the "end of art"? On the iconoclasm of modern art' in Bruno Latour and Peter Weibel (eds) **Beyond the Image Wars in Science, Religion and Art** (Cambridge MA: MIT Press, 2002) pp. 587-670.

16 Paulson, **Breaking and Remaking**: p. 16.

17 Jean Baudrillard, 'The Irony of technology,' in **The Perfect Crime.** Translated by Chris Turner (London: Verso, 1996) p. 71.

18 Let's take two other architectural iconoclasts: Le Corbusier and Rem Koolhaas. In the 'Introduction' to the second French edition of **Vers une architecture,** Le Corbusier asserts:
This book contains incisive writing. How does one discuss architecture with elegant detachment, architecture that results from the spirit of an era, at a time when this spirit still feels the unbearable effects of a dying era?/ Well, in order to carry on regardless of the crush of the millstone, draw lines that pierce it, like picks to punch holes in the millstone. Make holes. A hole here, a hole there. Now those are views. Views beyond the suffocating weight. Provide views, make holes. A useful, effective strategy. It is the tactic that I have chosen, something I almost felt compelled to do, actually.
In the 'Introduction' to the first edition of **S,M,L,XL** OMA, Rem Koolhaas, and Bruce Mau begin:
Architecture is a hazardous mixture of omnipotence and impotence. Ostensibly involved in 'shaping' the world, for their thoughts to be mobilized architects depend on the provocations of others – clients, individual or institutional. Therefore, incoherence, or more precisely, randomness is the underlying structure of all architects' careers: ... The more architecture mutates, the more it confronts it immutable core. Yet **S,M,L,XL** is a search for 'another' architecture, knowing that architecture is like a lead ball chained to a prisoner's leg: to escape, he has to get rid of its weight, but all he can do is scrape slivers off with a teaspoon.

19 Then why do they insist on controlling the discourse and managing the entrances and exits of those allowed to speak, determining whose voice is important, and what comments and criticisms acceptable? And what have they substituted instead?

horizontal line, vanishing and distance points and the resulting grid of orthogonals and horizontals that Brunelleschi worked out in Florence (1425) and Alberti described in writing, these ideal city images were utopian because the idea of implementation was an unreal expectation, they were merely visionary images of what might happen one day, when perfection could be attained.

In 1502 Leonardo da Vinci made a map of Imola based on the use of a horizontal surveying disk which allowed the accurate measuring of spatial dimensions of land and its objects, producing a mathematical abstraction of spatial reality. Called an ichnographic city plan – from Greek '*iknos*', meaning tracing or outlining, and '*graphein*', to write – its space was uniform and continuous in all directions. Leonardo utilized a plurality of hypothetical viewpoints all drawn perpendicular to the surface of the map. Such a map, or city plan, became the mode of cartographic documentation for the subsequent representation of European cities.

Alberti also developed a scale map of Rome to site any landmark accurately. He divided the circular horizon or circumference equally into spaced degrees, each connected to the center by a meridian which was in turn measured in evenly spaced parallels, thus creating a grid of nested circles. He could site any landmark on his map, noting its location at the nearest meridian and parallel and thus drew up a list of cartographic coordinates for every building and street in Rome. This map was absolutely abstract, a set of coordinates on a matrix. He called this cartographic grid a velum or curtain composed of perpendicular strands stretched across an open window, it was the grid through which the artist looked in order to copy the natural world that lay beyond.

So the process of tracing a map on paper continued down to recent history – the city map became an ideogram of how geometry measured and controlled perception of what is the 'urban' or the 'cityscape' and inscribed, as Foucault well knew, a grid of power/knowledge across its abstractions. More recently there has been a search for tools to engender new ways of viewing and mapping the city as a creative practice. Deleuze and Guattari offer a definition of mapping in *A Thousand Plateaus:*

> The map is open and connectable (sic) in all of its dimensions; it is detachable, reversible, susceptible to constant modification. It can be torn, reversed, adapted to any kind of mounting, reworked by an individual, group, or social formation. It can be drawn on a wall, conceived of as a work of art, constructed as a political action or as a meditation.[20]

They oppose mapping to tracing: the latter is closed in upon itself, propagating redundancies – while mapping is open-ended and experimental. It reformulates what already exists, looking for hidden logics underneath apparent forces (not just topography, rivers, roads, buildings, but wind and sun, local stories and historical events, regulatory forces and programmatic structures).[21] Mapping tries to visualize these interrelationships, looking for unfolding processes in a given milieu rather than imposing a static form on two dimensional space. There are flows of information dynamically interacting in space that develop in time; and stacks or layers of interactive processes to be superimposed upon each other into an amalgam of interrelationships.

Bruno Latour would call this a shift from looking at the city as an object to thinking of it as a thing: a shift in our critical equipment from questioning the social construction of scientific or urban facts, to taking a stubbornly realistic attitude dealing with polemical and political matters of concern. Matters of concern are constructed out of a complex and entangled history and gathering of a number of things into the object.

We take as an example of this thing-like gathering, the 'webby' quality of assemblages or the procedures of mapping, *S,M,L,XL* authored by OMA, Rem Koolhaas and Bruce Mau. This book, these projects of OMA (Office of Metropolitan Architecture) become a data space, a verbal-visual collage of alphabetical dictionary entries running down the margin of pages, juxtaposed with photographs that bleed out to the edge of their pages and these juxtaposed with written commentary about projects, autobiographical notes, events in the world, fairy stories and fictional accounts. It is hardly an architectural treatise.

Look at 'Congestion Without Matter', OMA's competition project for Parc de la Villette, Paris, France of 1982 – in this 'terrain vague' between the greedy needs of the 20th-century metropolis and the plankton of the suburbs, Koolhaas/OMA designed a program that offered 'Density without architecture, a culture of "invisible" congestion'.

A series of bird's-eye views in color of a model for Parc de la Villette, leads us into the project; one in particular, with a corner insert of Brandinelli's Adam and Eve. Is this to remind us of the Garden of Paradise from which we have been expelled, never to return? A few pages later we see dictionary entries along the left-hand margin with a double page photographic spread in colour of figures standing on an open field arranged in a spiral. These figures are voters in South Africa photographed by the Associated Press in 1994. In the margins continue the third and fourth entries about 'Lille'. The former explaining the various sports fields and walks to be found near the metropolis while the latter describes the site plan of Eurolille – as a monster encompassing London, Brussels and Paris. 'Liminal' defines a time and space betwixt and between meaning and action. 'Liguefaction' explains the latest OMA buildings as containers of gel rather than a series of geological formations or piles. And finally 'Lite City' begins with a drive through Houston.

These definitions and the photograph appear – at least on the surface – to be accidental juxtapositions, and even if they are chance encounters, they generate and disseminate meaning of their own. Standing in a line to vote, newly enfranchised South Africans – just an image of people and landscape – or a reminder of Modernism's project – its emancipation from tradition, from the tyranny of history and the Academies, its promise of improvement and reform? Connections

20 Deleuze and Guattari; **A Thousand Plateaus, Capitalism and Schizophrenia,** 2nd edition (London: The Athlone Press, 1996).

21 James Corner; 'The Agency of Mapping: Speculation, Critique and Invention' in Cosgrove D., (ed.) **Mappings** (London: Reaktion Books, 1990).

and linkages are important but kept open and indeterminate.
More bird's-eye views of the model follow until we discover that Houston's urban territory (note that the Lite City dictionary entry was left dangling several pages before) represents an art of erasure or desettlement. A less oppressive, less vulnerable kind of urban condition – park would not be an adequate word for this Lite City – offers catalytic chains and patterns of unpredictable events. Eventually we arrive at the first initial hypothesis: Parc de la Villette's program was much too large to create a park, in the recognizable sense of the word. The latter would have provided a replica of nature with some service facilities dotted about it. Instead this park would be an open ended, constantly changing and adjusting park (like the multiplicity and ambiguity of the dictionary entries that undercut stable and definitive meanings; or like the alphabet when used as an arbitrary encyclopaedic order that re-orders the universe in the manner it links words together and arranges them in space.
The park contains an underlying principle of programmatic indeterminacy: how to combine on a given field a series of activities that will interact and set off a chain reaction of new, unpredictable events (like the chain of voters in South Africa). Or how to create a social condenser, an architectural transformer, based on horizontal strips of congestion that constitute the park? The strips running East-West, house the major programmatic elements of the park, while layering creates the maximum length of borders and enables the maximum amount of permeability of each programmatic band.
Horizontal strips and vertical entries set up an investigative process: look up a word and consider the information, then transfer the data from margins to site. The horizontal and vertical establish the artificial confines of a gridded diagram of space. The grid, the CLAM grille, the graphic notational system, the data space that enable comparisons to be made on 33 different cities and then facilitate the projection of these comparisons forward onto the homogenized and abstract functional city of Modernity. This is Koolhaas' and OMA's acknowledged patrimony. But Koolhaas' system is less rigid than his modern ancestor's grille – it allows instead for free play. On top of the grid are layered a network of points and a layer of infrastructure, intended to interact, disorient, blur with and override elements in other layers – just as the page layouts do.
The spectator/reader faces two different projects – an alphabetical listing of words, and an abstract layering of grids and points – and acknowledges the random play between them. This is not a designed landscape as much as a framework that absorbs a series of potential meanings. And so we return to the game of making lists, juxtaposing fragments, drumming up different associations and analogies – an ordering of experience performed on a specific frame, determined by the logic of the site – drawn to experimentation and performance. But the text, like the strips and layers of Parc de la Villette, shifts meaning about from objective project description to personal anecdote, from random fact to

technical detail. It generates a discourse of tension between objects and ground plane, between artifice and nature. It is in the end an encounter, an adventure, a game, a shifting ground.

Matters of Concern Let me turn to another example of mapping that raises fundamental questions about assemblages in space. Stephen Read has commented on the saturation of urban images inundating the viewer from movies, photographs, advertisements, even literature.[22] He claims this pervasive visibility offers nothing substantial about the city, for we stand in the midst of processes we cannot see in their totality. The overflow and excessive noise produced by so much visibility only adds to the obscurity of the view. Hence images of the city will always miss essential aspects of urban existence that occur outside of our immediate visual or perceptual field and beyond our agency or volition.

Because the city has lost its opposite pole, the periphery, or its outside, it resembles a figure without its ground; hence it is difficult if not impossible to visualize. Instead of a bounded place, with limits and enclosures, Read concludes the city has a dynamic order, its form generated out of a field of moments, an open gathering together of heterogeneous elements. Connectivity between these events, is for the most part invisible; pathways from local to global evident only in the most obvious forms such as tourism, cellular phone networks, and the internet.

Inverting the theory of complexity which sees order emerging out of entanglements of micro-dynamics, or self-organizing autopoietic systems theory, Read argues instead that complex details emerge from simpler larger scaled processes and spatial orderings. Something already constructed produces effects: hence the city emerges from 'local thickenings' of pre-existing form; places created out of wispy traces of stuff passing through.

This city is likened to a machine, a construction built to the image of action containing points of relay between different 'bodies', be they animal, mental, social.[23] This is not Lefebvre's space of production but a productive space formed through interactions or interfacings between different horizontal layers; or topological extrusions of one space into another as a point extrudes into a line, a line into a square, a square into a cube.

Horizontal movements play an active role; they form relational substrata constantly transferring, opening out, in-forming. Points in various scaled relays build up into a 'matrix of encounters' that defines the urban. Hence the urbanist is no longer engaged in reading a map, or forming representations of a world seen from above or outside as if arriving from Mars. Instead this urban explorer examines a nested set of layers, probing and seeking pathways that lead from one stratum to another. The city then becomes a process that reinvents and reconstructs itself on the back of networks or substrata that are in themselves continually being constructed, revised or reordered.

This is quintessentially Michel Foucault's space of modernity: envisioned as a series, networks,

22 Stephen Read, 'The Urban Image – Becoming Visible', paper presented at Aesthetics of Mobility Conference Helsinki (January 2005); forthcoming in **Contemporary Aesthetics** (2006).

23 Stephen Read, 'Productive space' in **Crossover: Architecture, Urbanism, Technology**, edited by Leslie Jaye Kavanaugh (Rotterdam: 010 Publishers, 2006).

trees and matrices. It is not a matrix in which the nodes of enclosure are the focus, the cells that contain the information, but the relationships between the cells, the shifting upwards and downwards between layers in the series, the awareness that correlations of events are productive, in-forming, transforming as information passes through a series of points. This reading of the image of the city as indeterminate, an open process of becoming and a stream of events in which something unexpected, alien, uncanny even violent erupts, can also be read against Bruno Latour's concepts of 'matters of concern', 'gathering' and 'things'.

In 'Centres of Calculation' Bruno Latour writes about those on the first voyage to the Pacific making 'inscriptions' so that a second voyage could be undertaken.[24] It was important to create a code of what they saw, to trace it on paper and to send it back to the centres of control so that those who had never seen the land firsthand could draw accurate maps. The process depended on two types of local knowledge: one of them a network to transport knowledge back to the centre, the other generated inside the observatories and laboratories within the centre where the accumulated traces were reduced into lists, graphs, tables, and maps. Each stage of translation extracted elements out of the stage below, abstracting from the thing to the process, rewriting, representing, and discovering unexpected connections. Every trace was re-written as an equation or a geometrical form – a cascading of re-representations. Such is the task we are confronted with today: how to map out the network across which this information flows, how to generate images of this cascading flow, knowing that in the process of building models or facsimiles they in turn produce effects.

These are Latour's 'matters of concern': instead of debunking the representational forms that leave us with bits and pieces after so many prolonged image wars, he suggests that we get closer to the object of study, that we examine how 'matters of concern' enter our world.[25] Latour deploys the concept of 'constructivism' as the direct opposite of deconstruction: it offers a nested set of elements in order to improve one's sight, while deconstruction produces elements in order to delay the grasp of the whole.

In order to explain how machines, our models and facsimiles, produce effects, Latour resorts to a close reading of Alan Turing's fascinating original text 'Computing Machinery and Intelligence' (1950) in which Turing claimed a computer was indistinguishable from a woman typist.[26] Latour argues that language is a matter of building models or facsimiles, and that writers of novels or academic articles, always deploy a 'matrix of transformative metaphors' across layers of discourse from anthropology, technology, ideology, psychology etc. Discourse on scientific demonstrations is crooked and metaphorical, never straight and literal. Most readers of Turing's text think he is offering an outline of man/machine relations – or raising the question: can machines think? But Turing's text is, to the contrary, a baroque text filled with metaphors, anecdotes, asides, and autobiographical comments that compose a strange supposedly scientific article. Turing calls abstract machines 'mathematical fictions' rather than physical objects and ponders how far we can go in attributing machines agency? Devising a thought experiment, he builds a model with words: asking if computers supposedly can do only what we tell them to do or whether they have agency? His experiment is testing whether a computer can trigger, generate more ideas than we put into it. Can it surprise us with its consequences, can we attribute agency to it?

When mechanical objects are born they are born as things not objects – this is what Turing tells Latour – all objects are born as things. When we get close to the origin of important scientific discoveries, we get descriptions of things not objects, complicated entanglements, and matters of concern. Latour is making no distinction between language and the world, arguing that making facsimiles is carrying worlds into words. The question is what does it mean to reproduce something: an image of the city, a model of urban processes, or a calculating machine? What effects are generated by this construction of things?

If our contemporary model of space is constructed as a series of simultaneities, not an accumulation of slices of time that move inevitably towards the future, then Latour suggests a new set of questions emerge and a new set of effects to consider. We no longer are asking about the survival of the fittest, the nature of progress, or the arrow of time with its inevitable forward successions, but instead the question raised is how can we cohabitate this world together and yet allow expression to contradictory claims, interests, passions and differences? Latour believes ecology ruined the time of succession and ushered in the time of space, an intertwined form of cohabitation. In other words, as Foucault maintained, space has replaced time as the main ordering principle of our modern epoch, space as a series of contemporary simultaneities.

Progress and succession, revolution and substitutions are no longer part of our operating system. We know how to do things in time: to dissemble, divide, deconstruct and discard, to think of the city as a series of fragmented enclosures. But we do not know how to compose and assemble a sense of shared space, the space of our collectivity. Latour is arguing that progress and succession, revolution and substitution, are no longer part of our operating system. This is his matter of concern: the need to overcome dispersion, destruction, deconstruction, to stop adding ruin upon ruin and instead build new institutions, new models, procedures and concepts to collect and to reconnect the social. This is Stephen Read's matter of concern too, his 'imbricated ecology' in the space of the city and what the process of mapping is all about. This is how we build word experiments, study the effects of our models and project our imagings towards the city of the future.

Plans and Diagrams In the discussion of invisible processes that underlie the formation of the contemporary city, let us consider the substitution of the diagram for a city plan. Remember that Koolhaas compared the Generic City to a sketch which is never elaborated, nor

24 Bruno Latour, 'Centres of Calculation', **Science in Action**.
25 Bruno Latour, 'The Powers of Fac Similes. A Turing Test on Science and Literature', http://www.ensmp.fr/~latour/articles/article/94-POWERS%20TURING.html
26 Alan Turing, 'Computing Machinery and Intelligence', **Mind** (October, 1950), http://www.abelard.org/turpap/turpap.htm

improved but abandoned lying on the table. 'The idea of layering, intensification, completion are alien to it; it *has* no layers.'[27] With the passage of time the profession of diggers uncovering layers of prior civilizations on the very same spot, will not be able to approach the Generic City with their old set of tools. They will need new criteria to examine its traces for it leaves behind nothingness. How then to create 'the documentation of its evaporation'?[28]

That is the crisis this new breed of urbanists must focus on: how to critique the model that automatically produces the Generic City, how to discover the operations that program its evaporation and analyze the complex apparatus that distributes it globally as a mass-produced commodity? But how can a void become the object of study? To entertain a tiresome critique of planning and architecture committed to the pursuit of irrational ends says nothing at all about the operative effects of the Generic City. Since the code and object produced by this quasi-organic machine are far from perfect, it is better to examine the schematic diagram left abandoned on the table and the propositions it attempts to articulate.

A diagram is an abstract method depicting the relationship between points in space that may change over time, it is topographical, a series of points in an open-ended series, a tree, network, or matrix, as Foucault described. A diagram is deployed in order to graphically display relationships that course dynamically across the city, but they are by and large invisible, an intellectual construct and hence add to the problem of the invisible city.

A diagram is really a graph, and its origins are humble enough and related to the map of the city. In the 18th century mathematicians began to take networks into account. It began with a practical question: whether it was possible to cross all seven bridges over the Pregel river (in Königsberg) once and only once on the same round-trip. The river surrounds an island and on the right of the map of the city it separates into two branches – seven bridges span the river. All attempts to answer this simple puzzle failed. In 1736 Leonard Euler began to consider a mathematical solution to the problem: he proved the impossibility of finding such a route.

He replaced the map of the city by a simple diagram: the four land areas were denoted by the symbols A, B, C, D (the coordinate points) and the seven bridges by a, b, c, d, e, f, g (connecting lines). I.e. he defined a graph – but there is no path which contains each edge of the graph once and only once. Nevertheless Euler displayed that all structures in two-dimensional space can be represented by graph theory: all maps, trees, stars, junctions, rings, hubs, regions, and countries.

A flow-chart is also a diagram: It was John von Neumann (1903-57) who identified the key components of the computer as information processor: a central processing unit, a memory to store information, and an input/output device for bringing information into and out of the machine. He also developed the 'flow diagram' that charts the course of information transfers and operations. A flow-chart describes inputs and outputs, source and destination, it diagrams a sequential progression towards a specified goal. It is both dynamic and narrative.[29] Furthermore, a flow-chart or directed graph is a diagram linking points and lines which models and makes visible the relation between forces or processes in motion.

Architects have often relied on technical designs, diagrams or blueprints to describe and communicate with precision the dimensional and construction characteristics of a building. Their plans, sections, and elevations are based in geometry, or axiomatic projections based in volumetric descriptions. But contemporary diagrams, or graphs, do not come from architecture but from mathematical graph theory or information theory – and they are not representational but abstract machines. Foucault described the diagram in *The History of Sexuality:*

> The diagram or abstract machine is the map of relations between forces, a map of destiny, or intensity, which proceeds by primary non-localizable relations and at every moment passes through every point, or rather in every relation from one point to another.[30]
>
> This means that the diagram, in so far as it exposes a set of relations between forces, is not a place but rather a non-place: it is the place only of mutation. Suddenly, things are no longer perceived or propositions articulated in the same way.[31]

In recent times Ben van Berkel and Caroline Bos have been excellent diagrammers setting out many examples in the three-volume collection of *UN Studio – MOVE: liquid architecture*.[32] A diagram they explain is a visual tool used for the compression of information.[33] It freezes data into a pattern that can be analyzed to gain insight. In a dynamic diagram information is constantly changing as parameters are tweaked over time and these trace out different patterns in space. They make visible and calculable hidden processes that evolve over time.

Mathematics is full of such reactivations – insertions of a former discourse, technique, theorem into new domains, caused by basic omissions that come from within discourse itself. Thus contemporary architects may not be creating something new in their mapping and diagramming techniques, as much as they are returning to gaps and omissions within the texts of architecture, hoping to transform the discourse. But the architectural critics mentioned above have a passion for destruction when it comes to the city – to disrupt the continuous flow of history, the cascading of images, and like Nietzsche see all stable forms of knowledge go up in flames. Foucault too in his work on heterotopias of the asylum, the hospital, the prison, suffered the negative – focusing on the distributive networks of power/knowledge that excluded, repressed, censored, abstracted and concealed. He too lacked a will to go beyond opposition, beyond passivity to a

27 See Rem Koolhaas and Bruce Mau, et al.: **S,M,L,XL: Office of Metropolitan Architects, Rem Koolhaas and Bruce Mau**, edited by Jennifer Sigler (Rotterdam: 010 Publishers, 1995) p. 1264.

28 **ibid.**

29 Gunther Kress and Theo van Leeuwen, **Reading Images: The Grammar of Visual Design** (London: Routledge, 1999) p. 85.

30 Michel Foucault, **The History of Sexuality**, p. 93. Quoted by Deleuze, **Michel Foucault**, p. 36.

31 Michel Foucault, **Language, Counter-Memory**: 149-50. Gilles Deleuze, **Michel Foucault**, translated by Seán Hand (Minneapolis: University of Minneapolis Press) p. 85.

32 UN Studio, Ben van Berkel, Caroline Bos, 'Liquid Politic' in **Move: Imagination** (Amsterdam: UN Studio & Goose Press, 1999) p. 21.

33 Ben van Berkel and Caroline Bos; **Move** (Amsterdam: UN Studio, 1999) p. 19.

position of affirmation, reconciliation, and agency.
How then to create in the empty space where we are, in the mirror image of reflection, new relational possibilities? In his later work, the *History of Sexuality*, Foucault began to move away from the need to recover lost identity, or liberate the imprisoned nature of the self, or curb the desire for truth, towards something different, something that does not exist. He began to see in the mirror where the subject observes himself, a self constructed not just by passive but active affections.[34] How then might the cartography of the city, the diagram and the plan be reconfigured by a sense of making or producing reality instead of being condemned to passive reception?

Let us give to Michel Foucault the last word:

> Do not think (he advised) that one has to be sad in order to be militant, even though the thing one is fighting is abominable. It is the connection of desire to reality (and not its retreat into the forms of representation) that possesses revolutionary force.[35]

Just what might be an architecture of desire that addresses the city? How do we move beyond compensatory domains of invented communities, tourist destinations, gambling resorts, eco-tourist habitats, shopping centers, or whatever utopia of desire one can think of, and beyond the dystopias of war and destruction, nomadic barriers and territorial enclosures that mar so many contemporary cities? Or is architecture of the city confined to 'between-ness', constantly looking at a reflection of utopia/dystopia that it never quite grasps, and thus bound forever to opposition and ambiguity?

34 Brady Thomas Heiner, 'The Passions of Michel Foucault', **difference: A journal of Feminist Cultural Studies** 14, 1 (2005) pp. 22-52.
35 Michel Foucault, 'Preface' to Gilles Deleuze and Felix Guattari, **Anti-Oedipus: Capitalism and Schizophrenia,** Translated by Helen R. Lane, et al. (Minneapolis: University of Minnesota Press, 1985) pp xiii-xiv.

The Form of the Metapolis: Operational Mapping

Camila Pinzon Cortes

Introduction While around half of the world's population lives in urban agglomerations at the end of the millennium, we witness the triumph of the urban condition and in parallel, an overload of information and data about it. Most of the time the excess of information does not mean better knowledge, on the contrary, it might lead to 'misinformation, disinformation and out of control information'. [1] The several disciplines involved with projection in the contemporary urban agglomerations are desperately seeking for forms of assimilation and processing of all of this data. This search becomes even more anxious because it attempts to find or develop operative approaches, ways to act within an increasingly complex urban reality, complex because of the amount of data and variables that have to be observed. Within the attempt to develop new representation and analytical tools, 'mapping' offers possibilities to approach the contemporary urban reality operatively.

The term 'mapping' has become very popular in many disciplines. Today we are busy mapping the human genome, emerging global economic powers, or other planets of the solar system. The recent attention given to mapping is the consequence of the development of mapping and exploring techniques, but also of the information overload mentioned above, and of the emergence of new orders defined by invisible networks and connections. The new mappings attempt to represent these new orders. The question is that if everything is to be mapped, and if mapping implies selection, reduction, and exclusion of what is not represented on the map, then what should be mapped? What should be included and what left out? In urban areas, where we count on too much information, what is it that has to be mapped? What is needed to inform the design or project activity? Furthermore, the focus given to mapping data has relegated the formal aspects in the contemporary urban condition to the least level of importance, while data is, most of the time, translated directly into form in new interventions. Throughout this text I will try to argue for the necessity to return to the mapping of urban form, the mapping of physical and spatial dimensions as an alternative to the overload of information and as a possibility for operative approximations.

Mapping urban form in this case relates to 'description', but a description that 'reveals something new' as explained by B. Secchi. He also identifies a negative use of description that justifies mimesis, very common in the recent practices of city planning: 'a mimicry of settlement principles, of rules, of typological variations, of languages'. This use of description 'appears to be dictated by nostalgia which overlooks or pushes aside the most difficult problems'.[2] Description that 'reveals something new' can lead to a better understanding of structures that we are not so familiar with, and at the same time, reveal design possibilities or even become itself already a design activity. If we are dealing with an urban agglomeration that has exceeded the limits and

1 Lash (2001) p. 235.
2 Secchi (1993) p. 63.

definitions of the traditional city, a 'metapolis', the first step in order to be able to design within this urban structure is to describe it, and if this description reveals what is new, then it can become operative in planning desired futures.

When Ascher defines the metapolis, he shows how what is different in this post-metropolis phase is the discontinuity facilitated by communication and transport networks.[3] Therefore, an attempt to map form in this metapolis needs to acknowledge the relevance of these networks. But because the studies of urban form already constitute a consolidated approach to the city, I will attempt to present an alternative to actualize and contemporize this approach in order to be able to show relations and processes rather than static forms. Furthermore, this tradition of morphological studies concentrates on historical centres. If today, traditional historical centres are just a small percentage of the urban territory, and we talk about the metapolis rather than about the city, is it possible to study form outside these centres? The actualization and re-stating of the study of urban form is necessary because the form we need to study today is no longer the one that informed the classical studies of urban morphology of, for example, medieval towns. The form we need to consider is the form of the metapolis. In this metapolis, distances are relative and networks establish all sorts of distant relations.

Operational mapping

> It is the agency of representation that allows one to find hidden relationships and processes rather than simply 'image' them.[4]

Without ignoring the fact that mapping has never been an innocent activity, and that most developments in mapping follow first military objectives rather than naive attempts to 'know' and better represent the world, I will argue the possibilities of approaching mapping as a design activity. I will attempt to describe the opportunities of mapping the contemporary urban field operatively. If Pickles in *A History of Spaces* describes how 'It is the drawing and interpreting of a line that marks the cartographic impulse'[5] (p. 9), how then can this drawing and interpreting of the line allow design intentions in the contemporary metapolis?

Pickles relates how mapping is currently flourishing, even more in disciplines outside geography and cartography. For example, Hall (1992) in *Mapping the Next Millennium*, explores mapping techniques in several disciplines from astronomy to biology, using the new representation and processing techniques developed in the past century. Michel Serres writes an 'Atlas' [6] because in the world configured by invisible networks and new relations, 'even the same space changes and it asks for new world maps'. [7] How can we find our way when everything changes, when so many things and places are accessible to us from many networks without moving from our own home? We need to construct new maps and that is what he attempts with the writing of his Atlas.

Pickles also explains how 'for both geographers and cartographers the map has served in various roles: as archive for geo-referenced data, as picture of the spatial order of the world, as tool for investigating spatial relations, and as object of aesthetic and historical interest'. [8] In the same way, the recent excitement about mapping can be linked to these diverse uses of maps. To start with, there is a whole development and speculation related to the technologies and levels of exactness that have been achieved, principally in relation to the geo-referenced systems. When we have achieved such a degree of precision that allows us to map microscopic as well as astronomic dimensions, and we have developed technologies to relate information and data to the map, or to map that information, again the question is 'what to map?' And if we are aware of the reduction that a map implies, the question is also about what to leave out.

The diminishing of the margin of error achieved by mapping techniques does not exclude the fact that the map is still elaborated by mapmakers. If maps can serve as pictures of the spatial order of the world, they are the pictures of the world by someone or of a specific culture at a specific moment. Because of the increasing acknowledgement of this fact, there is a call for the need for criticism and to document a history of mapping, since mapping has always been linked to power and to spatial or ideological domination. Maps are not innocent, and thus their study needs to acknowledge the role of the mapmakers, because it can tell us much about their context as well as about the context of the map itself. As explained by Hall, when two maps of the same territory interpret it in a totally different way, that will tell us something about the clash of cultures that produced them. [9]

While historical criticism of maps and mapping practices becomes very relevant within geography and cartography, J. Corner shows how in the disciplines involved with planning and design of the built environment there has not been such questioning about the cartographic tools used for understanding as well as projecting urban areas. Moreover, we are still using the same mapping techniques developed in the early 16th century. They have not been subject to any criticism or innovation, becoming even 'institutional conventions'.[10] Mapping is in this case something that occurs as a survey previous to the design process, while Corner claims precisely the opposite. He calls for a new approximation to mapping where the possibilities that it offers are explored rather than accepted as conventions without question. He affirms that 'mapping' is 'the most formative

3 Ascher (1995).
4 Berger (2002).
5 Pickles (2004) p. 9.
6 Serres (1995).
7 **ibid.,** p. 12.
8 **op. cit.,** 5 (Pickles) p. 9.
9 Hall (1992) p. 395.
10 Corner (1999) pp. 216-217.

and creative act of any design process' and that 'the various cartographic procedures of selection, schematization and synthesis make the map already a project in the making'.

Again Pickles refers to the 'finger' in the Swedish geographer G. Olsson's theory. The finger is indexical because it points to something to draw attention to it. 'It delimits from a field a point, a place, an object for our attention. It stabilizes a particular meaning within a world of possible meanings'.[11] Corner describes this indexical aspect when he refers to the two main characteristics of mapping: First, a map is analogous to reality, or what Pickles calls lines of equivalence between the map and reality. Second, mapping is by definition abstract; it is abstract by being indexical because the information included in a map has been selected and isolated (maps are only 'one' version of that reality, a product of someone's specific selection). This abstract essence is what makes a map useful. A map that attempts to put together too many aspects of a territory loses readability; by attempting to say everything, it does not say anything. The multiplicity in the map is not given by the number of variables mapped, but by the relations and links that it uncovers.

The distance between the map and the reality to which it is analogous allows finding relations that become visible only through the process of isolation. The process of reduction is also a process of making evident aspects that were not, and of making spatial aspects not observed spatially before. If we observe the design or project activity in the same way, we can see how it also implies reduction: to design is to select, from many possible future options, one that seems for any reason the most adequate. This is a continuous process of discarding through the detailing and concreting of a design, always by means of representation. Thus, if mapping is taken as an essential part of the design activity, rather than accepting it as a convention, it can then become operative in studying the urban condition today. Instead of observing the main characteristics of mapping, partial, subjective and incomplete, as problems, they should be observed as essential to the process of exploring design possibilities for a specific area. Mapping can then generate ideas to act, by showing what is important for the mapmaker at a specific moment, for a specific place.

What to map? One aspect of the contemporary excitement about mapping is the claim for the need to map new geographies. These new geographies emerge from new global orders where political divisions, natural barriers, or concepts of borders and limits are redefined. For example, when we are talking about the global risks of the second modernity, as Beck[12] does, political and social borders are less relevant. These new orders require new cartographies. The limitations of cartographical representations, when so many invisible networks and connections structure our life today, are brought into discussion. The view from the top, or what Boeri[13] calls the 'Zenith arrogance', is criticised because it cannot give account of experiences, variable uses, appropriations and meanings of space.

Parallel to this claim for new maps, all sorts of 'atlases' have appeared, especially in the past 10 years: *Mutations*, *USE*, *The Harvard Design School Guide to Shopping*, *Costa Iberica*, *HICAT: Hiper Catalunya Research Territories*, or in the Netherlands the *KAN* and *LIME* Atlases, *Euroscapes* etc… Within these atlases or new mappings I identify three different tendencies that I will try to explain briefly, concentrating on the last one, and arguing the necessity of mapping form and relations when dealing with an urban structure like the metapolis, where issues of contiguity, continuity and borders are relative.

Mapping information, the globalized world The volume of *Wired* magazine, edited by Rem Koolhaas, where the Atlas of the new world or '30 spaces for the 21st century' appeared, brought to a climax a trend that, in a way, he had started with *S,M,L,XL*: a trend of architects producing atlases, maps and cartographies of several aspects, having in common a strong graphical accent. As Boyer relates it, there was a sudden extensive production of 'big books of architecture'. 'These books indicate that architects have become new gatherers of information, diagrammatic analyzers, and cartographers, in addition to being most attentive to mathematical models and topological surfaces'.[14] The particularity of these documents is that they combine design projects with statements and attempts to theorize, all of this framed in a highly graphical designed setting, where diagrams and maps become the structuring element rather than the text. [See figure 1]

There are two main motives behind these new mappings by architects. On one hand, there is an attempt to map new orders, orders of a globalized world, where aspects that become structural and relevant in defining relations do not coincide with the ones traditionally mapped. This is the case of AMO and Koolhaas in *Wired*. They attempt to map precisely those new global orders, new powers and forces in play at the global scale, by mapping for example MacDonald's restaurants, or Big Brother's reality shows. Secondly, as already studied by Harvey and Soja among others, there is a return to the reign of space and all the disciplines have started thinking and placing their knowledge in spatial terms.[15] Similarly Hall explains how questions of science like: 'Where do genes go on the chromosome? or how big is the ozone whole?' are all geographical and consequently they all require maps in order to be answered. 'Those maps might not all provide ultimate answers, but they almost surely suggest where to look for those answers'. [16]

11 **op. cit.,** 5 (Pickles) p. 3.
12 Beck (1992).
13 **cf.** Boeri (1998) and (1999).
14 Boyer (2005) p. 1.
15 Harvey (1990) and Soja (1996).
16 Hall (1992) p. 7.

Going back to the urban context, what all these architects and designers are doing by producing maps is, by graphical means, giving spatiality to information of all sorts. Putting information in spatial terms involves localizing it and relating it to existing maps and cartographies of the world. Unfortunately, most of these studies concentrate on the mapping of quantitative data and they mainly attempt to deal with issues of global competitiveness, or of how regions, continents or cities can compete. They remain then at a global scale and at the same time, even if they make this data spatial, the physical and spatial dimensions, the topographic issues, are disregarded.

Mapping congestion: nostalgia?

When the exotic imitates everyday, what's left to fantasize about? [17]

Before mapping emerging global orders in the 'Space Atlas' of *Wired*[18] magazine, Koolhaas mapped Lagos and initiated another trend: going to cities in developing countries to map congestion, liveable public spaces and unplanned processes. Since then, Tokyo, Istanbul, the Pearl River Delta, Belgrade and Hong Kong have been some of the subjects of 'new mappings'. Most of the time, the claim for the need of these maps is that the traditional mappings are limited, top-down, and authoritarian, and that the new maps need to record the multiple and continuously changing experiences, uses and meanings of space. They need to observe and represent the territory 'laterally'.[19] The problem is not the call for the need of new maps but the fact that it is necessary to change the context and study cities in Asia for example, in order to develop them. By having to go to other contexts to apply this 'new way to see', there is a certain degree of hidden nostalgia, especially from European architects and offices that are the ones involved in this mapping. [See figure 2]

The nostalgia criticized in the studies of historical European centres, nostalgia for something lost, moves the investigation into the congestion in Asian cities; that congestion is the one lost here. It is nostalgia for the street vendor, for the disorder that an overregulated Western urban sphere does not allow to emerge anymore. Claims about new ways to see the city, new representation methods, are all deeply rooted in nostalgia for a type of city. By observing the different, they are trying to grasp the lost. The discovery of the virtues of the traditional city, when it was already gone, and the reiterative going back to its virtues to judge or compare any other setting, might have been the point of no return for European Urbanism, but going to Lagos, or going to congested cities in developing countries is as nostalgic as the claim for the traditional city might be.

However, even if sharing a common desire for something lost, there are two types of nostalgia. The first one (for the traditional city) can be compared with the one argued by Jameson for 'nostalgia film' in postmodernism, a nostalgia different from historicism, and instead merely stylistic, linked to an image. [20] This nostalgia, represented by the re-creation of images, is illustrated by Boyer as related to the 'Tableaux vivant' of the 18th and 19th centuries. [21] These tableaux were composed not to recreate a historical moment but a static image. In Boyer's opinion, the approximation to today's urban reality carries a nostalgia for the city of the 19th century, but this nostalgia results in the attempt to reproduce isolated and disconnected, unitary images. However, Boyer's claim also carries a certain degree of nostalgia, but of another type; a nostalgia for a 'collective memory' that does not exist anymore.[22] In this case, the nostalgia of Boyer is not for an image, a form, or a static setting, but one for a space and a type of city as facilitator of the construction of a collective memory.

The argument of 'nostalgia' has often been used to disqualify the morphological observation of the city, because it attempted to recuperate something already lost even at the moment of its awareness. Certainly, the morphological observation focused on the historical centres and in this way it annihilated its possibilities as a contemporary analysis and design approach. As Hays[23] described it: 'While Tendenza's model of autonomy seems powerful and, in its basic contours, still correct, what was missed by its arguments is that the very conditions on which its "ontology" depends – namely the traditional European city – had, by the time of its theorization, already disappeared as a contemporaneous object of experience.'[24] However, I want to argue that while we focus on mapping so much data, the morphological aspect disappears as an object of study. Parallel to the mapping of data, morphological aspects still need be considered, not in the traditional centres, but in what Secchi has called the 'true domain of the new': the periphery, a space denied and considered empty, existing only because of its opposition to the centre, but the place where the urban experience occurs today.

Summarizing, while one group denied the periphery because they were too busy studying and re-affirming the historical centres, the other one abandoned it to go and study central and busy areas in 'other' contexts. The difficulty lies in the fact that the logic structuring the periphery is different from that of the traditional centres. This difference reinforces the idea of the necessity of mapping these places, the areas where urban experience occurs today, not only in the European case, but also in other contexts. Furthermore, the problem becomes more complex when we think that the notion of periphery, as it was defined in opposition to a centre, does not even exist anymore, having now a weight of its own, and being an active part of a new territorial structure: the metapolis.

17 Koolhaas (2003).
18 **ibid.**
19 Boeri (2003).
20 Jameson (1997).
21 Boyer (1994).
22 Boyer (1997).
23 Hays (2001).
24 **op. cit.,** 22 (Hays) p. 265.

Mapping form in the metapolis: void and relations

Within the collection of new atlases produced recently, there is one group studying form at the level of the metapolis, or at the level of territories. It concentrates on physical and spatial features rather than on quantitative data, arguing for the necessity of description. Within this group, territories in the Veneto, Catalonia and Flanders among other regions have been documented from the point of view of the form and process of the occupation of the territory, discovering organization-patterns differing from the ones of traditional cities. They emphasize description through mapping, illustrating the emergent interest in the mapping of the territory as a field of investigation and design. I will try to argue the relevance of this approach on a more general level, by explaining the necessity of mapping urban form in the metapolis, the necessity of an observation of form and relations in a moment where we experience 'the reign of the urban and the death of the city' as Choay so clearly put it.[25] [See figure 3]

The idea of the metapolis becomes a very powerful one because, of all the different names and terms that try to explain the contemporary urban condition (*edge city, città diffusa, dispersed city, megalopolis,* etc), the one developed by Ascher puts together both dispersed occupation and existent centres.[26] What is new for Ascher, are the types of relations within them. He explains how the form of growth that characterized the two previous modernities is either internal by densification or by extension into peripheries, while the form of growth in the metapolis is external in the sense that it means the incorporation into the area of quotidian functioning of a metropolis, villages, urban and open areas every time farther from it.[27] Metapolis is formed of 'distended, discontinuous, heterogeneous and multi-polar urban territories; there is no longer a clear boundary between the city and the countryside. New kinds of places and centres have appeared in the peripheries: commercial centres, urban research centres, logistic platforms (places where almost all facilities are available); public and private spaces have been reconstituted at all levels, from the inside of the house which opens to the outside world through new communication technologies, to the external spaces which are conspicuous by their exclusive logic'.[28]

If we are asking about the form of this metapolis, what emerges clearly is that ideas of continuity and contiguity become difficult to use as the basis for a definition of that form. Instead of the commonly used oppositions of city and countryside to form new units. The traditional morphological analysis, starting from those oppositions, focused on the built component of the city. This built component was classified in types, and these different types produced different fabrics. There are only two possibilities left for the open space: it is either clearly defined and contained by the built one, or it becomes the territory outside the city and thus left outside the study. In order to attempt to map form in the metapolis, the first element that needs to be included in the study is the open space, the unbuilt but not necessarily empty space which serves the more urbanized or more compact areas in many ways (one of the most evident is recreation). When different gradations of dispersion or compactness spread over a territory where borders are impossible to define, the underlying carpet that gives structure and continuity to these territories is the unbuilt, rather than the built component.

One example that illustrates how the study of the landscape can incorporate the void and mediate between all the different types of occupations of the territory is the studies of the Dutch landscape. These constitute a contribution to the understanding of the landscape as a unifying element between open and built areas, and to the valuation of the role of the open space in contemporary urban regions. The special characteristics of the Dutch landscape, mostly artificially constructed through major reclamation works, give a specific structure to the landscape. This structure, completely rational, remains as an underlying layer when rural areas are urbanized. Then, in a study of the urban as well as the rural areas, the same grid and the same system of added elements are recognizable. This gives a unity to the totality and allows a structural connection between open and constructed areas, as well as accepting the independent value of studying those artificially constructed open areas.

The 'networks' constitute the second protagonist when studying urban form at the level of the metapolis. The open intervals mean also openness for relations, facilitated by all sorts of networks. Thanks to these networks, relations in the metapolis do not depend on spatial contiguity anymore, distances become relative and a different type of continuity is defined. In a study for the South Quadrant of The Hague (1989-1990), the Dutch architect Neutelings defined the 'Patchwork Metropolis' (*'Tapijtmetropool'*).[29] He argued that in an urban region like the Randstad, the model of an urban area (red) against a green one, where 'to plan' implies simply deciding which of the green areas will be covered with red, was long ago considered inadequate. Neutelings suggested a way to understand this South Quadrant as a collection of pieces. Each piece has a specific programme and a physical structure. When thinking in this way, the contradiction and opposition between city and countryside is abolished. Each one of the inhabitants forms their own personal city thanks to the connections and accessibility provided by the system of networks, while a good level of diversity and balance between the pieces gives quality to the totality of the patchwork. Similarly, in a study for Antwerp's ring road, Neutelings talks about the ring as the new centre of the modern city; centre of the suburbs, where, according to him, the real urban life occurs today. Fishman had already developed a similar idea in the concept of 'city à la carte', the city that is singular for each individual and formed by his/her own specific destinations.[30]

25 Choay (1994).
26 **cf.** Ascher (1995) and (2001).
27 Ascher (1995) p. 60.
28 Ascher (2001).
29 Neutelings (1991).
30 Fishman (1990).

If the morphological study gives emphasis to the different relations and structures facilitated by these networks, it can start explaining relations rather than merely static forms. The study 'Morfogènesi de la Regió Urbana de Barcelona'[31] shows two predominant types of urban growth since the 1980s: by dispersion in the middle of the 1980s and, recently, by polarization. The difference between these two types of growth and the previous 'growth by aggregation' is the relation with the infrastructure networks. These types of growth, especially the one by polarization, do not relate to the existing city but to the infrastructure networks. These networks are the main driving force of the location of new urban developments, locating them not necessarily contiguous to existing areas, dispersed and discontinuous in the territory. These examples show how as structuring elements, as new borders to urbanization or as new centres, infrastructure networks acquire an importance that must be recognized if they are studied in relation to morphology in the contemporary metapolis.

The two elements described above, open space and the networks that furrow it, have to be integrated into an observation concentrating so far mainly on the static built component. Open space allows the relations that the networks facilitate, and they are both the essential structural elements of the territory of the metapolis.

Conclusion

> ...mapping space is 'a fundamental prerequisite to the structuring of any kind of knowledge. All talk about 'situatedness', 'location' and 'positionality' is meaningless without a mapping of the space in which those situations, locations, and positions occur. [32]

It is very clear that the emerging importance of mapping in many disciplines is related to a new spatial and relational paradigm. Mapping becomes a way of spatializing and localizing various types of information. Within these disciplines, in architecture, urban design and landscape architecture, the awareness of the possibilities of mapping rather than the acceptance of it as an established convention offers the opportunity to find an exit to the affirmation about the impossibility of acting, intervening, designing or influencing the urban condition today. Mapping can be operative if observed as a revealing activity that allows discovering and highlighting hidden relations and potentials.

31 Font (1999).
32 David Harvey (2001), as quoted by Pickles (2004).

But if everything is to be mapped, the problem is about the selection, about what to map. Related to this question, the periphery, denied previously in most of the studies of the urban condition, but being specially the space of contemporary experience, reclaims that mapping. It reclaims a description, an acknowledgement of its specific condition, and furthermore it reclaims strategies, design proposals. However, what we used to call periphery is not peripheral anymore but is an active part of the metapolis, as connected and as central as the traditional city but with different types of connections. This metapolis that represents new types of relations for the traditional centres but also for the old peripheries needs to be mapped. This mapping seems to provide ways to research around possibilities to act, firstly through description, not done until now, but a description revealing or bringing into light new relations; secondly, through an understanding of a different logic that structures form in the metapolis, and the development of intervention possibilities within this logic, different from the one normally assumed for the traditional cities. Finally what is important to observe if we attempt to map this metapolis is that the unbuilt is the core rather than the built, the unbuilt facilitates relations, flows and multiplicities. It is the open space and the relations it allows that need to be mapped if we are attempting to discover what is the pattern that organizes transformation in the metapolis.

Bibliography

Ascher, F. **Metapolis ou l'avenir de villes.** France: Editions Odile Jacob, 1995.

Ascher, F. **Town planning in the wake of the new urban revolution**. Brussels: European City Visions Workshop, 2001.

Beck, U. **Risk Society. Towards a new modernity**. London: SAGE Publications, 1992.

Berger, A. **Reclaiming the American West**. New York: Princeton Architectural Press, 2002.

Boeri, S. **USE Uncertain States of Europe: A Trip through a changing Europe**. Milan: Skira, 2003.

Boeri, S. Marini, E. Lanzani, A., 1993. **Il territorio che cambia. Ambienti, paesaggi e immagini della regione Millanese**. Volume edizioni, AIM-Abitare Segesta, 1993.

Boeri, S. 'Eclectic Atlases, Four possible ways of seeing the city' in: **Daidalos** 69/70 (1998/99).

Boyer, C. **The City of Collective Memory: Its Historical Imagery and Architectural Entertainments.** Cambridge Mass: MIT Press, 1994.

Boyer, C. 'Playing with Information: Urbanism in the 21st Century', in: Read, S. Rosemann, J. et al. (eds) **The Future City,** Routledge, 2005.

Choay, F. 'Le règne de l'urbain et la mort de la ville', in: **La Ville, art et architecture en Europe, 1870-1993**. Paris: Editions du centre Pompidou, 1994, pp. 26-35.

Corner, J. 'The Agency of Mapping: Speculation, Critique and Invention', in: Cosgrove D. (ed.) **Mappings,** London: Reaktion Books, 1999.

Fishman, R. 'America's New City', in: **The Wilson Quarterly**, #14 (1990), pp. 24-48.

Font, A. Llop, C. Vilanova, M. **La Construcció del territori metropolità: morfogènesi de la regió urbana de Barcelona**. Barcelona: Àrea Metropolitana de Barcelona. Mancomunitat de Municipis, 1999.

Hays, M. 'Ideologies of Media and the Architecture of Cities in Transition' in **Cities in Transition,** Rotterdam: 010 Publishers, 2001.

Hall, S. **Mapping the Next Millennium: The Discovery of New Geographies.** New York: Random House, 1992.

Harvey, D. **The Condition of Postmodernity: An Enquiry into the Origins of Cultural Change.** Cambridge Mass: Blackwell, 2001.

Koolhaas, R., and Mau, B. **S, M, L, XL**, Rotterdam: 010 Publishers, 1995.

Koolhaas, R. 'The New World, 30 Spaces for the 21st Century', in **Wired** 11-06, June 2003.

Koolhaas, R. (ed.). **Content**. Köln: Taschen, 2004.

Jameson, F. **Postmodernism or the Cultural Logic of Late Capitalism**. Durham (USA): Duke UP, 1991.

Lash, S. 'Informationcritique', in: **Cities in Transition.** Rotterdam: 010 Publishers, 2001, p. 235.

Page, M. 'Book reviews. The City of Collective Memory: Its Historical Imagery and Architectural Entertainments', in **Planning Perspectives**, Volume 12, Number 1 / January 1, 1997, p. 111–133.

Pickles, J. **A History of Spaces: Cartographic Reason, Mapping, and the Geo-Coded World**. New York: Routledge, 2004.

Serres, M. **Atlas**. Madrid: Ediciones Catedra, 1995.

Secchi, B. 'Descriptive city planning', in: **Casabella** no. 600, 1993.

Secchi, B. 'The Periphery', in: **Casabella** no. 583, Oct 1991.

Solà-Morales, M. 'The Culture of description', in: **Perspecta** no. 25,1998.

Soja, E. **Thirdspace: Journeys to Los Angeles and other Real-and-Imagined Places.** Oxford: Blackwell, 1996.

Stichting Rotterdam-Maaskant Foundation, **Willem Jan Neutelings Architect**. Rotterdam: 010 Publishers, 1991.

pping congestion: nostalgia? Photo credits: Pepijn Verpaalen.

Mapping information: the globalized world. Source: Author (2006).

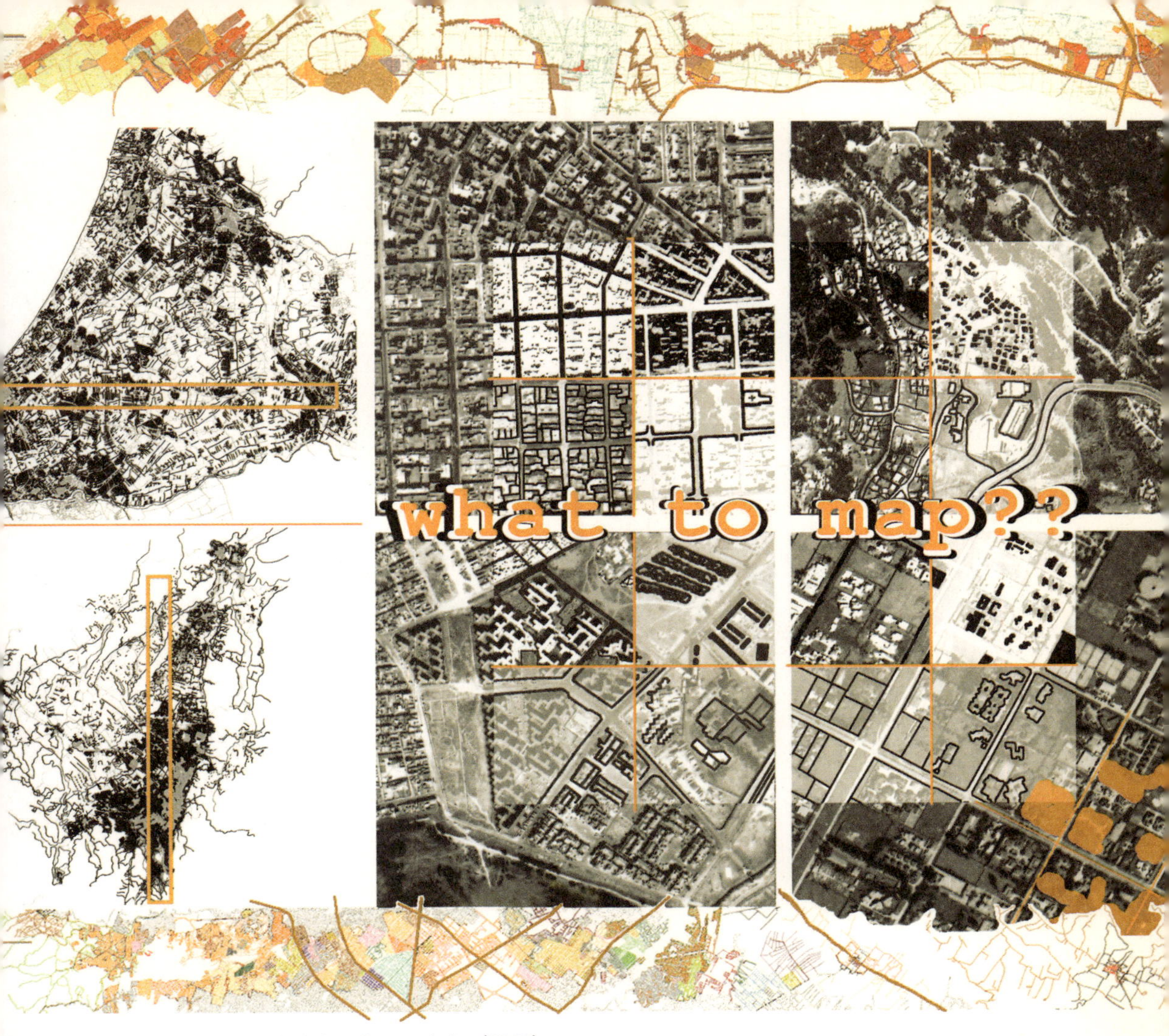

pping form in the Metapolis: void and relations. Source: Author (2006).

Shanghai: Brave New World
An Investigation into the Post-Colonial East-Asian Urban Condition

Gregory Bracken

In no city, West or East, have I ever had such an impression of dense, rank, richly-clotted life. Old Shanghai is Bergson's élan vital in the raw, so to speak, and with the lid off. It is life itself.[1]

Part One: Overview

The immediate theme of this paper is the city of Shanghai, which will be investigated within a framework of the wider post-colonial east-Asian urban condition. Comparative studies of Hong Kong and Singapore will also be undertaken, but in order not to make the scope of this investigation too wide, the former colonies of other Western powers in the region, for example, the Dutch or the French, are not examined here. The paper's aim is to outline some of the parameters and directions for this study.

Guidebooks invariably refer to Shanghai as the 'Paris of the Orient', but with its warrens of winding streets, lined with robustly weightlifting neoclassicism, it more resembles London; Shanghai is full of such contradictions, it is confusing and multi-faceted, the very fact of its being a capitalist engine in a communist country is a startling enough starting point. Further, as China's power and influence continues to grow internationally, could Shanghai become the capital of the twenty-first century, in the way that Paris was capital of the nineteenth, and New York of the twentieth?

Shanghai needs to be studied and mapped now. Asian scholars have long been looking to the West, it is time for Western scholarship to look East. Asian urban strategies are producing urban environments of incredible complexity and dynamism. Shanghai is China's new industrial powerhouse, it also has a Western footprint; parthenogenetically built up over a century following its seizure from the Chinese in 1842, this remained virtually untouched between 1937 and 1990, since which time, there has been staggering growth and change.

In the nineteenth century, the label 'Made in Britain' reflected that country's industrial and imperial might, a time when the world enjoyed the *Pax Britannica*. The twentieth century saw goods exported internationally with the logo 'Made in USA', again a reflection of that country's industrial power. Increasingly we are seeing the label 'Made in China'. Twenty-first-century China is interesting in that we now have an awakening giant of an economic powerhouse with its capital (at least in commercial terms) at Shanghai. 'What will happen', asks Ted C. Fishman in his provocative book *China Inc.*, 'when China can make nearly everything that the US and Europe can, at one-third the cost?' He then goes on to point out that, 'the burgeoning output of China's vast low-cost factories not to mention the ever-increasing appetite of its 1.3 billion[2] consumers are rapidly altering global commerce.'

One of the main tasks in this study will be to investigate the current conditions on the ground in Shanghai, at all levels of scale, in order to map the city's trajectory as it most likely becomes the capital of the twenty-first century, and to advance understanding of the post-colonial east-Asian

1 Aldous Huxley, **Jesting Pilate: The Diary of a Journey**, 1926.

2 Whenever the figure one billion is mentioned it is to be understood as American usage, i.e. 10^9 and not the European 10^{12} (in Europe, 10^9 is known as a milliard).

urban environment, and its potential effects on the contemporary global urban condition.

An Approach to Mapping Urban Complexity One of the keys to understanding Shanghai is mapping, not just static maps, but maps of movements, flows and patterns, the lines of flight in the city as it were. Certain specifics need to be looked at, such as architectural typologies, a list of these will be highlighted in Part Two and will include such contrasting types as the indigenous *shikumen* houses, and the new skyscrapers. Patterns of movement in the city have been analysed, including roads, water, public transport and pedestrian routes, as well as patterns of movement between Shanghai and other cities in the global network, for example, the transport of people, money, ideas, etc., which will be outlined briefly in Part Three, as will the history of these movements.

Mapping is one of the main tools of this project. Maps are revealing, they should be, but sometimes it is for what they leave out. Cook's map of Shanghai in the early twentieth century left out the streets in the Chinese City, there is simply a blank oval on the page, presumably no tourist ever felt safe enough, or curious enough, to want to go there.[3] As Arie Graafland has pointed out, maps have been used since earliest times to gain political power. Mercator's projection became a legend because a navigator could draw a straight line between two points and determine the course to sail. But Graafland shows that architects and urbanists use maps for other purposes, and that the perceptual apparatus brought to bear is never completely neutral to its observations.

Graafland, in discussing the issue of maps, quotes Harvey on 'latitudes of money and power' and 'longitudes of resistance', and how these, precisely because of the transcending possibilities of global framing, can register other forms of social difference, a notion that he points out as also being strongly present in the work of Manuel Castells and Saskia Sassen. Sassen's comments on globalisation in particular is another important research clue helping to correctly place Shanghai within the global network of world cities.

But Shanghai needs to be understood not just from a spatial perspective, as outlined in the mapping projects above, but also from a temporal one. Its timeline from the past through to its potential future trajectory. The city is a palimpsest, each trace of what has gone before can be useful in explaining what is there now, and, potentially, what is to come, though it is not in the purview of this project to make predictions. A study of the city's history as well as that of the country as a whole is essential, particularly as a Westerner looking East. This part of the study will be outlined and begun in Part Four of this paper.

Finally, in Part Five of the analyses under consideration here, some of the conclusions that are likely to result from these studies, as well as potential directions for further study, such as ontological analysis – the better to understand the mindset in an Asian city – will also be outlined.

Part Two: Shanghai

It has long been a cliché in China that the cleverest people come from Shanghai, but when one recent mayor of the city was asked if this was indeed true he replied, 'No, the cleverest people in China come *to* Shanghai.'

Until very recently Shanghai[4] appeared as if it were still 1937, the year the Japanese occupied all of the city except for the French Concession and the International Settlement. Four years later, in December 1941, these enclaves too were taken. Western life, as well as all building projects, came to a halt. Thirty years of Communist rule after 1949 likewise kept the city from developing. Architecturally speaking it's the least Chinese of China's cities, and one of the few important world cities to have escaped the second half of the twentieth century so intact, at least until recently. Ironically, it is the very revitalisation of the city under the new 'open door' economic policies, as well as the return of the foreigners, that are the greatest threats to Shanghai's architectural heritage today.

Shanghai, with a population of over 13 million, is one of the largest cities in China and a cultural, commercial as well as a political hub. It was always a cosmopolitan metropolis, but even during its colonial heyday Westerners never accounted for more than about 10% of the city's population. Shanghai, as well as being China's major centre of water communications, is also heavily industrialised. Historically it was China's main textile-producing centre, but more recently it has diversified, especially into chemical production, shipbuilding and engineering works. Located on the 31st parallel north, Shanghai has a temperate climate, with four seasons: Spring is from mid-March to mid-May; Summer mid-May to mid-September, when it can get humid and quite hot; Winter is from mid-November to mid-March, when it's chilly but seldom snows; Autumn is September-October and is the most comfortable season, though it can get typhoon-driven rain. China itself has a monsoon climate, with a long dry season consisting of autumn, winter and spring. Rainfall occurs mainly during the summer with at least half the annual rainfall occurring during June, July and August. In some areas the proportion can be as much as 90%.

China has recently begun to emerge as a world power, it's the third largest country in the world, and the most populous, with about one-fifth of the world's total population. It dominates the Pacific coastline of continental Asia, and shares over 14,000 kilometres of land frontier with more than a dozen other countries, including Russia and India. Despite opening up, China still remains little known or understood. Relatively few foreigners, even the ones living there, seem to learn its language or study its culture or history. Although foreign trade and tourism increased dramatically during the 1990s, they are only very slowly leading to any changes in foreign perceptions of China. Barriers of ignorance and misconception, long in place on both sides of the East-West divide, are not easily overcome.

Though the area around Shanghai has been occupied for 6,000 years, the city itself is a recent

3 At this period, for Westerners to show any interest in Chinese culture or history was to risk being thought of as 'going native'.

4 Shanghai as a name, as far as I can tell, is unique in that it is also a verb, albeit a rather dubious one. 'To shanghai' someone was the nineteenth-century practice of press-ganging men into working on board ship against their will. This was usually done by finding sailors so drunk that they had passed out on the street, which was also often a result of their being drugged. Once awake they had no option but to work their passage to the next port.

one by Chinese standards. The name means 'above the sea' and was first applied during the Song dynasty in the late thirteenth century, when the original fishing village had gradually grown into a busy market town. An enviable geographical position, halfway up China's Pacific coast and at the mouth of the Yangtze River, ensured its growth into one of China's key ports by the sixteenth century. At almost 6,500 kilometres, the Yangtze is the world's third longest river. A major shipping artery, it's large enough to allow ocean-going vessels to sail for several hundred kilometres upstream. After flowing out of Yunnan it carves it way through the famously beautiful Yangtze Gorges in the mountains of eastern Sichuan and western Hubei, it then meanders for hundreds of kilometres across fertile lowland plains dotted with lakes before debouching into the sea less than twenty kilometres from Shanghai.

The Japanese were the first to trade with China but the activity of their pirates in the sixteenth century forced the Shanghainese to build city walls. These stood until 1912. Westerners first became interested in the city as relatively late as the 1830s, when it was a domestic port of some importance. The First Opium War, leading to the Treaty of Nanking (now Nanjing) in 1842, opened up five so-called 'treaty ports', including Shanghai and Hong Kong.

The history of the colonial era will be dealt with in more detail in Part Four, this section is intended to cast some light on Shanghai's growth and development since the economic reforms of the late 1980s and 1990s have begun to take effect, allowing the amazing renaissance that has enabled the city to be thought of as a serious rival to Hong Kong in the global city network, also an issue that will be touched upon in more detail in Part Three in the *Note on Globalisation*.

Shanghai Now In 1990 China's first (and largest) stock market opened in the new Pudong district, which faces central Shanghai across the Huangpo River. China's economic reforms are the result of Premier Jiang Zemin and Zhu Rongji's innovations, both of whom came originally from Shanghai. Since that time, as if to make up for generations of inactivity, the pace of change in Shanghai has been rapid. It seems to have reverted to the same sort of staggering growth that characterised its first hundred years.

Currently the city exists in a dizzy state of equilibrium between government control and market forces as its trajectory accelerates towards capitalist ideals. More than any other metropolis, Shanghai has become synonymous with the most brutal kind of urban redevelopment. 'By 2000,' states Richard Turnbull, 'half the buildings from the late 1940s, the vast majority colonial, had been razed to make way for 200,000 high-rises.' He refers to the city as 'the world's largest construction site'.

Darryl Chen calls Shanghai 'more a process than a static cityscape, with its explosion of object buildings tempered by new infrastructure, parks and conservation the city presents an almost unique control-model kind of urban subject matter among the world's major metropolises.' Chen also warns against drawing hasty conclusions in a city which lends itself so easily to cliché and whose presence in popular imagination is potently fuelled by what he calls 'a mythologized past'. One must beware of nostalgia in this study, but Shanghai as 'Icon' could well prove a fruitful topic.

The government is investing heavily in urban infrastructure, what Chen calls the 'hardware of any global city'. It opened its first metro line in 1994, it now has three, and is currently constructing three more. It is also home to the world's first commercial Maglev line, linking the new Pudong Airport to the city. Overhead expressways have snaked their way across the city since the 1990s, as have new river bridges, and an outer ring road. Shanghai is also home to China's first Formula One racetrack, and has successfully bid for the World Expo in 2010.

And as for the new buildings of Shanghai, the architects working on them read like an international *Who's Who*: Richard Rogers: master plan for Pudong business zone; Foster and Partners: Jiushi Corporation Headquarters; Skidmore, Owings & Merrill: Jin Mao Tower; Kenzo Tange: Bank of Shanghai; John Portman: Tomorrow Square; Kohn Pederson Fox: Plaza 66; and the World Financial Centre (currently under construction, when completed in 2007 it will be the world's tallest building). There is also the local talent of Xing Tong He, architect of the Shanghai Museum as well as mastermind behind Shanghai's successful bid for Expo.

The question obviously has to be asked if all of this is sustainable, or even manageable? Another area for concern is Shanghai's existing architectural stock, and although some steps have been taken to conserve the city's traditional architecture, the famous waterfront of the Bund and many of the *shikumen* courtyard houses, indigenous to the city, are being retained and restored for reuse; many other areas are simply being razed to make way for redevelopment.

S*hikumen* are a sort of compact version of the traditional Chinese courtyard house, they take their name from their decorative stone entrance gates. They might also make an interesting and useful study of how urban constraints can affect traditional design. Xintiandi is an area of *shikumen* houses in the old French Concession that were attractively restored in 2000 by Wood and Zapata. Though some of the houses have been 'faked', using old bricks retrieved from rubble, this is, in my opinion, a scheme that has been more successfully executed than similar efforts in other Asian cities, for example, Singapore's Far East Square. This could make for a useful comparative study. But interesting as all of this is, in order to understand what is going on in Shanghai now we must avoid focusing too much on individual buildings, or set pieces, especially on grounds of aesthetics alone, Shanghai as an urban phenomenon is so much larger, and it to this larger scale that I will turn in the next part of this paper.

Part Three: analysis

Methods Methods of analysis need to include mapping the city's infrastructure. These will include its road network, public transport networks, waterborne transport, pedestrian and bicycle movements; street life, including locations for Tai Chi, newspaper reading, ballroom dancing, skateboarding and English conversation practice; building types, their heights, age and style; the location of icons and landmarks, as well as the different places of religious worship; divisions of residential and commercial activity, official and unofficial; type, size and use of city blocks; and any other mapping techniques that might be felt to be useful. Another type of exploration will entail the mapping of specific routes through different parts of the city, that of Nanjing Road has already been begun, with some interesting findings, such as the significant differences in size and scale of the city blocks east and west of Tibet Road. These lines of difference will be extrapolated into the rest of the city to see what information they might disclose. Nanjing Road East resembles London's Oxford Street, and this is where the city blocks are dense and regularly gridded. Nanjing Road West is a much stranger urban phenomenon, there is no precedent that I can think of, it seems unique with its bizarre mix of old and new, communist and capitalist, eastern and western, large and small scale, fashionable and dingy. This is definitely an area that requires further study.

Comparisons Shanghai has once again become a major world metropolis, what will its new ascendancy mean for regional neighbours Hong Kong and Singapore, as well as other Pacific Rim cities such as Tokyo, San Francisco, Los Angeles and Sydney? Not to mention London and New York, and, of course, Beijing? Shanghai and its colonial sisters, Hong Kong and Singapore, may be in the Orient but they were very definitely founded as Western cities. The nineteenth century, through its industrial development and colonial expansion, was arguably the most prodigious period of city building since Imperial Rome. Like most colonised cities, Shanghai (along with Hong Kong, Singapore, and Georgetown in Malaysia), was developed in a way that I will posit could be referred to as parthenogenetic. Parthenogenesis is a biological term usually referring to a certain mode of reproduction, invariably in populating a colony (of ants or bees) by means of a fertile queen. To compare and contrast differing urban strategies employed by Shanghai, Hong Kong and Singapore, in their heritage areas, waterfronts, former industrial zones, etc., could be very informative in allowing us to see how a Western urban footprint grows and changes in an Eastern environment.

Examples for Comparative Studies

Heritage and Gentrification 400 structures and 11 districts have been identified as 'fine historic buildings and zones' in Shanghai, including the detached villas with gardens in the former French Concession. The Xintiandi area is a high-profile development where architects preserved and reconstructed two city blocks of *shikumen* courtyard houses and opened a public spine through the middle to create a classic mixed-use development. Unlike similar developments in places like Singapore, such as Far East Square, Xintiandi introduces quality open-air urban spaces at a time when Asian cities in particular seem to be relying ever more on the enclosed shopping mall. Far East Square, like Xintiandi, is a matrix of once charming streets but it is one that has been most inelegantly roofed. Of course, the Xintiandi redevelopment raises its own questions, security guards exclude shabbily dressed locals, leading to a blurring of what is public space and what private. Graafland in *The Socius of Architecture* defines 'gentrification' as the process by which the uneducated make way for more qualified residents in certain neighbourhoods of a city. And while this gentrification preserves some of the area's courtyard houses, ironically its success has caused neighbouring land values to rise to the extent that surrounding *shikumen* communities have been demolished to make way for redevelopment.

Waterfronts Shanghai's waterfront, the Bund,[5] has not suffered the endless reclamations that have completely altered Hong Kong and Singapore's relationships with their waterfronts. Shanghai sits on the Huangpo River, a busy waterway that will never be narrowed, and this is why the Bund has been left intact, almost incredibly so, given that even the buildings on it remained unchanged throughout the second half of the twentieth century. It now makes for an interesting heritage district, and while Asian city planners are realising that heritage adds value – it seems that now even the past has a future – it's another area that could yield much if studied, especially when compared to the other cities mentioned above.

Traditional Housing Traditional housing in Shanghai from the mid-nineteenth century onwards consisted mainly of *lilongs*, or dense networks of connected two-storey buildings occupying a city block with shopfronts facing out onto the street. The residences above them were accessed through internal alleyways, the *lilongs*, which had gates onto the main streets. They were organised through a hierarchical system of semi-public, semi-private, and private laneways and courtyards throughout the block (not unlike Beijing's *hutongs*), where residents could talk, cook, eat and play, forming a strong social fabric which extended the family unit into a network of family, friends and neighbours. Chen maintains that the apparent lack of formalised public space in the history of Chinese architecture could perhaps be explained by this model, it might also help explain why the urban square, so popular in Europe, seems not to exist in Asian cities (Tiananmen Square in Beijing is an exception, but is hardly typical of the genre). Recently, the razing of these neighbourhoods for redevelopment, and the transplanting of entire communities to government-subsidised housing in the suburbs, is having a devastating effect on this way of

5 'Bund' was originally the Hindi word for a riverbank.

life. This is something that needs looking at immediately. Gated communities and suburban replica villages are also making an appearance in the suburbs of Pudong, Gubei and Hongqiao, another pattern that needs to be examined. In short, Shanghai's urban fabric is under siege, it needs to be mapped in order to understand what is going on, and perhaps to help preserve that which would be a pity to lose.

A Note on Globalisation 'Over the centuries,' Saskia Sassen writes, 'cities have been at the cross-roads of major, often worldwide processes. What is different today is the intensity, complexity and global span of these networks, the extent to which significant portions of economies are now dematerialised and digitalised and hence the extent to which they can travel at great speeds through some of these networks, and, thirdly, the numbers of cities that are part of cross-border networks operating at vast geographic scales.'
Cities like Shanghai, Hong Kong and Singapore constitute a system rather than simply competing with each other. Markets are integrated, maximising growth in all centres. 'A crisis in Tokyo or Hong Kong does not create advantages for other centres, there is little to gain for the larger financial system in Hong Kong's or Tokyo's decline.' So says David R. Meyer. In examining Hong Kong's role as a strategic node for capital exchange between China and the rest of the world, he highlights the extent to which it is social connectivity that has produced this strategic role. Whether Shanghai can reproduce this social connectivity is an interesting question.
Intermediaries, Meyer posits, build transactions on trust in order to minimise risks of exchange across international boundaries, and this they do through friendship, family, ethnic or religious ties. In Hong Kong, social networks comprise the fundamental governing structure of exchange. Intermediaries require face-to-face exchange to acquire information from one another, to develop strategies and to acquire trustworthy partners. Control rests in the social networks of capital that meet in Hong Kong, and these networks are rooted in long-standing relationships and bonds of trust linking firms locally, throughout Asia, and across the globe. Hong Kong's government, according to Meyer, has been the facilitator of these developments rather than a formal director of them. Can Shanghai achieve something similar?

Part Four: History

Chinese Shanghai Central to any study of Shanghai is an understanding of its history. For the purpose of this paper, this has been divided into three main eras: 1) colonial growth 1842-1937, which will be the main era explored here; 2) Japan and the Communists, when, in urbanistic terms, nothing happened; and finally, 3) rebirth, since 1990, the effects of which were looked at earlier in the *Shanghai Now* part of the paper. But before we can look at the colonial

history of Shanghai it might be useful to look at the history of China in general.
Shanghai was founded on the China trade, namely the export of tea, porcelain, cotton and silk, this entrepot function gained it the nickname 'Gateway to the Celestial Empire', but the imbalance in trade with the European powers, particularly Britain which took to tea more than most, was in danger of bankrupting them (the China trade is now also thought to have been a major contributor to the fall of Rome), so Britain cast about for something to import, notoriously deciding on Bengali opium.

Shanghai might better have been described as the 'Interface of Empire', with the British, French, Russian and German empires, not to mention the burgeoning American one, all scrambling for a piece of the action.[6] They saw China as the next Africa, which had been ruthlessly carved up a generation earlier. But China was not Africa, China was a single nation, and a great one, with an ancient culture of major historical importance. Empires are all about the control of routes, particularly for trade, the Romans and later the Chinese did this by land, the British and other Western powers by sea, and Shanghai was perfectly positioned to capitalise on such a maritime trade.

Chinese civilisation is ancient, arguably the longest continuous civilisation in the world. But compared with ancient Egypt and Mesopotamia, China was rather primitive until relatively late. Evidence suggests that metallurgy began in China 1,000 years later than in Mesopotamia, and the earliest (organised) Chinese state is unlikely to have come into existence before about 2000 BCE, by which time many Mesopotamian city-states were ancient and several Egyptian dynasties had already fallen. The development of Chinese civilisation actually shows a remarkable parallel with that of Europe, with the first period of strength and unity in China under the Qin and Han dynasties, roughly at the same time as the domination of Europe by Rome.

Colonial Shanghai 'If God lets Shanghai endure,' one nineteenth-century Western missionary is quoted as saying, 'he owes an apology to Sodom and Gomorrah'.[7] Shanghai came into being as a Western entity on 29 August 1842 with the Treaty of Nanking, which ended the First Opium War. Ironically, since it was opium that had caused the war in the first place, and it was opium that could be said to have built colonial Shanghai, even causing it to be called the 'Whore of Asia', in the 1842 treaty opium is never even mentioned. The Chinese called it 'foreign mud', and even though it had long been enjoyed by their moneyed classes, it was the British who spread it to every level of society, with devastating social consequences.

By the middle of the nineteenth century, despite more than 300 years of direct contact with Westerners, the Chinese had almost entirely failed to learn anything about them, and Western powers were able to wrest such advantageous concessions from the Chinese because they had grown considerably richer and stronger in the meantime. When the first British merchants

6 The Dutch, former colonial masters of Taiwan, had consolidated their position in the Dutch East Indies (Indonesia) and by the nineteenth century do not seem to have been interested in China any more.

7 **Shanghai: Gateway to the Celestial Empire**, Stella Dong.

arrived in Shanghai in 1843, they were given 140 acres along the river, north of the Chinese city, as the British Settlement. The Americans had an unofficial settlement in Hongkew, north of Soochow Creek. Shanghai citizens were considered friendlier and more peaceful than the Cantonese, where the Western powers had their initial footholds in China, and the city immediately supplanted Canton (Guangzhou) as China's leading port.[8]
A cornerstone of Western power in the treaty ports was the notion of extra-territoriality, or 'extrality' for short. Foreigners were immune to Chinese law, being subject to their own ones at home, at least in theory. Despite such inducements, the foreign population did not exceed 100 until 1848. Chinese Shanghai had existed as a city as early as the tenth century, and, as we saw earlier, by the sixteenth it had become one of China's major ports. The two Shanghais, Western and Chinese, had little to do with each other, indeed the residents of each enclave even went by different names, the Chinese were Shanghainese, whereas the Westerners were known as Shanghailanders.
The 1858 Treaty of Tientsin, which ended the Second Opium War (also known as the Arrow War) was ratified in 1860, and finally opened the Yangtze to Westerners.[9] In 1863, the Shanghai Municipal Council was founded to administer the affairs of the British and American Settlements, which had merged and become known as the International Settlement. The French Concession also declared itself a municipality at the same time, but this was under the French colonial government in Hanoi. The port was by now the sixth-largest in the world. The 1858 treaty also stipulated that the Chinese government must allow a tariff on opium imports, (effectively legalising the drug trade), which meant that opium could now be stored in Shanghai itself, which it was, on two converted sailing hulks moored off the Bund for everyone to see. Opium shops and smoking parlours sprang up all over town. But opium wasn't the only source of wealth, the American civil war (1861-65) had cut off Europe's supply of cotton, so there was a boom in the Chinese cotton trade, and in the first year of the Yangtze's being opened to Western trade Shanghai's customs revenue tripled. Property speculation also made many people rich (as it still does today in the city), the cost of an acre went from about 50 pounds in 1850 to 20,000 by 1862. With rapid growth fuelling all this speculation, not to mention the different enclaves governing themselves without an overall plan for the city, development was haphazard to say the least. The decision in 1907 to phase out opium over ten years didn't have any adverse effect on Shanghai's continued growth, which remained prodigious. The city's population doubled to a million between 1895 and 1910, and then nearly tripled again by 1930.[10] By the 1930s, the port had become the world's fifth-largest, handling 51% of China's imports and 30% of her exports. The Great Depression was barely felt, land prices tripled in five years, making rents along the Bund, by now the most famous skyline east of the Suez, more expensive than the Champs Elysées or Fifth Avenue.

By this time the Japanese had become the largest group of foreigners in the city and they had begun to demand control of the International Settlement's Municipal Council (on which they had seats since their defeat of China in the war of 1894-95 which had also made them a treaty power). On 18 September 1931, a small bomb exploded on the Japanese-owned South Manchurian Railway in Mukden (the capital of Manchuria).[11] This is now thought to have been planted by the Japanese themselves as a pretext for occupying the province, which they did by December. They renamed it Manchukuo and placed China's last emperor, Puyi, on its throne as a puppet ruler.

Then on 18 January 1932, a group of Japanese monks was attacked in Chapei, two were killed in the incident. Three days later the Japanese issued an ultimatum for the arrest of the perpetrators and an end to the anti-Japanese boycott that was going on at the time (a protest at the annexation of Manchuria). Despite Shanghai's mayor accepting the demands, the Japanese invaded Chapei anyway. The five week battle was the world's first experience of urban warfare. Chapei, the city's industrial heartland, was almost completely levelled, but it wasn't the success the Japanese had hoped for, mainly thanks to the proximity of the largest press core in Asia, who were busy transmitting the horrific images around the world. On 5 May Japan was obliged to remove all but garrison troops from Shanghai.

Shanghai in the 1920s and 1930s was notoriously lawless, one of the reasons for this was the 1918 prohibition on opium, which allowed this entrenched trade to fall into the hands of gangsters (something similar happened with alcohol in America at the same time); but the main reason for this lawlessness was the existence of three separate jurisdictions in the city: the International Settlement, the French Concession, and the Chinese territory, each possessing its own government and police. Lack of a central law enforcement authority meant that a thief could escape capture simply by crossing the street from one enclave to another, the police in the district where he had committed the crime couldn't follow him.[12] In addition to this, of course, most Westerners enjoyed the added protection of extra-territoriality.

The Lonely Island On 7 July 1937 the Japanese staged another 'incident'; they were missing a soldier, and they used this as an excuse to bring troops into China. The 'undeclared war' had begun. (The soldier in question is said to have been found two days later in a Beijing brothel). On 12 August the Japanese advance fleet arrived in Shanghai and the following day sporadic firing started. On 14 August, a stream of refugees ten miles long was making its way across Garden Bridge, the only official entry point into the International Settlement, when Chinese bombers, trying to bomb the Japanese warship *Idzumo*, panicked when its guns were trained on them and accidentally dropped their payload onto the Bund, right in front of the Cathay Hotel and through the roof of the Peace Hotel next door. Unfortunately, because of the huge number

8 ibid.
9 ibid.
10 ibid.
11 This incident is featured in the Tintin book **The Blue Lotus**, which, when eventually allowed for sale in China in 2001, sold out in a matter of days.
12 This colourful facet of Shanghai life is also featured in **The Blue Lotus**.

of refugees passing by at the time, casualties were appalling: 729 killed and 861 wounded. More bombs were dropped shortly afterwards at the intersection of Avenue Edouard VII (Yunnan Road) and Tibet Road, where the Great World amusement centre was distributing free rice and tea, another 1,011 were killed and 570 injured. This was the worst civilian carnage anywhere in the world up to that point.[13]

Two months of fighting followed, again mostly in Chapei. By the time the Rape of Nanking occurred, on 12 December that year, where 300,000 civilians were raped and murdered, Shanghai's port and trade had been destroyed, along with most of its industry. By the time the Japanese celebrated their Victory Parade along Nanking Road on 3 December, the foreign concessions were being referred to as the Lonely Island.

Then on 8 December 1941 (which was 7 December in the USA), the Japanese bombed Pearl Harbour, and the Second World War proper had started in Asia. Shanghai's foreign concessions were immediately taken over by the Japanese and the city found itself under one administration for the first time in a century. All clocks were set to Tokyo time,[14] (as they later were in Hong Kong and Singapore as they fell later that December and the following February respectively). Of the 8,000 citizens of Allied countries who were still living in Shanghai at the time, all had to wear armbands with 'A' for American, 'B' for British, etc. Ethnic Asian citizens, such as Filipinos, didn't have to as they were considered part of Japan's Asian Co-Prosperity Sphere. In July 1944 the first American aircraft was seen over Shanghai, and in November air raids had begun. Japan surrendered on 16 August the following year.

A brief post-war boom lasted until about the middle of 1946, but Britain's prestige as a colonial power in Asia was gone. An American cruiser was moored at their No.1 Buoy on the Bund, the No.2 Buoy, which had traditionally been the American one, was assigned to the Chinese, but as they had no ships they let another American ship take its place as well. Almost immediately, the smart money began to move out, a lot of it went to Hong Kong. Then on 24 May 1949, with the Nationalists fleeing to Taiwan, Shanghai fell to the Communists.

Despite the fact that the Communists had founded their party in Shanghai's French Concession in 1921, the city did not fare well under them. They regarded it as a sink of capitalist iniquity. Hong Kong, which remained a British colony until 1997, suddenly found itself China's main conduit to the outside world.

Part Five: Conclusions

The Tiananmen Incident Hu Yaobang died in April 1989, he had been the Communist Party General Secretary before being dismissed in 1987. Students started marching to commemorate his death and by May these marches had turned into riots. It's estimated that 400 civilians lost their lives, as well as 600 soldiers.[15] The Communist Party is not likely to let loose the reigns of power any time soon, but then China's history does not seem to have necessarily prepared the country for a Western-style democracy. Maybe this is no bad thing. A thorough investigation of China and her people might throw some light on their situation and the sort of governance that seems to be working now.

Hong Kong, Macau and Taiwan The former British colony of Hong Kong, wrested from the Chinese in 1842, was returned to them in 1997. Macau followed two years later. Both are now Special Administrative Regions of China, and will remain so for half a century. Taiwan is still regarded as a renegade province, neither the Nationalists nor the Communists ever regarded its separation from China as permanent or desirable. This matter is bound to be resolved one way or the other in the not too distant future, what this will mean for Shanghai remains to be seen.

The Future Information is not the same as knowledge, to extract one from the other, you have to, as the word suggests, 'inform'. This study will require, and will indeed no doubt produce, a lot of information, largely empirical data that will need to be analysed, hopefully leading to some useful conclusions. The past needs to be examined: a temporal analysis; the present needs to be mapped: a spatial exercise; and from both we will hopefully be able to trace Shanghai's trajectory into the future in a tempero-spatial drawing together of all these disparate elements.
Koolhaas in *Delirious New York* calls Manhattan the twentieth century's Rosetta Stone; could Shanghai be a key to understanding the twenty-first? Koolhaas has also admitted that since he and his colleagues have started looking at the Chinese city their designs have changed. I, likewise, intend to keep an open mind throughout these investigations. What I will be trying to get at here is the underlying truth of Shanghai's situation, truth in Heidegger's sense of 'aletheia' or unconcealment. And maybe then we'll be able to come to a better understanding of what it means for human beings to inhabit an urban environment.
Environments, Ingold states, are constantly coming into being in the process of our lives. We shape them as they shape us. They are, therefore, fundamentally historical, as well as being culturally constituted. Bearing in mind that an environment is never complete, that they are forged, as he suggests, 'through the activities of living beings', then so long as life goes on, they are continually under construction. It is this process of construction and reconstruction that will be central to this study.
Finally, this can, and should be, primarily an investigation into the urban environment with regard to what it means for human becoming rather than merely for human being.

13 **Shanghai: Gateway to the Celestial Empire**, Stella Dong.
14 Old Shanghai: Gangsters in Paradise, Lynn Pan.
15 **China: A Traveller's History**, Stephen G. Haw.

Bibliography

Chen, Darryl, 'View from Shanghai', **Architectural Review**. February, 2003.

Dong, Stella, **Shanghai: The Rise and Fall of a Decadent City**. New York: HarperCollins, 2000.

Dong, Stella, **Shanghai: Gateway to the Celestial Empire**. Hong Kong: FormAsia, 2003.

Fishman, Ted C., **China Inc.** New York: Scribner, 2005.

Graafland, Arie, **The Socius of Architecture: Amsterdam, Tokyo, New York**. Rotterdam: 010 Publishers, 2000.

Haw, Stephen G., **China: A Traveller's History**. London: Cassell, 2002.

Ingold, Tim, **The Perception of the Environment: Essays in Livelihood, Dwelling and Skill**. London: Routledge, 2005.

Koolhaas, Rem, **Delirious New York**. New York: The Monacelli Press, 1994.

Mayhew, Bradley, **Shanghai**. Lonely Planet, 2004.

Meyer, David R., 'Hong Kong: Global Capital Exchange' in **Global Networks, Linked Cities**, ed. Saskia Sassen, (Chapter 9).

Pan, Lynn, **Old Shanghai: Gangsters in Paradise**. Singapore: Cultured Lotus, 2000.

Pan, Lynn, et al., **Odyssey Illustrated Guide to Shanghai**. Hong Kong: Odyssey, 1992.

Sassen, Saskia, **The Global City: New York, London, Tokyo.** Princeton University Press, 2001.

Sassen, Saskia (ed.), **Global Networks, Linked Cities**. New York: Routledge, 2002.

Turnbull, Richard, 'View from Shanghai', **Architectural Review**. December, 2004.

CHINA (c.1900)

Beijing

Treaty Ports
hanghai
lingbo
uzhou
moy
Guangzhou

Colonies
Port Arthur (Russia)
Wei Hai Wei (Britain)
Jianzhou Bay (Germany)
Taiwan (Japan)
Hong Kong (Britain)
Macau (Portugal)
Qinzhou Bay (France)

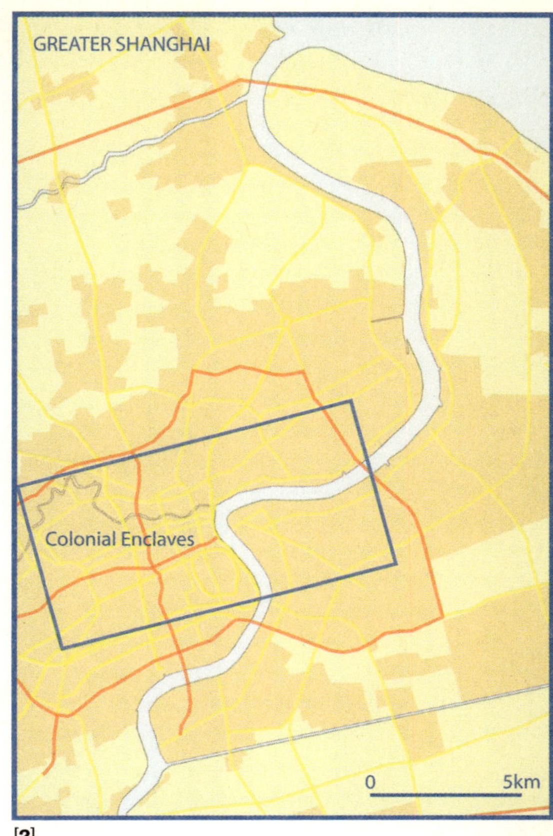

[2]

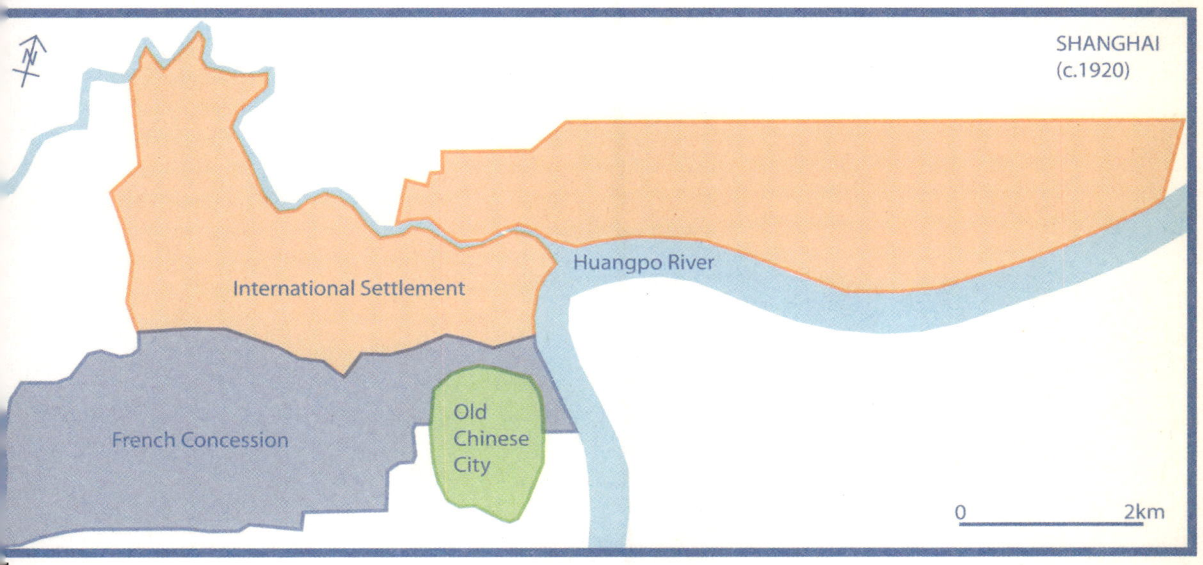

China (c.1900): Colonies and Treaty
rts. Source: G. Bracken.
Greater Shanghai. Source: G. Bracken.
Shanghai (c.1920): Colonial Enclaves.
urce: G. Bracken.

[4]

[7]

[5]

[6]

[8]

[12]

0]

[11]

4 Pudong. Source: G. Bracken.
5 The Bund. Source: G. Bracken.
6 Xintiandi. Source: G. Bracken.
7 Yu Yuan Park. Source: G. Bracken.
8 Shikumen (off Wenmiao Rd). Source: G. Bracken.
9 Fuxing Park. Source: G. Bracken.
10 Lilong (off Guangdong Rd). Source: G. Bracken.
11 Colonial mansion, Ruijin Hotel (former Morriss House). Source: G. Bracken.
12 Colonial commercial building, the Bund (former HSBC). Source: G. Bracken.

The Meaning of Habitat in a Changing Architectural Context

Javier Peinado Pontón

Human being consists in dwelling and, indeed,
dwelling in the sense of the stay of mortals on the earth [1]

Introduction This paper reacts to an interest in more explicitly incorporating the concept of *habitat* into the mainstream discourse of contemporary urbanism and architecture, in order to enhance the viewpoint of the individual and not only care for the abstract guidelines of planning and regulations, when studying or to intervene in the environment where humans actually or prospectively live.

HABITAT is an intellectual construct in process. Etymologically stemming from latin *habitare* (to dwell) and so related to *habitus* (habit) and *habere* (to have), its use in English and in French has been documented since the late 18th century to allude to a place of habitation by the basic act of inhabiting, i.e., living in a determined place or *de facto* possessing it. It has similar uses in modern Spanish.

At least three avenues or lines of thought come together in the concept of *habitat*. One runs from biology and the environmental sciences; the other, along its institutional use in planning and research, and the third one is related to the academic environment, be it by its etymological genealogy or by the allusion to urbanized spaces of habitation. These avenues acquired institutional forms during the 1970s, when the United Nations Organization incorporated the term in order to frame its projects of technical cooperation in sub-standard human settlements and the development of traditional domestic economies of third world countries.

In the field of architecture, the concept of HABITAT can be associated with naturalistic, organicist trends like those supported by Frank Lloyd Wright, Lewis Mumford or Ian McHarg. Today, this naturalistic vision of the built environment is showing new overtones due to demographic pressures, to ICT changes and, as a whole, to globalization in the wide sense of the word.

In the discussion among, on one side the so-called 'unified institutional ideology' that supports current world economics, and on the other side the post-structuralist criticism of philosophers like G. Deleuze and J. Stiglitz, *habitat* seems to be a concept useful to signify a specific territory which keeps on being able to sustain the civilized life of human beings, in spite of current disrupting pressures. Therefore, a reclarification of *habitat* is established, and positioned against implicit meanings in the context of current mega-trends that are deeply changing what we have understood as 'cities' through history.

Meanings In Latin, *Habitat* is the third person singular of the verb *habitare*, which means to inhabit, to dwell, and is therefore related to *habitus* (habit), and *habere* (to have).

1 Heidegger (1951).

Its use in the French and English languages has been documented with two senses: one, in use since the end of the 18th century to designate a geographical environment which is adequate for the life of vegetable or animal species, and the second one, spread during the 20th century, is 'a way of organizing and settling made by man in the environment where he lives'.[2]
This second meaning allows relating the term to territorial ordering, urbanism and architectural design, including in addition, urban equipment and other elements of the human environment. It has similar uses in Spanish, meaning first the place of habitation of any living species.[3] By extension, habitat becomes the ecosystem where a human individual, group or community lives, including the way it is characterized by the combination of natural and cultural elements. According to *Webster's Dictionary*, in modern English habitat means: 1a: the place or environment where a plant or animal naturally or normally lives and grows; b: the typical place of residence of a person or a group. 2: The place where something is commonly found. 3: a structure that affords a controlled environment for living in extremely inhospitable locations, such as an underwater research laboratory.
The amplitude of these definitions shows that it is a complex expression, related to the spatial study of human societies as well as of animal and vegetable species. During the 20th century, the term has shifted from biology and the natural sciences to fields of knowledge concerned with people and space as studied from different approaches: biology, geography, anthropology, economics, politics, and architecture and urbanism. The following diagram depicts habitat as a support of human life: a complex field of knowledge where society, nature[4] and individual's subjectivity overlap, as well as distinct approaches to knowledge building.
[See figure 1]

The term 'habitat' can be used more broadly in ecology. It was originally defined as the physical conditions that surround a species, or species population, or assemblage of species, or community.[5] Habitat implies sharing in a dynamic way; it is not just a species population that has a habitat, but an assemblage of many species living together in the same place, who essentially share an environment which allows them to live a sustainable existence. Ecologists regard the habitat shared by many species to be a biotope, and call biome the set of flora and fauna living in a habitat and so occupying a certain geography, but they make no clear distinction for the human species. There is an ongoing discussion amongst specialists in the built environment aiming to reach sustainable development, and the environmentalists who conceive the 'natural' world as a harmonious whole that human development is threatening to disrupt.

One of the earliest textbooks about habitat is *Habitat, Economy and Society; A Geographical Introduction to Ethnology*;[6] based on the comparison between differ-

ent ethnic groups. In this book Forde attacks the idea that the environment determines the cultural and economic line of development of a society. In spite of the close correlation between human activities and environmental conditions and resources, many important social practices are not related to physical environment but are based in specifically human factors, like culture and economy, which are considered in the term 'habitat'.
There is a clear parallelism between 'habitat' and the concepts of 'eco-system' and 'environment', the basic difference being that these two give priority to the surroundings' intrinsic qualities, while habitat refers more to their capability to support a life with quality, which entails a special emphasis on the requirements of the inhabitant. Another difference is that ecology takes the thermodynamic approach to knowledge building, and environmentalism gives priority to the non-anthropic balance of the environment, while habitat is a relational concept that articulates social, environmental and subjective factors in a complex.

When talking about the human species, habitat refers to the territory where the human being is located, physically and imaginarily. It means the specific location which the human being inhabits, not only in terms of the instrumental, physical and functional actions of housing, but also in terms of what that place represents for the individual and collective recognition and identity, which is socially acknowledged or instituted.[7] The basic act of inhabiting a territory is *de facto* possessing it.

Use In technical documents after the 1950s, the word habitat is associated with reports about demographic and living conditions, like density and indicators of health, education and quality of life.[8] The versatility of the term, derived from its uses in French, was probably a main reason to consolidate its use in the United Nations Organization, where it is associated with the concept of human settlement, and urban habitat is understood as the concentration of people in cities. The United Nations Human Settlements Programme, UN-HABITAT, is the United Nations agency for human settlements. Its declared mission is to meet the mandate of the UN General Assembly to promote socially and environmentally sustainable towns and cities with the goal of providing adequate shelter for all. This is considered a necessary condition for human development, being human development equalled to freedom, as stated in the 'Habitat Agenda' and the Istanbul and Istanbul+5 Declarations.
The link between human development and the supportive environment has been debated from the economics viewpoint by Nobel Prize winner Amartya Sen, who reaffirms that 'human development, as an approach, is concerned with what I take to be the basic development idea: namely, advancing the richness of human life, rather than the richness of the economy in which human beings live, which is only a part of it'.[9]

2 **Robert Dictionnaire** (1970), **Encyclopaedia Britannica** (1991).
3 Real Academia Española (1970).
4 'Nature' is here understood as the material setting of the world: the complete embodiment of the 'built' and 'natural' landscapes.
5 Clements and Shelford (1939).
6 Forde (1949).
7 Giraldo (2004).
8 Rivera (2003).

And what is the use of freedom? Once existing, he/she who exists tries by all means to keep existing. This seems to be a most basic impulse for all and everyone who is in this world. From there comes the struggle in every person for structuring himself/herself, as well as to make the environment adequate to his/her needs in sustainable ways. In the Darmstadt Symposium on *Man and Space* held in 1951, Martin Heidegger presented his lecture 'Building Dwelling Thinking' (*Bauen Wohnen Denken*) which has become some kind of a classic in the literature related to architecture. According to David Farrell-Krell, editor of *Heidegger, 1951/2000*, the focal issue in this paper is the relation of 'building' to 'dwelling' and the kind of 'thinking' that results from paying attention to that relation: '...human being consists in dwelling and, indeed, dwelling in the sense of the stay of mortals on the earth'.[10] Habitat is the place where one can dwell, where one can stay in place; therefore, habitat is the place where one can be human.

In a lecture given on 02. 06. 2005 at the Berlage Institute of Rotterdam, Peter Sloterdijk said that dwelling is to develop habits. He also noted that Paul Valéry proposes in 'Eupalinos, or The architect', the first real theory of immersion, and that by our daily immersion in the adventurous regression of dreaming, the habit of freeing ourselves is reassured, the habit constructs habitat. In '*En el mismo barco,*'[11] Sloterdijk states that 'A litigant paradox is hidden in the concept of humankind, which can be stated as: it corresponds to us, being next to those to which we do not belong..." meaning that by freely developing, every human being has an inborn drive towards differentiating himself/herself from any fellow man.[12] This tendency to differentiation leads every individual in post-industrial society to become a least probable (as well as most divergent and exacting) being in the world.
Contemporary habitat should be able to support such a huge demand for potential differentiation by being a creative integration of aesthetics and science, not anymore fixated in the pre-industrial images of city and landscape, nor lacking artistic sensibility. When the value at issue is the unconditional freedom to differentiate, humankind can only be led by imagination. Radical imagination is a necessary condition for autonomous creativity.[13]
Commonly employed words to designate urban spaces are not capable of expressing this supportivity; terms like 'environment' and 'ecology' deal with the 'objective' aspect of the issue, but are insufficient to take into account the complexity of the human habitat.[14] This refers to much deeper discussions on symbolic and cultural issues, since human spaces are spaces of meaning and sense which obviously relay on physical places, but are not only concerned with them.
Egenter (1996) is proposing an anthropological approach to deal with the complexity of habitat, based on Bollnow's concept of space:[15]

In short, habitat research provides us with an inductively gained complex nucleus of data which can be organized into a sequential typology based on changing parameters. It applies to very different cultures – today and in history – and provides new explanations... Beneath the tremendous formal differences among various cultures, there is a surprising continuity in the ways man structures his habitat... In contrast to this, the structural differentiations of various types of human habitats are remarkably few. What is most striking with this habitat theory of culture is the fact that it provides reasonable explanations for what is described as endlessly differentiated manifold by the conventional humanities.[16]

In the realm of architecture, professionals in the naturalistic stream of organicism use the term 'habitat' when wanting to integrate culture and nature, housing and environment, architecture and climate, and so on. Since the 1960s, the discussion of social implications in low income housing, and of the problems of urbanization in developing countries, are considered as well as part of the urban habitat discourse.
In growing cities of developing countries, the essential task of planners is directed to spatially distribute increasing growth. According to participative politics, this should be done by changing the planning activity, from being restrictive and controlling into being proactive and creative. It requires tools at the regional scale, like political and financial basis for planning. In that context, housing is assumed to be the human habitat *par excellence*, with the potential to articulate the private and the public, the intimate and the social.
Identifying the systems that interact in housing as a complex whole, is the starting point in order to be able to affect the processes that are conditioning the construction of urban habitat, and to direct them towards the realization of a viable project of liberating society.

Urban habitat as a body Anthropological studies show that since prehistoric times, humankind has applied patterns and proportions of the human body, translating them into guidelines for designing urban environments (Rapoport, A., Eliade, M., and others). The symbolism in anthropomorphic correspondences was believed to guarantee order, equilibrium and harmony. In classical culture, the human body represented the image of God, and this symbolism carried the will to transcend matter and connect the place to a cosmic universal order whose existence was faithfully believed. Out of this belief, the identification of the human being not with a real but with an ideal body derived towards a model of the body whose geometric

9 Sen (1999).
10 Heidegger (1951) p. 351.
11 **'In the same boat'**; original title: **'Im selben Boot. Versuch über die Hyperpolitic'**, Suhrkamp Verlag, Frankfurt am Main 1993. Translation in this paper of paragraphs by Sloterdijk made by the author, out of the edition in Spanish (Sloterdijk, 1994).
12 Sloterdijk (1994).
13 Castoriadis, (1983) and (1989). Taken from a discussion on the imaginary institutions of society carried out in Giraldo, Fabio and Malaver, José (1996).
14 Giraldo (2004).
15 Otto Friedrich Bollnow, **Hombre y espacio.** First published (1963) in German with the title **'Mensch und Raum'** (Kohlhammer, Stuttgart). A review is available in three languages, in: Egenter, Nold: 'Architectural Anthropology' Research Series Vol. 2, **Foundations for Anthropological Research into Architecture.**
16 Egenter (1996).

translation was pure forms, like in the platonic worldview. 'The sequence "city/body/geometry" transformed itself into a "universal city/ideal body/precise geometry", setting up a convention that modernity would assume without any major questioning'.[17]

Contemporary knowledge rejects the existence of universal concepts or entities. Therefore, allusions to God or any mystical reality have been eradicated from its discourse. What is more, the fullness, unity and coherence of the ideal body have been denounced to be means to impose power dictums on citizens. It does not mean that the body is not anymore a source of inspiration in urban contemporary culture: after many years of rejecting pain and ugliness as alien, and of morally reinforcing the values of health, sport and beauty, a new way of relating city and body to each other appears in Western culture: it is the interest in the city as a sick body. The sick city offers a shocking complexity with values of its own. Among these values, it is important to stress the renewal of ethical considerations that the prevalence of an economic rationale tends to render invisible.

Most contemporary studies on urban geography share the intuition that economic inequality is something inherent in urban life. According to the Report of the 'Rio Summit',[18] urban poverty will be the most significant, and politically the most explosive problem of the 21st century, since it brings together generalized criminality, ethnic tensions, popular uprisings and street riots. Urban poverty has causes that are rooted in the very structural rationale of late-capitalism (Stiglitz, Sassen, Carmona and Rosemann, and others in the Alfa-Ibis program).

In intellectual circles, the idea that 'social inequality is normal' is becoming usually accepted, which implies that conflict is ingrained in the contemporary city, that is, that its illnesses are chronic,[19] and being there to contend with those maladies implies getting involved with the excluded and homeless of the dual city. The sick city becomes then the city of the resisting, the engaged. An environment which is neither supportive nor nurturing, and therefore is not what can be called a human habitat.

Another form of illness in the urban body is the lack of definition and perception of its limits. Fuzzy borders make increasingly difficult to distinguish between centre and suburbs, or between suburbs and countryside. This diffusion of the once compact city into a city web, a boundless extension of conurbations made up of a number of development clusters is presented with an optimistic outlook by Sieverts.[20] But the fact can't be overlooked that it implies the ill exacerbation of individualism and social and spatial segregation, together with increased traffic congestion.

Processes where global, unplanned but highly organized patterns emerge out of the seemingly unrelated actions of large numbers of apparently free individuals are coming to the foreground in virtually every area of knowledge and reflection.

The concept of self-regulation acquires new dimensions when the awareness of probable self creation in complex systems, like the urban body, emerges as autopoiesis.[21]

Fascinating analogies between collective actions of people, and those of collective associations of unexpected kinds are being discovered, which promise to contribute new insights toward the understanding of our urban habitat. Some authors and practitioners are considering the concept of 'body without organs' proposed by post-structuralists G. Deleuze and F. Guattari, as a promissory metaphor to explore how some cities manage to successfully perform their functions, and to look for ways to foster such dynamics.

What is new in this approach is that the control might be made, not by means of the pre-designed coordination of clearly separated and specialized components as the 'Chart of Athens' proposed, but thanks to cyclic processes of self-regulation based on light and temporary associations controlled by flexible and *ad-hoc* forms of order. These processes of constant activity and evolution are quite congruent with the mixture of forms and functions characterizing the fluid, undifferentiated compound that is late-capitalism.

By the end of the 1960s, diverse events led to the breakdown of what generally and without question had been accepted before: the 'theories' and programs of Modernism in architecture and urbanism. Landmarks in this process of paradigm change were: the pronunciation of Jane Jacobs on the deterioration of American cities[22]; the failure of historicist postwar-reconstruction of German cities based on principles of modernism, documented by Alexander Mitscherlich[23]; Charles Jencks' chronicle of the demolition of Pruitt-Igoe, a prizewinning, barely 20-year-old ten-storied residential development in St. Louis, USA.

What followed then was the general acceptance of the end of modernism and the beginning of post-modernism in architecture and urbanism. Since then, a huge and all-including wave of change is causing great perplexity among people in charge of planning, managing and thinking the cities of the 21st century. This is a dynamic situation which is being accelerated by the deregulation of the global economy and the amazing development of networks and telematic technologies (ICT).

In an attempt to provide a map of this changing territory, an analysis of world cities is made in '*Ciudad hojaldre*'[24] by García Vásquez (2004) in order to define different current 'visions' of the urban structure, in the same line of the seminal book *L'Urbanisme. Utopies et realités*,[25] as his author declares. Four visions or conceptual frameworks are described in this panoramic book by

17 All quotations of García Vásquez in this paper, translated by the author from Spanish in García Vásquez (2004) p. 132.

18 Rio Summit is the informal name for the 'United Nations Conference on Environment and Development', held in Rio de Janeiro, Brazil, in 1992.

19 Sennet (1970).

20 Siervits (2003).

21 Johnson (2001).

22 As in Jane Jacobs, **The Death and Life of Great American Cities.**

23 **The inhospitality of the modern city**, available at: http://www.hhm.k12.nf.ca/teachers/rbanfield/Modern/Modern.htm

24 Translated as 'Puff pastry city'.

García Vásquez, namely: the culturalist, the sociological, the organicist and the technological visions. They together show how far the spaces in contemporary cities are from the inclusive and supportive environments which were provided (at least for the upper classes) by the classic, renascent, or romantic cities of past times.

Be it in Berlin, the culturalist emblematic 'European city' which became the failure of the planned historicist city; or in socially fragmented Los Angeles, in organicist ill-bodied and dual Mexico City, or in technologically dystopic Houston, many people are confronted by the lack of habitability in the places and spaces where they have to live. Christine Boyer[26] is convinced that a political intention exists behind the process of fragmentation which the real city is going through. According to her, the strategy of not re-constructing the unitary whole seen as the Modern city, but only its areas with high economic potential (which usually depends on symbolic values), leads to a society which lacks structure and critical conscience.

In this way, the post-modern statement which says that the absence of a centre and of hierarchy supposes freedom and alterity or otherness, would be a 'virtual' justification that forsakes political questioning, to refrain from participation in critical and social controversies. Then, the citizen is bound to retire into living within a non-compromised superficiality.

This dystopic and non-transcendent urban heterogeneity, under which injustice prevails, is a rather possible scenario. But it is not unavoidable, provided that an actual hyper-politics[27] be devised to lead the leading minds of humankind towards fostering and keep going 'the oldest of all arts, the repetition of men by the work of men'.[28]

Conclusion Habitat is no new word, but its horizon of meaning is widening as the world conditions of the environment, technology, politics, and economy evolve towards increasing complexity. Accelerating advancements in ICT, in economic relations, and in interaction among ethnicities and cultures, which are characteristic of current globalization, negatively affect the habitability or living conditions in cities. Resulting contradictions lead to inadequacy of usual terms and concepts to signify the human habitable environment. A need to transcend the reductionism of the sectoral approach to planning and project making, forces the search for dwelling environments able to provide not only the material conditions needed to support biological existence. The essence of being

25 Choay (1983).
26 As taken from the Christine Boyer – Delft School of Design Seminar Series at Delft University of Technology, Faculty of Architecture (2005).
27 Sloterdijk (1994).
28 **ibid.**, p. 103.
29 Author's free transcription from Sloterdijk, 2003: **Experimentos con uno mismo, conversación con Carlos Oliveira**, Pretextos, Valencia, España.

human is our ability to lead a social and cultural life, and the support to this development must be emphasized in the production and management of space apt for human habitation.
It is here proposed to retake and extend the use of the term 'habitat', using it in order to designate an environment which is actually habitable because it is sustainable as well as including and supportive of the civilized life of its inhabitants. Consider this sense of habitat as a tool of governance to confront the task of building a society which accepts the load of mediating between its ancestors and its descendants in order to attend the need to 'cultivate and build up a new habitability, which is non predator with respect to the surroundings and the alterity[29].
Habitat is then a relation of conditions articulating individuals, society and nature without remaining only in their physical qualities, but seeking as well to encourage the encounter of people in places. Habitat is a way of use and appropriation of the physical place.

Bibliography

Bollnow, O. F. **Hombre y espacio.** Labor: Barcelona, 1969. Originally published in Germany [1963] as: **Mensch und Raum.**

Castoriadis, C. Vol. I, 1989 Vol. II. **La institución imaginaria de la sociedad**, and, Tusquets Editores: Buenos Aires, 1983.

Choay, F. **L'Urbanisme. Utopies et realités**, Éditions du Seuil: Paris, 1983.

Egenter, N. **Otto Friedrich Bollnow's anthropological concept of space. A new paradigm is under way**, 1996. [Online] available from: http://home.worldcom.ch/~negenter/012BollnowE1.html, [Accessed 25 March 2005].

Forde, C. D. **Habitat, Economy and Society; A Geographical Introduction to Ethnology.** 8th ed. – London: Methuen, 1949.

Garcia Vasquez C. **Ciudad hojaldre. Visiones urbanas del siglo XXI.** Edit. Gustavo Gili: Barcelona, 2004.

Giraldo, F. **Hábitat y desarrollo humano**, unpublished draft, UN-HABITAT/CENAC: Bogota, 2004.

Giraldo, F. 'Hábitat y sostenibilidad', in: **Colombia ciencia y tecnología**, Vol. 21 N° 2, pp. 40-50. Colciencias: Bogota, 2003.

Giraldo, F. and Malaver, J. 'El laberinto del pensamiento y la creación', in: **Ontología de la creación.** Ensayo y Error: Bogota, 1996.

Heidegger, M. 'Building Dwelling Thinking', in: **Martin Heidegger, Basic Writings, Revised and Expanded Edition**. Farrel Krell, David Edit. Routledge: London, 2000.

Johnson, S. **Emergence. The connected lives of ants, brains, cities, and software.** Penguin Books: London, 2001.

Rivera, J. A. **Hábitat. Estado del arte.** Universidad Catolica de Colombia: Bogotá, 2003.

Salingaros, N. **Principles of Urban Structure.** Techne Press: Amsterdam, 2005.

Sen, A. **Development as Freedom.** Oxford: Oxford University Press, 1999.

Sennet, R. **The Uses of Disorder: Personal Identity and City Life.** W. W. Norton: New York, London, 1970.

Sieverts, T. **Cities Without Cities.** Spon Press: London, 2003.

Sloterdijk, P. **Experimentos con uno mismo, conversación con Carlos Oliveira**. Pretextos: Valencia, España, 2003.

Sloterdijk, P. **En el mismo barco. Ensayo sobre la hiperpolítica**, Ediciones Siruela, S. A.: Madrid, 1994.

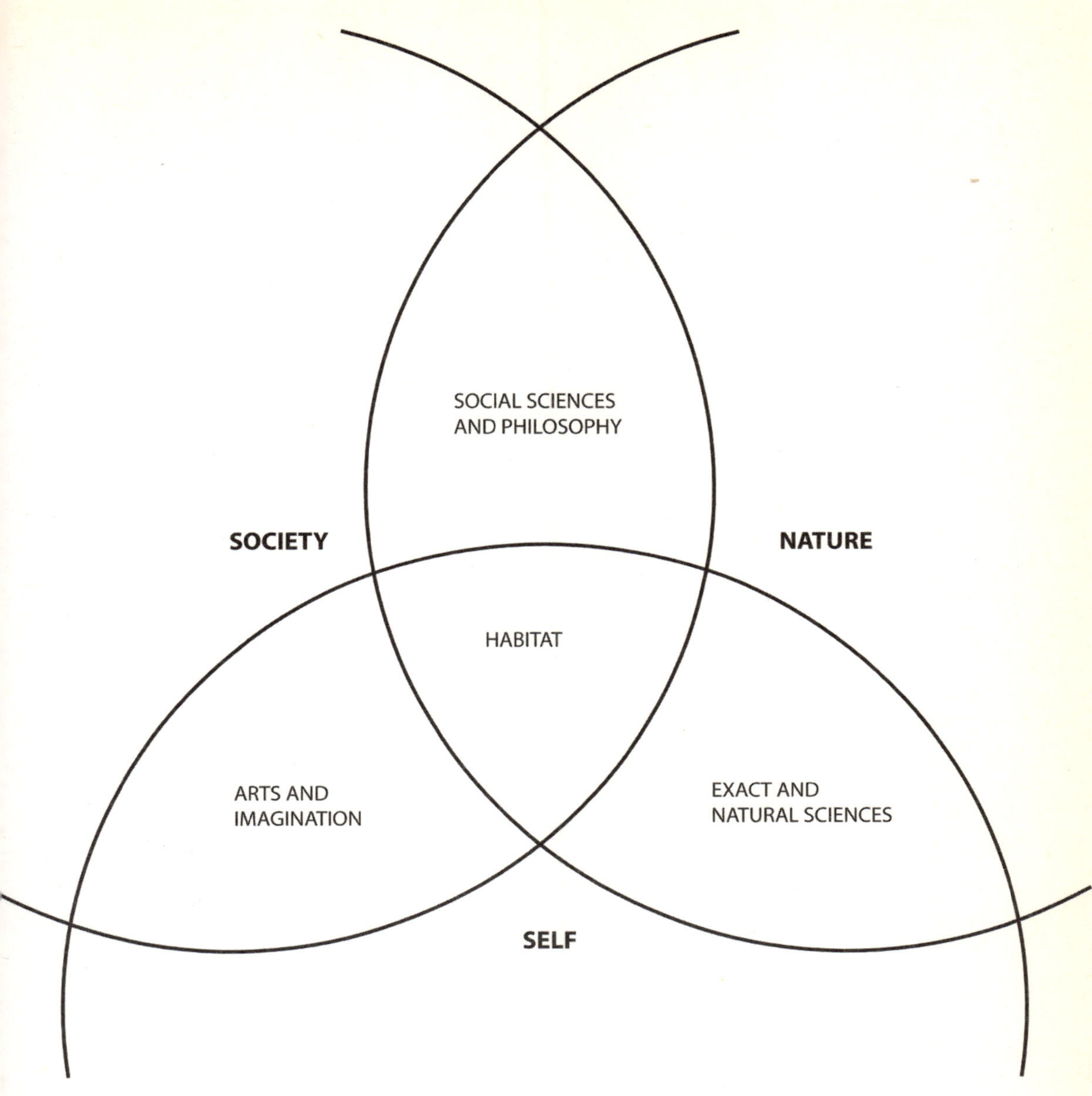

Habitat as a field where different domains of knowledge overlap. Source: author's elaboration, 2005.

'like already measured thread rewound onto a spool': a(n)notation on Bergson's two forms of multiplicity

Deborah Hauptmann

Introduction One of the recurring issues within the DSD seminars revolved around questions pertaining to the concept of *multiplicity.* At least we can use this term for the purpose of this essay as this work will outline a way of grasping the problem of the 'one and the many' in terms developed within the work of the French philosopher, Henri Bergson. Bergson provides a theory which explicates what he refers to as the 'two forms of multiplicity'; utilizing these concepts as one of the arguments on which he bases distinction between spatial and temporal categories, formulated under the terms of *discreet* and *continuous* multiplicities. Thinking this as *forms* and *relations,* we will further introduce Bergson's notion of the virtual.

This contribution will offer simply a close reading of Bergson, primarily from his early work *Time and Free Will.* The essay will provisionally allow for an interpretation that remains close to Bergson's thinking of space as homogeneous and time as heterogeneous. Although with Bergson, and certainly with Deleuze and similar thinkers, a much more complex way of thinking the dynamics of space is indeed possible, this essay intends to provide primarily a basis for first decomposing the composite of time and space, or, the one and the many, in order that in recomposing it we might operate with a clearer understanding of the elementary characteristics and attributes of our contemporary ontology of the virtual. Deleuze, in paraphrasing Bergson, summarizes the composite as such:

> The important thing here is that the decomposition of the composite reveals to us two types of multiplicity. One is represented by space (or rather, if all the nuances are taken into account, by the impure combination of homogeneous time): It is a multiplicity of exteriority, of simultaneity, of juxtaposition, of order, of quantitative differentiation, of difference in degree; it is a numerical multiplicity, discontinuous and actual. The other type of multiplicity appears in pure duration: It is an internal multiplicity of succession, of fusion, of organization, of heterogeneity, of qualitative discrimination, or of differences in kind; it is a virtual and continuous multiplicity that cannot be reduced to numbers.[1]

Although this contribution will not include any specific references to architecture and urbanism; I will simply offer the following observation. It does appear that the need to understand the distinction between these two forms of multiplicity within the disciplines of 'spatial thinking' seems to have become pressing in that a lack of clarity on the issue appears to encumber our view of the city as emergent and dynamic phenomenon capable of both acting and being acted upon; the urban entity as it offers powerful stabilities while at the same time generating a series of seemingly fragmented *moments* of a captured yet still generative force. From this question of centrality continue to arise even in the face of the seeming agreement that the city is now composed of multiple and diverse parts. Each (part) capable of generating a unique 'centrality', each amongst

1 Gilles Deleuze, **Bergsonism**, translated by Hugh Tomlinson and Barbara Habberjam (New York: Zone Books 1991) p. 38. (Orig. pub. as **Le Bergsonisme**, 1966).

the others forming an overall dynamic which cannot be explained by merely thinking the multiple within more traditional notions of 'plurality'.

Finally, this essay will conclude with an extended literary excerpt from William Faulkner; this provides what is, to my mind, a most exemplary illustration of what will be referred to in this essay as the second form of multiplicity, that of the *continuous* (Bergson) and *virtual* (Deleuze).

On Unit and Unity In *Time and Free Will* (1889) Bergson introduces his famous notion of 'two kinds of multiplicity'.[2] In the first chapter of the book Bergson provisionally concludes a discussion on 'psychic states' arguing that we cannot discuss psychic states, aesthetic feelings, affective sensation or moral feelings in the manner of a scientific quantifiable. With many examples he demonstrates that 'feelings', while they may be expressed in terms of greater and lesser intensity, cannot be calculated in direct correspondence with the physical function proper to external cause – not, at least, if we maintain that the lesser can be contained in the greater as in the case of an extended magnitude. This is not to say that intensive states do not seemingly have the effect of changes in degree of intensity; but, this is due to our habit of conceiving pure (temporal) states – which are affective – in terms of space, or, in other words, in analytical terms, whereby qualitative differences in kind are construed as quantitative measurements of degree – accomplished through representational symbols. Bergson writes:

> For, in proportion as a sensation looses its affective character and becomes representative, the reactions which it called forth on our part tend to disappear, but at the same time we perceive the external object which is its cause, … this cause is extensive and therefore measurable: a constant experience which began with the first glimmerings of consciousness and which continues throughout the whole of our life, shows us a definite shade of sensation corresponding to a definite amount of stimulation. We thus associate the idea of a certain quantity of cause with a certain quality of effect; and finally, as happens in the case of every *acquired perception*, we transfer the idea into the sensation, the quantity of the cause into the quality of the effect. At this very moment the intensity, which was nothing but a certain shade or quality of the sensation becomes a magnitude.[3]

Nonetheless, Bergson allows, for the sake of argument, that we can discuss two types of 'quantity': one intensive, admitting of 'more and less' and the other extensive, lending itself to measure. Additionally however, he provides that while the second is supported on representation and '*acquired*' perception, the former admits of otherwise, of what he terms a '*confused*' perception. 'The idea of intensity is thus situated at the junction of two streams, one of which brings us the idea of extensive magnitude from without, while the other brings us from within… the image of inner multiplicity.'[4] With this Bergson introduces the idea of a 'concrete multiplicity', as that which unfurls itself through time, or more precisely, for Bergson, as that which is unfolded in pure duration.[5]

In the second chapter of *TFW*, entitled 'The Multiplicity of Conscious States, The Idea of Duration', Bergson introduces the problem of the singular and the multiple in terms of spatial and temporal orders and uses the case of the mathematical numeric in order to identify the confusion between quantitative and qualitative categories. Here, number is understood as both an individual collection of units and a unity of multiple parts. Conceived either inclusively in a single image or in succession as discrete elements, the mistake, he consistently argues, is in thinking that succession places these elements in time (*durée*) as opposed to space.[6]

I will now follow Bergson carefully in the construction of his argument. Number, Bergson writes, 'may be defined in general as a collection of units, or, speaking more exactly, as the synthesis of the one and the many'. Every number can be considered as 'one' in that it is given a name and can be identified by a simple intuition which brings it forth. I can mention the number 3 for instance and we can all bring forth an adequate representation of it. Equally however we also know that this number can be decomposed into a collection of units (1 + 1 + 1), and on *ad infinitum* if we take into account not merely counting in other (whole) units, but the mathematical principle of division. What is important at this moment in the argument is simply to realize that any such units are 'identical' to one another. Equally however, there are also many cases of enumerations where we can draw note of distinctions with regard to the individual units. One example Bergson gives is this: when we count the soldiers in a battalion we are dealing with a numeric identical with which we achieve a 'unity' (the most simple relation of part to whole); however when we call the roll of names, we are distinguishing particular features which, although they can be enumerated, cannot in any way be accumulated to a numeric totality. The problem which emerges from this seemingly non-problematic description is this: while 'the idea of number implies the simple intuition of a multiplicity of parts or units, which are absolutely alike'… (somehow)… they must be 'distinct from one another, since otherwise they would merge at once into a single unit.'[7] Things which are constituted by duration and motion are not

2 Henri Bergson, **Time and Free Will: An Essay On The Immediate Data Of Consciousness**, Translated by F.L. Pogson (Montana: Kessinger Publishing Company) 1919 edition. (Orig. pub., **Essai sur les donneés immédiates de la conscience,** 1889).
3 **ibid.,** p. 42.
4 **ibid.,** p. 73.
5 With this term 'concrete' we might already anticipate a confusion when it comes to thinking in the disciplines of architecture and urbanism, in that the concrete is most often placed over and against the abstract. Of course this dichotomy is naïvely reductive when utilized to construct a distinction between that which can be perceived and that which can only be conceived, in other words, when used to distinguish that which is tangible or that which has 'form' so to speak, from that which is non tangible or that which is merely 'relational'.
6 Henri Bergson, **Matter and Memory** (New York: Zone Books, 1988) p. 71. Here he articulates this relation succinctly, writing, '(q)uestions relating to subject and object, to their distinction and their union, should be put in terms of time rather than space'.
7 Bergson, **Time and Free Will**, pp. 76-77.

given as objects but only appear to arrive as such through the process of 'mental syntheses'. In our consciousness states permeate one another, imperceptibly organize themselves into a whole, and in this way they are able to bind the past to the present. Conceived as a virtual, qualitative and concrete multiplicity, this duration only possesses the potential to contain the numeric. As Bergson puts it so succinctly:

> In short, we must admit two kinds of multiplicity, two possible senses of the word 'distinguish', two conceptions, the one qualitative and the other quantitative, of the difference between *same* and *other*. Sometimes this multiplicity, this distinctness, this heterogeneity contains number only potentially, as Aristotle would have said. Consciousness, then, makes a qualitative discrimination without any further thought to counting the qualities or even of distinguishing them as *several*. [8]

The question thus arises, what is the mechanism we utilize when conceiving of numeric extension? In order to perform such a simple operation as counting we have to retain the successive images of a thing (be it concrete – a soldier in a battalion, or abstract – the symbolic representation and repetition of the number 12 for instance), we set them alongside each other in spatial juxtaposition as an 'extended image'. The problem here is simple, as Bergson observes, we have fallen into the habit of believing that we are counting in time as opposed to in that of space. I will try to anticipate your rebuttal – 1 (second), 2 (seconds), 3 (seconds)... on *ad* (temporal) *infinitum* – yes. But, with Bergson we have to include the argument that 'clock-time' is nothing more than a spatialization of instants which pre-suppose spatial extensity and not temporal intensity, or the life of 'real duration'. 'Note that the mental image thus shaped implies the perception, no longer successive, but simultaneous, or a *before* and *after*, and that it would be a contradiction to suppose a succession which was only a succession, and which nevertheless was contained in one and the same instant.'[9]

I will digress on this point with an example – it is 12:58 and your train is leaving for the airport at 1:05 (thus there is numerically 7 units of time, measured in an arbitrary figure we call minutes, between this moment and the moment by which you depart). How is it then that this numeric extension could be 'experienced' as a 'unit' of varying intensities? Two scenarios will illustrate this – one, you are safely sitting on the train, your luggage stowed and (although in full anticipation of the journey ahead, which forms its own unique intensity) you open a book and begin to read. Two, you are running through the city, luggage in tow, colliding into one obstacle after the other, from the red-lights which catch you at the cross walks to the kindergarten class waddling along the side-walk hand in hand forming a block as distinct as the construction site which you just had to detour around, all the while checking the seconds on your watch as they relentlessly tick by at a 'seemingly' ascending rate of passage. The question is simple: are these two 'states' of 'temporal extension' precisely equal within the particular consciousness which perceives them? Whereas we can say objectively, that the numerically extensive passage of time will be identical in either case. The answer is clearly that they are not equal in experience nor are they identical in perception.

On the Discrete and the Continuous Here Bergson introduces an additional term for this idea of number which 'implies a visual image in space': *discrete multiplicity.* And he will later set this against the other idea of multiplicity which will come to be known as a *continuous multiplicity*. The former being related to quantitative distinctions and belonging properly to the domain of space and the latter to qualitative differentiations and belonging to the domain of time understood as duration (*durée)*. Further, the discrete multiplicity is by definition divisible (as discussed above, number can be infinitely divided) and the continuous multiplicity by nature indivisible. This brings us back to the problem of the 'unity of the whole' (every number being both a collection of units and a unity in itself as a synthesis of the units which compose it). Bergson writes that '... there are two kinds of units, the one ultimate, out of which a number is formed by a process of addition, and the other provisional, the number so formed, which is multiple in itself, and owes its unity to the simplicity of the act by which the mind perceives it.'[10] Yet, we are returned to a similar point as mentioned before with the problem which seems to be not a problem at all, namely, that if the mind, in its simple act of unification, forms this perception of 'the whole' then it must be so only by virtue of the fact that there was a 'multiplicity' for it to unify. If we extend this further, providing that the moment I analyze this composite and including the fact that arithmetic, in utilizing *provisional* units, allows for these units to be subdivided without limit, then the question returns us to the fact that we could not even conceive of a 'unity' made up of fractions if we did not implicitly regard it as an extended object, as Bergson puts it, as 'one in intuition but multiple in space'. And to remind us where we are going with this argument Bergson inserts a seemingly curious passage: 'You will never get out of an idea which you have formed anything which you have not put into it; and if the unity by means of which you make up your number is the unity of an act and not of an object, no effort of analysis will bring out of it anything but unity pure and simple'.[11]

We will further this distinction before going on to other aspects of this argument. If we wish to conceive of the 'whole', this provisional unity, as an indivisible act, and staying with the argument of numeric distinctions, we will find that this conception, thus represented to us by the naming of a unity – 3 for instance – is also 'represented under the form of a mathematical point which is separated from the following point by an interval in space.' Bergson suggests that:

8 ibid., p. 121.
9 ibid., p. 106.
10 ibid., p. 80.
11 ibid., p. 81.

> (W)e must distinguish between the unity which we think of and the unity which we set up as an object after having thought of it, as also between number in process of formation and number once formed. The unit is irreducible while we are thinking it and number is discontinuous while we are building it up; but, as soon as we consider number in its finished state, we objectify it, and it then appears to be divisible to an unlimited extent. In fact, we apply the term *subjective* to what seems to be completely and adequately known, and the term *objective* to what is known in such a way that a constantly increasing number of new impressions could be substituted for the idea which we actually have of it. [12]

And now we can return to the passage above which was referred to as 'curious', for here Bergson will introduce the critical distinction between what will come to be referred to as 'virtual', 'actual' and 'realized'. As mentioned above, the general appearance of an object (here Bergson uses the term 'body') as analyzed in thought will not yield anything more than what is already visible in the mental image which we have formed of it.[13] Yet the 'actual' perception of subdivisions in what is undivided, as we have just seen, is precisely what is referred to as 'objective'. That which properly belongs to the mind (in the argument on numeric conception) is the 'indivisible process by which it has the capacity to concentrate attention successively on different parts of a given space'.[14] However, this 'successive concentration' operates as an extended form of perception, thus it spreads itself out in space, space then becomes the very 'material' with which the mind builds up the idea of number, and thus, applies this conceptualization of the spatialized numeric within the very heart of thinking the divisible and the indivisible, the unit and the unity.

In keeping with Bergson we must further understand that duration (as well as the *continuous multiplicity*) is not simply the indivisible, nor is it the non-measurable. Duration, has its distinction from space in that within the process of change, duration divides only by changing in kind as opposed to degree. It is not that it defies all notions of measurability; it is just that it must vary its metric principle at each moment of division.

Further, with this we can include the Bergsonian proposition regarding space whereby he suggests that things are not in space, but rather it is space that is in things. In other words, we must not conceive of space as an abstract field upon which things are spread out (as in Cartesian space); but we must understand that it is by virtue of the fact that things themselves have extension, that space as such necessarily follows from such extensity, that space is in fact in things. Keith Ansell Pearson reformulates this proposition, writing:

> It is necessary to give an account of our categories of being and spatial habits of representation, to show how they are part of human evolutionary existence; space, for example, is a schema of matter which represents the limit of a

movement of expansion that would come to an end as an external envelope of all possible extensions. In this sense it is inadequate to say matter and extensity are 'in' space, it is rather the other way round.[15]

To reiterate, we have seen that there are 'two types of multiplicity' in Bergson. One, the *discrete,* by which we speak of material objects which are localized in space and to which the concept of number immediately applies; and the other, the *continuous,* which refers to states of consciousness, and cannot be regarded as numeric unless given symbolic representation which subsequently also places them in space. (Deleuze will rename these, as well as further extend their theoretical reach, under the terms of 'actual and virtual multiplicities').[16] But before giving an example of a continuous multiplicity we will follow one step further in the development of the argument in order to bring forward one of the distinctions which I believe to be highly pertinent in thinking through the notion of the 'virtual' in its contemporary form.

On Subject and Object Dealing directly with what I have referred to elsewhere as the subject/object collapse,[17] Bergson writes that we make a distinction between these two types of multiplicity when we discuss the impenetrability of matter, whereby 'we sometimes set up impenetrability as a fundamental property of bodies, known in the same way and put on the same level as (for example) weight or resistance.'[18] Suggesting that when we try to picture one body penetrating another (a 'picture' that computer software today allows fluidly as evidenced in the work of many architects today) we must assume an 'empty space' in which particles can fill this space, merging into the interstitial voids left by the one and/or the other. In fact, our thoughts can prolong this process indefinitely in preference to picturing two bodies occupying the 'same place' at the 'same time'. If impenetrability is an actual quality of matter, Bergson argues, 'there is no clear reason why we should experience more difficulty in conceiving two bodies merging into one another than a surface devoid of resistance or a weightless fluid. But... in reality, it is not a physical but a logical necessity which attaches to the proposition: "Two bodies cannot occupy the same place at the same time".'[19] The assertion which insists on the impenetrability of matter does so due to the fact that notions of number and that of space have been inextricably linked, so much so that in stating the properties of matter, we are, in fact, reducing these properties to only those which exist properly as properties of number.

12 ibid., pp. 83-84.
13 Bergson extensively elaborates this concept in his later works as well. For instance, in thinking on the notion of 'image' **as** 'matter' in his book **Matière et Mémoire** of 1896.
14 Bergson, **Time and Free Will,** p. 84.
15 Keith Ansell Pearson, **Philosophy and the Adventure of the Virtual: Bergson and the Time of Life** (London: Routledge, 2002) p.11.
16 Deleuze suggests that Bergson takes this distinction from his reading of the mathematician G.B. Riemann. Ansell Pearson further elaborates the basis of Riemannian theory in his **Philosophy and the Adventure of the Virtual,** pp. 15-16.
17 'The Third Turn: The Space of Immersion', in **Medium Architektur** (Weimar: 9th International Bauhaus-Kolloquium, conference proceedings, 2003).
18 Bergson, **Time and Free Will,** p. 88.
19 ibid. (see chapter II in general, pages 88 & 89 specifically, on this point).

Nevertheless, it is equally certain that when it comes to feelings, sensations and ideas, we can readily accept the notion of permeability. The permeability of feelings, of continuous and concrete multiplicities, can be easily grasped when we think of music. Although a musical composition can be symbolically represented – laid out within the 'discrete' spatial frame of the musical score – as well as played by virtue of units measured in a precisely spatialized-time; the experience of listening to, for example, an aria (Bergson also uses the example of the chiming of a clock) cannot be reduced to numeric measure. For although we know that one note ends and another begins, they persist within our conscious perception, they prolong each other in a time proper only to lived duration. Now, even if we attempt to objectify this 'experience of permeability' and argue that a note can be played staccato and thus distinguishable from the note which follows or proceeds it, this does not change our conscious perception of this note which endures throughout the entire composition as we cannot retain the music, which is that which we experience, if we extend the intervals between the notes to the point by which their relation to the composition no longer retains its 'unity'.

Science, Bergson argues, 'works exclusively with measurements, and the measuring of time consists in counting simultaneities'.[20] In dealing with time the concern of physics is with the extremities of time and the illusion is generated that the extremities of an interval are identical with the interval itself. What takes place in the interval – an actual duration – is neglected and lost sight of, and this means that the counting of simultaneities can only take the form of a counting of instants. Bergson goes further, arguing that it does not matter at what speed time runs, if the number of extremities is indefinitely increased, or if the intervals are indefinitely narrowed, these changes would have no great impact on the calculations of time carried out by the physicist:

> The speed of unfolding of this external, mathematical time might become infinite, all the past, present, and future states of the universe might be found experienced at a stroke; in place of the unfolding there might be only the unfolded. The motion representative of time would then have become a line; to each of the divisions of this line there would correspond the same portion of the unfolded universe that corresponded to it before the unfolding universe; nothing would have changed in the eyes of science.[21]

Bergson also goes on to state that our own experience, our own perception of this change in speed would be immediately recognized in consciousness.

The mind is capable of conceiving a succession without distinctions, thinking of it as a 'mutual penetration, an interconnexion and organization of elements, each one of which represents the whole, and cannot be distinguished or isolated from it except by abstract thought.'[22] However, the problem for thought seems almost overwhelming, *Duration* is nonrepresentational and just as we *think* it, so too it becomes spatialized.

The composite of space and duration in which we act, in which we actuate (or presence) our memories into perceptions, is given to us by experience, not merely 'lived' experience, or 'immediacy'; but the very 'condition' of experience. Duration is experience, but equally it is experience enlarged and gone beyond. For Bergson questions of experience go not merely to the 'state of experience' but the very nature of the 'condition of experience': a condition which can only be reached, as Bergson argues, *beyond the turn*, where we engage with our will not the simple effects of action but the pure affect of all action (both virtual and real).[23] Ansell Pearson succinctly puts it in this way: 'The human condition refers not to an existential predicament but to accrued evolutionary habits of thought and patterns of action which prevent us from recognizing our own creative conditions of existence and which restrict the domain of praxis to that of social utility...'[24]

At this point we have moved from the composite of the whole and the part (the one and the many, the unity and the unit) to that of time and space. And from here we can now move to a final reflection. Walter Benjamin, in a passage from his seminal essay of 1936, 'The Work of Art in the Age of Mechanical Reproduction' writes: 'During long periods of history, the mode of human sense perception changes with humanity's entire mode of existence. The manner in which human sense perception is organized, the medium in which it is accomplished, is determined not only by nature but by historical circumstances as well.' By historical circumstance Benjamin intended technological advancements, as having the power to alter the very mode of human experience and subsequently the nature of human perception. Bergson, foreshadowing Benjamin, also questions: 'If, in order to count states of consciousness, we have to represent them symbolically in space, is it not likely that this *symbolical representation will alter the normal conditions of inner perception*?' He continues: 'In the same way, our projection of our psychic states into space in order to form a discrete multiplicity is likely to influence these states themselves and *to give them in reflective consciousness a new form*, which immediate perception did not attribute to them'.[25]

If we wish to separate out our feelings and sensations, our ideas, it is necessary to count them, to reduce them to number and represent them symbolically in space, as homogeneous units 'which occupy separate positions in space and consequently no longer permeate one another.'[26] In other

20 Henri Bergson, **Duration and Simultaneity,** 1999, p. 40 (orig. Durée et Simultanéité, 1922).
21 **ibid.,** p. 41.
22 **ibid.,** p. 101.
23 This issue is elaborated in: Bergson's **Matter and Memory**. See also: D. Hauptmann, 'Interval & Image in the Embodiment of Memory: On Henri Bergson's Matter and Memory', in **OASE,** issue 58, 'The Visible and the Invisible', Amsterdam, 2002.
24 Ansell Pearson, **Philosophy and the Adventure of the Virtual,** pp. 9-10.
25 Bergson, **Time and Free Will**, p. 90 (my italics).
26 **ibid.**

words, in order to continue this false or 'inaccurately stated problem', which confuses quantity with quality, we continue to apply to our experience of time (*durée*) the notion of succession, yet understood as discrete and discontinuous sections, as extensive and homogeneous; in fact, we thus spatialize our experience of time as simultaneity. And it is this conflation of time and space which prevents us from understanding the condition (as opposed to the state) of the subject/object categories as delimitated on the plane, within the multiplicities and singularities of what has become to be simply referred to as *the virtual*.

By way of conclusion In lieu of drawing conclusions to the concept of multiplicity in the form of recounting the arguments as presented above, this essay will take a different turn by offering examples of how the continuous can be seen to express the both/and of time and space within two different examples from art. First, with a summary reading of a contemporary art work by Christina Linaris-Coridou, entitled, 'Woman in Blue Reading a Letter', an interpretive work based on the original work by the same title of Johannes Vermeer; secondly, with an introduction to an excerpt from a novel by William Faulkner. [Figures 1 and 2]

I will presume, for the sake of brevity, the reader can anticipate an interpretation of the original work of Vermeer through the concept of spatial and temporal multiplicities. This includes, for instance, the letter as it provides for a duration that is continuous (intensive and indivisible); both in terms of the virtual act of its reading as well as its writing – by a hand which is absent in space and the thought which is past in time; the framing element of the map as it provides an example of a discrete multiplicity (extensive and divisible) in the form of time-space compression; as well as the pregnancy of the woman in blue which furthers the complexity of the durational intensity already implicit in the various moments of action made present in the image. Advancing this reading one step further through the work of Linaris-Coridou, I will offer considerations on the additions and subtractions provided by her interpretive work. With regard to the letter, with the insertion of the ruler fragment the discrete is firmly inscribed; as if the intensive acts both present and absent (past and future) might be extensively measured. Yet, in the margins of the composition a fragment of 'a' letter is inserted which brings the 'time of the reading' to the immediate present (of the current viewer). The other fragments added to this composition provide for similar immediacies taken from the body of the subject in the original painting; two fragments of her dress are extracted (the yellow ribbon and a swatch of blue fabric) bringing to the work a tactile manifestation of a now absent material presence. Again, with this we see a temporal past made continuous through what might be considered as a material discrete. With regard to the subtractions, the erasures, the effacements: over half of the original image has been all but removed, leaving only a silhouetted 'memory'. In the actual space of this absence the artist has inserted a Greek text: 'it exists and it does not exist' referring to the immaterial yet existent (soul) which temporally endures (durée) in the absence of space (actually, in the absence of the requirement of any form of pure space leaving only the 'expressed of the soul' in pure time). In other words, with the work of Linaris-Coridou we not only witness the movement between the continuous and the discontinuous, we are engaged in a double movement between memory and matter, between the virtual and the actual.

With the second example, taken from Faulkner's *Light in August* we also see a sympathy with the virtual multiplicity, actualized not as event (pure reserve in Deleuze), but also as memory and matter, yet in this case the virtual image must be understood as both pure space and pure time. Here Faulkner tells the story of Lena, a child of the depression, uneducated, unemployed, orphaned at twelve, pregnant and searching for the father of her unborn child, a man named Lucas Burch. The novel tells the story of this young woman's journey in search of a memory, for once, not so many months before, Lena recalls: 'he said he would send for me'. At this moment of the below excerpt, Lena is sitting on a hill, along a dirt road where she has been walking, she has seen a wagon which she knows will be traveling down this road on which she awaits for the simple kindness of a weary ride:

> The sharp and brittle crack and clatter of its weathered and ungreased wood and metal is slow and terrific: a series of dry sluggish reports carrying for a half mile across the hot still pinewiney silence of the August afternoon. Though the mules plod in a steady and unflagging hypnosis, the vehicle does not seem to progress. It seems to hang suspended in the middle distance forever and forever, so infinitesimal is its progress, like a shabby bead upon the mild red string of road. So much so is this that in the watching of it the eye loses it as sight and sense drowsily merge and blend, like the road itself, with all the peaceful and monotonous changes between darkness and day, like already measured thread being rewound onto a spool. So that at last, as though out of some trivial and unimportant region beyond even distance, the sound of it seems to come slow and terrific and without meaning, as though it were a ghost traveling a half mile ahead of its own shape. 'That far within my hearing before my seeing,' Lena thinks. She thinks of herself as already moving, riding again, thinking *Then it will be as if I were riding for a half mile before I even got into the wagon, before the wagon even got to where I was waiting, and that when the wagon is empty of me again it will go on for a half mile with me still in it*. She waits, not even watching the wagon now, while thinking goes idle and swift and smooth, ... Thinking, '...*I will be riding within the hearing of Lucas Burch before his seeing. He will hear the wagon, but he won't know. So there will be one within his hearing before his seeing.... And there will be two within his seeing before his remembering.'*

Perhaps in thinking through the questions of the divisible and the indivisible one might also ask what is within the hearing before the seeing, what is within the seeing before the remembering as it might direct us towards an other urban and architectural understanding that refuses to conflate the part and the whole, unit and unity; and, ultimately, decompose so that it can properly recompose the most critical of composites which we refer to as time and space.

Woman in blue reading a letter. c. 1662-1665, Johannes Vermeer, oil on canvas, 46.5 x 39 cm.
Source: The Rijksmuseum.

Woman in blue reading a letter. 1996, Christina Linaris-Coridou, Collage: hemp, color photocopy on fabric, cotton, wood and paper, 53 x 59 cm. Source: Collectie C. Orfanidis.

Immaterial Relata in the Urban Construct

Alexander G. Vollebregt

> Intellectualism…is blind to the mode of existence and co-existence of perceived objects, to the life which steals across the visual field and secretly binds its parts together.[1]
> Immaterial: irrelevant, unimportant, of no importance, of no consequence, beside the point, neither here nor there, makes no difference, doesn't matter.[2]

We live in an urbanised world. If urbanity is perceived as the result of man's intervention in an otherwise natural environment, then one could argue that in effect, there is no natural world anymore. The term 'ecosystem' that we formerly used to describe the fragile ecological state of natural affairs through which our worldly activities are actualised, has been substituted by a new global 'economic system'[3] from which our governed worlds are forced to capitalise; a process of urbanisation which exploits every natural, human and material resource, satiating its own drive towards sovereignty. This urban sprawl[4] – a cancerous process of *artificialisation* – disrupts the ecological skin of this earth while draining its submerged resources. A resultant synthetic tissue is superimposed; an overlay of contained worlds conjured up as housing neighbourhoods, commercial districts, civic centres and recreational parks, resulting in an unnatural, dissociated, highly regulated and closed urban system. And to what end, one may ask? Is this process of evolution in any way sustainable? While in natural environments we witness how life-forms create synergetic systems as symbiotic relationships emerge, in our own urban environment we seem to opt for an approach in which our agents operate as controlled parasites, exploiting their close encounters, exhausting their milieu and blind to the urban disequilibrium they create. Standardisation, regulation and optimisation seem to be the hidden concepts from which this process departs, and from where our increasingly mobile life-worlds unfold towards a life, out of balance.[5]

The detrimental consequences of a rapidly overdeveloping malignant ecology are witnessed at every turn. The fact that we even have so-called 'developed nations' versus 'developing nations' naturalised in the notions of first, second or third world countries is in itself cause for concern. We struggle to come to terms with a seemingly complex environment. The contemporary urban transformation processes – fuelled by political, economical and social forces, and further

1 **Phenomenology of Perception,** Maurice Merleau-Ponty.

2 Microsoft Office Word 2003 Thesaurus.

3 Economy in this sense refers strictly to the economy of finance; where value and worth are circumscribed by their monetary value, thus empowering the establishments of financial distribution.

4 'Urban sprawl' in this instance refers not to the process of simple sub-urbanisation, the conventional peripheral housing neighbourhood developments, but to the expansion of the current urban concept in general over an otherwise natural and sustainable ecology. Gregory Bateson stated that if this me-versus-the-world attitude wherein the human species continuously exhausted its natural environment would be the estimate of our relationship to nature, and we have the advanced technology, our likelihood of survival will be that of a snowball in hell… we will die, either by the by-products of our own hate, or simply of overpopulation and overgrazing (**The Global Brain,** 1995), these are the similar behavioural characteristics we can find back in the cancerous cells which can eventually consume the entire human body.

5 This process of urbanisation is beautifully illustrated in Godfrey Reggio's 1982 film **Koyaanisqatsi – Life out of Balance** in which 'an apocalyptic vision of the collision of two different worlds' is depicted; 'urban life and technology versus the environment' (http://www.koyaanisqatsi.org). The visual and audio **tour de force** encapsulates seven years of film footage in which the physical results of modernisation are portrayed.

advanced by technological and digital innovations – have intensified the complexities apparent in our metropolis: a 'historical process of implosion-explosion (...) the tremendous concentration (of people, activities, wealth, goods, objects, instruments, means and thought) of urban reality and the immense explosion, the projection of numerous, disjunct fragments (peripheries, suburbs, vacation homes, satellite towns) into space'.[6] Spatial strategists struggle to keep up with powerful and uncertain forces that effect/affect our lives, but the contemporary urban problematic cannot be sufficiently understood with modernistic epistemologies pertaining to our built environment. We are faced in actual fact with an urban phenomenon that we still fail to comprehend, as 'realities'[7] alter with changes in the connective tissue of our worlds.

In order to efficiently correlate with the forces that guide this urban evolutionary process, a new perspective towards 'the urban' needs to be generated. A paradigm shift is required that makes sense of and even embraces the multiplicity of unknowns with which we are confronted. New insights are called for that help expand our awareness to the growing multiplicities inherent in our transforming cities which embody an appreciation for and opens us to the possibilities that these complex relationships offer. The progress of our cities, paired with the mutations in our globalising societies has reached a state in which the urban and its process of urbanisation has become something of a 'black box'.

> The architect and the urbanist, sometimes confused as partners in an ambiguous duo, sometimes as twins are warring siblings, as distant colleagues and rivals, examine the black box. They know what goes in, are amazed at what comes out, but have no idea what takes place inside.[8]

Spatial planners and designers implement seemingly well-researched interventions yet are perplexed when the result does not comply with their projections. The discrepancy here does not lie within their lack of motivation or any financial restraint, but is rather due to their lack of understanding of the urban phenomenon itself. Their comprehension towards what constitutes the urban is blind to the mode of existence of actualised urbanities. Unveiling these blind fields in the current perspective is essential if we truly wish to understand and facilitate a sustainable urban future.

Focusing on the *immaterial relations* of the city allows us to understand the urban beyond its purely physical manifestation. A reality based solely on the foundation of the constructed urban - a result of layers of interventions striving to engender an optimal *setting*, from parks to civic centres to housing neighbourhoods to commercial districts – is blind to the processes which in effect hold the system together, namely the urban *construct* of relations. One may ask for whom this optimum operates, and to what extent these optimums are an integral part of the inter-relationship of an urban system. How can we even speak of an optimum while both global degradation and social deprivation are actively progressing? Our governing intellects – our 'ministers of knowledge'[9] –

responsible for the urban development processes, are limited by a problem-solving approach focussed on objects rather than relationships. Their proposals and interventions are confined in a binary reality; one that focuses on 'what is' or 'what is not', and not on 'what may become'. This impaired mindset restrains them from perceiving an alternate reality where new opportunities may lie. Dealing with the city in this framework is restricted to 'patching up' urban problems, like dressing wounds, resulting in yet one more fragmented layer over an already splintered urban patchwork. Perhaps a new form of understanding can be generated by investigating the in*form*ing relationships that can be opened up by shifting away from a purely factual binary perspective.

The visual is our most powerful sense. Our mind is 'fooled' by the evidence of our senses as we *see* a dry wooden stick *bend* as it submerges into a pool of water. Though our current intellectualism has been constructed by a rationale that prohibits the possibility of a stick actually bending, a temporal reality can seemingly still penetrate our thoughts; only to be removed as the stick itself is removed from the water, or by eradicating the thought altogether by forcefully inducing a correctional system of logics. We are habituated to perceive (and thus conceive) an object-based reality, our perceptual perspective has been obstructed to see past the constructed order. We see objects, materialised containers and store them away into databanks only to re-invoke them in order to pass judgement over our environment and construct our worlds out of them. But this mental map of imagery can overlook which matters most, namely the worldly operations constructive of an everyday urbanism, the *urban relata*. We live life-worlds, in constitutive relations with both space and time. Refusing to make this conceptual shift, refusing to acknowledge these relational life-worlds, we remain in a contained urban illusion where the foundations of our belief is based solely upon the objects we perceive. We choose to believe what we see, but fail to see what we believe.

While the sun may shed light over our urban fabric, it inadvertently lays a veil over the stars. Though we know they are there, while their visual presence has been removed, we fail to acknowledge their existence. They have become in actual fact temporally absent. Maurice Merleau-Ponty stated that if objects may never show us more than one of their facets, that is because we are ourselves in a certain place from which we see them and which we cannot see. If nevertheless we believe in the existence of their hidden sides and equally in a world which embraces them all and co-exists with them, we can perceive *realities* that sustain their co-existence and communicates to it all the pulses of its duration.[10] Incorporating multiple perspectives, perceiving the urban as a relational construct, one may also start to conceive it as an open embodiment of processes; a relational and inter-dependant synergetic urban system.

6 Lefebvre (2003) p. 14.

7 I distinguish three 'forms' of reality; a **physical** reality which finds itself in our materialised world (i.e. the urban products upon which many 'truths' are based), a **virtual** reality which can be found in the inter-relations generating these products and around which temporal actualisations emerge (i.e. the urban processes), and a digital **informational** reality which slowly, yet surely, makes its presence more and more evident.

8 Lefebvre (2003) pp. 28–29.

9 De Certeau (2002).

10 Taken from Maurice Merleau-Ponty's study into the experience of the body and classical psychology in **Phenomenology of Perception** (2002) Routledge Classics.

This paper does not intend to put forth a purely romantic proposition towards a new Babylonian utopia, but simply wishes to opt for an environment that is both socially and technologically just; an urbanity that generates opportunities while facilitating desires, spawning cultures of creativity striving for quality as opposed to quantity. For this to be achieved, we need to strive to see an urban configuration that operates as an open-ended system, maintaining its structural integrity, while embracing and mediating subjective intentions and desires.
In order to do so, we need to look beyond the physical form of the city, or what we define as form. In figure 1 four ways are shown to re-present the form of a square. Each form, both similar yet different to the original Cartesian model of a square is constituted through a set of relations, be they intrinsic, extrinsic or combinatorial. The possibility of endless representations of the form of a square opens a way to begin to understand the countless ways in which one could opt to perceive the urban environment. However valuable a set perspective may seem to appear – aesthetically or statistically – it fails to visualise the multiplicities inherent in its becoming. As part of a relational system, it has the authority to construct or obstruct a myriad of possible futures and appropriations. This may serve as a starting point to opening up our perception and eventual re-conception of the urban. In fact the variability of representation is not part of the multiplicity potential of singularities[11] – it is simply that all realities are constructed in time-space vectors of involved engagement with the world. Multiple worlds are a simple product of the particularity (and non-repeatability) of individual life trajectories.

Lefebvre proposes that we examine the problem by looking at the urban, not as a city, nor as metropolis, but as an immanent 'urban field':

> To explore this field, to see it, change is necessary, the abandonment of earlier viewpoints and perspectives. During this new period, differences are known and recognized, mastered, conceived and signified. These mental and social, spatial and temporal differences, detached from nature, are resolved on a much higher plane, a plane of thought that can grasp all the elements. Urban thought (not urbanism), that is, the reflection of urban society, gather the data that was established and separated by history… it rediscovers the community and the city, but at a higher level, on a different scale, and after their fragmentation. It recovers the key concepts of a prior reality and restores them in an enlarged context: forms, functions, urban structures. It is constituted by a renewed space-time, a topology that is distinct from agrarian and industrial space-time. Urban space-time, as soon as we stop defining it in terms of industrial rationality appears as a differential, each place and each moment existing only within a whole, through the contrast and oppositions that connect it to, and distinguish it from, other places and moments.[12]

The city reveals itself to be a relational and active space; not a preconceived utopia that engineers societal and urban (trans)formations.

> Today, the urban reality itself, with its problematic and practice, is hidden, replaced by representation (ideological and institutional) that bear the name 'urbanism'... The urban considered as a field is not simply an empty space filled with objects. If there is a blindness, it does not arise simply because we can't see these objects and the space appears empty. No, the urban is a highly complex field of tensions, a virtuality, a possible-impossible that attracts the accomplished, an ever-renewed and always demanding presence-absence. Blindness consists in the fact that we cannot see that shape of the urban, the vectors and tensions inherent in this field, its logic and dialectic movement, its immanent demands.[13]

We are currently operating in an era[14] where the emergent reality, intensely invigorated by new space-times – generated through *movement* and *communication* – has exponentially complexified the urban field generating tensions concerning its relations. It would be not only insensitive, but thoroughly naive for any profession to engage with the city without a careful consideration of its immanent demands. The acknowledgement of its immaterial relations and consequences is essential if we are to attain a truly sustainable urbanity. A re-conceptualisation of the urban as constituted is critical if we are to address its rising problematics. For this to be realised, the city must be seen as process and product; a multitude of layers and processes with intrinsic and extrinsic relations producing ever-interrelated products that any binary based epistemology founded on gridlocked notions would ever be able to fully comprehend. To visualise the urban as a field of 'becoming' allows for a sensible understanding and eventual intervention in the contemporary city. The Urban Field Diagram depicts one such visualisation. [see figure 2]

The vectors and flows of movement and communication are steered by (mostly) hidden socio-spatial and socio-*technical* networks which in turn generate 'hidden' places. *Placeness*[15] in this perspective, is thus not inserted by way of program or defined by conceived borders *made* perceived, as in a closed and dependant system, but is ephemeral, mutable, open; a fluid and dynamic process of actualisation in an extensive interactive flux. As such, the actual *form* of the city is not the configuration of buildings and infrastructure, but is generated by relations and communications *in the midst of* the urban, converging to generate transient crystallisations of placeness. Our movement as human agents, as well as the movements of images, goods, information, finance, ideas, constitute the true *texture* and weave of the city. Form is not the materialisation of the built urban fabric, nor is it generated by the overlaid program inserted to activate the city; it emerges by way of our co-engagements within the city through the appropriation and performance of space (mediated through technological infrastructures) by relations. These performed relations constitute what can be referred to as the *urban materia* – a live substance that precedes

11 See Annemarie Mol, **The Body Multiple: Ontology in Medical Practice** (Durham: Duke UP. 2003).
12 Lefebvre (2003) pp. 36–37.
13 Lefebvre (2003) p. 40.
14 Entity-relationship-attribute.
15 'Placeness' in this sense is the eventual process from which space as a neutral entity acquires meaning. The intensity (and value) of this meaning – its horizon – effects to what extent place-presence is acknowledged as such for the related societies.

and gives form to the dependent matter of the city. The interplay of human and non-human agency by way of these relations and their performance in networks produces the urban reality of the contemporary metropolis. The enabling or disabling *surface* in which its complex operations take place is our concern as urban practitioners.[16] An abstracted representation denoting such an association is illustrated in a spatial relations diagram wherein a field of opportunities and limitations provides the spatial realm in which interchange is actualised. [see figure 3]

Spawning a new urban... The urban scene is constituted through the urban condition; a condition that is constructed primarily out of two aspects, namely that which is created as a result of 'hard' or relatively permanent material, economical, political, technological and social networks of the *everyday* construct, and that which is generated out of 'soft' or relatively temporary networks that are the result of *everyday* urban dynamics. Urban dynamics, or flows, that in effect generate the form of the city ground themselves in local settlements.

These flows could be referred to as the *veins* or *arteries* of the city, comprised of everyday movements of people, economies, and ideas; effecting the processes that influence the workings of the metropolis as an *urban body*; whether represented through the city as an urban membrane that synthesises the *real* urban fabric with the *virtual* operations it generated in the flows; or by way of the human body, understood as an *urban being* that not only inhabits the urban field, but is constituted through conditions to which it is habituated. A growing awareness that the urban being is progressively generated through relational and process driven conditions helps us to re-conceptualise our understanding of the urban and its agents, allowing us to perceive *city* as process-product; a multi-layered urban, where relationships intrinsically effect processes in adjacent layers gradually yet continuously altering the entire configuration. This layered organisation engenders a complex system, an *urban matrix*, which illustrates urban convolutions that by definition cannot be represented as a simple flat interface[17] without unintentionally levelling out the intricate operations that constitute its eventual urban condition. Was it not Albert Einstein who said that we cannot solve problems by using the same kind of thinking we used when we created them? If we are to acknowledge the dynamic complexities inherent in everyday life-forms, then we too must look for new means to search (not research), re-present and communicate these intricacies before attempting to engage with them. For now we are at the forefront of a new urban reality, which can find its *DNA* embedded in several realms; a crystallized sphere of the physical, an emergent sphere of the virtual actualized over time, and an informational sphere generating new modes of communication and movement spawning new forms of digital spatial inhabitation, while simultaneously retaining the potential to facilitate the absolute and unconditional accessibility and interrelatedness of all digitalised information.[18]

As previously illustrated, the form of the city is not restricted to a physicality we perceive *in* time, but can be found in the visible form that emerges *over* time. The urban physicality that we fabricate does not represent our everyday urbanisms. The snapshot image capturing the urban composition, typologies and zones represents only a managed and aesthetic urbanism, in actual fact they only function as the *skeleton* upon which *real* urban life comes to pass. The true urban body, a life-form that rises and sets each day, is one that can hardly be represented or understood within current urban epistemologies. The tools we utilise – founded on statistics and dualities – are the result of an outdated, static and misconceived urban understanding. A novel and sensible point of view may spawn which acknowledges the urban body as a space accommodating active *becomings* within convergent processes; constant communication producing event-horizons that ripple over spaces and times, constrained within an evolutionary spatially-interrelated urban matrix.

Clarifications for the contemporary urban problematic lie perhaps not so much in offering purely reactive answers, as it may lie in posing the right questions. The focus of this search should not find itself entangled in the heart of our built urban fabric, but is rather concealed in our own disillusioned perspective, our own urban blind fields. If we are to pose new questions, we must first be able to perceive alternative urban realities; a shift in urban attitude that strives to harmonise its constituents. Perceiving the city as an urban system, layered with physical, virtual and digital spheres, allows us to analyse and synthesise an extensive configurational surface that may generate *urban equilibrium*. Urbanism would then not operate as an *optimising* market machine, but would aspire *efficiency* by mediating its components. Seeing the city as an evolutionary system, the new urbanist would relinquish the attempt to manufacture an ideal urbanity, but would rather strive to facilitate its workings by engaging *within* its configuration of actuality, virtuality and informationality.

Is it so impossible for us to imagine an urban that is economically viable, environmentally sound, and socially inspiring? Urban philosophers, theorists and critics of the 20th century constantly proposed further investigation into the residual; the idiosyncrasies that leaked out of the constructed order. Merleau-Ponty, Heidegger, Lefebvre and Deleuze all refer to a hidden reality. Modelling[19] and understanding the city as a processual field – through which *place* is activated as

16 Vollebregt, A., **Hidden Places, Hidden Powers**. In: S. Read and C. Pinilla, eds **Visualizing the Invisible: Towards an Urban Space** (Amsterdam: Techne Press: 2006).

17 Further research into software development which helps to sufficiently represent complex urban systems is currently underway. Our outdated means of representation through mapping and diagramming filter out substantial informing insights. We need to replace our old ways of thinking and presenting, with new ways of seeing and visualizing.

18 The expansion of the informational evolution is already generating advanced forms of knowledge-information resulting in higher levels of global awareness on a worldwide scale. Based on a holistic, open-source and inter-dependant perception, it has already spawned innovative websites as **www.Google.com** and **www.Wikipedia.com**. Simultaneously it has also inspired such evocative books as those by Peter Russell entitled **The Global Brain Awakens** and **The White Hole in Time** wherein through an observation of the evolution and organisation of life itself, the world, with its living cells, is portrayed as a 'single living organism'.

19 Modelling in this sense refers not to the conventional model of the constructed urban, but to a result of complex dynamic relations and not merely induced through simple superimpositions – allows for the relational and dynamic affordance of the city to be visualised; gradually substantiating our proposed materialised interventions. This active extensive space, producing local emergent placeness in the midst of our conceived reality connects us and our perceptions to the urban system as a whole. Just as the complex processes of our bodies converge to produce the identities by which we are perceived as bodily *cells* in the urban, the metropolis too converges towards us as an urban body. We see an urban life-form composed of inter-dependant constituents that are related and invigorated through movement and communication, generating the urban tissue, or the 'flesh' of the city. This *urban metabolism* is the origin where the life of the city and its cells transpire, and where the organisation of urban life is conditioned. Our attunement, as urbanists, to this reality is essential, not to conjure up yet another utopic framework, but to understand and embrace the city's sensitive interrelationships so that we can search for the conditions through which located realities come to be. We seek an integrated urbanity striving to understand the relation between globally governing necessities and locally creative places and citizens; a 'natural' and open urban ecology through which we can sensibly realign past, present and future becomings.

model the urban construct in order to visualize its interrelatedness. Proposals for interventions would require to not only be simply **located** in space, but sensitively **situated** in space-time relations.

Bibliography

De Certeau, M. **The Practice of Everyday Life**. Berkley CA: University of California Press, 1998.

Deleuze, G. **Difference and Repetition**, translated by Paul Patton. New York: Columbia University Press, 1995.

Deleuze, G. et al. **The Logic of Sense**. Continuum, 2003.

DeLanda, M. **A Thousand Years of Nonlinear History**. Zone Books, 2000.

DeLanda, M. **Deleuze and the Open-ended Becoming of the World**, essay was given as a lecture on the Conference: 'Chaos/ Control: Complexity', [online] ZiF Bielefeld June 27th, 1998. Available from http://www.diss.sense.uni-konstanz.de/virtualitaet/ delanda.htm.

Foucault, M. 'Other Spaces', in: **Lotus International**, 48/49. Milan: Gruppo Electa spa.

Global Brain, The. DVD short film. Directed by Chris Hall. Based on the book **The Global Brain** by Peter Russell. Global Brain Inc, 1995.

Harvey, D. **Spaces of Hope**. Berkley CA: University of California Press, 2000.

Harvey, D. **Justice, Nature & the Geography of Difference,** Blackwell Publishers, 1996.

Heidegger, M. **The Essence of Truth: On Plato's Cave Allegory and Theaetetus,** Continuum, 2002.

Jacobs, J. **The Economy of Cities,** Vintage Books, 1969.

Koyaanisqatsi – Life Out of Balance. DVD Documentary. Directed by Godfrey Reggio. Santa Fé: Institute for Regional Education, 2002.

Koyaanisqatsi – Life out of balance. Koyaanisqatsi [online]. Available from: http://www.koyaanisqatsi.org [Accessed March 15, 2006].

Lefebvre, H. **The Urban Revolution**, translated by Robert Bononno. University of Minnesota Press, 2003.

Lefebvre, H. **The Production of Space**, trans. Donald Nicholson-Smith. Blackwell Publishers, 2001.

Merleau-Ponty, M. **Phenomenology of Perception**, translated by Colin Smith. Routledge Classics, 2002.

Mol, A. **The Body Multiple: Ontology in Medical Practice**. Durham: Duke UP, 2003.

Read, S. 'The Urban Image – Becoming Visible,' in: **The Body in Architecture**, edited by D. Hauptmann. Rotterdam: 010 Publishers, 2006.

Pinilla, C. & Read, S. A. (eds) **Visualizing the Invisible: Towards an Urban Space**. Amsterdam: Techne Press, 2006.

Sassen S. **The Global City: New York, London, Tokyo,** Princeton University Press, 2001.

Sennett, R. **The Fall of Public Man,** W.W. Norton & Company, Inc, 1974.

Soja, E. W. **Thirdspace: Journey to Los Angeles and Other Real-and-Imagined Places**, Blackwell Publishers Inc, 1996.

Vollebregt, A. G. **De[sign]ing Thirdspace**, lecture given as part of the Urban Body studio. February 15, 2005. Spacelab, Delft University of Technology.

Vollebregt, A. G. 'Hidden Places, Hidden Powers', in **Visualizing the Invisible: Towards an Urban Space**, Read, S. & Pinilla, C. (eds), Amsterdam: Techne Press, 2006.

Vollebregt, A. G. **Spatial Instruments in an Age of Transforming Spatial Logics**, paper presented and published as part of the **5th Space Syntax Symposium**, Van Nes, A. (ed.) Delft University of Technology. June 2005. Amsterdam: Techne Press, 2005.

Urban Field

[1]

Public Space
Transactive
Movement
Interactive
Communication
(ProActive)
Lived
(Virtual)
Form
Texture
Conceived
(Real)

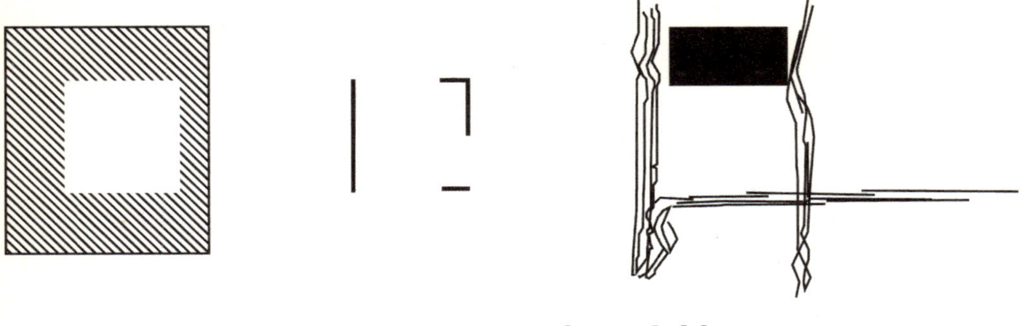

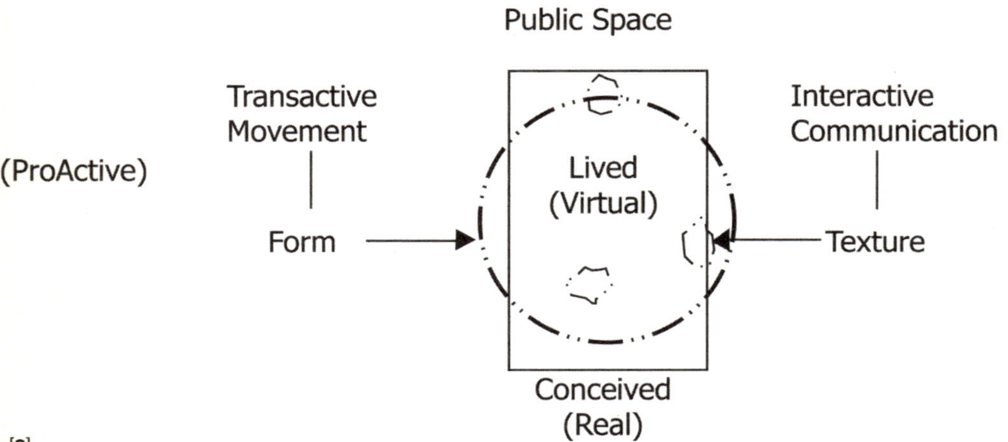

[2]

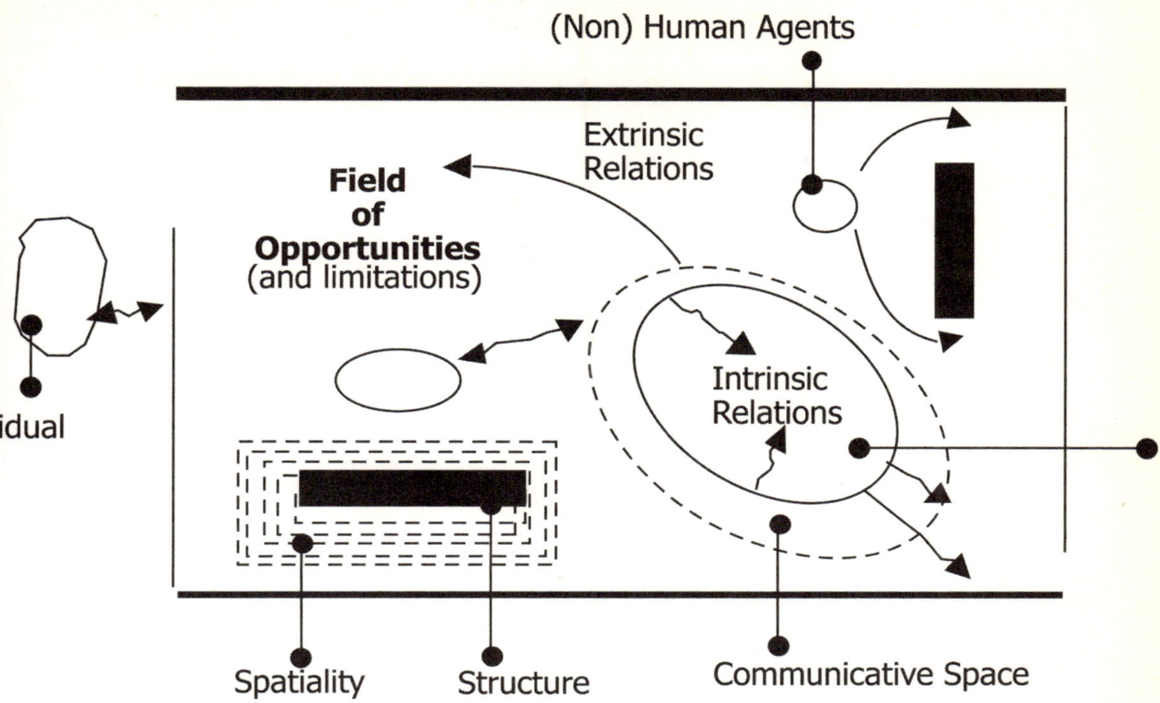

1 4 squares. Source: **De[sign]ing Thirdspace** (2005).
2 An Urban Field Diagram. Source: **De[sign]ing Thirdspace** (2005).
3 Spatial Relations Diagram. Source: **De[sign]ing Thirdspace** (2005).

Critical Hybridization – ‘No Place like Home’

Viktor Kittlausz

Transformations of Place and Space As analysed by quite some scholars the development and application of new information and communication technologies play a fundamental role in the restructuring process of capitalism since the late 1960's. They have contributed to an acceleration and globalization of the economy and an increase in the circulation of a plurality of symbolic codes. Telecommunication networks allow the management of highly differentiated units of social practice which are distributed around the globe in the course of international division of labour. Each of these units is focusing on very small aspects of a production process and needs to be re-integrated into larger functional systems. Thus the complexity of today's social practice has increased immensely and produces many unwanted side-effects. It calls for an actualization of the ways the boundary conditions of social practice are negotiated. The social and spatial consequences of these developments are considerable.

In the process of modernization the knowledge of everyday experience is increasingly infiltrated by media, which enlarge the horizons of temporal and spatial relations and at the same time increase the need for mediation; what arises is the demand to integrate experiences made through media into the practice of everyday life, which is furthermore mainly situated at places. For the following considerations this is an important observation, so let's take a brief look on some aspects of what is meant by place here.

Places can be considered as circumscribable spaces which are saturated with experiences and memories, whereas space can be seen as a category, which points to the openness of the spatial horizon with all its potential for movement and projections of expectation and anxiety.[1] Place can be regarded as a dimension of experience in and with the body. This experience is nurtured by the individual perception of oneself and of the environment. Place attains a special meaning in one's own experience by representing a structure to which one habitually refers to physically and in communication. It represents one part of a configuration of objects within a greater spatial structure. Place is a lived space because it is integrated in relatively solid biographically certain arrangements of experience and knowledge. It is generated continuously anew in everyday practice through interaction and communication. Places get recognizable through objects (houses etc.) and people, which we encounter again and again at certain places.

The sociological concept of space worked out by Martina Löw[2] refers to the mutual relation between production and appropriation of space. Löw describes space as a relational order of social goods and people. Space is constituted through practice as a relational order which itself structures practice. Löw distinguishes analytically two processes: 'Spacing' and 'synthesis' which are both at the same time involved in the practice of spatial constitution. The relational order of space is based on placings of social goods and people; placings are always carried out in relation to other placings. In the performance of synthesis this order is realized and appropriated. Spacing thus refers to placing goods and people, placing buildings, streets etc., but also to placing primarily

1 **cf.** Müller and Dröge (2005).
2 **cf.** Löw (2001).

symbolic markings to make ensembles of goods and people recognizable as such. And if a man straightens up in front of another one, this can be regarded as a spacing-process as well as connecting computers to networks to form informational spaces. The concept of synthesis points to the processes of synthesizing spatial configurations through relating perceptions, ideas and memories.
Löw differentiates analytically between three forms of synthesis: a synthesis in perception, in memory and in abstraction, though these hardly appear in pure form in the everyday practice. Concerning place, in perception the different features of a space are connected to a familiar structure of order and lead to the formation of a place which doesn't have to be questioned and thus eases the task of orientation and finding stability. The familiarity of the place is supported by the collection of experiences with this place which are condensed in memories and as such influence the constitution of space in general. By abstract ideas which are expressed, for example, by objects on a sheet of paper, or, the monitor of a computer spatial practice is considered and orientated without leading necessarily to concrete placings. The city in its totality is a rather abstract space which is too overly complex to be comprehended at once. Rather its complexity is reduced by dividing it up in a net of more or less familiar places. Through experience space forms itself by the combination and configuration of the places which are in everyday practice experienced one after another and as such subdivide the simultaneity of all the different processes which constitute space. The knitted order of places offers prospects of this space and establishes a more or less reliable order. The dis-simultaneity of the different perspectives reduces subjectively the complexity of city space and breaks it down into an order determined by preference. Through this the habits of the individuals are stabilized and installed into a 'sub cultural' system of experience and knowledge.[3]
In the formation of places, as much as in the formation of ideas of space, knowledge gained through experience plays a vital role, and this knowledge is nowadays to a considerable extent gained through the use of media. That is why there is a need to re-consider sociological concepts which try to grasp the role of place in the reproduction of society, like Bourdieu's concept of 'habitus'.
In Bourdieu's conception the forming of habitus is tightly connected to a place based life-world, which accounts for its stability by providing a stable set of structures that determines 'the range of practices available, or not available' for individuals as well as the space for improvisation.[4] Nick Couldry proposes to re-formulate the concept to account for the increasing role of media communication in the processes of identity building and social reproduction. Today media plays a vital role in the formation of trans-local 'virtual' forms of habitus, which might get in conflict with other forms of habitual uses more related to place-based practices like in the family.
Facing the spatial transformations enhanced by the possibilities of global communication-networks it points to the difficult task of reconquering a feeling for

one's own location as well as to construct and reconstruct marks of orientation. Questions are raised as to how the complexity can be reduced, while becoming at the same time aware of effects which are negotiated at faraway places, and how individual and collective competences can be developed in responding to the new demands. In attempting to face these demands media themselves are becoming more and more important in productively mediating the difference between the presence at places and the dimension of space, which reaches into the unknown.

Critical Hybridity Through the possibilities of electronic media formerly separate areas are related and the connection between the concrete place and the 'place' of social relations is loosened. In this regard Marc Augé talks about a crisis in the thinking of space which offers reason for concern and hope at the same time. The excessive consumption of space through media is associated with an individualization of relating to spaces. However, at the same time it can also be accompanied by a reduction of the concrete space of everyday life or the effective spaces. This is painfully true for those who are jammed in refugee camps or settlements and slums in the outskirts. The gap between the variety of the represented spaces, the increase in spatial relations, and the narrowness of the individually available and effective spaces grows. Particularly the metropolitan areas are filled with people who are disembedded from their regions of origin and with symbols from all corners of the world. The 'uprooted' must try to design for themselves a life with the material and symbolic means and social connections which they find in the new environments. They are much more dependent on relating to other people with a similar cultural background and to uphold far distant connections to their regions of origin in order to sustain cultural programs.

The processes of cultural transformation hinted at here are accompanied by changes which might be – failing a better term – characterized as processes of hybridization. Without striving for a 'tight definition' of the term I will point out a few more aspects of the processes and relations it might refer to and which have effects on the ways spaces are constituted. Hybridization points to the transgression of territorial boundaries which used to be – and in quite many regions still are – considered a precondition for a distinctive culture which can establish and reproduce a coherent identity different to others. The frameworks of making sense of oneself, of the world and one's place in the world, of the processes of identity building have changed profoundly.

In the course of modernization culture becomes reflexive, its programs and sets of relations aren't perpetuated by tradition any more without being questioned. Especially media and mobility have contributed to an acceleration of cross-cultural exchange and processes of cultural mixture and thus to the development of new hybrid forms of culture as well as to an urge for 'clear' distinctions and 'pure traditions'. Different cultural practices from different regions all over the world are brought into comparison and thus can no longer claim to carry ultimate and universal

3 cf. Dröge (2000).
4 cf. Couldry (2005).

truth. Furthermore the tight connections between places and cultural programs, between the borders of a nation and its culture are loosened and give way to circulations and mixtures of different symbolic codes and cultural expressions across borders. But increasing mediatization of experiences, through which we structure our views of the world and ourselves, doesn't mean the dissolution of any culture, but rather, brings forth the possibility *and* need to reflect on it critically; culture becomes a task *and* responsibility of the individual and collective construction.

In the process of symbolic codes circulating and reaching far distant places, the places themselves have undergone profound changes through the accelerated mobility of certain groups of people in processes of migration, in tourism and business travel. Processes of cultural transformation which are characterized by the ambivalence of fixity and movements of people, goods and images, by continuity and profound changes and the accompanied increasing confrontation of cultural differences might be considered as 'hybrid'. Hybridity has nothing to do with biological and essentialist connotations here, rather it points to processes of cultural mixture and to the possibilities of relating to different trans-local cultural programs in the process of identity building. The rich reservoir of anxieties attached to the foreign and alien is one of the main problems which arises out of the tension between the task of identity building and conditions of cultural mixture. The term hybridity can emphasise the difference between neutralizing cultural difference by the dominant host culture and bringing cultural differences into a reflexive process of co-constitution.[5] The latter could be enhanced by offering possibilities for the continuation of different cultural backgrounds *and* communication and exchange of differences.

As concrete physical spaces are penetrated with pictures of the media, with data layers which allow far distant relations, new media allow the immersion into 'virtual' spaces leaving the body behind at its location while the mind wanders off. This too leads to new mixtures of spatial qualities and impose new demands on our perception; they ask for the development of new ideas of space. Mixtures of different symbolic systems in space surely aren't a new appearance and as the urban space could in general be considered as a 'hybrid space', the term 'hybridity' addresses the actual forms and trends of an amplified intermixing of different spatial layers and layers of actions which can reach far beyond the places where they are triggered. It is quite obvious that the use of mobile telecommunications affects the production of and the proceedings in 'public' spaces. It is less obvious how major moves in currency assessments – which are steered through means of telecommunications in real time – have effects on the associated economies and particularly on the people who try to earn their living in these economies.

Hybrid spaces can thus also be characterized as spaces in which quite a variety of

different systems of signs and symbols are coming together, intermix and configure spaces which are tied into complex expert systems. Related to this intermixing are the new possibilities of computation as they are intensely applied in the wide usage of digital images. Here, not only different 'worlds' are easily combined without leaving traces of the different heritages of the used 'visual material', but also the borders between 'existing' and imagined dimensions are blurred. These digital images can change in time and thus point to the artificiality of permanence.
The presentation of spaces on electronic screens or projection surfaces confronts the perception with new demands which have consequences for the constitution of space. For the individual perception this means there is a variety of more or less familiar elements in different forms of media simultaneously present in space which all 'ask' for attention. At the same time there are also quite a few effects of far distant activities present at places which are not visible and to which most individuals cannot respond, even though they might be affected by them.

In the processes, only hinted at here, different value systems, cultural forms and programs, and cultural differences are questioned and become 'critically' reflexive. Cultural differences can be reconsidered out of a certain distance to the dominant cultural 'attractors' (traditions) and are thus sliding into a situation of comparison which might challenge their further function as reference for orientation and commitment. All these aspects have – in not yet clearly conceivable ways – affects on the processes of constituting space in which concrete, media and mental spaces are interrelated.
The processes of cultural transformation referred to here with the term 'hybridization' are characterized by a general exposure to uncertainty. With the wide range of differences coming together arises a 'critical' potential which is in itself ambivalent. It is critical in the sense of threatening unquestioned traditions. At the same time it is critical in offering mixtures of cultural forms and practices as well as new possibilities to switch perspectives out of which new cultural programs may emerge. The expression 'critical hybridity' acknowledges that difference is always already right there to invite or circumvent a conversation. It points out that the condition of hybridity is marked by the need to construct individually and collectively flexible cultural programs for orientation and commitment which are configured around 'stable' (as opposed to static) sets of priorities – cultural, ecological, economic etc. In the following I will briefly point – on a general level – to three ambivalent 'critical' dimensions of actual processes of hybridization.
One 'critical' dimension can be seen in how the actual processes of hybridization affect the realms of individual and collective *knowledge*. Concerning the new possibilities of the digital and telecommunication media, what can be observed is an increase in the variety of communicative offers and in the variety of media through which these can be obtained. This development is simultaneously connected with a new formability of the communicative environments. Out of

5 cf. Papastergiadis (2005).

the perspective of the user all the new and old audio-visual media develop into one electronically mediated communication space which seems to be global. With the merging of until now separate communication channels on the one hand new communication possibilities arise. On the other hand considerable orientation problems are coming up. Particularly the problem of being able to assess the relevance of information, and this can lead to a general reliability problem. The reliability of information gets – in tendency – weakened still further by an increasing economization of the communicative offers and by a functionalizing of the users to receivers of advertising messages.[6]

These rapid transformations are highly ambivalent and bring about changes concerning the connectivity of communicative processes and the knowledge, expectations and conventions involved. As with the increase of knowledge the quantity of what is unknown seems to increase as well – which leads to a general condition of uncertainty; the diversification and multiplication of media offers contribute to the mentioned de-stabilization of tradition and an increase in the possibilities of interrelating and crossing over elements of different cultural programs. Quite a lot of information about different cultural and social backgrounds is available through media coverage and can be obtained and thus will influence what is seen and what remains invisible. It can, but doesn't necessarily, contribute to reduce the anxieties often attached to the unknown other. But it will not be possible to gain knowledge concerning all the offers of cultural difference one is confronted with. This may be due to the sheer quantity of offers, to conditions of life or personal capabilities. Still, in order to productively cope with the immense reservoirs of information available non-exclusive systems of access and support as well as barrier-free cross-cultural translations become more important.

Another 'critical' dimension concerns the rather *emotional and aesthetic dimensions* of experiencing differences. The coming together of a plurality of differences is quite typical for the life in big cities. Here one gets accustomed to others, to strangers, without necessarily gaining knowledge about them, at least not in the sense of knowledge which could be written down and appropriated through re-construction. It concerns a 'knowledge' which is acquired less consciously and without bringing it on certain terms, but which is still relevant in the continuous processes of identity building and orientation in everyday affairs. In media communication such aesthetic aspects play a central role in offering materials, symbolic codes and patterns for the processes of individual and collective world making. In media spaces an increase in mixing of entertainment and information can be observed which can be read as an attempt to reduce social complexity. Furthermore it can be read as a reference to the general trend of an aesthetization of information and an 'informatization' of the aesthetic. What can be noticed in this, is that the aesthetical perception and aesthetic consciousness play a significant role in our knowledge oriented reflection of ourselves and

the world, and the other way round, the aesthetic dimension carries 'knowledge' about things, people and their relations to each other. It provides marks of orientation, which we rely on in everyday practice, even though not necessarily consciously. The interrelation of cognitive, aesthetic and emotional aspects in reflecting oneself and the world needs further investigation to enhance the development of abilities in reading what is set in scene in more or less intentional ways of affection. Next to freely accessible systems of knowledge, instruments of support are required for the translation of different cultural programs through aesthetic means, which provide different approaches in the exploration of an overly complex world.
Yet another 'critical' dimension concerns the *motivations and aims* which play such a vital role in orientation, in reading and responding to the given and presented. It points to the 'complicated' relation between us, our perceiving and acting and the things around us. It can also point to the involvement of our imagination and 'mental spaces' in perception and in the constitution of the social worlds and at the same time to the involvement of the things in what we see know and do. As mentioned before the mixing of formerly separate aspects can be accompanied by problems of orientation and at the same time by the emergence of new perspectives on things as well as changes *in* motivations and aims since alternatives and new possibilities are coming into view.

Processes of Mediatization Central for the communication and prolongation of any cultural form and program are media. Even though there might be a wide consensus about the end of the 'grand narratives', the processes of making sense continue on all levels of social practice. In this, cultural programs, media and social practice are inseparably interrelated. Media understood in a wide sense of meaning here as 'materials' useable in reliably communicative processes are needed for an implementation and the continuation of cultural programs, which again need to be applied by a living culture to enfold their capabilities of orientation and connectivity. If we consider the culture of a society (which is actually just a very crude construct which refers to a very complex field of cultural practices and differences) we might talk of cultural (symbolic) codes and programs which are applied in order to interpret semantically the socially constructed worldviews and to correlate emotional attachments and overall aims related to these views.[7] In differentiated societies there are different sets of cultural programs, like the culture of arts, religion, knowledge, economy etc., which together make up 'the' culture of 'a' society. Each of these programs can operate quite autonomously and might even gain such an importance that the cultural system as a whole is threatened (for example if religious or economic programs become more and more dominant to occupy other social fields, like the legal system and politics).
As Siegfried J. Schmidt, to whom I loosely relate here, points out, when the cultural programs are applied they tend to be hardly changeable while they are adaptable in the long run. When applied they are characterized by blind spots, which are the prerequisite for them to appear as

6 cf. Krotz (2001).
7 cf. Schmidt (1997).

the natural course of action and thus can ease the always precarious process of individual and collective identity building. In order to enfold their capabilities of orientation and connectivity they rely on being continuously applied and implemented and for this, media are fundamental. Media are thus characterized here as basic ingredients in processes of communication and of observing society, as ingredients which are used to apply cultural programs in order to allow their function as elements of orientation and connectivity. But what happens when the diversification of media and the accompanied possibilities of connecting and re-presenting what is far away in time and space bring the media of cultural communication in a process of drifting by themselves (as hinted at above with respect to the new formability of the communicative environments which bring about questions concerning the reliability of their contents)? One side effect of this process of cultural transformation is the rise of cultural anxieties and tendencies of setting up rigid frames of re-adoptions of supposedly pure traditions. These more general remarks concerning the mutual relation of cultural programs, media and social practice have to be completed with less obvious interrelations which are the unquestioned preconditions of the functioning of 'advanced' societies as well. As systematization and embodiment of knowledge, expertise and wishes technology (architecture and technical media can be – in some regards – subsumed here) is decisively involved in our everyday practice. It can thus be considered as a medium of our relations to the world and ourselves. In nearly everything we do we are tied into or connected to socio-technical expert systems. These far reaching systems regulate the glocal processes of exchange, they bring relief and convenience for quite a large number of people. At the same time they perpetuate negative side-effects which are the unaccepted prerequisites of everyday action. Even though individuals and groups refer only sporadically directly to experts, the knowledge stored in expert systems and things has an effect constantly on most areas of everyday action. Anthony Giddens indicates that the central importance of expert systems for our everyday life is on our part not necessarily accompanied by a closer knowledge of these systems and that we must built up confidence in them. Only through this we can obtain the relief we strive for by inventing technology and expertise in the first place.

Modern institutions are fundamentally connected to mechanisms of confidence in abstract systems. The possibilities to technologically bridge large distances rest on such institutionalized relations. In societies in which social relations aren't reproduced through a set of firm traditions, this confidence must be partially produced actively. The process of socio-technical arrangement is accompanied by tensions and breaks and requires corresponding mechanisms of mediation; active confidence in the sense of Giddens is an important one of them. However, at the same time a lot of tensions remain and circulate through the late modern world in form of risks for individuals, for groupings and regions, especially if confidence towards certain things is propagated by some interests which are not shared by others, as in the case of nuclear power.

About seventy years ago in his book *The Public and Its Problems* the pragmatist philosopher John Dewey pointed to the indirect consequences which arise from such entanglements and to the need for public debate and political processing of these developments. Dewey turned to the question, how to become aware of the indirect side effects of social action to be able to evaluate it and to bring it in tune with the needs and interests of the people who are affected by this social activity. Since the persons affected are for the most part not in direct contact with the acting persons, intermediary layers and networks are required. Through these – and that is what Dewey was aiming at as well – an exchange could be made possible between sciences and everyday practice. For this a change in the academic life would be required, though. The application of science in the life world would presuppose that it would be acquired and communicated by and in the broader public realm. As the precondition for the existence of a true and effective public this again would require to use science to find out how to do this. We could ask why not study the mechanisms and structures more thoroughly which prevent the public from becoming a participative public.

Dewey stresses the point that (social and other) sciences need to continuously examine the processes in society in order to deliver the material which is needed to built up an informed and durable opinion in public matters. Taking the variety of social, cultural and cognitive preconditions into account, Dewey demands the education of an 'art of communication' which should be of central importance in the process of social mediation, in order to develop democracy as a social 'design principle' by its continuous cultivation as a social life-form. How can publics train themselves for democratic culture in an art of communication about public matters, which bear indirect consequences for social practice? What instruments and systems can science and practices of experts deliver to bring this process on the way more informed more democratically? As indicated with the short sketch of the relation between culture and media above, we can on a very general level say, this would need a cultivation of democratic cultural programs, using media in order to continuously remember to apply these programs.

With regard to the omnipresence and 'power' of socio-technical systems one of the central problems concerns how we can respond to the claims of these systems and how to respond to their unintended side effects. From this can be derived the necessity to work out a critical distance towards the 'practical constraints' produced by the claims of technical systems, to open up a space for a social reflection of the developments and to negotiate the preferences which are carried on silently in systems and artefacts.

Affairs of Attention Attention is the prelude in the construction of memory. Through discipline attention can be raised to a 'higher level of concentration' and can take the form of a wilful and long-term orientation. According to Aleida Assmann, in the attempts to master the information currents there are signs that indicate a tearing apart of the connection between getting alert and building up memory. In times of huge quantities of fast circulating information in the media it is hardly possible to condense attention to memory. What is needed today, are techniques of very quick and specific access to information and of reacting presently on selective attractions in the process of clicking through data configurations.[8]

When something unexpected happens quite often a change in perspective is associated.

Becoming alert in the light of the unexpected can be referred to by distinguishing two dimensions which Georg Franck uses in his considerations to an 'economy of attention'. Franck draws on the distinction between 'awareness' and 'attention'. He emphasizes the difference between the condition of an 'awake attentiveness' and a 'focused attention'.[9] Awake attentiveness is considered to be an intransitive condition, a feeling of one's own existence, a noticing, a feeling that there is something rather than nothing. On the other hand, in a state of focused attention an object is intensely addressed while other perceptions and thoughts are dimmed out. In the attention of everyday practice both qualities are combined with different weightings depending on the situation.

Attention appears to be a scarce good which in connection with the chase of the media for our eyes and ears can only be distributed but not increased. Therefore an increase in the supply of media goes along with an increase in the competition for the restricted resource of attention. As Franck points out, the innovative idea that turned publication media into mass media was the idea to give the audience information to get their attention. The new digital simulation techniques contribute to the overall tendency that an increasing and substantial part of reality is specifically created in order to attract attention. The quantity of attention which a person or an object gathers stands in proportion to the subjective ascription as reality. The subjective impression becomes socially objective as soon as it manifests itself in considerable numbers of subjects and is communicated between these.

The electronic media are often considered as a system of social self-observation, in which everything can be presented and brought to comparison. This observation points to the novelty of the (interactive) electronic media in comparison to the rather fixed sets of meaning delivered by myth, religion or by the 'invisible hand' of the free market as the virtual centers for getting rid of the paradoxes of social practice. But in media practice a huge number of topics and especially continuous practices of critique are structurally excluded from the media-spaces, while the living attention of the users is absorbed by the diversity of offers. This

is because most media are fundamentally relying on private economic systems or are under control of power holding institutions and thus are not able to criticize their fundaments. Under these conditions – even though the scope of offers is widened – it is hardly astonishing, that not all topics get a lasting place in the 'spaces of media'. What achieves public attention through the mass media doesn't necessarily correspond to the problems modern societies are faced with and which would need much more continuous attention to be worked on. Due to the continuous work of a large number of activists of so called social movements, some of the excluded topics and severe problems of today's societies can temporarily gain attention just be swallowed by the next advertisement.
The question raised is which topics can gain social attention and which not? And who decides about the selection? And these are quite fundamental questions considering the principal limitedness of attention available. Informational and entertainment offers in the media deliver material for communication, agreement forming as well as models of individual and collective (political) identity. They provide a space for society in which the inventory of collectively shared ideas, values, operative norms and meaning is staged and witnessed newly again and again. Media content thus functions as a consolidation of the social and cultural status quo. But media have a potential to point their attention to the severe problems of society and the possibilities for change informatively and emotively. What is vitally missing is an independent subsystem of media which can provide the public space for a continuous critical reflection of the social.

Turning to the subjective side of attention the considerations of Aleida Assmann[10] to what she calls an 'aesthetic attention' are very informative. Assmann distinguishes two basic 'roots of attention' from which other forms can be derived. The first form, as strategic attention, is concerned with the mastering of everyday practice and organizes the safeguarding and validity of the person. The second form, as transcending attention, strives for an increase in perception, for interpretation and new knowledge and meaning. Assmann holds the thesis, that the splitting of the attention in these two forms is basic to human existence and that neither of the two forms can be subordinated. The strategic form of the attention is always activated, where danger and profit is around, where there are matters of power and success involved. Two needs are at the root of the strategic attention: the need for safety and the striving for visibility. It focuses on techniques of self authorization, by risk mastering or self-portrayal.
When the transcendent attention opens itself to the horizon of the 'alien' and the 'stranger', this presupposes, that the work of the strategic attention is already, at least partly, done. Again there can be distinguished two forms: In its philosophical form transcendent attention is astonished about the things around and leads to finding new things and, driven intellectually, to gaining knowledge, to criticism and scepticism. However, it is always only a temporary condition as

8 cf. Assmann (2003).
9 cf. Franck (1998).
10 Assmann (2001).

such. The astonishment consolidates at first in the religious dimension of the transcendent attention, in techniques of prayers and meditative contemplation. According to Assmann younger forms of attention, the ethical and the aesthetic attention can be derived from the basic forms. In the ethical attention the longing for self-portrayal and exposition of the strategic attention is turning to others. The aesthetic attention on the other hand is derived from the practice of religious prayers. Like religious attention it draws its transcending strength out of a competence to switch perception from daily affairs to the unusual, from the empirical to the mental, from the ordinary to the extraordinary, from the abstract to the sensual, from the useful to the meaningful.[11]

This brief survey of aspects of today's conditions of attention, of becoming alert and to build up memory points towards a set of problems and contradictions. As mentioned before the need arises to build up temporarily a distance to the never stopping activity of everyday social practice. This is to be able to reflect and evaluate what side effects are generated and where the social practice seems to head to. The building up of memories for necessary changes and for what we are aiming at becomes a task, as well as to question which priorities we have been setting up in the past in order to re-consider the aims of yesterday which of course might still – e.g. in expert-systems, artefacts and images of social development – be active and effective, even though we wouldn't want to set them up anew. Space and time is needed for considering the overall parameters which are applied in the frameworks of social practice and which are – in tendency – marked as 'natural ones' by the interests which profit most if everything goes on as it is.

'Virtual Places' The oxymoron 'virtual reality' can indicate that reality embraces virtuality, that in reality there is always virtuality too. The notion of the 'virtual' as introduced by Charles Sanders Peirce seems to be quite illuminating here. To Peirce a virtual x isn't an x, however it has 'the efficiency (virtus)' of an X. Picking up Peirce's thought here, virtual objects can be distinguished from potential objects, which have the same 'nature' as a certain object but, as one could say, don't bring about a certain 'effect' in a certain context, even if they potentially could do so. For example, different persons of comparable qualification have the potential to take up an advertised management job, but only one person will actually do the job. By contrast, a scarecrow could be considered as a 'virtual' person who acts in the field and is able to keep birds away more or less effectively. In his philosophy of mind, Peirce points out, thoughts develop meaning and get 'effective' only in relation to other thoughts. No present actual thought has any meaning, any intellectual value by itself. The value lies not in what is actually thought, but in what this thought may be connected with in representation by subsequent thoughts. Thus the meaning of a thought is something virtual. Cognition or representation doesn't arise out of a

single state of mind, rather it results out of the relation of different states of mind.[12]
If one relates loosely to Peirce's notion of the 'virtual', as one aspect of what the term 'virtual' might refer to, the 'virtuality' of thoughts, ideas and of artefacts can be taken into account as well as the interrelatedness of different mental and physical aspects. By emphasizing the idea of the 'efficiency (virtus)' of virtual objects, and ideas which can have similar 'effects' like comparable real objects, it will be possible to view and explore virtual and real realities departing from one ground. At the same time it becomes recognizable that time is not only linear, but can somehow change direction, e.g. in anticipation and in wishing. The activity of anticipation in everyday practice happens for the most of the time unconsidered. Activities and prospects, the wishes, worries and anxieties we cast out and to which we respond, so to speak, come back to our presence from the future; as much as experiences from the past stain our present perceptions. As possible future scenarios our ideas of the future form a part of our orientation framework which is effective, without being actual. This applies in the context of everyday worldly practice just as in outlines of life prospects. These 'virtualities' are in principle open for change and other courses, but they are nevertheless – in their present situational configuration – effectively playing a role in our present actions, thoughts, feelings and judgments.

According to the philosopher Helmut Plessner, man holds a utopian position, which is at the same time without a bottom and in which he is exposed to the question of being: Why is there something rather than nothing? We are not able to look down to the bottom of being clearly (Unergründlichkeit); thoughts *in* which we think are not transparent to us. This calls the undisposable 'rest' (Unverfügbarkeit) into mind. Plessner points to a conception of the subject which takes the instability of the human constitution into account. In it, the center is characterized by an open space, or a 'place' without a fixable location, bringing about the movement of the self, which reflects itself through the relation to others. At the same time this doesn't start a process of a complete dissolution of the subject. It rather points to the constant task of building, deconstruction and re-building individual and social identities and worldviews. The eccentric situation of the subject marks a space in a field of co-relations which, in its unrest, is open to occupations through the common constructions of values, norms, wishes and promises. The possible identification of each with something, what one is not by himself, refers to a restless longing as one aspect of the 'eccentric position', which makes processes of identification possible in the first place. At the same time, this position raises a demand for identification, and therefore we need to look in the outside world for answers.
We are, one could say, without a fixed location and thus have to find and construct places in space, which makes us susceptible to pre-figured meaning offers, which bring us relief from this task and responsibility. At the same time the symbolic-medial form of human organization (the

11 ibid.
12 cf. Skagestad (2006).

way we get together) is basically marked by a tension between the establishment of places and a constant drive to exceed and rework the environment through social interaction or to find and configure new ones. Considering this precondition, the search for an accommodation, the attempts to establish in the outside world, can also be understood as attempts to stabilize the interior. In this process the accounts from the environment and the productive mastering of these accounts are to be mediated constantly. The appearances of the outside are used as material in the generation of identity and meaning to bring about a coherent story *of* and *to* oneself and the world.

Everyday practice is characterized by movement through different places and spaces more or less familiar and more or less concrete (as one 'moves' through spaces presented via media or uses the ability to follow one's own imagination). In this, all sorts of things speak to us, and to some of the potentially unlimited number of offers we respond. We respond more or less consciously, more or less attentive; it is quite helpful that our unconscious archives of experiences manage the processing of most of the proposals without us taking notice of it. In these *inner* archives the accumulated experiences of the past and the imaginations thrown towards the future are stored. In these archives quite a variety of attractors are active, their interplay and quantities changing from situation to situation and of course there are hidden agendas which structure the ways how and to what we respond, when we need to raise our attention, and when we can habitually solve what we are asked for. In our more or less unconscious archives of experiences we carry condensations of time through space (or it's the other way round). These condensations of experiences structure our actual experiences, but don't determine our responses in an absolute sense. Between proposal and response there is an un-closable gap (that is what Plessner's notion of the 'excentric position' of man points to as well). How these situational gaps and the altogether 'open middle' are furnished, is influenced by a variety of conditions, e.g. subjective cognitive and emotional abilities, accessibility of all sorts of media, bodily or weather conditions, forces present in the surrounding and so on. These conditions have impact on the individual and collective tasks of continuously building and re-building identity by responding to offers in certain situations.

As mentioned before, place as a specific form of space can be considered as a familiar structure saturated with experience. It is a spatial configuration which doesn't have to be questioned and in which orientation is relatively easy. The residential place many would refer to as home is a place which is considered to offer security and ease in the process of world-making. In his 'private space' the resident understands his space as delimitation against the outside and as delimitation of a living quarter at the same time. As Bernhard Waldenfels[13] points out, building doesn't exhaust itself in the making, but grants and offers space. A 'space to move' which stands out because of the difference between inside and outside, which opens up a space for experimentation, for play. Here, the personal experience of everyday requirements, of being moved in a net of different influencing forces is suspended. It gives way for movements of the self in the 'living' space, which offers a space for responding creatively to the claims of life in a different way. This is because a border is drawn which allows us to shut off temporarily the stream of proposals of the outside world; at least 'private' spaces can be used in this way. On the other hand this drawing a border, this shutting off, can lead to an 'alienation' from the actual social conditions and processes outside; the production of 'ignorant spaces' as in the gated communities is an expression of such a retreat. But of course there are more productive and open ways to shape this quite common and real need for a place which grants a space outside the stream of having to function according to the systems of the social process.

Extraordinary experiences might lead to the question of what seems to be natural and thus might open up new perspectives. In order to lead to lasting changes in attitudes, beliefs and practices, time and space is needed to let the extraordinary become an impulse for a continuous re-working of the ordinary. In the 'private' spaces one has possibilities of externalizing one's own process of identity building through the configuration of things, of memories, thoughts and ideas attached to things. These individual *exterior* archives allow a relief from the task of always having to respond or at least to react to the more or less unfamiliar. In this relief lies the possibility of reflecting the experiences, to relate them to the webs of thoughts and feelings, memories and ideas, beliefs and preferences. New orders develop out of existing orders even though they haven't been contained in these before. In this contingency lies the chaotic trace which is part of every order. Orders contain in themselves aspects of the unordered, an in-between which can be described as a movement of reaching beyond the existing order.[14]

The 'private' space has to be considered in its relation to the outside, to other spaces and to the spaces of media as well as to mental spaces of imagination. Spatial qualities only show themselves if the familiar place is connected with a moment of the heterotopic, a somewhere else. Under conditions of today's media private spaces can't be strictly separated from outside influences. Far away realities and imaginations never thought of before creep through the ether into the new fire places. As hinted at above, in the course of increasing trans-local circulation of a large variety of symbolic codes even the 'home base' is increasingly becoming hybridized. This becomes clear if we consider the moral complaints over the 'disruptive role of media' through which cultural patterns, thoughts and ways of behaving are coming into the home which haven't been imaginable before.[15] At the same time the processes of constructing identities and world views relies on mediated communication, which means the materials for this construction work are collected out of spaces which reach far beyond the personal home. Even though possibly concentrated at specific sites, places like home (e.g. residential spaces) can't be reduced to certain

13 Waldenfels (1999).
14 **cf.** Waldenfels (2002).
15 **cf.** Couldry (2005).

locations any more. They might be distributed over quite a number of different places and include symbolic codes, media spaces and mental images. They can be considered as 'bases' in which possibly far reaching relations are integrated into more or less stable configurations; here experiences of different qualities gained through face to face and mediated communication are condensed to form knowledge, memories, wishes and aims. This continuous work of mediating differences and of identity building is of course also done while moving through other spaces, but still, 'places like home' hold special qualities of conditions for this work which are 'virtually present' as sustaining relations even when we are on the move.
As in the constitution of space in general, the condensations of memories play a vital role in the actual perception. But in memory not only real experiences are collected and configured, here impressions of fictional stories and images, one's own imaginations, wishes and anxieties are assimilated as well and stain the individual ways of experiencing the world around. As indicated before, the 'home base' is connected to the individual archives of experience one carries through space in everyday practice. What we consider in this base – the work we do here of more or less consciously relating and integrating different experiences into the backdrop of our past and the imaginations of the futures – belongs to the influences which take part in the constitution of our practice and identity in social space. And still, it is the dialectic of the inside and the outside which provides the productive tension and enhances the critical possibilities of trying to make sense of oneself and the world. Any cultural program – if uprooted or not – needs a space for its reproduction which is to a certain extent 'exclusive'. One opportunity offered by space transcending mediated communication is to loosen up the tight connection between identity and place. Identity building can thus be seen as a task to be worked on continuously and trans-locally, even if many still will claim certain places as the 'authentic' ones for their specific cultural traditions. By accepting the hybrid condition of cultural mixture in many parts of the world, and by not confusing 'bringing cultural differences into a reflexive process of co-constitution' with 'neutralizing cultural difference by a dominant host culture', it comes into view that places *and* other media are needed which allow the reproduction of more or less consciously chosen cultural programs and at the same time provide points of connectivity for communication and exchange with others.

To provisionally come to the end of these essayistic lines I turn to the question raised at the beginning of this text concerning how to conquer again a feeling of ones own position in a global 'space of flows'. But being unable to give an answer I would like to transform it into a task Paul Virilio (1996) pointed to some years ago. According to Virilio the newest developments of digital telecommunication provide an electromagnetic dimension for the imagination, which can be understood as an expansion of space. Architects now would have to build the real space in a way that both the physical and virtual spaces can enter into a correlation with each other. Architecture will have to solve the task, to house the virtual space within its concrete three-dimensionality. For a re-gaining of a sense for one's location in the mediatized world, the new digital communication media (complementing the older ones) provide potentials to conceive the 'home base' in its condition as a 'virtual place', which has its actual grounding in a concrete location – which might change – and is at the same time connected to nets of exchange whose lines reach far into space *and* time.

Above I hinted at three ambivalently 'critical' dimensions of hybridity which can briefly be related to this task, or rather the many tasks contained in it. To unleash the critical potential of the actual conditions of hybridity, on a general level new systems of support are urgently needed, such as systems of support concerning the mediation of knowledge to a wider public in the sense hinted at above with relating to Dewey. To productively cope with the immense reservoirs of information possibly available via media, non-exclusive barrier-free systems of access and support are to be formed. In this regard it has to be considered that the actual media space is marked by structural deficits excluding important concerns and the possibility of fundamental critique. Sustained by science and organizations of consumer protection and social engagement these systems of support could provide knowledge about invisible and visible side-effects of socio-technical expert-systems and operations trigged at faraway places much more 'radically' and continuously. Independent subsystems of publicity are needed to fill the gap in reflecting social developments and to give the excluded their voices. These systems need to be independent of governments and the market and thus rely on public support.

Systems of support concerning more aesthetical and emotional forms of reflexivity and 'knowledge' which contribute to cross-cultural exchange and understanding are urgently needed as well. By using aesthetic means of exploration such cross-cultural translations could contribute to an enhancement of 'emotional and aesthetic knowledge' and understanding. Furthermore it becomes important to develop individually and collectively competences in reading what is set in scene with certain intentions attached to it as well as reading what might be effectively present without being visible. For this Assmann's conception of an aesthetic attention might offer productive points of connection in gaining a competence in 'switching' one's attention.

Since processes of hybridization question aims of the past and the present as well as future scenarios they can not just be reproduced by tradition anymore. Wishes and aims, cultural programs and forms of communication need to be de- and re-constructed individually and collectively on the run. For this, stable but never fixable memorials for being able to continuously and critically work on the priorities and motivations and the visions cast out are required which can function as attractors in the never stopping stream of events. Otherwise we might even forget where we have already passed by and to ask once in a while 'what for'.

Bibliography

Assmann, A., Assmann, J. **Aufmerksamkeiten.** Archäologie der literarischen Kommunikation VII München: Fink, 2001.

Assmann, A. **Druckerpresse und Internet. Auf dem Weg von einer Gedächtniskultur zu einer Kultur der Aufmerksamkeit: Oberfläche, Geschwindigkeit und Supermarkt.** In: Frankfurter Rundschau vom 18.01.2003.

Augé, M. **Die Sinnkrise der Gegenwart.** In: A. Kuhlmann (Hrsg.): Philosophische Ansichten der Kultur der Moderne. Frankfurt am Main: Fischer, 1994. pp 33-47.

Beck, U., Giddens, A., Lash, S. **Reflexive Modernization – Politics, Tradition and Aesthetics in the Modern Social Order.** Oxford, UK: Blackwell Publishers, 1994.

Couldry, N. **Media and the Transformation of the Habitus.** Paper presented at the University of Bremen in 2005.

Dewey, J. **The Public and Its Problems.** Athens: Ohio University Press, 1991.

Dröge, F. **Ort und Raum. Über die Raumkonstruktionen und ihre Vermittlung.** Bremen: Universität Bremen – ZWE, 2000.

Franck, G. **Ökonomie der Aufmerksamkeit – Ein Entwurf.** München, Wien: Hanser, 1998.

Krotz, F. **Die Mediatisierung kommunikativen Handelns. Der Wandel von Alltag und sozialen Beziehungen, Kultur und Gesellschaft durch die Medien.** Wiesbaden: Westdeutscher Verlag, 2001.

Löw, M. **Raumsoziologie.** Frankfurt am Main: Suhrkamp, 2001.

Müller, M., Dröge, F. **Die ausgestellte Stadt. Zur Differenz von Ort und Raum.** Basel, Boston, Berlin: Birkhäuser Verlag, 2005.

Papastergiadis, N. **Hybridity and Ambivalence. Places and Flows in Contemporary Art and Culture.** In: Theory, Culture & Society, Vol.22(4), London, Thousand Oaks, New Delhi: SAGE, 2005. pp. 39-64.

Plessner, H. **Conditio Humana.** In: Golo Mann; Alfred Heuß, Propyläen Weltgeschichte – Eine Universalgeschichte, Band I. Berlin, Frankfurt am Main: Propyläen, 1961.

Skagestad, P. (o.J.): **Peirce, Virtuality, and Semiotic.** Wie bereitgestellt unter: http://www.bu.edu/wcp/Papers/Cogn/CognSkag.htm; 12.01.2006.

Virilio, P. **Im Zeitraum des Trajekts.** Andreas Ruby im Gespräch mit Paul Virilio. In: Der Architekt 3/1996, pp. 171-173.

Waldenfels, B. **Sinnesschwellen.** Studien zur Phänomenologie des Fremden 3. Frankfurt am Main: Suhrkamp, 1999.

Waldenfels, B. **Bruchlinien der Erfahrung: Phänomenologie, Psychoanalyse, Phänomenotechnik.** Frankfurt am Main: Suhrkamp, 2002.

Bio-urbanisms and the problem of form in contemporary urban discourse

Gerhard Bruyns

Thinking form It is difficult to imagine that during the 19th century there once existed a whole debate, within the mathematical discourse dealing with issues around *truth*, *image* and *form*. From two opposing sides of the same proverbial coin, both scientists and mathematicians attempted to prove the validity of mathematical functions, through either the reasons of logic (constructions and equations), or through the reasons of image (seen as form). The philosopher and physicist Henri Poincaré reflected on the role of qualitative and visually directed work in mathematics. Poincaré's attempts to derive principles of motion within solar stability, influenced him to think that all proofs of the mathematical equations had to be visually represented as image, as well as 'equate' within the rules of logic.[1]

Historically speaking, within the development of empirical philosophy – that included notions of thinkers such as Locke, Berkeley and Hume – the issue concerning 'true *Form*' itself remained a central theme. For the empiricists, all theories and hypotheses had to be reflected against observations of the natural world, rather than being based on perceptions or feelings.[2] The essence of *Form*, or what a true *Form* represented, became as it were, trapped between the world as object (seen as knowledge), and the world seen through the lenses and perceptions of the individual that inhabits it.
As a consequence, a whole history of methodological-empirical investigation and scientific debate followed, attempting to prove the relationships between scientific proofs and natural *Form*, as it is observed.[3] [see figure 1]

Discourses such as quantum mechanics,[4] physics, geology, technologies and even art, shifted in perspective and approach to revised methodologies so to address an object of 'Formal' research. Questions concerning *Form* included extreme levels of scales, from an electron level, that shifted from orbital positions, to scales of the celestial systems and planetary motions.[5] The true question surrounding all of this, was not to separate entities of *Form* or any of its 'inherent' logics, rather, it proposed an alternative search into the established links between the principle of formation[6] and the ruling logic that linked [as subsidiary] logics, the images, and its truths into a coherent whole.

It is clear, that within recent times and its available technologies, as well as in an ever widening scientific debate, the quest for establishing any truths of *Form*, is still ongoing.
Sociology, as an example, labours at clarifying a current social *Form* and its supporting structures, as it is *in-formed*, through certain forces such as global economies, ethnicities, demographic compositions and street level interactions.
Theories such as the *Actor Network Theory (ANT)*, developed by Bruno Latour,[7] seek out forma-

1 Galison (2002) p. 301.
2 Robinson (2004).
3 Healy (2005).
4 Galison (2002) p. 306.
5 **ibid.**, p. 306.
6 See Rupert Sheldrake's, 'Hypothesis of Formative Causation on Morphicfields and Morphogenes', in **New Science of Life**.
7 Latour (2005).

tions and formal arrangements of the social level by way of the social distributions, organizational, scientific and technological structures.[8] ANT incorporates processes and events, onto a 'complete social' form, by way of the actors, the 'operative' networks in place, as well as principle theories that drive the objects as encountered in daily life.[9] As an example, Latour established the social formations at the neighbourhood level, whilst reading it against a variety of external phenomena, such as mobility, demographic compositions and economic markets. His '*Paris Invisible City*' project renders invisible processes of the social, visible, as an activity of semantically 'de-signing' of the social form and the urban context.[10] [see figure 2]

In contrast to the discourse of sociology, quantum physics still remains fixated on establishing the absolute building block of the world, or the universe for that matter.[11] The proposed Newtonian mechanistic view of the universe in which the world was demarcated into two basic components of the objects and empty space, was inverted by the introductions of the wave and particle notions of matter. *Object-space theories* expressed the world as solid object surrounded by empty space at all scale levels. In contrast, Rutherford's and Heisenberg's experiments demonstrated the basis of wave and particle theories, that had confirmed that the very 'object' or unitary 'solid' matter of the world, did not act like solids, but mere abstractions, in wave like formations.[12] As a result, new proposals where made for altered concepts to 'fundamental principles of the world', such as 'super'-space or wormholes, as well as attempts in pinning down a true formal construction of the 'shape' of time.

Closer to home, for architecture and urbanism itself, the question around *Form* and its relations is still undecided. We question current urban forms, shapes and space, in relation to architectural and urban technological application, seen as design interventions to change, alter and shape architecture, space and the city. Furthermore, specific urban perspectives seek clarity and definitions of the current urban space, and devices as operative frameworks through which to interpret these logics of *Form*. Stefano Boeri, has in recent publications highlighted an encompassing multiplicity of the urban, in sets of comparisons between [1] spaces of the city with [2] other aspects such as: the urban and territorial shape, urban processes of economy, movement and demographic compositions, drawing comparisons between the amount of coffee being consumed to the transmigration mobilities of the truck drivers in Europe. The *Uncertain States of Europe* reflects and ponders an alternative spatial shape, as a product of upheavals[13] within the territorial system of the European context.[14] [see figure 3]

This paper therefore addresses a current research question of the ruling logics and constructive elements that constitute the present spatial form. It attempts to highlight the supporting roles that certain morphological elements have as a spatial structure; and as an effect, produces the urban realities, or architectures, we encounter as urban form on a first hand basis.

Secondly, to commence with a brief overview of the object in question, the city, as well as positioning the new urban context in perspective with the modernist approach of planning, with its inherent shift on aspects such as the interpretation of the dynamic city, or its 'ecological' spaces within the processes of the contemporary timeframe. As a synopsis, the discussion addressed here, is an attempt to extend an existing debate on the merit of a spatial technology, in which space is seen as a principle design element, within which to alter, steer and transform the urban condition itself.

Historical Form for the City From within the perspective of the architecture, the thrust of the morphological discourse for the most part has been situated around the relationships between the physical objects of the city and its volumetric spatial arrangements.[15] The classification of the building, as a type, became a reflection to the *type and style* to which urban patterns were formed, and spaces produced.[16] As a mere development from the typomorphological interpretation, typological applications became a basic technical apparatus for intervention within the urban and settlement types, for various resolutions of urban scales.[17]

Zone and building were fused within a singular functional framework. Objects and the urban [zones] of programmes became interdependent within interpretation, translation or interventions strategies.

Gauthiez[18] elaborates on the origins of the two dominant streams of urban morphological theory and practice, which are set out chronologically, by a *pre- and a post-WW II* approach. The earlier, pre war, theory was for the most part influenced by a Germanic tradition, based on historical interpretations, which applied a perspective of the city through its *planimetric* units, building blocks, and plots as physical units of urban form.

Interpretations of these units were later expanded by the German geographer Schlüter, 1899, beyond the singular typological building unit, into the city-zone or town parts, for the urban scale. The zones where demarcated as a contextual grounding for urban description related to urban function and its related typology. One can say briefly that this perspective took the build-

8 cf. Annemarie Mol and Marianne de Laet's article on 'The mechanism of a fluid technology'.
9 I refer here to the PhD research project on Amsterdam's Warmoesstraat, that attempted to de_sign the social in one particular street, by Gregory Bracken, Gerhard Bruyns and Ceren Sezer, SpaceLab, Delft University of Technology. 2005.
10 Latour (2006).
11 Talbot (1981).
12 ibid., p 51.
13 Examples of Boeri's upheavals are: exfoliations, pulsations, osmosis, thinnings, disseminations, and so forth, and are elaborated in detail within the Uncertain States of Europe publication (2003).
14 Boeri (2003).
15 Vernez Moudon (2003) p. 23.
16 Kropf (2004) and Vernez Moudon (2003).
17 Vernez Moudon (2003) p. 29.
18 Gauthiez (2004) p. 74.

ing unit, as a type, beyond a unitary description, and was transplanted onto an urban scale of the zone, that became indicative of the area function and an urban zone itself. What was of significance in this extrapolation of scale, was the very specific nature of the descriptions of *centre* and *periphery* as places that became transplanted onto an urban model, so that what took place on the outside and the inside remained prescriptively separate by definition.

We can observe, however, in the work of Strübben, 1907,[19] that a different view began to emerge during the pre-war thinking; as it might be said he was the first to appreciate the importance of critically looking at urban space, within urban analytical practises. Strübben's method dealt with a dialectical setup of a typological analysis of building, as a first principle, and as a second, an insistence on viewing and reflecting upon the built typology, in relation to the transportation networks. The introduction of such a methodological step in which urban transformation was read against the relations that were established between buildings and infrastructure, was a first of its kind, and has had a great following within the current urban discourse.[20]

For the post-war period of morphological discourse, it is possible to speak of a paradigm shift. Notions on observing space within this period, progressed from the unitary object alone, as per pre-war period, to a scale that reflected upon the territorial scale at large. Even if an architectural – typological – emphasis within the interpretation was used as a basis, the discussion became, as a first difference to pre-war morphology, a discourse of a much larger field of urban settlements, in contrast to city understood as a bounded entity. Such a view is especially evident in the work of the Italian architect Luigi Piccinato (1899-1983), which has been incorporated within the Muratorian and Canaggian schools of thought, within morphological analysis:

> The urban territory is to be seen as composed of varied sectors or zones. In each built zone must be determined the types of buildings that, precisely proportioned and distributed, give the character of the zone itself.[21]

Where previously the approach had focussed on the function of the building and relied on historical analysis, the post-war perspective opened onto the overall function of the territorial plan and its spaces.[22] Space, its configuration and variations thereof, had by this, become a crucial component to a discourse concerned with pin-pointing an exact and ultimate urban form, even though the interpretation itself was still lock within the aspects of the objects that defined it (plan, unit, street plot and architectural building type).
A temporal concern is evident in the work of M.R.G. Conzen (1907-2000). The aspect of integration of streets, plots and building units, as well as town and settlement structure, expressed within various periods of space and time, became

for Conzen the interpretive tool of insight into urban form. For Conzen, this temporal signature of 'city form' is taken as an alternative route in dealing with processes of formation, in contrast to the block-like static perspectives of the Italian school, as mentioned earlier. [see figure 4]

As a second alternative to a 'static' urban formal interpretation, we reflect upon the approaches at present. A current perspective on spatial form reflects altered states of seeing and understanding the world. The introduction of time to a world view, has made a considerable impact on basic perspectives and model of understanding. Instead of seeing the objectified or types of objects, as being the definitive model, the altered course has been one to include the aspect of '*in-from-ing*', rather than a singular shape alone.

The *typological* has in essence been replaced by the *topological* narrative. As the two following quotations show, the question of form and information are themselves constituent for the way in which dynamic properties and technologies are criss-crossed in new discourses around the urban, in variations on the classical city and its urbanization process. New conglomerations and swarms of settlements, referred to as upheavals in Boeri's terminology, is an exact account for the developing and increase of urbanisation for human beings on the global level.

> Our own study of organic form, which we call by Goethe's name of Morphology, is but a portion of that wider Science of Form which deals with the forms assumed by matter under all aspects and conditions, and, in a still wider sense, with forms which are theoretically imaginable.[23]

> Building don't matter anymore. The future of architecture and design is dependent upon your ability to develop models that can generate a whole series of projects, models that are designed to be instrumentals, that are filled with meaning and ideas, and encounter everywhere and nowhere in your architecture.[24]

The formal and the in-formed As an introduction to Form, we find an extensive historical debate, on the Form(al) seen from within various discourses of biology, mathematics, quantum physics and metaphysics.[25] In particular, it is clear that for the discourses of Architecture and Urbanism, the effects of these fine and elaborate meshworks of theories and interpretations, have not left their mark unnoticed. Research enthusiasm has not diminished regarding an inquiry concerning a better understanding of what the 'form and meaning' is for architecture, nor in the desire to establish any true 'formal' qualities of the city.

19 **ibid.,** p. 75.
20 With reference to the work of Stefano Boeri on Milan (1993).
21 L. Piccinato as cited and translated in Gauthiez (2004) p. 79.
22 Le Corbusier's approach to architecture reflect this very clearly in his **Vers Une Architecture** (1923).
23 D'Arcy W. Thompson (1961) as cited in Steadman (1989).
24 Quote from Ben van Berkel & Caroline Bos's new publication, **UN Studio: Design Models** (London: Thames and Hudson. 2006).
25 Healy (2005).

Concepts and notions of *Form* throughout history has been varied. *Form*, in its most basic sense is taken from the Latin word *forma*, and refers in general to the external shape, appearance and configuration of an object. Plato produced a definitive distinction between *Form* and *Idea*, seen as archetypes and abstracts, which has historically been applied as an 'archetypal' interpretational basis for the world or any structures. Platonic *Form* is in essence a perspective on the world seen as a collection of objects, as opposed to form seen as an idea. *Form* of Idea observes a 'mental' world order – or alternatively – an arrangement constructed from within orders of the mind. [26]

The Germanic language presents us with a similar distinction of formal worlds, either as *Form* as an abstraction of the world – seen as '*a particular concept*', or alternatively, Form seen as *Gestalt*; based upon the perceptive and sensorial experience of the phenomena in the world.[27]

In addition, Bateson's [1972] introduction of the Gnostic notions of the *Pleroma* and *Creature*, extends the interpretation of 'formal reading', as a mechanism that translates self-imposed orders we give to the world, irrespective of discourse or technological applications; as for example within the domains of architecture, biosciences or urbanism. Within the field of the *pleroma*, the world is seen as an objective form, whilst the world of the *creatura* is a world defined by the individual's perceptive mind. The crux of the matter in all three formal positions is in effect an interpretation of a world we have constructed, in which the named object – *pleroma space* – is nothing more than a reflection of the collective and individual imaginations, whilst being *in-formed* in a space, which is *itself* a form of construction.

Morphology: knowledge (-ology) and form (morph)[28]

Biological science has contributed its own specific approach to a biological formal enquiry. The founding father of the biological morphology, Johann Wolfgang von Goethe (1749-1832), who's analytical quest for finding the *urform* or the 'true' biological form, *Urpflanze*, from which all species of plants had evolved, has been adopted by architects, planners, and geographers to elaborate on the same archetypal forms of the built environment.[29]

As stated, classic morphological interpretations of the urban fabric, focus on the urban form as composed of the streets, building sizes, shapes, architectures and density of any urban settlement, in relation to a distributive plan of objects to a functional description of the context.

Adding to Bateson's concept of the alternative '*ways of seeing*', discourses such as history, geography and anthropology have since the end of World War II, applied traditional morphological analysis to search for alternative interpretive narratives for settlements within various time periods. As an example, geographers have made attempts to clarify current urban form, through what is present and visible in the built landscape, whilst archaeology has sought to explain historical (formal) plans that have long disappeared. For historians the purpose is much more evolutionary; seeking out the effects on forms of a specific place, positioned within its chronological dimensions. For urbanism, and planners in particular, formal plan and compositional interpretations have become technologies within their own right, where the planner seeking design logics for possible future scenarios that might assist the discourse in future development strategies.[30]

A crucial moment rests upon the clarity of what specifically is observed as object of study and as a *Form*. For urban scholars, the question regarding the present types of urban form remains central. Do all cities function the same, or, are the same spatial structures present within the First and Third World urban environments? More so, what are the basic formal interpretations of urban space, and what does the contemporary space of the city look like?

A spatial form At first, any attempt to summarize an overall contemporary urban form, is no longer possible. The modernistic framework of understanding the city, with a centre, a periphery and neighbourhoods, has proven unequipped to lay bare any conclusive 'holistic' shape.

Expansions of urbanized fields, across large territories leave no distinctions between what is city, neighbourhood, industrial zone, periphery, or small village, and if so, the observance of contradictory programmes situated in close proximity to one another, blurs the 'traditional' image of the city even more.[31] The 'break' through the medieval wall has given way to modern planning practices and technologies as various infrastructure lines transgress beyond the historical city, towards the outskirts and even beyond.

Sprawl has become the new city itself,[32] as it consumed the landscape and all its qualities of heterogeneous spaces, discontinuous elements, multiple poli-nuclear and a vast amount of infrastructures across the landscape.[33]

Regarding the clarity of describing the *spatiality of the city*, urbanism has not yet concluded on the problematic of naming this dispersed and shapeless structure. '*Metapolis*', 'Multicity'[34] and '*Netzstadt*,'[35] are but a few alternative descriptions or naming for the urban condition. These current examples seem to reflect mere attempts that address certain qualities or components of the urban field, while '*Landschitecture*' *[landscape combined with architecture] or 'citerritory' [city in relation to the territory]*,[36] relate to the relationship between the city and the non-city, rather than a concrete shape. [see figure 5]

26 **Stanford Encyclopaedia of Philosophy**.
27 Forty (2000) p. 149.
28 Meyer (2003) p. 11.
29 Forty (2000) p. 147.
30 Gauthiez (2004) p. 80.
31 Also see Stefano Boeri's work on Milan (1993).
32 Secchi (2004) and Bekaert (2002).
33 Gausa (2003) p. 439.
34 **ibid.**
35 Baccini (2003).
36 Gausa, et al. (2003) p. 19.

With the abandonment of the modern project's zoning distinctions, and with an alternative naming of the city, urban scholars, as well as designers for that matter, seek new approaches or techniques for intervening within any urbanized context.[37] My intention here is to add to the descriptions of the differential urban forms, as found within the current debate, and to highlight the importance of two basics in reading the contemporary urban field.
Furthermore, each of the three units of form, seen as [1] space, [2] infrastructures and [3] programme can be viewed as the 'primary' forms that composes a total urban context. It is therefore possible to read or interpret these primary elements, individually, through their own characteristics and tendencies, or as a collaborative form once overlaid upon one another. I therefore propose to fuse the element of *space* with that of the *infrastructural mobilities*, as to construct an interpretive framework for the urban condition.

Space and infrastructure Space within the 'traditional morphological framework, is positioned as a compositional 'after' effect, due to the arrangements and structures that are *in-placed* by the architect, urban planner and transportations engineer.
In contrast to the 'traditional city perspective', the alternative *non-city-form* of the '*citterritory*', has in some way been inverted, almost dependent, on the space of the city, primarily. By the inversion of the building-footprint drawings, so easily used by architects and urbanists, the space or the void is made visible as a structuring element within a total form of the city. Cortez addresses this approach by way of similar studies on the morphological approaches in current urban forms.[38]

> This is not an idea of form that is 'one', but that is 'like one'. It is difficult to hold in the mind's eye. It is elusive except when we see it. All its faces and sides have equal importance...There is an element (material or structure) that gives that unity that the 'old pregnant' figure can no longer provide... It is a form, therefore, indebted to the fluctuating processes that the (sic) shape it.[39]

Various theories, such as Field, Mobility and Network theories are in support of space as a primary structuring element within the urban reading of Form. For Urry,[40] who is a specialist in the complexity discourse, the metaphor of the network is most appropriate to address the formation of space by way of the types of mobilities and fluidities that operate within the city. Urry elaborates on the networks of the travelling individuals, internet, information, money, automobility, as well as health hazards as part of the global fluids of individuals and materials within the city and its spaces. Inherently, space and infrastructural mobilities are there fused into one operative device, which would allow for a shift of space as an effect, to a spaces that affect, as part of a technological devices in urban Form and urban transformations.

Examples of analytical work on the spatial Form of the city are available. I would like to make reference to the work of both, Stefano Boeri and Xaveer De Geyter. Stefano Boeri has periodically produced reflection on urban from, through both a de-compositional analysis of morphological elements, as well as through methods of process that play within the urban Form. Boeri's publication of '*Il Territorio Che Cambia – projects on the Milan region*' [1993], '*Multiplicities*' [2001], and most recently, '*Uncertain States of Europe*' [2003], have all been reflexive in the comparison of space as an urban Form at first. In the most recent work, Boeri, attempts to produce logics or mechanisms, termed as *dispositifs*, to clarify and structure spatial Form against social processes within one framework, as varieties of spatial types within the contextual scale of Europe.
For Xaveer De Geyter [2002] the contemporary city is an effect of 'After-Sprawl', a mega space on a European scale, focussing on the open and residual spaces as left by the 'extended-spread-effect' of urban elements. In contrast, De Geyter's focus' remains centred on the composition of territorial 'operational-formations', such as the *Randstad* – Holland, the area of *Brussels – Antwerpen – Gent* in Belgium, *Zürich – Basel* in Switzerland and *Veneto* in Italy, as well as the strict 'negative spaces' – or voids – that exist as a result of the sprawl effect.

> In the mid-20th century, those who thought about cities believed that they were clearly organised, simply ordered, and thus predictable, capable of being designed and planned in such a way the quality of life of their residents would be directly improved by manipulating their physical form. This was the view widely held by architecture and, of course, the social sciences. It was grounded in the belief that the social world, and their representation of its objects (such as cities themselves), was coherent and comprehensive in the same way that the physical world has been understood since the Enlightenment. It was argued that the triumph of rationality through the application of a scientific method could be transferred completely and emulated in the social world. The result was a deliberate attempt at social engineering, as well as in the sort of architectures and urban planning that has dominated western societies over the past 50 years, and now, the developing world. As we approach the third millennium, all this looks a bit naïve... Our understating of the small scale systems does not provide us with nor does it clarify our understanding of the large scale.[41]

These former examples, are in distinct contrast to the Modern planner's approach. Modernism saw *Form* and space, much like the construction of the social, as a projective practice, which if

37 Read (2005).
38 Pinzon Cortes (2006) p. 94.
39 Frederico Soriano, in Fisuras 3 1/3 (1995), as cited in **Metapolis**, by Gausa (2003) p. 236.
40 Urry (2003).
41 Michael Batty, as cited in **Metapolis;** under '**m city or multicity**'. **Metapolis**, p. 424.
42 Fishman (1977), Kostof (1991), Forty (2000).

done appropriately, could ensure a utopian world. In contrast to the interpretation of Form up until the late 19th century, which saw Form as a mere mass or shape, the modernist project associated Form with that of an ideology. For that reason, Modern urban planning techniques, became significant instruments within the production of; [1] an ideal Form that placed or zoned an [2] ideal society, within a framework of masterful planning, as done within the *Garden city, Broadacre City* and the *Modern City*.[42] Having been made aware of the historical perspective regarding *Form*, the question now remains as to how current practices address this seeming crucial aspect in city making.

Current practices on reading urban Form

> The term [*morphic field*] is more general in its meaning than morphogenetic fields, and includes other kinds of organizing fields in addition to those of morphogenesis; the organizing fields of animal and human behaviour, of social and cultural systems, and of mental activity can all be regarded as morphic fields which contain an inherent memory.[43] [Own emphasis]

For Meyer,[44] two key factors are crucial in understanding urban formal investigation itself: a) the essence of urban *Form* and b) the driving logics of orders that structure spatial compositions. To establish an essence of urban form, Meyer states, requires a two-level decomposition, of which plan criticism is seen as the first, whilst any explanation to clarify the origins of the *Form* itself, is seen as the second. The motivation of interpretation of this nature, is done for the reason, in Meyer's view, as a construction of knowledge itself and a devolvement of skill in urban strategies. In general *plan criticism* addresses composition aspects of the territory, by way of a highlighting the *object*, seen as the unitary building block and the total city, through its architectures. In addition to the mere object, the *space* of the city is dialectically defined, or rather informed, as the structure of the architectural object defines and produces urban 'space'.

Submerging deeper into a discourse of urban formal investigation, we find an established morphological tradition worldwide as evident in Italy, Switzerland, Germany, France and England. Specificities of methodologies of morphological schools, apply very specific principles to reasoning on spatial structure itself.[45] In particular the *typomorphological perspective*, produces theories that hypothesize a dual relationship between *'object vs space'*, by incorporating *type* as a principal key in its clarifying logics. The counter balance between the physical and its void, at the scale of the neighbourhood and the territory, are placed in opposition to one another, whilst marrying a typological view with processes such as social, economic and urban zoning types.[46]

In conclusion, typomorphological descriptions produce theories as well as discuss tendencies, through primary relations between the built *Form*, the volumetric arrangements, and the social compositions of the city. These relations are set within a temporal dimension, seen as the effect of *urban settlement patterns*, from three distinct, *Canaggian*, scales, of the [1] building unit scale (groups of buildings), [2] the neighbourhood scale-the city scale, and finally [3] the region or territorial scale.[47] This research has identified a problematic, not within the scales or the units of analysis, but within the interpretational framework of the city. Certain logics of place and location, seem invalid to account for specific emergent urban phenomena, as spontaneous economic and market developments occur at inexplicable geographical locations.[48] hereby would attempt to clarify a basic method of approach in achieving such a spatial reading.

Space itself, as the logic In contrast to the traditional approaches, as for example typomorphological interpretation of the city, this research has taken an alternative direction on investigation of the urban *Form*. As an alternative, what is proposed here is an interpretation of space, at its first levels, deviant from a traditional methodology that is solely based on 'typological logics' or urban compositional aspects. Space has to be rethought in relation to urban scales of settlements, its architectural unitary mass, as well as the social, political and economic forces that occur within it's domain. [see figure 6]
A second result is a trade-off for the modernist top-down paradigm, in favour of an ecological urban perspective. What the modernist framework did in terms of positioning a constructive device for producing ideal worlds forms for society,[49] economy, architectures[50] and even the city, the 'biological-ecological' model has replaces with a framework of dynamics and emergence theories.[51] Thrift [2005] states in his paper entitled, '*Form born to made: technology, biology and space*', that the biological view directly *in-forms (teaches)* our technologies and spatial thinking in the current world, irrespective of which scale is being looked at or which *technology* is being applied. For the city, this perceptive shifts all interpretation to a *topological perspective* that resonates principles of relational dynamics, away from Cartesian flatness itself.

The space of the old is no more. Traditional space, previously 'constructed', is at present prioritized as a *Form of Space* in its own right. As a primary backbone to the urban conditions, space has been positioned as platform that conveys and facilitates urban dynamics. Space has become the machine,[52] *a dispositif*,[53] a device and mechanism that operates beyond its own existence and

43 Sheldrake (1988) p. 112.
44 Meyer (2003) p. 11.
45 Vernez Moudon (2003).
46 **ibid.** This notion is a direct result of the post-war theories and methodologies as discussed earlier.
47 Vernez Moudon (2003) in Urban Analysis Guidebook, edited by L. van der Burg (2003).
48 Bruyns & Read (2006) p. 63.
49 Graafland (2000).
50 Forty (2005) p. 166.
51 Urry (2003), Kapra (1985), Bateson (1972). A first indication of the direct influence of the biological sciences in the urban formations, as discussed previously in Sheldrake's **morphic-field theory** – see note 6.
52 Bruyns and Read (2006).
53 Originally a Foucauldian term, translated as '**mechanisms**' of formations within various

seeks to produce effects outside itself, on all levels of scale. Manuel Gausa contributes to this understanding, by elaborating on the notion of *dispositioned* states as being:

> The contemporary change in paradigms and the new idea in time, provide for a new 'informal' order, more elastic- based no longer upon compositions or positions, but rather upon dispositions, open to individual variations and, therefore, to diversity, to a dynamic and plural articulation of information.[54]

Gausa advances the theoretical guides within a practical application, which includes the multiplicities and formations as part of an operative framework of analysis, and design. *HiCat; HiperCatalunya, Research territories* is a collaborative research effort in which various discourses[55] contribute to define territorial formations, as well as applying a reflexive method that produces a layered analysis, that constructs the grounding rules for interpreting the urban conditions and spatial formations.[56] A vast collections of maps and diagrams illustrate these types of formations for the territory in question, and contributes to the debate on urban analysis as well as urban *Form*.

Practicalities of this research Particularities of this framework operate within 3 basic components of analysis, and a fourth for logic formation.[57] The analytical components are defined as the [1] mobility networks or infrastructures of movement, [2] scalar systems of operations, [3] urban compositional and dynamic elements, whilst [4] the logics formation is seen as a conclusive section that extracts and produces grounding work for interpretations of the ecologies of urban *Form*.

As a first element – mobility networks and infrastructure are used primarily to interpret and highlight urban *Form* and spatial urbanisation. Manuel Castells [1998] has illustrated the effects and the influences of network per sé, within the contemporary paradigm, as reflected in the constructions of society, economy, technologies, and territorial urban environment of the network society with its network city.
Historically, Jane Jacobs has made reference to the settlement formations of Anatolian villages along the lines of the long distance trading routes, establishing the merit of reading mobility lines as basic components in urban *Formal 'production.'*[58]

Form, in this proposal, is primarily a Network *Form*, and is therefore interpreted through the pattern and circuit distributions of the urban grids, as lines that promote and accommodate mobility at large. Characteristics of the network/grid allows for *scalar, temporal, spatial and contextual* effects to occur through a distributive pattern, as built up through sets of scalar lines of mobilities, juxta-

posed upon one another.[59] Similar scales are placed into individual layers, with a 'formal' result of the total grid expressed in scales of; [1] the metropolitan, [2] the city scale ('*supergrid*'),[60] and [3] the local (neighbourhood) scales of movement.[61] This decomposition becomes the backbone to any comparison between [a] space, [b] the compositional morphological elements, and [c] the empirical data.[62]
Space Syntax techniques assist directly within the interpretational and the clarification of the spatial lines itself. The vector diagram and axial map are simplified versions of the urban grid, and are used as basis in a mathematical model to establish hierarchy, relations and formations within the urban system. More specifically, the formations referred to here are seen as products of topological relations that show connectivity and accessibility in space, but more crucially, the centres of urban *Form*, or '*centralities*'. [63] [see figures 7, 8, 9]

Sequentially, as a second component to this multi-layered configuration, the analysis would have to position the infrastructures within larger or smaller urban systems of movement and urban flows. Urban systems are operational at various scale levels, whether these systems are operational at the local level of the neighbourhood, the global, metropolitan scale of the territory. Examples of operational scale levels for the European context are systems similar to those Xaveer De Geyter has so specifically analyzed within his urban analytical work.[64] The territorial system of the *Flemish diamond*, the *Ruhr-Gebiet* in Germany, or that of the *Randstad* are strategically situated within expanded flows of mobilities seen as the connections of airports, railways, highways, provincial road, and local neighbourhood arterial routes that disperse across vast territorial distances.
Depending on the resolution of observation, the complexity of the system can be enlarged or reduced to suit descriptive needs. The *New European Union*, with its borderless conditions, could be seen as one such system of scale, followed by national scales, provincial scale, city scale, regional scale, and ultimately the neighbourhood scale.

A third, but final component to an analytical stage, is focused on extracting layers of composi-

disciplines and sciences. Much has been written on Foucault's work, especially theoretical interpretations of the '**Archeology of Knowledge**' (1972), where the term originates from. The term used in the '**Metapolis: Dictionary of Advanced Architecture**', '**disposition**', closely resonated the original term within an urban setting and discourse.

54 Gausa (2003a) p. 174.

55 The discourses referred to here are: biology, economics, anthropology and law.

56 Gausa (2003) p. 19.

57 As examples: Research on Switzerland – **Netzstadt** – Baccini (2003), **Research on the Catalan territory** – **HiCat** – Gausa (2004), Explorations of the Milan Region – **Ill Territorio Che Chambia** – Boeri (1993).

58 Jacobs (1970).

59 Kakihara (2002).

60 Read (2002), 'supergrid' is also termed the 'middleground'.

61 For a complete description of a layer clarification, see Bruyns and Read (2006).

62 The procedural Space Syntax integration analysis was influential in establishing a hierarchy of the mobility infrastructures.

63 Read & van Nes (2003).

64 Bekaert (2002).

tional information. Although this method is divergent from a traditional reading of urban *Form*, it however requires basic grounding work as expressed by the traditional practise of morphological analysis. The 'formal' aspects comprises of layers that show: all buildings, all roads, plot configurations, plots used or plots that have an architectural object located on the land-parcel, and finally, open space. As an alternative, this research proposes a reshuffling of the order of reading urban *Form*, and to commence with the infrastructures of mobility at first, hence the open spaces, plots configurations and conclusively, the building or architectural units themselves.

The empirical 'dynamic' sets, notate and map information in order to measure spatial strength. Various sets of data are collected and, as the same with the aforementioned morphological compositional set, reflected upon territorial spatial *Form,* i.e mobility infrastructures. Examples of data include, all commerce activity found on the street level, population density data, and conclusively, scales at which the commercial activities are operational at (similar to the scales used to classify mobility within the urban grid).
For each set, and each spatial scale of movement (see network description) a separate image is produced to critically reflect upon any pattern of formation, distribution or emergence tendencies as forms of the new urban. The crux of the 'ecological' interpretation is established on the mere basis of seeking 'spots' or spaces, where urban programme alternate between any two scales, at any given time. [see figures 10, 11]

To follow and exit... It is my preference not to write a definitive conclusion to this paper, as the debate on spatial interpretation has been introduced, historically defined, and at this period, open to greater fields and sources for interpretation. Like with Poincaré, the objective remains to 'harmonise' the two extreme scales of vision by which we are confronted; the scale of the particle (the unit or individual) with the scale of the system (greater operative logics). Our task ahead would have to be a diligent operation to be able to test these relations between the empirical and the theory, from the particle level, to its universal grounding logics. Any governing or visible spatial logics need to be expressed in terms of the space (as a *prime* urban from), and reflected upon by way of the effected distributed pattern (seen as the in-formed emergence).
The shift from *infrastructure* to *ecological-movement-structure*, is a crucial altera-

65 A similar concept on a patchwork metropolis was introduced by Willem Jan Neutelings' 'The Carpet Metropolis'.
66 Macro and micro morphological analysis is taken from A. N. Whitehead, as cited by Vernez Moudon (2002) p. 37.
67 See note 8.

tion to make as it effects our mental capacities of naming and deriving logics of both urban and spatial *Form*.
Previously, where the infrastructures of a mobile network where seen as the links between spaces, places, programmes and zones,[65] the position of the network itself, has become 'attractor-like' as a basic systems, towards which macro- and microcosmic 'sediment-like' elements are drawn.[66]

Finally, any ecological interpretation of the new structures of urban formations, or 'eco- structures', as Gausa terms it, inherently transforms and in-forms, an engineering tool, into a '*dispositioned*'[67] mechanism through which space becomes technologically equipped. Such an example is the link between space and any distributive pattern, in terms of the dependency of the microscopic elements of the distributed unit, to the network system itself, as a primary link to the world that facilitates processes of urban growth, mutation of the smaller elements, or even demise of certain units. As a final remark, it is fair to state, that place and public space therefore become bound to a region principle, by way of all the spatial mobility lines that move into, and beyond the horizon of a singular geographic point. Mono-functionality, homogeneity, and singular zoning demarcations are in principle, abandoned in favour of the freeing up of any strict spatial control, to allow for a 'natural' process of formations or '*landscapes of* ecologies', to emerge through whichever means available. A final question within the dilemma of space becomes, a question of how to address the urbanised landscapes of the First, Third or Fourth Worlds, as well as deciding on which spatial *off-ramp* to take. [see figure 12]

Bibliography

Baccini, P. & Oswald, F. Netzstadt, Designing the Urban. Birkhauser: Basel, 2003.

Bateson, G. **Steps to an Ecology of Mind: Collected Essays in Anthropology, Psychiatry, Evolution, and Epistemology**. New York: Ballantine Books, 1972.

Bekaert, G., et al. **After Sprawl: Research for the Contemporary City**. Rotterdam: NAi Publishers, 2002.

Berkel van, B. & Bos, C. **UN Studio: Design Models**. London: Thames and Hudson. 2006.

Boeri, S. 'Notes on a research project,' in **Mutations**. Edited by Koolhaas, R. Barcelona: Actar, 2001.

Boeri, S., Lanzani, A., & Marini, E. **Ill territorio che cambia: Ambieti paesaggi e immagini della regione milanese.** Edited by Renatto Minetto. Milan: AIM, 1993.

Boeri, S. (ed). **USE: Uncertain States of Europe**. Milan: Skira, 2003.

Bruyns, G. & Read, S.A. 2006. 'The Urban Machine,' in: **Visualizing the Invisible**, edited by Camilo Panilla and Stephen Read. Amsterdam: Techne Press, 2006. p.52.

Capra, F. The **Tao of Physics: an exploration of the parallels between modern physics and eastern mysticism.** 2nd edition. Boston: New Science Library, 1985.

Castells, M. **The Rise of the Network Society**. 2nd rev. Blackwell; Oxford: Blackwell, 2000.

Forty, A. **Words and Buildings**. New York: Thames and Hudson, 2000.

Fishman, R. **Urban Utopias in the Twentieth Century; Ebenezer Howard, Frank Lloyd Wright, and Le Corbusier**. New York: Basic Books, 1977.

Galison, P. ' Images Scatter into data, data gathering into images,' in **Iconoclash; Beyond the image wars in science, religion and art**. Edited by Bruno Latour & Peter Weibel. Karlsruhe: Centre for Arts and Media, 2002. pp. 300 -319.

Gausa, M. 'Dispositions,' in: **The Metapolis Dictionary of Advanced Architecture; city technology and society in the information age**. Compiled by Susanna Cros. Barcelona: Actar, 2003a. p 174.

Gausa, M. 'Metapolis (multicity),' in: **The Metapolis Dictionary of Advanced Architecture; city technology and society in the information age**. Compiled by Susanna Cros. Barcelona: Actar, 2003b. p 430.

Gausa, M. **'No-form',** in: The Metapolis Dictionary of advanced architecture; city technology and society in the information age. Compiled by Susanna Cros. Barcelona: Actar, 2003c. p 236.

Gausa, M., Guallart, V., and Müller, W. 'Research Territories; state(s) of reference; Matapolis', in **HiperCatalunya: territories of research and territories of crossing**. Barcelona: Actar, 2004.

Gauthiez, B. **The history of urban morphology**. Urban Morphology, vol.8, no. 2, 2004. pp.71-89.

Graafland, A. **The Socius of Architecture; Amsterdam, Tokyo, New York**. Rotterdam: 010 Publishers, 2000.

Healy. P. **Images of Knowledge; An Introduction to Contemporary Philosophy of Science**. Amsterdam: Sun, 2005.

Jacobs, J. 1969. **The Economy of Cities**. New York: Vintage Books, 1969.

Kakihara, M. and C. Sorensen, 'Mobility: An Extended Perspective', in **Thirty-Fifth Hawaii International Conference on System Sciences**. USA: Big Island Hawaii, 2002.

Kostof, S. **The city shaped: urban patterns and meanings through history**. London: Thames and Hudson, 1991.

Kropf, K. 'M.R.G. Conzen, Gianfranco Caniggia, Oscar Wilde and Aesop: or, why urban morphology may be right but not popular'. **Urban Morphology**, vol. 8, no. 1. 2004. pp.26-28.

Latour, B. **Reassembling the Social: An Introduction to Actor-Network-Theory**. Oxford: University Press, 2005.

Latour, B. Paris: **Invisible City.** 2004. Available on website: http://www.ensmp.fr/~latour/virtual/index.html#. [Accessed; February 15, 2006].

Meyer, H. 'Plan Analysis,' in: **Urban Analysis Guidebook**, edited by L. van der Burg. Delft: Technical University of Delft, Faculty of Architecture. 2003. p.11-21.

Neutelings, W.J. 1992. **Patchwork City**. Rotterdam: 010 publishers, 1992.

Pinzon Cortes, C. 'Morphological analysis of the contemporary urban territory: Is it still a relevant approach?', in **Urban Transformations and Sustainability**, edited by F. van der Hoeven and H.J. Rosemann. Amsterdam: Delft University Press, 2006. pp. 94-112.

Van Nes, A. & Read, S.A. **Local Machine. A 'design guide' for real Urban Centrality.** 2003. Available on website: www.spacelab.tudelft.nl. [Accessed 15 February 2006].

Robinson, D and Mayblin, B. **Introducing Empiricism.** Royston: Icon Books, 2004.

Secchi, B. 'The European city', in Proceedings of EAAE Conference **'The European City'; Architectural interventions and Urban Transformations**. Delft: TU Delft, October 27-30. 2004. pp. 16-25.

Sheldrake, R. **The Presence of the Past**. New York: Times Books, 1988.

Steadman, J. P. **Architectural Morphology; An introduction to the Geometry of Building plans.** London: Pion Publishing, 1983.

Talbot, M. **Mysticism and the New Physics**. London: Arkana – Penguin Group, 1981.

Thrift, N. **From Born to Made: technology, biology and space**. Transactions of the Institute of British Geographers, 2005.

Vernez Moudon, A. 'Thinking about micro and macro morphology.' **Urban Morphology**, Vol. 6, no. 1. 2002. pp. 37-39.

Vernez Moudon, A. 'Getting to know the Built landscape: Typomorphology,' in **Urban Analysis Guidebook**, edited by L. van der Burg. Delft: Technical University of Delft, Faculty of Architecture. 2003. pp. 23-43.

Urry, J. **Global Complexity**. Cambridge: Polity, 2003.

Next page:
1 A question of Urban **Form**; Athens from a distance. Source: Author. 2006.
2 Questioning a Social **Form**. These figures are examples taken from a research exercise that examined variations of the Social Form, within the Warmoes Street in Amsterdam. This project was inspired by Bruno Latour, as an attempt to **de_sign** the urban context, and elaborates on the spatial qualities that contribute and support social formations of the city, seen as practices of [1] a resident, [2] of a religious convent, [3] homosexual activities and [4] the drug dealer.
Source: **Vectors of Visibility** research project, Warmoes Street, Amsterdam. Authors: G. Bracken, C. Sezer and G. Bruyns. Delft University of Technology, 2005.

Narrative 1:
St Jansstraat
Local
the resident, his wife and children
Spatial
stories
Narrative 1
The Resident
Spatial
Geographic
Spatial Depth
H
M
L
Narrative 2:
the Zusters van Augustinus van St Monica
Local spatial relations
a convent, bread, and the men they feed
Spatial
stories
Narrative 2
the Zusters van Augustinus
van St Monica
Spatial
Geographic
Spatial Depth
H
Speculation
M
L
Overlapping SvA and narcotic activities
Narrative 3:
Sexual practises: Homosexual
Local
men, some tools and some spaces
Spatial
stories
Narrative 3:
Orchastrated practises: Sexual particularities
Spatial
Geographic
H
SB
FB
CO
M
L
Narrative 4:
Street Narcotics
Local
visible and invisible commerce of the 'high'
Spatial
stories
Narrative 4
Narcotics:
Spatial
Geographic
Spatial Depth
H
Speculation
M
L

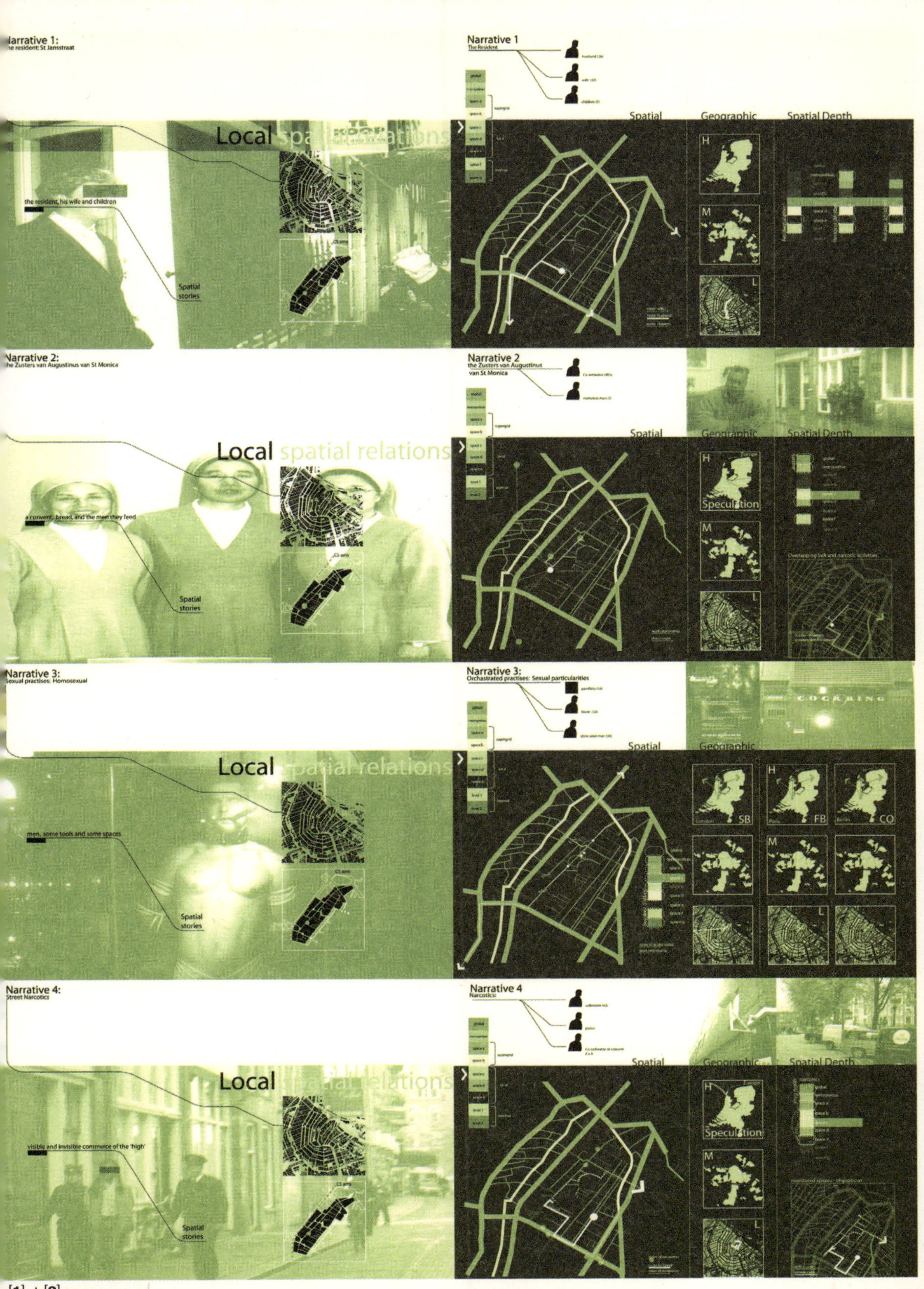

[1] ▲ [2]

[3]

[4]

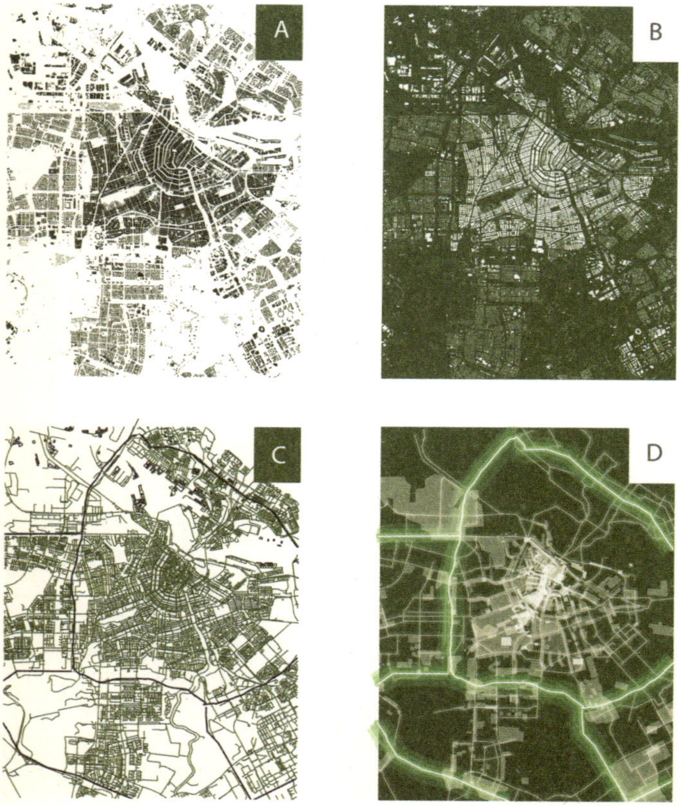

A

B

3 A line drawing, as an Urban **Form**, of al the mobility infrastructures of the Amsterda region, which was influenced by Stefano Boeri's research on urbanization of the Mil region (1993). Source: Author. 2006.

4 [A] The traditional formal arrangement o urban space, composed by the architecture lines and volumes.

[B] The urban space of the city, expressed the 'void'.

[C] Infrastructure as space: translations of mobility infrastructures of the city, as a first space of the urban field.

[D] An urban spatial form of movement hierarchies.

Source: Author. 2006.

5 An urban problematic of **de_signing** th city; as a form and space of the **'Metapolis** 'Multicity', **'Netzstadt', 'Landschitecture', 'citerritory'.** Source: Author. 2006.

[5]

xt page:
A new model for interpreting urban spatial m: the Amsterdam mobility armature pressed in its movement dynamics. This ure establishes a basis to which urban enomena could be compared to. Source: thor. 2006.
De_signing of the movement armatures in nsterdam (and region);
level 1: a global scale grid (the railway nature).
[B] Level 2: a metropolitan grid (the national highway armature).
[C] Level 3: The 'supergrid' or city grid
[D] Level 4: Local / neighbourhood mobility grid.
Source: Author. 2006.

8 For the region of Amsterdam: a comparison between the spatial armature and all street level commercial activity. Source: Author. 2006.

9 De_signing spatial **Form** for the region of Amsterdam. This figure represents the four commercial levels that correspond to the scale orders as expressed in figure 7. Each shop is surveyed to establish the scale at which it functions. Those commercial establishments that operate predominately on the tourist level are indicated with a red dot. Orange indicates the high scale activity, whilst the middle is represented by yellow and the local scales in green. Source: Author. 2006.

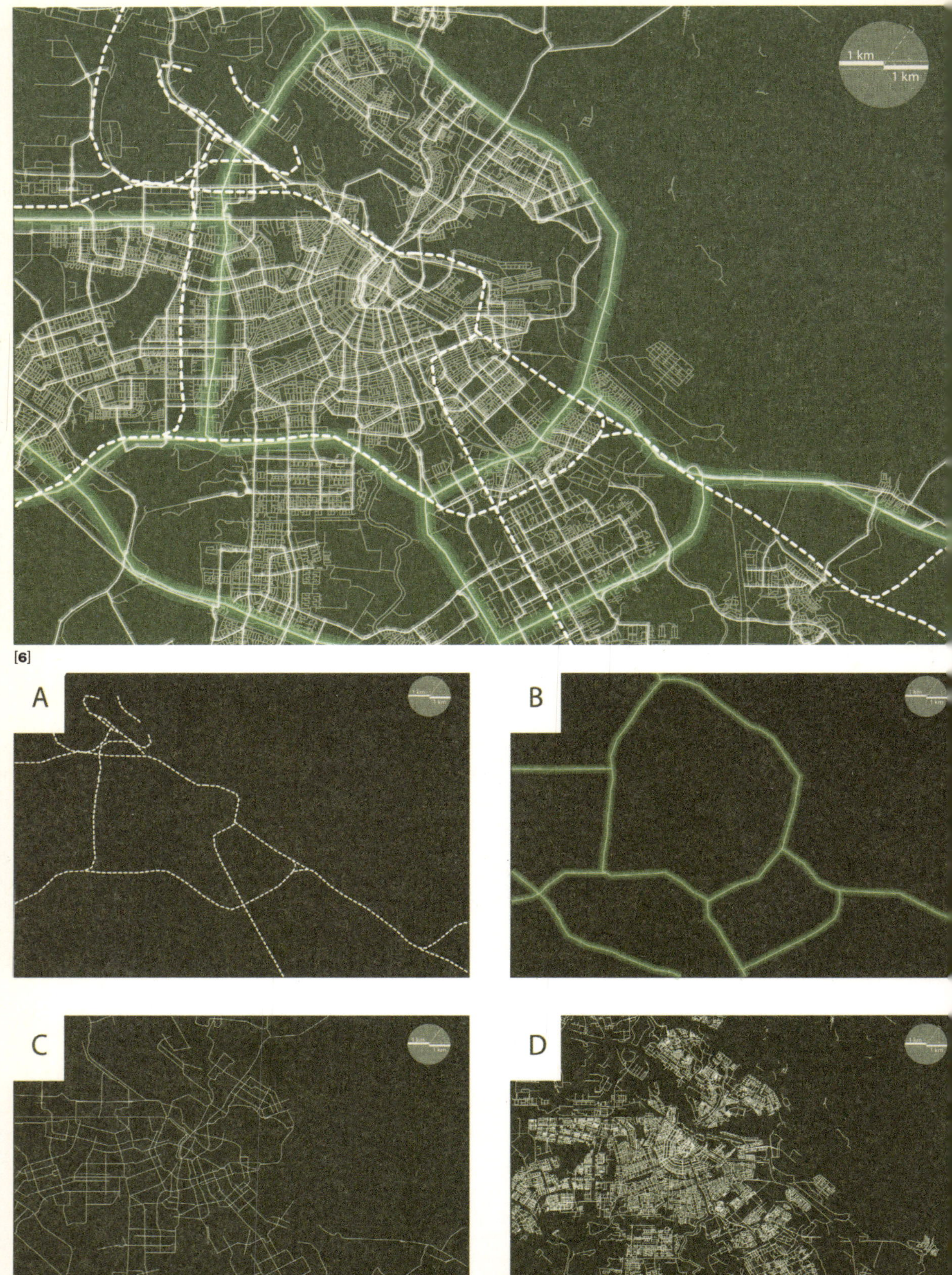
1 km
1 km
[6]
A
B
C
D

1 km
1 km

[9]

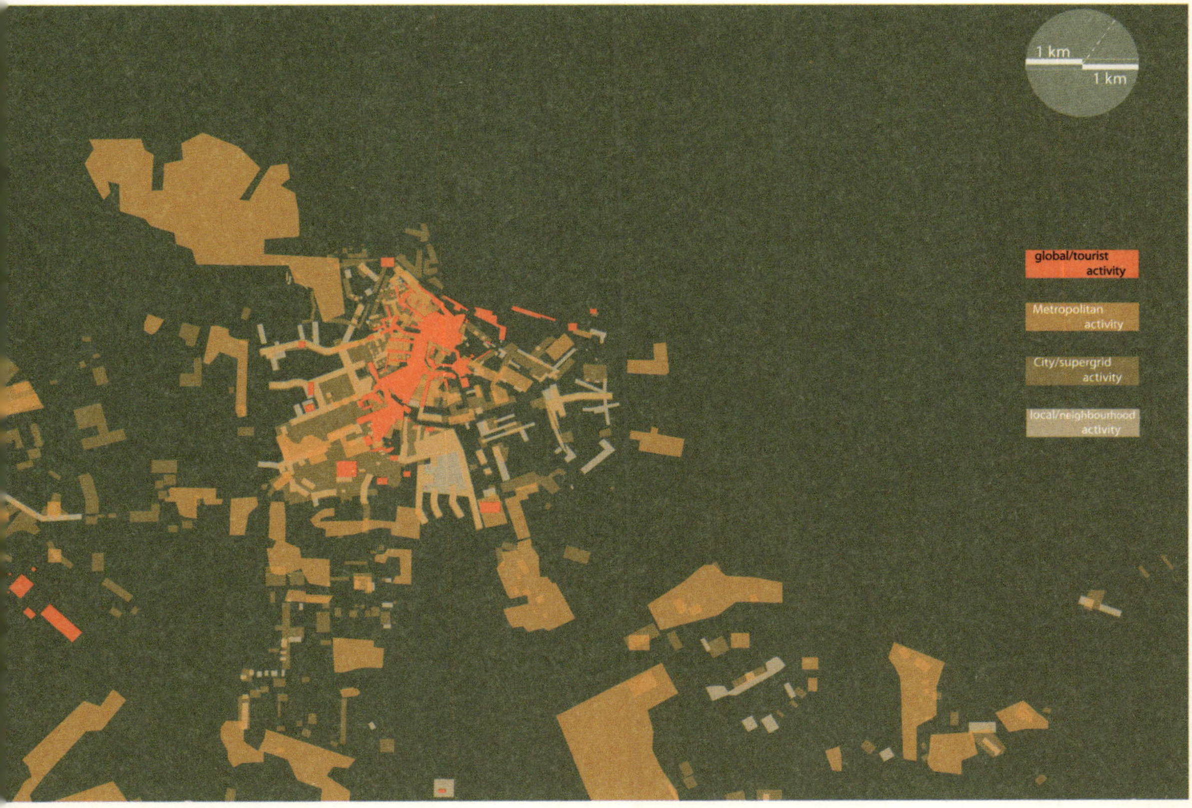

1 km
1 km

global/tourist activity

Metropolitan activity

City/supergrid activity

local/neighbourhood activity

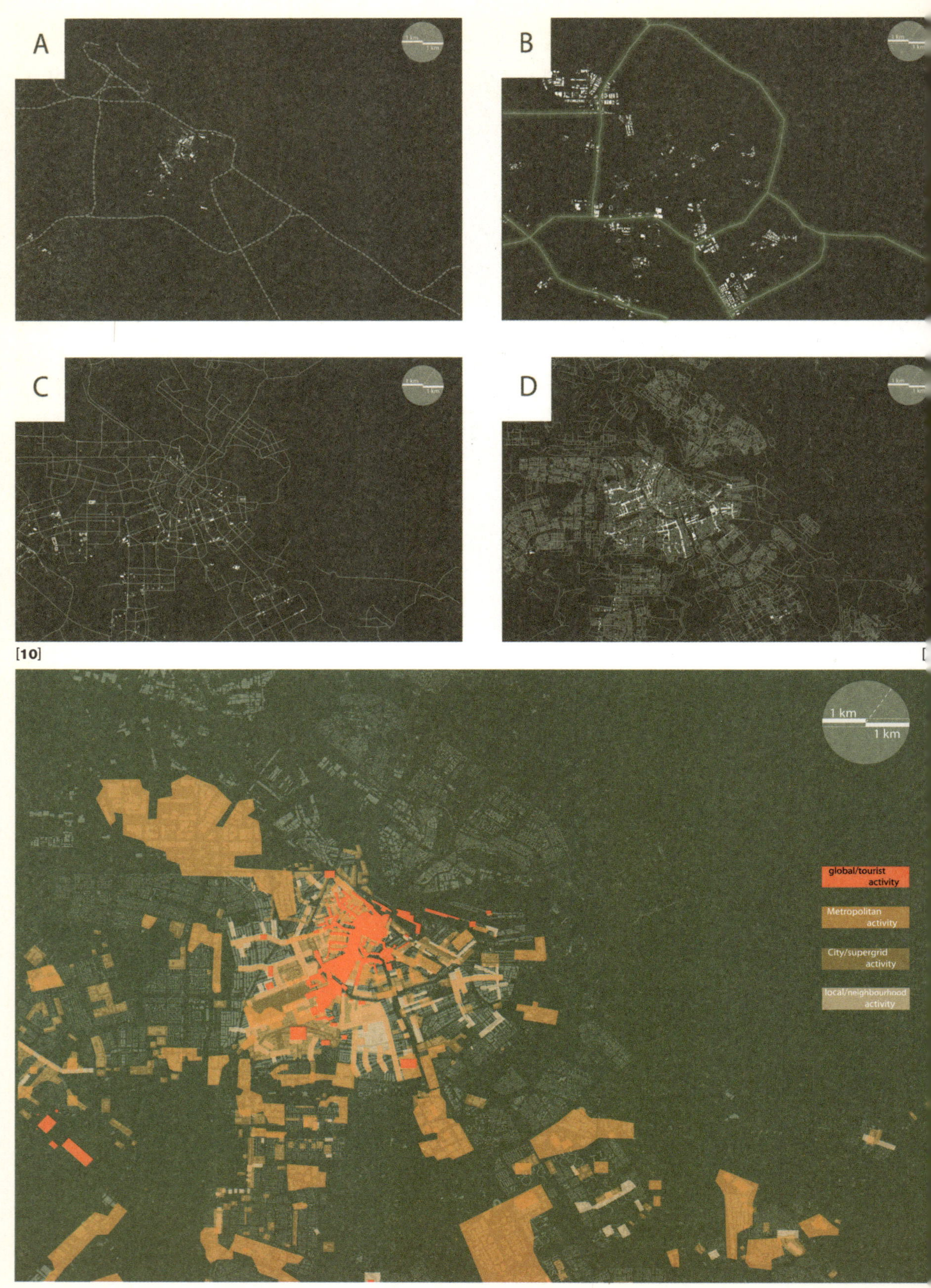
A
1 km
1 km
B
C
D
[10]
1 km
1 km
global/tourist activity
Metropolitan activity
City/supergrid activity
local/neighbourhood activity

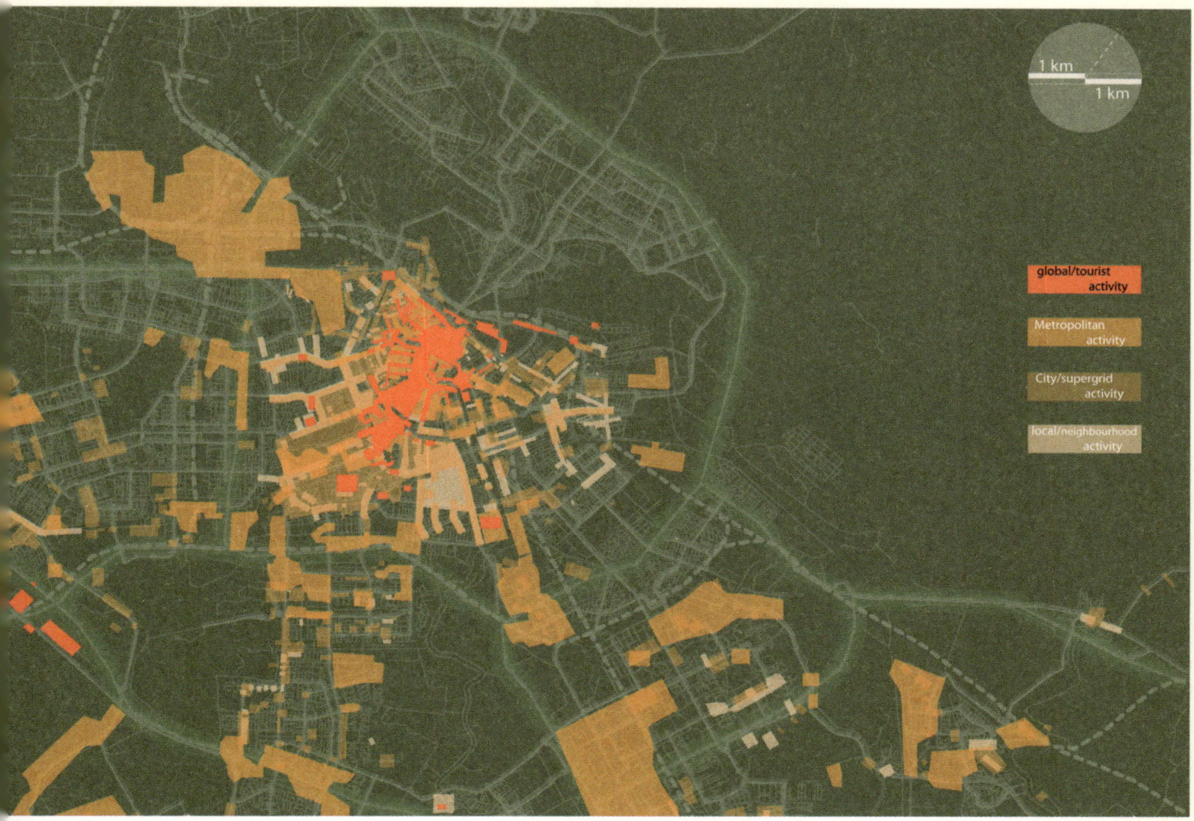

2]

[13]

10 Mobility model vs. the spatial **Form**; a comparison between the individual levels of the mobility grid, and the corresponding commercial activity. Each of these layers represents individual ecologies of spatial operation.
[A] The global mobility scale and the corresponding commercial activity as used by the tourist industry.
[B] Metropolitan scale functions and the corresponding mobility grid/armature of the city.
[C] The middle scale functions, which operate on the city level, and the corresponding mobility scale grid/armature.
[D] The local grid/armature and the corresponding commercial activity.
Source: Author. 2006.

11 Locating spatial **Form,** in relation to the architectural **Form** for Amsterdam and region. Source: Author. 2006.

12 Locating spatial **Form,** in relation to the mobility armature for the city of Amsterdam. Source: Author. 2006.

13 A schematic representation of the vertical ecology of place formation. One place as constructed by the four hierarchies of space, and the mobility grid that supports this formation. Source: Author. 2006.

The runaway train of aesthetics; or understanding the concepts of 'beauty' and 'aesthetics' from an evolutionary perspective

Brent Batstra

Aesthetics is a runaway train; this is what we can experience when the theory of evolution is taken into account while studying aesthetics. Another refreshing experience, able to shake aesthetic theorizing out of its lethargic slumber, is to find that aesthetics has to do mainly with feedback systems of fashion.

However, contrary to most other fields of knowledge, the theory of evolution is seldomly taken into account in theorizing aesthetics. At moments, when it is taken into account, it is often mistaken in its use, as a method to describe aesthetics from the one-sided viewpoint of natural selection, resulting in the common idea that aesthetics is only about the 'survival of the fittest'. This is misleading because for Darwin heritable differences in survival power were as important in evolution as heritable differences in reproduction capacity.[1]

The main core and new insight promoted in this article is that the concept of beauty and aesthetics does not belong to natural selection but to sexual selection.

This article explains the bold statement that aesthetics is a runaway train and still has its 'meaning' in life without reducing aesthetics to a struggle for life.

We can say: If natural evolution shapes life, then sexual evolution shapes the shapes (of life).

Sexual selection: the birth of a new idea

Darwin wrote three pages on sexual selection in his masterpiece *The Origin of Species* (1859), the rest was dedicated to evolution through natural selection. It was not until *The Descent of Man and Selection in Relation to Sex* (1871) that he worked out his new theory of sexual selection.[2] The *main question* of this late work had already been formulated during his travel with the Beagle (1831 – 1836), when Darwin realized that all kinds of extravagant and beautiful ornaments – for instance the golden colours of bugs, or the elongated rump feathers, which cover the tail of the peacock – are not for the sake of survival. When peacocks are feeding, fighting or fleeing their elongated feathers are kept straight to their body.

These ornaments are useless for everyday routine by which animals escape natural selection. His new theory of evolution by natural selection could not explain these seemingly superfluous luxuries. However he knew they only could exist because they helped the animals in question in some way, and they certainly did not exist to delight our eyes or to be a symbol of godly providence. After his return to England it seemed to Darwin that every English garden was awash with peacocks, and their tails constantly reminded him about the shortcomings in his theory.[3]

Darwin overcame his 'peacock-nausea' by elaborating his theory of sexual selection in *Descent*, in which he devoted approximately 550 pages – more than half of his book- to sexual selection.[4] He proposed two main sexual selection processes:

- Males compete among males for the 'possession' of females.[5]
- 'Choosy' females who select among male suitors.[6]

1 **cf.** Miller (2000) p. 39.
2 **ibid.,** pp. 36-37.
3 **ibid.,** p. 35.
4 **ibid.,** p. 36.
5 **ibid.,** pp. 39-41.
6 **ibid.,** pp 39-41.

This article will elaborate only on the second process, namely the female sexual selection.

Darwin's theory of evolution

To call something *evolution* in a Darwinian sense three aspects have to be considered:
1) There has to be *variation* in the members of the studied phenomenon; Darwin always considers the studied phenomena as living 'things'. (Genetic) variation is needed because it opens the possibility of selection. If there is no variation within a population, and taken that it could only live at a certain precise temperature, a radical drop of temperature would mean that the population as a whole would cease to exist. If this were the case evolution of life would not be possible, because of environmental (external) change.[7]
2) *Selection* is the second aspect. Selection (due to scarcity, predators, disasters, excessive negative mutations weakening the species, etc.) takes from a mutated population the weakest individuals in those circumstances. Selection is inevitable if there is life, because unlimited growth will eventually find its limits. These limits are called selection.[8]
3) *Heredity* is the third condition for evolution, because only with random reproduction (thus without accumulation of 'design' through inheritance), no coherent new individual of a certain population will be born and the species face rapid extinction.[9]

Difference and common features in Darwin's three types of selection

Darwin recognizes three kinds of selection The first is *artificial selection*, which he observed with the work of farmers and pigeon-breeders. In artificial selection, humans **select** specific traits on the grounds of economic, aesthetic, or culinary values. Thus they look for **variations** in individuals, and choose an individual on grounds of their experience that these individuals would pass their good values on to the next generation (**'heredity'**).[10]

The second is natural selection. This term implies that (we do as if) selection is 'made by nature'. Under ***'selection'*** we here understand all kinds of 'forces' that put pressure on the individuals of a species, and hence some individuals will die and others will survive. Such pressures can be scarcity (of food, sunlight, water etc.), or predators (who select the weaker specimens), or natural disasters (such as meteorite impacts). '**Variation**' occurs on two levels; firstly through natural selection, secondly on the genetic level through 'mistakes in copying' (mutations). '**Heredity**' here means that the offspring of survivors accumulate their dispositions.
The characteristic of natural selection is that it is all about competition with

respect to relative survival ability within a species (when scarcity arises) or between species (when two species -due to scarcity- have to fight for remaining 'products').[11]

Opposed to natural selection, sexual selection only occurs between individuals of the same species. The competition between individuals is for the sake of the highest relative rate of reproduction.[12] Taking a bird's species as example, where males do not contribute in raising their offspring. And furthermore they differ in tail length (which is inevitable, because biological traits always show **variation**). Mostly much variation is **heritable** due to genetic differences between individuals. Thus males with longer tails normally will have offspring with longer tails. At this point it may be possible that some female birds develop a preference for tails that are longer than average. (It does not matter *why* this preference evolves; it only matters *that* it appears). Once this preference arises, one can speak about sexual selection through mate choice.[13]
Darwin realized that sexual selection (heritable differences in reproduction ability) was as powerful a force in the evolution of species as natural selection (heritable differences in survival ability).[14] He understood that due the 'active choice mechanism' in it, like in artificial selection, it could easily lead to, and explain very diverse existing evolution patterns. Therefore he had found a 'mechanism', which could explain fashion, cycles, taste and beauty in nature, as well as rapid divergence between closely related species, and the growth of extreme 'ornaments' like the tail of the peacock.[15]

Illustrations of sexual selection and natural selection

This article will elaborate on aesthetic phenomena from their sexual selection 'roots'. For this we need a clear understanding of the difference between natural selection and sexual selection in regard to 'a built environment'. This paragraph presents some examples from the realm of animals and humans to illustrate the difference.

Beaver dams and termite hills may be considered as pertaining to natural selection.[16] They are not related to beauty or sexual selection. These 'buildings' are only constructed for the sake of survival. They meet the first motives why species use 'built environments', namely for protection. In nature the foetus and the newly born are in need of the most protection. We see therefore that animals have holes for their young, or nests, or all kinds of secret hiding places for their eggs etc. These ('built')-protection-places need to fulfil certain 'minimal' necessities. They need to be

7 cf. Dawkins (1976), chapters 2 and 3; Ridley (1999), Preface and chapter 1; Miller (2000) pp. 70-72.
8 cf. Dawkins, Miller; Breackman (2001), chapter 3.
9 cf. Miller; Breackman; Dennett (1995), chapters 2 and 3.
10 cf. Miller, pp. 38-39; Breackman.
11 ibid., pp. 38-39; Breackman ch.3.
12 ibid., pp. 38-39; Breackman ch.3.
13 ibid., pp. 70-72; Breackman ch.3.
14 ibid., p. 39.
15 ibid., pp. 39, 35-36.
16 Dawkins (1982) chapter 11.

solid, they need to keep heat (or cold) in, and they need to be defendable. We also see there is in nature a general kind of distinction between labour and dwelling. For example if we consider the most frequent and necessary activity, namely drinking as work, we see the young not being raised nearby drinking places, and certainly in the first weeks of their lives they drink at home from their mother.

These 'built environments' (extended phenotype phenomena) are 'purely' functional. That is to say they are the 'result' of an evolutionary energy cost-profit balance. Therefore, it is self-evident that inefficient 'structures', which do not comply with energy requirements, necessarily will be abandoned (due the pressure of natural selection).

The main distinction between a built environment due to natural selection or sexual selection is that the former is only made **for the sake of survival, and the latter is built for the sake of replication success.**

The best example of the latter is the bowerbird. The male bowerbird builds an elaborate bower of twigs and ferns. Some build whole wooden 'palaces' using twigs of the same length for the roof – between two trees standing about two meters apart – and setting up pillars for support. Others build bowers and decorate them with objects of unusual colour. The Archbold bowerbird's best decoration feature is the very scarce feather from just above the eye of the King of Saxony (a bird of paradise). All bowerbird males use their bowers by trying to seduce females therein. The female inspects the bower and mates if she likes the workmanship and the decoration. The bowerbird's buildings are not for the protection of their offspring, because the females build their nests without the help of males. Once a male bowerbird has mated with one female he is already in the race for mating with others. The buildings of the bowerbird males are an extended product of sexual selection only. Buildings here are the products of the need for display. Buildings are status objects, which indicate power and this finally indicates good genes.[17]

Comparable to the bowerbird's case in the human realm is Mies van der Rohe's Barcelona pavilion. The pavilion is also not a building for living; it has no use, except to display, and exhibit. People appreciate it; they judge it through criteria of workmanship (how the 'white' coloured veins of the marble slabs are placed in accordance with each other, i.e.), people judge it through the 'right' harmony of colours etc. (this we call decoration when bowerbirds are concerned). But what really happens, on a deeper layer, when people are taking all of these features as criteria, is that the building shows how well the architect is synchronized to the preferences of his time. He appears to be one of the best. This is what is called the indicator theory in sexual selection theory.

The following conclusions can be drawn when applying both possibilities for building as mentioned in this paragraph on man-made buildings in general:
• Firstly, we can state that when humans searched for safe places to live (sleep and raise their young) or started building these places, it was for the reason of natural selection.
• Secondly, when they started to use ornaments, or to build follies for instance, it was for the reason of sexual selection.
• It would be a categorical mistake to count ornaments in the ranks of natural selection.[18]

Using sexual selection theory to overcome categorical mistakes in theories on aesthetics

When evolution theory is taken into account in aesthetic theory, the mistake is often made to describe it from the common idea that aesthetics is only about 'survival of the fittest'; a phrase coined by Herbert Spencer.[19] Even Darwin took over Spencer's phrase in later editions of *The Origin of Species* to replace sometimes the term *natural selection*. Therefore Spencer's phrase is misleading, it only stresses on survival power, while for Darwin heritable differences both in survival power and in reproduction capacity (sexual selection) are of equal importance in respect to evolution.[20] Features due to sexual selection tend to completely different forms of appearances because they originate through completely different factors and 'aim' at different goals than features of natural selection. This distinction is much disregarded in theorizing aesthetics and beauty. Many theories on these topics explain aesthetic features from the viewpoint of natural selection, or from economic principles (which themselves find their ground in evolution theory), while the features (ornaments, beauty etc.) they try to explain are solely the product of sexual selection.

Functionalists, for example, based the theory that squandering energy is negative on economic motifs or on social utopian visions (for instance Bauhaus); however these latter visions are also economically underpinned. Their main argument is as follows: ornaments on houses cost extra energy to make, and are not needed for a house to fulfil its function as a house. Therefore, from the economic 'rule of thumb' follows that energy spoilage is undesirable thus ornaments are bad, which they also happened to see as the equivalent of ugly.[21] This condemnation of the ornament in general does not treat the ornament from its own 'category', namely sexual selection, but from natural selection (however that they used natural selection as ultimate criterium, this they probably did not know). The implication of what they did was not only that they judged ornaments from another category, but also based and explained their theory of aesthetics, known as

17 cf. Ridley (1993) p. 143; Miller, pp. 267-270.
18 Even when social reasons are given for the existence of ornaments, such as 'ornaments are demarcating certain places', or 'they indicate certain hierarchies' (Ridley, 1996, **The Origin of Virtue**, mainly chapters 5, 6, 8), these ornaments are as demarcations, or as power and status divisions, indirectly based on the indicator theory of sexual selection. The sexual selection theory applies here too, because the reasoning is that hierarchy in status stands for power and this stands for good genes.
19 cf. Breackman, p. 65; Miller, p. 39.
20 cf. Breackman, p. 112; Miller, p. 39.
21 Tzonis (1972) ch. 11; Müller (1977).

machine aesthetics, on a category foreign to it. They call something beautiful if it is economically good; the unornamented is beautiful because it is economical. This means, in evolutionary terms, that one says 'I find the predator killing his prey beautiful'. One can say this, but one has to remember that this judgement itself does not come from the realm of the natural selection at work there. The judgement originates in sexual selection. It is only with eyes and tastes evolved through sexual selection, that we can judge it as aesthetic. Thus economics, or the social, or natural selection can never be taken as the basis for aesthetic judgements, as Bauhaus theory did.[22] On the contrary: through sexual selection taste has evolved by which we can judge for example economics as beautiful. If we do make such a judgement this would only tell us something about our own evolution by which we developed a taste, which likes economics.

Beside aesthetic theories, like that of Bauhaus, making the fallacy of using the wrong 'category', there are aesthetic theories which try to explain aesthetics from their own right; they refuse to ground it either in economy (the wrong category), or in an indicator function (sexual selection). This means they don't 'ground' it at all; they cannot explain how it originated, and instead their arguments are circular.[23] They state the concept of beauty beforehand, then they study aesthetic phenomena from their conceptual framework, and the results they draw from these phenomena they see as proof for their conceptual framework. Their refusal to 'ground' their concept of beauty in a 'lower level of explanation' means that they stay metaphysical in their explanations.[24]

Liberated from circular aesthetic reasoning, the further aim of this article is to work very carefully from the 'category' of sexual selection alone. This however remains difficult because it goes against many well-established ideas.

Despotic fashions, treadmills, and runaway trains

The first question any sexual selection theory has to answer is: How and why do ornaments arise? In the evolution of life there is constant variation on the genetic level (called mutations) with each new generation. This means 'each male trait begins as a chance mutation. If it happens to hit a sensory bias of the female it starts to spread.'[25] This is a feedback system in evolution. It works as follows: suppose that peahens prefer long tails, a preference which at this point need be no more than an arbitrary fashion.[26] But 'once most females are choosing to mate with some males rather than others and are using tail length as the criterion...then any female who bucks the trend and chooses a short tailed male will have short tailed sons. (This presumes that the son inherit their father's short tail.) Yet all other females are looking for long-tailed males, so those short-tailed sons will not have much success.'[27] At this point the arbitrary fashion becomes a despotic one, because each peahen is on a treadmill and dares not jump off as condemns her sons to celibacy; so she needs 'sexy' sons.[28] As a result of peahens' preference of taste, peacocks are now also in the treadmill, they will get more grotesque encumbrances. Both genders now have become prisoners of their own mutual self-reinforcing feedback loop.[29] 'In Fisher's words, "The two characteristics affected by such a process, namely plumage development in the male and sexual preference in the female, must thus advance together, and so long the process is unchecked by severe counterselection, will advance with ever-increasing speed."'[30] It was Ronald Fisher in 1930 who saw the explanatory power of these *feedback systems* between choosy females and ornamented males. He mathematically proved that feedback systems are exponential. Therefore any arbitrary fashion, which becomes a despotic fashion, is potentially an unlimited exponentially 'growing' feedback system, from which no escape is possible. 'The only limit is extinction', according to Miller: 'if the courtship trait becomes so costly that it imperils the survival of too many individuals, the species may simply die out...Perhaps the ancient Irish elk went [sic] extinct because their sexual ornaments – antlers over six feet wide – proved too burdensome.'[31] This is why every despotic fashion is a potential deadlock. The exponential 'growth' due a despotic fashion is called the runaway-train-of sexual-selection theory, which could end in extinction.

Good genes The second question posed at evolution theory is: How and why does female taste arise? If female preferences can lead to extinction, why should evolution then favour female preferences? Until now we only know that female preferences happen to be there and function as an explanation for the 'growth' of all kinds of ornamentation and male skills. But what is the reason behind these dangerous female preferences? The two main theories on this topic are:

1 The 'good-genes' indicator theory

2 The 'sexy-son' theory

Both theories can exist next to each other, or even in combination. They are not naturally exclusive per se.

22 For example in trying to fuse the artist and the architect together (cf. Müller, p. 148), Bauhaus – in Darwinist terminology – actually tried to subsume sexual selection under natural selection.

23 See for instance the essays **Der Ursprung des Kunstwerkes**, and **Die Zeit des Weltbildes**, in Heidegger, M., **Holzwege**, Vittorio Klostermann, Frankfurt am Main, 1950.

24 For example where architecture has to originate in fantasy [thus in metaphysics] according to W. Gropius and B. Taut, otherwise architecture and its aesthetic ideas will be determined and limited through its use as technique (cf. Müller, p. 62) [thus grounded in natural selection].

25 Ridley (1993) p.162; cf. p. 140.

26 **cf.** pp. 134-5; Miller, pp. 34-99; Breackman, ch. 3

27 **ibid.,** pp. 134-135.

28 The terms 'son' and 'celibacy' are from what some call rather exclusively the human realm. They are used in this article for both humans and animals in an **as if** way of speaking as is common in Darwinism. For a good discussion of this see Dennett, chapter 8. The term 'sexy' I will use later in the term 'sexy-son theory'. However there is no common name for this theory, I follow Matt Ridley in this. Helena Cronin, who has written a standard book on the history of sexual selection calls it 'good-taste', I prefer sexy-son because it directly relates to the goal on the basis of what choice is made, while good-taste leaves this open.

29 **cf.** Miller, p. 53; Ridley, (1993), pp. 135, 138-142.

30 Ridley (1993) p. 135.

31 Miller (2000) p. 42.

Evolution is about variations, 'some good some bad'. The good-gene indicator theory states that in sexual selection the best genotype is selected, by 'looking' at the phenotype (= the body grown out of the DNA; genes), and its extended phenotype (= the tools a body uses, which are separate from it).
Since the 1980s, scientists influenced by the theory of sexual selection, gathered an overwhelming amount of empirical corroborating evidence for the theory that certain clearly sensible features of males are an indication of good or bad health. Scientists, for example, discovered that it is carotene which colours combs and wattles, the orange colour of guppy fish, the house finch's and flamingo's plumages. This carotene can only be extracted from food, and the peculiarity is that parasites affect negatively the ability to extract carotenoids from food and deliver it to the tissue of the animal involved.[32] Researchers concluded as a rule *that within a species, the more flamboyant a male's ornament is, the lower will be his parasite burden.*[33] The general conclusion, which is expressed in the good-gene-theory, is that ornaments are indicators for good-genes, because they form a handicap for the bearer and if he can cope well with it, then it is a clear visible sign for his health. Thus if only the carriers of the best genes are also the carriers of the best ornaments, then this display is extremely useful for choosy females. It is known that females generally favour males with fewer parasites; this holds for sage grouse, bowerbirds, frogs, guppies, crickets, pheasants, jungle-fowl, amd swallows among others.[34]
We see that it makes sense to select the other sex on their display, because finding a mate with the best genes promises the best offspring. Therefore, to get the best genotype, females discriminate on the basis of sense information (colour, form, sound, etc.) of the phenotype.

An example of the good genes theory related to buildings in nature is the bower of a bowerbird. Bowerbirds build a bower, not for living, but only to impress female bowerbirds. A fit bowerbird must be able to make a good bower and to maintain it, and to protect his bower against the robberies of other males. Therefore it must be fitter than a bowerbird with a worse bower. This means that the bower, the extended phenotype of the bird, is an indicator of the bowerbirds good- or bad-genes.

Good-gene-indicator theory applied to human buildings tells us that a simple, poorly constructed building, which only offers safety, does not get our aesthetic appraisals; the builder is not much prized. If an architect makes from a simple building plan a building that not only offers safety, but is a joy for the eye as well, then the architect of such a building is praised for his good job and his status rises. For a high-rise building, or a bridge, or a train station or whatever challenging structure, it is clear that these built-forms **are** more impressive on their own account already. When these built-forms are now also extravagantly or heavily ornamented, or just very sober but carefully detailed, then the impressiveness now relates – through its extraordinary features – to the impressive mathematical and physical under-layer, which again must be even better for such an impressive building not to collapse. The architect will get more appreciation. This analogy therefore tells us that impressive buildings are in this respect expressions of the good-genes of the architect (and the owner). This is what the good-gene-indicator theory states.

The sexy-son theory The sexy-son theory states that there are male ornaments preferred by females, which are not indicators for good-genes. This theory starts with the female preference as explained by the indicator theory; so females do not pick out features arbitrarily anymore, because they have preference tastes favoured by their evolution of picking out the good genes indicators (since females and their offspring falling for the wrong indicator have faced evolutionary extinction). The question to answer is: How can females with evolved preference tastes make the mistake of selecting males on the grounds of indicators which do not relate to good genes? The answer is rather simple. What worked in the past is no guarantee for what will work in the future; evolution gives no guarantees. So if new random features emerge (which is the case in every new generation), it can happen that females pick a feature, which accidentally has no relation with good genes. Perhaps the newly chosen feature looks very much like a good gene indicator, and females are misled by this. However, we know once females start to favour one feature the runaway train starts its 'unstoppable' ride. Females cannot 'get off the train', unless they want their sons to become unpopular and live a celibate life.[35] Therefore if females have chosen a feature they have to follow the chosen fashion. We saw (in the paragraph *Despotic fashions, treadmills, and runaway trains*) that when a runaway train is formed it is worse bucking the trend than that there is no relation between the trend and good-genes. If an individual bucks the trend and chooses for better genes against the runaway train's direction, then her offspring will face celibacy and her genetic line faces extinction. So all individuals will follow the trend, also if this means that they finally all are going to die, because they all favoured the wrong indicators. The main criterion has become: get sexy sons, follow the fashion, and do not buck the trend. It thus can happen that a runaway train is not based on good-genes, but solely due to fashion.[36] This is what 'fashion for the sake of fashion' in evolution implicates.

This does not mean it is fashion only, because once such a trend 'grows' exponentially, the chosen ornament or skill will become a high burden for males. So eventually it becomes an indicator showing males who can 'carry the burden and who cannot'. However if there is no direct relation with genes and it is only a matter of display, males can cheat. Therefore, when males only have to 'price their goods through advertising', and females have to copy other female's choices, due to

32 **cf.** Ridley (1993) p. 151.
33 **ibid.,** p. 147.
34 **ibid.**
35 **ibid.,** p. 135.
36 **ibid.,** p. 142.

group pressure, for fashion's sake, it is more probable that males start 'cheating' (because it is easier than carrying a high burden). Bowerbird males can more easily cheat, for example by stealing materials from the bowers of other males. In humanity the relation has become even more extended and polluted. All kinds of 'intermediaries' have come in between the display and what it indicates (good-genes).[37]

What this theory states in relation to humans is that all kinds of fashion following trends originate in indication theory. But, tastes which originated through choosing the right genes, do not necessarily have to stay linked to good genes anymore. There is a gap between the origin and the actual, or present, taste. Because of this gap tastes can be aimed purely at fashion for the sake of fashion. Mankind has evolved in a direction which widens this gap even more. Therefore it seems as if beauty or aesthetics has grown to become a level of its own, which has no direct link anymore with sexual selection. However, this distinction does not hold in the end, as we have seen. So the question 'How to deal with this problem?' can be put forward, but to answer it would exceed the subject matter of this article.[38] Therefore this article takes human fashion-following behaviour into direct relation with the sexy-son theory.
Another point we have to realize in relation to mankind is that the appearance in evolution of 'fashion for the sake of fashion' is a strategy. This strategy however is not rooted in good genes, therefore it can only prosper in times of abundance, and otherwise the burden with which males are saddled would be too great. Only in times of abundance males are able to 'carry the trend' for a longer time.

Examples of this 'for fashion's sake' theory we have in abundance in the history of architecture. The builders of the great cathedrals were lured into a kind of treadmill to build the highest, biggest and most elaborate cathedral; it is only because they did not live in a time of abundance that their runaway train stopped before a cathedral collapsed. In France we can still witness the ruins of an unfinished super-cathedral as the silent remnants of this treadmill. And in the epoch of the baroque we can recognize a treadmill of ornaments, which was finally broken by a change in economy and in fashion.[39]
In 'our time' we can see several runaway trains; one of them is the 'battle' for the highest structures, which continues as the battle for the highest building; other 'battles' are for the most impressive museum, or the most complex mega-struc-

37 cf. Miller, p. 104-107.
38 This problem, about the different levels in evolution theory, is discussed very well by Dennett, chapter 9.
39 Here one can easily argue that fashion followed economy, again this is beyond the scope of this article. This argument is dealt with in my PhD research in the chapter **Three strategies**.

tures, or the most ingeniously technological *tour de force*, etc. All these 'battles' are kinds of runaway trains, which drive us greatly because of our passion for 'bigness-fashion' (superlatives are more common in times of abundance), according to the sexy-son theory. These 'battles' are still continuing in our times of abundance. There is no counterselection (yet), because of the abundance of money (energy) in certain circles of human society.

Conclusion

Superficially, this article engages in sexual selection theory in relation to aesthetics, and it looks for the possible implications when it is applied to humankind and its built environment. The results are the following:

Firstly, it shows that this application may be done, something, which has possibly not been attempted before, and not with the aims of this article.

Secondly, it proposes to look at aesthetic theories and at the concepts of *aesthetics* and *beauty*, from the 'category' of sexual selection. The advantage this gives is that these concepts do not have to be metaphysical anymore, but can be grounded (in a lower level of explanation). As a consequence, aesthetics will finally start to belong to the realm of science. This article has taken the first step, by trying to *perceive* aesthetics as a product of evolution. This shift in perception of the aesthetic can lead (eventually) to the conduct of crucial experiments on the theory.

Thirdly this article implies that the discourse and theory on architecture can become more 'pure'. Non-falsifiable theories should be abandoned, and architecture can start to analyse itself from the basis of the two introduced 'categories', *natural-* and *sexual selection*. From this starting point, the indicator-theory and sexy-son theory are applied to get a better understanding of the importance and the role which style and fashion play in architecture.

Fourthly, this article carries an implicit 'warning'. By rethinking aesthetics from an evolutionary stance the awareness can grow that contemporary aesthetics, including architecture, is on a runaway train which runs, not on a 'genetic-level' anymore, but for fashion's sake only. Getting insight into the mechanisms of evolution could raise the awareness that one can jump off a runaway train driving for fashion.

Yet the question remains; who will be the first to jump?

Bibliography

Breackman, J. **Darwins moordbekentenis** [Dutch – Darwin's murder confession]. Amsterdam: Uitgeverij Nieuwezijds, 2001.

Dawkins, R. **The Selfish Gene [1976]**. Revised edition. Oxford New York: Oxford University Press, 1989.

Dawkins, R. **The Extended Phenotype [1982]**. Revised edition. Oxford University Press, Oxford New York, 1999.

Dennett, D. **Darwin's Dangerous Idea [1995]**. 2th ed. Penguin Books, 1996.

Miller, G. **The Mating Mind [2000]**. New York: Anchor Books Edition, 2001.

Müller, M. **Die Verdrängung des Ornaments**. Frankfurt am Main: Suhrkamp Verlag, 1977.

Ridley, M. **The Red Queen [1993]**. Penguin Books, 1994.

Ridley, M. **Genome**. **Great Britain:** Fourth Estate Limited, 1999.

Tzonis, A. **Towards a Non-Oppressive Environment**. Boston: i Press, 1972.

Critique, theory, praxis: escaping the modernist dialectic
Propositions: learning from then, producing for now

Lara Schrijver

Contemporary issues are deeply rooted in the 1960s. How and why some of the projects failed at the time can illustrate why they are in part being resurrected today.[1] The ambiguity in the work of the 1960s has not been adequately examined – it has simply been utilized either to ridicule the unrealistic venture of the utopian project or to hide behind the safety of waiting for the world to change. Although I concur with David Harvey when he states that postmodernism's eclecticism was not a thorough way of engaging with the cultural transformations in perceptions of space and time, I'm not sure that the American Marxist discourse can offer the plurality he considers fundamental to the postmodern condition.[2] As long as a single discourse is considered preferable to others, plurality is by necessity undermined.

In short: I believe that the democratization that took place in the architecture of the 1960s (through such images and mechanisms as a valuation of individual opinion and the everyday life of the street) was significantly indebted to the rise of the mass media and the way they were incorporated in architectural practice. Mass imagery offered a release from the more 'purified' forms of high modernist discourse, and introduced a mode of communication with the man in the street. Yet the liberating aspects of this excursion outside the bounds of 'high architecture' also opened a Pandora's box of public relations, complicity with vested commercial interests (replacing traditional power structures), the problems of advertising and the tendency to relinquish expertise in favor of 'what the people want' (uncritical populism).
In other words, what the 1960s left us with is a mixed blessing: the promise of individual freedom is exhilarating when set against the authoritarian society of the 1950s, yet rings hollow when public cohesion seems lost, when there is little communal structure to help define this individuality. The idea that mass imagery and the ephemeral, fleeting quality of the mass media might help form a new aesthetic for a more communicative architecture is admirable, but becomes suspect when architects avoid responsibility for their work by simply replicating mass culture rather than making clear and well-argued choices. Finally, the notion of technology as an instrument of liberation is crucial to the ongoing developments in both the modern and the postmodern, but that does not mean we can close our eyes to the less pleasant consequences of technological progress – in that sense, we cannot hold to a neutral instrumentality of technology, but must acknowledge the autonomy it has also displayed.

These issues are the foundation of the society of the spectacle – they circumscribe the 'paradigm shift' of the 1960s, and indicate the similarities between questions that were raised. Although groups such as the Situationist International (F), Venturi Scott Brown and Associates (USA) and Archigram (UK) were all working within extremely different cultural contexts, there was a more globally-oriented, transatlantic debate that had everything to do with the position of the indi-

1 For example, although the Situationist International (F, 1957-1972) was only marginally influential beyond their own circles at the height of their activity, they have since been rediscovered and revitalized. First in 1989 with an exhibition at the ICA in Boston curated by Elisabeth Susskind; and in the past decade, there has been an enormous amount of Situationist writing posted on the Internet, as a logical questioning of the 'spectacular' conditions of the late 20th century.
2 David Harvey (1990) pp. 10-12.

vidual in an authoritarian form of modernism and the question of a critical stance at the advent of late capitalism, determined by mass media and commercial interests. This position of the 'critical' is thus defined by resistance against the spectacle, while all else becomes a form of affirmation. On the one hand, we then have complicity with the media spectacle in the form of not only star architects but also celebrity chefs, celebrity fashion designers and even celebrity castaways on Survivor Island. On the other, we have a general form of resistance such as that posed by the SI against the spectacle. This resistance however also paved the way for an apolitical stance as exemplified in deconstruction. Since it is based on resistance as its fundamental strategy, it never takes a stance for anything but always remains *against*, thus remaining by definition apolitical.[3]

Potential models What I am aiming at is to find a different conceptual structure here, something that theorists and practitioners will find useful to work with as a new set of ideas, and which may help illuminate forms of practice that are innovative yet underexposed. The basic characteristics of this model are many, but they include a tendency towards plurality rather than the dialectic, and a place for aesthetics as more than just representational or matter of taste, as productive in their own right. It is built on the notion of a 'material practice', encompassing the contamination of reflection and production, as appropriate to a contemporary culture steeped in contamination rather than modern purity. The combination between theory and praxis is viewed as helpful in trying to move beyond cynical reason. The notions of contamination and plurality are essentially postmodern, while the interpretation of aesthetics as productive can be considered modern. The notions of material practice and the combination theory/praxis settle this into the contemporary debate, which is seeking a form of engagement with reality.

Suggestions towards a 'sensibility' from other forms of culture outside of architecture might include: skateboarding as a subversive urban activity, especially when it appropriates corporate space, or the idea of culture jamming in between commodity culture and aesthetic resistance, a contemporary form of *détournement*. Another point of interest might be hacker ethics with the belief in equality on the Internet, yet also subverting power structures by targeting Microsoft in its position as a powerful corporation. Furthermore, in many areas of aesthetic production there is a revaluation of craft, expertise, and beauty as a form of resistance to overly politicized work, possibly since overpoliticization offers only a single interpretation. In this sense, private reflection is productive, and contemporary imagery possibly allows that by being less linear or direct.[4] Moreover, high technology and new materials are also being utilized as more than a mere image of functionalism or of modernity.

Beyond cynical reason Above all, this also questions the role of theory in the architecture discourse.[5] While the nihilistic analyses of the 1970s and 80s revealed the failure of the 1960s in the most painful way; and while they also contributed to a highly conscious mode of architectural practice (awareness of underlying presumptions on gender etc.), they also left a gaping hole where the orientation towards a better future once had been. The pure analysis (to the point of destruction) of underlying societal meanings in architecture neglects the importance of aesthetics and of architectural meaning.

In recent years, many publications have testified to the need to once again reconsider a positive, active role for theory. These suggestions again resonate throughout various sources of architecture theory, from architects' writings to philosophical and cultural studies. A key text as yet undiscussed in the architecture debate is a rigorous questioning of the contemporary position of 'critique' by Bruno Latour, which will be discussed in detail below. Others negotiating the terrain of 'critical theory' and its position in a late capitalist world of spectacle are Michael Hays, Kate Nesbitt, Sarah Whiting, George Baird (in architecture), and Douglas Kellner and Douglas Rushkoff (in media studies) to name but a few.

Michael Hays has suggested a strategy called 'scanning' to help define the work of Diller + Scofidio; this would view architecture more as a 'tool of social cartography.'[6] This strategy as described by Hays performs a critical function in its assessment of underlying sociocultural assumptions, yet also retains some agency in its (positive) invention of new modes of thinking (and creating) architecture. The salient aspect of 'scanning' as defined here is its distinction from critique simply by being embedded or complicit with its surroundings – it works within the mechanisms of the market, yet also documents problems within this very context. To Hays, Diller + Scofidio 'are aware that even the more self-conscious and sophisticated tactics of rebellion and negative critique seem to be, in our time, not so much co-opted by "the system" as they are a strategic part of the system's internal workings.'[7] Sadly, he also proposes that if architecture is primarily valued as a tool of social cartography, the 'architecture henceforth need not achieve or even propose a building,' while it would seem that this is precisely where the major potential of architecture lies – in its bridging of social commentary and construction of the environment.[8]

3 An escape from both media complicity and pure deconstruction is suggested by Jean Lyotard's loss of meta-narratives (**La Condition Postmoderne**). Accepting a loss of meta-narratives allows a middle ground between committing entirely to the spectacle in all its forms and resisting the consumer society wholesale, by demanding that each response is to a **specific** condition and **specific** instance.

4 As early as 1958, Lawrence Alloway comments on the importance of personal experience of significance; Alloway (1958) pp. 84-85.

5 The phrase 'cynical reason' as borrowed from Peter Sloterdijk revolves around the cynicism that ensues when the 'enlightened' rational being is entirely buffered from any impact, any form of critique thanks to theory. In other words, the senses of both meaning and value begin to fade. This is closely related to the smug position of the critic as will be addressed below in relation to Bruno Latour.

6 Hays (2003) pp. 230-233.

7 Hays (2003) p. 231.

8 Hays (2003) p. 230.

In a recent publication George Baird examines the current position of 'criticality' in relation to the field of architecture, suggesting also that this is the moment that a renegotiation of the position of theory within architecture is inevitable.[9] He even relates this to a distinction between the European and American practices of theory and architecture. He notes that criticality in its traditional form is under attack, and that critics such as Michael Speaks, Robert Somol and Sarah Whiting are all trying to formulate something other than the (by now traditional) resistance against conditions of commodity and spectacle. This would lead to the formulation of a new program for architecture practice (called 'projective' by Whiting and Somol) that leaves behind the Marxist or leftist notion of criticality.

The sociologist Scott Lash points out that in contemporary society, part of the problem is that the 'speed and ephemerality of information leaves almost no time for reflection.'[10] Here I would argue that we might want to reconsider the relationship between critique and reflection. Maybe it is less about slow, careful 'disinterested' reflection on a single object or concept, and more about a slippery form of reflection based on pattern recognition and comparison, on discovering and examining what I call resonances in order to reflect on a more strategic (as opposed to essential) level. This is called a 'slipping in and out' of critical modes of thinking as Whiting uses, or an 'embedded critique' as I've called it. Whatever the label may be, it undermines the notion of a fixed essence, but still demands definition and specificity. Related to this is his observation that information 'makes no claims to universality but is contained in the immediacy of the particular.'(p. 233) This also recalls one of the aspects of the failure of 1960s utopias: by extending individual revolution to a universal condition, the specificity of the particular was lost.

Most important in the renegotiation of critique is perhaps a subtle comment by Sarah Whiting that indicates just how crucial the intermingling of practice and theory has become in the contemporary debate. To her, utilizing architectural expertise is crucial: 'architects must engage, lead, catalyze – *act*, rather than *react*. Our expertise lies in defining forms, spaces, and materialities; we should not be afraid of the results and subjectivities (read: *biases*) that such definition implies. Unlike other disciplines in the liberal arts, architecture's relationship to critical theory is not entirely concentric. Rather than bemoan this fact or conclude that theory has no bearing on architecture – two options that guarantee architecture's intellectual suicide – architects interested in the progressive project have no choice but to take advantage of our ability to slip in and out of critical theory's rule.'[11] The call to action is unmistakeable here, and tends perhaps even to the modernist and 1960s manifestoes; yet the idealism is tempered by her awareness of the limitations of the field. There are biases inherent in the forms and materialities of architecture – she simultaneously acknowledges this and reminds us that that need not lead to impotence. Her emphasis of architectural expertise reins theory back into a relationship with the actual production of architecture, and her willingness to accept that something must be *defined* or made specific to have an impact allows a more active engagement with the world than a permanent position of resistance.

The suggestions above share a belief in forward-looking without the modernist *tabula rasa*, and in critique without the permanently antithetical stance of deconstruction. Each of these propositions is difficult for its shades of meaning, and dangerous for its potential to become the next dogma. The need for words of description is inevitable, but the labels again risk becoming the next big hype. Therefore, when I suggest such notions as realism, pragmatism, embedded critique, I hope their meaning and intent remain the primary focus rather than the catch-phrase. Here also, history may fulfill a vital role: for by understanding history as an essential part of our present, as part of the very fabric of our society, it may become more than either a selection of (meaningless) historical forms, or an inescapable weight determining our actions.

What is also apparent in almost all of these discussions is the difficulty of positioning critique within the society of the spectacle. Conditions of consumer culture and the omnipresence of the media return in each analysis, and the relevance of critique in this relatively new conglomeration of market forces and public relations is not in question, but the intent of traditional critique is: the radical revolution of overthrowing an entire system seems untenable, yet a critical eye remains paramount. It is within these conditions that an assessment of the 1960s' forms of critique seems to the point (if not downright necessary). In following the Frankfurt School and Marxism's ideas on critical theory, 'critical' has become identified with resistance and negation, while what I am suggesting here is less about resistance and more about critique from within. If public space has become too entangled with corporate interests, it is more useful to design a public space that transcends these interests than it is to not design anything at all, or than it might be to merely point out that something is complicitous.

Critique and consumer culture Most of the notions of criticality as handled in contemporary (transatlantic) discourse are founded on a Marxist position embedded in consumer culture. Taking pleasure in consumer culture and various forms of mass culture is accepted, but the analysis of these forms of cultural expression is typically premised on ideas of reification and a need for critical assessment to penetrate beyond the surface affect. The tenuousness of this position is usually emphasized within the text through a discomfort with the slippery conditions of media and commodity culture, often positioning architecture as either hopeless affirmation or the locus of resistance.

9 Baird (2004).
10 Lash (2001) p. 233.
11 Whiting (2003) p. 502.

The strength of the few hints given by Whiting is that they discard these notions of the critical in favor of a position of neither autonomy nor servitude but rather a critical and affirmative function: the possibility to slip in and out of critical theory, as she calls it. Again, I take the 1960s as the grounding of this transformation since it both wallows in the profusion of the time yet formulates a program of (general) critical resistance (to modernism, to the spectacle, to standardization).

Whiting's position appears to offer the kind of relationship with consumption that Hays mentions as a relationship no longer defined by resistance and negation but transformed into something other.[12] And this seems a way to sidestep the congealed definitions of revolution that continue to be based on 1968. Revolution now may well be found in culture jamming rather than burning the streets. In architecture, it may well be based on creating the best building for a specific program. Perhaps the problem is no longer to build a radically different environment (which also, in the forms suggested by Archigram and the situationists, embodies a singular logic, negating their own rhetoric of indiviudality and difference), but rather to build a beautiful environment.

Theory and critique in the age of spectacle To help frame my suggestions which are still by necessity incomplete due to their contemporary focus, I would like to borrow some suggestions from Bruno Latour. As noted above, a need for a different direction has been expressed in various forms. Yet architecture theory has not yet been able to fully address this. It seems that Latour, among others has at least some suggestions on a 'sensibility' that may prove fruitful to architecture.

One of the 'problems' in architecture discourse today is the notion of the critical and whether it is not too nihilistic an endeavor. This leads to suggestions such as a 'projective practice' (Whiting and Somol) which is understood to incorporate both critical elements and a component of agency. However, I turn here to Latour because he offers a different suggestion for critique.[13] My hope for what I have called 'embedded critique' is here simply used to reframe our current understanding of 'critical'. As noted above, 'critical' in this discourse is often conflated with negation and resistance. Or, as Latour puts it: 'What if explanations resorting automatically to power, society, discourse had outlived their usefulness and deteriorated to the point of now feeding the most gullible sort of critique?'[14] He identifies certain problems with the very structure of critique in cultural studies that derive from the type of analyses I have discussed in the architecture discourse of the 1960s. Latour also immediately warns against a facile appropriation of earlier arguments such as those used by situationism or Archigram for contemporary problems. Although the resonance in their questions may be striking, a critical eye is always necessary. The failure of an earlier solution 'does not mean … that we were wrong, but simply that history changes quickly and that there is no greater intellectual crime than to address with the equipment of an older period the challenges of the present one.'[15]

Another reason to turn to Latour for suggestions on a different approach in architecture is his emphasis on realism. As a critic, he distances himself from purely theoretical observations that remove themselves from the world at hand. He posits: 'The question was never to get *away* from facts but *closer* to them, not fighting empiricism but, on the contrary, renewing empiricism. What I am going to argue is that the critical mind, if it is to renew itself and be relevant again, is to be found in the cultivation of a *stubbornly realist attitude* – to speak like William James – but a realism dealing with what I will call *matters of concern*, not *matters of fact*. The mistake we made, the mistake I made, was to believe that there was no efficient way to criticize matters of fact except by moving *away* from them and directing one's attention *toward* the conditions that made them possible. But this meant accepting much too uncritically what matters of fact were.'[16] The idea Latour posits here of a 'stubbornly realist attitude' encompasses a realism that goes beyond the traditional understanding of empirical realism. Latour is referring primarily to the sciences, defined by an empirical realism that was eventually reduced to *only* measurable and quantifiable entities. His desire to move beyond this to a 'stubborn realism' is about taking other factors into account as well (not instead of but in addition to measurable traits), such as social influences or (conventional) meaning. I use the phrase 'critical realism' here to maintain the sense of careful observation and reflection implied with the word 'critical'. As an extension of his argument, 'matters of concern' entail seeing the object as more than a merely quantifiable entity, or a 'matter of fact'.[17]

This strong sense of what I am calling a 'critical realism', concerning itself with both the observation of reality and the critical view of what constitutes that reality, seems precisely where architecture discourse will find a productive strategy, by both acknowledging the reality of the world it is building in, yet remaining aware of how it is constituted. Moreover, Latour's distinction between matters of concern and matters of fact is a beautifully precise formulation of one of the problems of the discourse: that somehow matters of fact have been either radically affirmed in an objective scientific tradition, without the opportunity for questioning their context, or radically negated in architecture theories like deconstructivism, where every 'fact' was consituted *only* by its context, and thereby lost its own status in reality.

In the rhetoric of the 1960s, these problems begin to surface in critique not necessarily when it appeals to disbelief (as a mode of skepticism to aid in resisting facile presumptions), but when it

12 Hays (1998) p. xiv. See for full quote below, note 18.
13 Latour, (2004), pp. 225-248.
14 **ibid.,** pp. 229-30.
15 **ibid.,** p. 231.
16 **ibid.,** p. 231.
17 Following this line of reasoning, the social issues that the modernists addressed in their manifestoes, in principle 'matters of concern,' were reduced to 'matters of fact' by their tendency to quantify.

appeals to what Latour calls 'powerful agents hidden in the dark acting always consistently, continuously, relentlessly.' (p.229) These 'agents hidden in the dark' are continuously lurking at the edges of Debord's critique of the spectacle – the dominance of capitalism is indeed acting relentlessly and consistently, and therefore in a sense already undermines the possibility of critique. This tension between the dependence on critique for liberation, and on the other hand the 'secret powers' that mercilessly define our world is an unproductive illusion still plaguing some ideas on the role of the critical in architecture. It simultaneously posits the need for an active resistance while fatalistically accepting the pointlessness of this resistance. The impasse in this position suggests that perhaps the problem today is not that resistance needs to be reactivated, but rather that critique and agency need to be redefined. Critique in its traditional sense puts everyone in a bind: are you seeing what you think you see? Is there not another level of reality behind that, controlled by some evil forces of domination? And therefore, is not meaning as you know it completely without value? Agency as defined by a leftist scheme of power and alienation is simply impossible in the society of the spectacle. Yet is it not true that within the spectacle there is also agency? Is a consumer-boycott not a form of agency with respect to corporations? And is the act of building by definition not a form of agency?

Strategies The primary reason to discuss this issue of critique and theory so extensively is that a revised strategy could aid in escaping some of the 1960s dichotomies mentioned earlier. The failure of the 1968 revolution deepened the chasm between theory and architecture; by navigating the middle ground and revising the relationship between theory and practice we may find a way to move beyond the polemical reductions of pure radicality. This has become ever more important in the age of late capitalism, where the consumer society has fundamentally transformed conditions of production. Following a comment by Michael Hays: 'It may well turn out that a different, younger audience, whose relationship to consumption is altogether altered, whose memories may not include any notions of resistance or negation, may have to produce another kind of theory premised on neither the concept of reification nor the apparatus of the sign, both of which have their ultimate referent in the vexatious territory of reproducibility and commodity consumption.'[18] Note here the key concepts of consumption, resistance, negation, the sign; all of which are omnipresent in the 1960s discourse on architecture. The roots of what Hays is suggesting as a new direction for theory lie in the 1960s, and before that in the 1920s.

Although I believe we should look to our own field for the critical questions and the expertise to resolve them, there are perhaps some suggestions we can take from other disciplines for strategy. The examples above of the shifting of architecture theory and the debate are intentionally culled from the architecture debate – they indicate what the issues are *within* the discipline. Moreover, the discussion of how we got here is through the architecture debate, albeit framed through mechanisms of mass culture and the media. The knowledge of the history of the discipline and the expertise of the field in its fullest extent – from rhetoric to image to building – is crucial to developing the discipline in a sensible way. Yet since critique itself has become such an important element in this constellation, I also believe it wise to look just over the fence and examine some alternative strategies. Hence the introduction of thinkers such as Kellner, Rushkoff and Latour, diverse as they are, to offer some possibilities of reframing the arguments, not the content, of architecture production.

Images and words We could also question whether part of the so-called impasse or crisis of contemporary architecture lies not so much in architecture but more in two things: the simplistic rendering of the power of words and images and their relationship; and also the professionalization of the discourse in the twentieth century. Especially the latter has presented some problems in the relationship with imagery, since each image was taken to signify an infinite expanse of problematic assumptions, mostly socio-political. Yet the significance of aesthetics and the image itself was demoted to a lowly spot in the hierarchy of meaning. This allowed an extensive analysis of meaning without ever needing to enter the difficult arena of the power of imagery, unless that image was somehow dominant in a dangerous fashion. Yet the poetry inherent in the aesthetic experience was set aside in favor of the social construction of meaning.

The complexity of the relationship has increased – images are now not only settled within a specific cultural context, but also in a global setting. Yet the common complaint is that the richness of an earlier aesthetics has disappeared. This could indicate that contemporary imagery is lacking in imagination or aesthetics, or it could indicate that the vocabulary we have is not (yet) prepared to address it.

Individuation in the collective Along the same lines of traditional critique, the city itself can be deemed to be in crisis. However, the vocabulary used to address the city is often still defined by the distinctions between the rural (collective) and the metropolitan (individual). Instead, by examining the manifestations of an urban form of *Gemeinschaft*, a new set of definitions could be found to address the place of the individual within a collective without destroying his individuality. This redefinition of community might also involve the visual symbolism of contemporary everyday life as support for social conventions. We might even see in this a return to the communicative nature of visual understanding of the (pre-) nineteenth century. This turn towards images as communicable (as opposed to consumable) could then fulfill a counter-function to the total loss of public space. Above all, the mutual interaction between an

18 Hays, (1998), p. xiv (introduction).

individual and the collective should remain at the forefront of any discussion. Here again, the importance of a level of realism becomes clear: each individual has a right to self-realization through individuation, but contrary to what was claimed in the 1960s' manifestoes, each individual also has a responsibility within the collective which is not necessarily served by individual emancipation.

Technology in various forms Technology too may find new forms of criticism from within. Although the quintessential expression of modernity has been through technological metaphors of speed and the machinic, the reassessment of technology as a metaphor in the 1960s has also opened up a different view. Yet a pure negation based on an apocalyptic view also denies the very real progress that has been offered through technologies. The introduction of the Internet in China, despite attempts by the government to regulate and police it, helped information exchange.

Critique, the visual, and the radical Critique is in fact a problematic notion: by extending the avant-garde idea of a principally *critical* function of the visual, of symbols and of imagery, the 1960s discourse presented a problem in addressing the visual. The aesthetics of visual production are not reducible to only a critical function, nor does a critical attitude encompass only one strategy: it may have as much to do with transforming aesthetic convention as it does with social liberation, or with questioning contemporary developments. The continuous *mutual* influence of tradition and innovation is important in creating a productive interplay between the conventional and the critical. In this sense, the radicality of the 1960s revolution was ambiguous – it presented tradition and vernacular as a revolutionary intervention in the discourse, yet by virtue of its radicality it also was reminiscent of an earlier revolutionary position which was opposed to an embedding in tradition. On that level the 'purity' (again for lack of a better word) is very much at the heart of today's problematic: if the everyday and the pragmatic and the real were somehow more incorporated in a discourse, the general rules of revolution and return could be modified to a point of specificity. This would mean accepting that innovation takes place on a small scale equally to the large (and mediagenic) scale of manifestoes and publications.

Critique and the moment The critiques I have discussed are simply moments, and perhaps that indicates precisely that some of the grand narratives have disappeared: instead of critique leading to a stable or defined reality, it is now a moment in time. This does allow it to retain its historical dimension, but not in the Hegelian or Marxist sense, where there is a discernible progression in the course of history. The notion that revolution is a lead-in to a permanent state, and that it is a pure process, divorces from the reality of its roots, seems no longer tenable (even if only judged by its own premises).

In the end, maybe the spectacle can do little more than teach us that critique itself is ephemeral. That when it does its job well it will be superseded by transformed conditions and need or seek a new target. The critical moment is fleeting but also a permanent condition.

Is contemporary architecture indeed primed for this awareness and the ability to operate within the ephemeral? Judging from some journals of architecture (Archis, Grey Room, A.D.) the ephemeral moment is still treated as something that can be given eternal form (as in blob architecture). Diller and Scofidio are perhaps the only firm who have made an ephemeral form in their Blur building, even though the notion of the ephemeral is avidly sought.[19] Is theory even ready to be aware that each critique will be superseded or no longer relevant shortly, yet also remain conscious of the absolute necessity of agency? Permanence and architecture are at odds with the revolutionary program of critique, and have been for some time. Is it now perhaps time to revise the form of critique rather than the form of architecture?

Critique and PR Media-saturation is often blamed for an inadequacy of the contemporary debate to really address issues. The perception that an image is worth less than 'the real thing' feeds this skepticism. Yet is it not more a matter of complicity with the media rather than media-saturation as a general condition? When magazines begin to publish the personal statements of architects *as* their critique of a building, one could wonder how it might still be possible to maintain any form of critical position. There is a sense of the corporate in the contemporary debate with the professionalization of the journals as a platform, placing marketing techniques at equal importance to a careful discussion of architecture. At the same time, by their very isolation as a platform, they only take the world around them into account in a limited fashion.

General conclusions This paper has discussed a number of diverse phenomena that are intimately connected, such as the media spectacle, the idea that passivity is concomitant to the spectacle, and the difficult position of the critical within an image-based culture. These are all issues that are rooted in the 1960s, and have become increasingly crucial to contemporary discourse. Each theme is interesting in itself, but in this paper, I have been interested in delineating and understanding the resonance between these phenomena.

As a result, one of the concluding questions remains: is agency absolutely pointless in the society of the spectacle? Are we doomed to create only some kind of constructed PR for capitalism? Or is there a mode of 'critical practice', of 'praxis' that can be *in* the world yet critical? Is a 'critical realism' as described by Latour possible, and does 'projective practice' escape the constrictions

19 Or, following a well-known slogan by Koolhaas: Where there is nothing, everything is possible, where there is architecture, nothing (else) is possible. Koolhaas (1985).

of pure commodification? This position would attempt to hold a median between critique and idealism, yet do so with the context as a given.

This requires some adjustments – though nothing necessarily drastic. A reexamination of where we stand today – and a refusal to play purely formal games, yet also a refusal to subjugate aesthetics to social rhetoric. This proposal is close in spirit to 'material practice', to 'projective practice', etc. Yet what I argue here is not radical, and therefore not necessarily attractive as a media representation. It is not clean, clear-cut. But it is useful – it goes into details, asks more questions than it can provide answers. I am also trying to connect here to tendencies in other disciplines, and to draw a line from developments begun in the 1960s (such as freedom of the individual and critical thinking) and find the limits of these ideas as well as their potential. All this within the media spectacle, both *despite* the influence of the media, of the image, of the spectacle, and *because* of it.

Although my suggestions here have not yet found material form (this does remain, after all, a theory) I hope that a more subtle negotiation of the conditions of late capitalism, of the spectacle, of commodity culture, a strategy that is not based on radical revolution but rather on a form of embedded critical view, will bring architecture both closer to its own discipline (in terms of building) and remain true to the notion of not being purely affirmative (in the sense of merely replicating existing conditions). Should we be afraid that the media will overtake the meaning of architecture? Or should we be afraid that the media have offered a new platform for architects to replicate their manifestoes more effectively? Or should we be 'sliding in and out' of the logic of the spectacle, looking for the gaps where the confrontation between architecture and its image produce new meanings, new forms of independence for its users and (maybe even above all) new moments of beauty in the world at large?

In conclusion, Latour describes a new potential role for the critic, which I believe resonates with the notions of projective practice and embedded critique:

> The critic is not the one who debunks, but the one who assembles. The critic is not the one who lifts the rugs from under the feet of the naïve believers, but the one who offers the participants arenas in which to gather. The critic is not the one who alternates haphazardly between antifetishism and positivism like the drunk iconoclast drawn by Goya, but the one for whom, if something is constructed, then it means it is fragile and thus in need of great care and caution.[20]

20 Latour (2004), p.246.

Bibliography

Alloway, L. 'The Arts and the Mass Media.' **Architectural Design**, 28(2). 1958. pp. 84-85.

Baird, G. 'Criticality and its Discontents.' **Harvard Design Magazine** [online], 21. 2004. Available from: http://www.gsd.harvard.edu/research/publications/hdm/back/21_baird.html [Last accessed December 16, 2005].

Harvey, D. 'Looking Backwards on Postmodernism,' in: Post-Modernism on Trial, **A.D. Profile**, 88. London: Academy Editions, 1990. pp. 10-12.

Hays, K. Michael, ed. **Architecture Theory since 1968**. Cambridge, Mass: MIT Press, 1998.

Hays, K. Michael. 'Inventories of Suspicion,' in: **Hunch**, Berlage Institute Report, 6/7. 2003. pp. 230-233.

Koolhaas, R., (1985). 'Imagining Nothingness,' in: **S, M, L, XL**. Rotterdam: 010 Publishers, 1995. p. 198.

Lash, S. 'Informationcritique.' in: **Cities in Transition**. Rotterdam: 010 Publishers, 2001. pp. 232-247.

Latour, B. 'Why Has Critique Run out of Steam? From Matters of Fact to Matters of Concern,' in: **Critical Inquiry**, 30. 2004. pp. 225-248.

Whiting, S. 'Going Public,' in: **Hunch**, Berlage Institute Report, 6/7. 2003. pp. 497-502.

Urban space as generator of distinctive urban cultures An introduction to a research project on Analysis of Ecologies of Urban Communities

Ceren Sezer

Introduction In the Las Palmas building in Rotterdam, the exhibition 'Between the Waterfronts: Istanbul-Rotterdam' displayed a collection of artworks from Turkish and Dutch artists in 2004.[1] When I visited the exhibition, I found one of the works more striking than others. It was a series of photos combined in order to give a large visual perspective of an event, 'The Muslim Sacrifice Festival' in Istanbul. A group of people with women, men and children in front of the 'modernist' image of the city with high apartment buildings and a busy highway nearby were sacrificing cows, oxen, sheep, and rams in order to practice their religious ceremony. The main idea of this practice, as it is stated in the Koran, was to share the meat of sacrificed animals with poor people in order to strengthen the support between social groups in this four-days religious festival. [See figure 1]

The chosen spot for the event was practically perfect: As it is commonly preferred in rural areas, a 'soil ground' with a slight slope so that the blood of the animal can flow through a small hole and from there be absorbed by the soil easily. And more importantly in terms of location: It was a kind of residual space with easy access from all around the city, an area planned as a 'green band' near the highway. Although it is surrounded by high fences, this couldn't stop one from entering the area since it is the best place for the practice, which is rarely found in between concrete and the dense fabric of the city. Somehow, people just noticed the potentials of this place; they deliberately selected it for their specific purpose, and they simply used it ignoring any kind of given attributes to the space.

This photo evoked many questions in my mind: What can this image impose on us, urbanists, architects or whoever seeks to introduce meaningful relations to the city? How can we account for it? What does it tell us about the city? Can we define it within any kind of categorical schema: is it urban, is it rural, or can the distinction of traditional-modern help us to understand it? Can we locate it on a geographical map, or what is the way to represent it?

To my understanding, the investigation of this sort of distinctive spatial practice can neither be analyzed within cosmopolitan encounters of rural-urban, traditional-modern, local-global nor in an aerial perspective of the city which homogenizes diversity and promises unity. Rather, there is a need for a close look; a street-scale investigation, exploring various usages of space and situating them in the different scales of movement space. I believe, the representation of the space (in the mind or on paper) can reveal dispositions that it consists. Therefore, this way of reading the city can be translated into a spatial instrument in the form of a map. We urbanists can provide these tools and contribute to the understanding of the urban space as movement space, distinctively, even technically providing insights for diverse spatial practices.

1 See the Catalogue of the exhibition in Las Palmas: 'Between the Waterfronts: Istanbul-Rotterdam', Rotterdam: Stichting Trafik, 2002, pp. 98-99.

Following this idea, this paper will present an experimental research process which aims to investigate the city as a generator of distinctive urban cultural practises – particularly of those immigrant groups – on the back of dynamic material processes. This aim will be carried out by constructing a theoretical and analytical framework in order to investigate mobilities of migrant groups within everyday activities such as shopping, social gathering, working and so on. By theoretical, I mean to deploy a spatial model, which investigates the spatial practises within generic movements and webs of urban space. The analytical tool I use relies on first-person observation, on movement patterns in the city, which is documented by photos, movies, and interviews, represented by space-time diagrams and relational maps.

The following questions will be posed and the aim of this essay is to suggest how they might be answered: What is the role of the city as movement space in the constitution of distinctive urban cultures? What are the material and spatial conditions, that generate productivity in urban space? How can we analyze these processes in order to explore potentials of creativity in diversity in urban population? Finally, what is the role of public space in terms of publicly accessible space, in the whole discourse? This is a considerable agenda, and in the limited space of this paper, I can do no more than touch on the many questions raised.

Background: Istanbul as a Migrant City It is difficult to portray Istanbul within general terms. The main reason behind this might be that Istanbul is constantly changing; it is always in motion, always performing temporalities without giving permission to portray all its unity. It is a 24-hours active city; crowded, noisy, and dirty. It is spectacular, charming, and full of illusions that renders observers dizzy: what once used to stand there, can be gone in a glimpse; a sign, an object or even a street. In this sense, the city always gives us the feeling of 'incompleteness'. This makes Istanbul considerably different from many other European cities; by resisting any kind of control, regulations or stability. Among many possible sources of this dynamicity, my main concern will be with the variety in the city population. More specifically, how people from different backgrounds living in the same city construct the space in different ways in the everyday course.

Within its more than two-thousand year old history, Istanbul has always been a cosmopolitan city with diverse populations. There are two major reasons for this diversity: The first was the political condition of the city as the capital of Roman, Byzantiam and Ottoman Emperors, which extended national borders. Secondly, the geographical position of the city, being connected to the Black Sea trade by the Bosporus Sea, and a natural inner port, The Golden Horn, made

Istanbul as the biggest permanent market between India in the East and Europe in the West. This condition attracted diverse trade communities.[2]

The diversity of the population changed over the course of history due to political reasons. The most contemporary change that we can note is after the foundation of the Turkish Republic in 1923. During that time, Istanbul was a city of – mostly – Armenian, Greek and Turkish populations. However, during the 1960s the nationalistic policies of the government forced the non-Muslim population to emigrate. Additionally, the industrial developments in the city and need for labour-generated mass migration from rural Turkey. In the 1980s, the city of Istanbul almost had a 99% Muslim population of which ¾ was of rural origin.[3]

In 1980, the government introduced a series of reforms to liberalize the Turkish economy to follow international and global tendencies. These policies mainly required new infrastructural investments in order to attract foreign companies to Turkey, and especially to Istanbul. However, policy makers were not aware of all the consequences of this scale of transformation, such as mass migration. Specifically in the case of Istanbul, migrant groups had serious difficulties in terms of habitation, work, etc, once they arrived within the city. A reason for this difficulty was due to an unwelcome attitude of the native inhabitants towards the new influx of migrants, who were generally regarded as invaders and troublemakers.

Circumstances triggered a deep social inequality within different populations of the city: On one hand, a minority group with high education has access to global changes with high quality jobs, luxury living conditions and high consumption power. On the other hand, a majority of the population witnessing these changes had difficulties to find even a proper job to provide the basic needs for living.

However, these vulnerable groups managed to find a sort of 'creative' way to maintain their position in the city, through informal networking.[4] These networks were mostly based on patriot relationships supporting family members, relatives, and neighbours to find housing (mostly illegal housing) or a work opportunity (mostly through the informal economy): not in the best standards, but at least providing minimum needs. Also through these informal settings, formerly settled immigrants had opportunities to get rich unlawfully by selling their illegal housing to the newcomers.[5]

Some gathering places such as teahouses, mosques, open markets, or community houses are where these networks are mostly constituted. Teahouses and mosques are obviously male-domi-

2 Keyder (1999) pp. 9-40.
3 **ibid.**
4 Erder (1999) pp. 192-206.
5 See Isik and Pinarcioglu (2001).

nated environments where the presence of a woman – as I also noticed during my field work – seemed misplaced and peculiar. Teahouses are mostly situated in the residential neighbourhoods. They are meeting places for chatting and information exchange with friends while drinking coffee or tea and playing some table games as well (it is very crowded when the most exciting soccer game is on the TV screen). In some cases, teahouses are more institutionalized like employment offices where one can find specific type of working groups (such as construction workers, carpenters, wall-painters) to hire for particular needs. [See figure 2]

Mosques, on the other hand, are places for periodic religious meetings. In Muslim custom, there are five times for praying a day, which can be practised at home or when one is far from home, in the religious buildings. Women can also pray in the mosques. Because they are mostly at home, they do not need to go to mosque as often as men do. These regular meetings in the mosques constitute some social networks through visiting the same mosque of the neighbourhood. Some of the mosques even have teahouses nearby or in the same building where these relations can strengthen by having a chance to chat after praying.

Networking sustains a kind of 'urban village' where disadvantaged groups support each other by providing a variety of opportunities for economic and social survival, extending their connections to the different parts of the city within daily life mobilities. These webs of relations constitute the vivid city life of the 16 million-population of Istanbul of which 80% originates from another city. [6] These networks can be investigated by analysing various performances in the public space where images, signs, music or events can freely celebrate the hybrid emergences. In other words, the distinctive urban practices (such as the sacrifice ceremony near the highway I presented at the very beginning) call for a spatial investigation through analysing their location in the city and mapping mobilities of its performers, who meet in that specific time-space frame, can give us insights for the complex spatial operations in the city. As many other examples can be raised in the case of Istanbul, this is what makes the city difficult to read and yet motivates an academic curiosity to investigate it. [See figure 3]

A brief review of researches on immigrant groups The recent studies regarding immigrant groups in West European countries and Turkey might fall under two general approaches: The first is social analysis of communities within the traditional categories of society, such as ethnic, racial, and religious or class groupings.[7] The second is spatial analysis of ethnic group concentrations, which are mostly indicated by residential clusters, and physical investigation of these formations.[8]

Although these studies provide important insights for the social and physical situation of immigrants in different urban contexts, they can be critized on several counts. Firstly, there is a tendency to problematize immigrant groups in general. The big problem of 'immigrants' in the 'host' city seeks for only one-way solutions: Integration of one group into another group. This approach homogenizes diversity in immigrant groups and limits the understanding of possible relationships between different urban groups. Secondly, the immigrant is treated as a static subject who can be defined by origin, race, ethnicity, income, age. These traditional classificatory schemas of society need to be revised within the transformative global changes. Finally, investigating urban space within the zonal-territorial definitions, such as residential clusters, does not provide a ground for the analysis of dynamics and potentials of urban space.

From even a minimal reading of Latour[9] and Urry,[10] the conventional understanding of 'spatial' and 'social' needs radical revision. As Latour stated in his book *We Have Never Been Modern* the distinction between human and non-human, social and technological, local and global, micro and macro which is strengthened by the 'modern' way of thinking is insufficient to understand mechanisms of the contemporary world.[11] The developments in information/communication technologies, increasing movement of speed and accessibility tend to collapse such a distinction.[12] Instead, there is a need to understand networks, which entails daily mobilities, not between locations in the urban space but between places constituted in the interfaces of different movement scales. Given this, it might be even questioned if this consideration of Latour and Urry is sufficient for an understanding of the urban condition.

In this context, the definition of cultural identity I would like to propose is as 'emergent' processeses as a relation between real and virtual networks of the urban space. By emergent, I understand social, economic, and political processes, which needs explaining within a concept that is sensitive to their being open-ended. This also goes with Latour's conception of the experimental.[13] Secondly, by relation between networks I want to make the idea of layering more 'complex' so as to reflect the complexities at every level of self-organization and takes again into account the open processes of the urban. In drawing down the distinction of the virtual and real, I draw attention to the way in which urbanity is a 'real' of such complex emergences.

I want to point to a single example, which gives a sense of an 'emergent' process that is difficult of localize at an abstract level. This phenomenon might be seen well in the constitution of 'Arabesk' music and culture in Turkey by informal networks until the 1980s, before market-driven forces drastically influenced the distribution of the music.

6 **op. cit.,** no. 4 (Erder) pp. 192-206.
7 See Simon (1998) and van Kempen (1994).
8 See Deurloo and Mustard (1998); van Kempen & Ozuekren (1998).
9 See Latour (1993).
10 Urry (2003), (2000).
11 Urry (2000) pp. 97-122.
12 Urry (2003) p. 3.
13 See Latour in Healy (2006).

The term 'Arabesk' is defined by Ozbek[14] as a music genre which represents the motions of people from rural areas who were confronted with the urban and also excluded by the urban during the first mass migration flows to Istanbul in the 1960s. Ozbek argues, Arabesk is also named as 'periphery music' referring to the music performed and nurtured by migrant groups who live in poor districts of the city. Further, she says, the state and many scholars labelled 'arabesk' as a music without any musical value, only expressing distress and depression of vulnerable groups who are struggling with the difficulties of city life. This condition is interpreted as a result of urban-rural confrontation and was an unwanted aspect for state-run cultural programs. Consequently, state TV and radios, which were only media channels in that period, excluded the '*Arabesk*' until 1980s.

However, these restrictions could not stop the rise of Arabesk. It is played in teahouses, nightclubs, baths, brothels, shops, small workshops, construction sites. It was also very common to listen to Arabesk in private/public transportation, carrying migrant workers from peripheries to the rest of the city. Eventually, it is carried along from big cities to smaller cities and also to the rural areas by migrants themselves who visit their villages regularly. Through informal networks of migrant groups, Arabesk is distributed all around Turkey representing a sort of 'odd', not 'urban' way of life, which is attributed to migrants. Therefore, although in the beginning the term was used only for a music genre, later it represented a whole migrant culture in the peripheries of Turkey.

What this example raises to me is the constitution of an urbanity, by a distinctive group through their informal networking. Travelling by means of dwelling in different movement scales of the city, from home to work, to village etc, provides the constitution of relationships, which sustain an urban culture. These examples indicate the importance of mobilities in the usual course of everyday life. Therefore, the spatial tool 'mobility' can be used in order to understand mechanisms of cultural processes.

Mobility as a spatial tool in the exploration of urban communities In the very basic sense, mobility might be understood as having an ability to move. However, what makes mobility different from movement is, that mobility causes change, stimulates transformation, whereas movement occurs under control in a constant situation. Burgess makes this contextual distinction in his article 'The Growth of the City'[15] where he argues the relation between mobility and mechanisms of social growth and physical expansion.

Burgess and his colleagues Park and McKenzie, who were the leading figures of the Chicago School of Sociology in the 1920s, aimed to develop new instruments with the purpose of understanding urban space and social activities. Their approach is particularly interesting for me, because they studied the mobility of a city population, changes in physical structures and the construction of urban communities, segregation in populations and measurement of these dynamics from the perspective of 'human ecology'. They defined the city as the 'ecological community', borrowing the notion from the science of plant ecology, in which competition/interdependence between different groups and accommodation determines the size of the human community.[16] They assumed that the major consequence of these processes is the 'natural areas' which they defined as territorial organizations that emerged 'naturally' on the basis of mutual interdependence of its inhabitants. In that context, co-existence, and geographical propinquity were the key factors in the formation of an urban community.

I believe that the Chicago School's investigation of urban ecologies can be a guide for us to theorize spatial organizations of immigrant populations constituted through networking. What they named as 'natural area' might refer to an urban neighborhood with a high immigrant population. However, their assumption on 'community' formation based on co-existence and geographical distance needs revision considering today's increased and diversified mobilities.

The contemporary urban sociologist John Urry expands the mobility concept in his book '*Sociology Beyond Societies*'[17] with the aim of investigating materially constructed social processes. According to him, the analysis of diverse mobilities in socio-spatial practises will provide comprehension of the very complex constitution of mobilised cultural forms, such as of those immigrant groups. He further claims that the urban groups cannot be investigated within the traditional sense, which sees 'community' as a human-centred geographically-bounded set of relationships. Instead, they should be examined as circulating entities considering the new forms of mobilities.

Urry examines four types of mobilities. The first is the corporeal travelling of people in which he discusses different levels of bodily mobilities such as walking, or travelling by train or car. The second is the physical movement of objects. Here, he assumes that objects should not be viewed as given or fixed, but rather as performed within complex relationships between places. The third is the imaginative mobility of images on TV or radio or any kind of visual mediator. The last type of mobility is virtual travel, through digital communication systems such as computers.

In this sense, Urry's argument opposes the Chicago School, which analyses urban groupings through geographical distance. Although both approaches see mobility as a guiding concept, the Chicago School considers only corporeal mobility, whereas Urry opens up other forms of mobil-

14 cf. Ozbek (1997) pp. 192-211.
15 Burgess (1967) pp. 47-63.
16 Mellor (1977) p. 206.
17 Urry (2000) pp. 49-77.

ities. Moreover, Urry argues that these diverse mobilities sustain multidimensional sets of 'overlapping communities' whose members are not human subjects but rather hybrid entities, which involve networks of connections between humans and other components. According to him, 'societies are necessarily hybrids.'[18]

Urry's notion of 'hybrid' directly corresponds with what Latour terms 'quasi objects' in his book *We Have Never Been Modern.*[19] According to him, modern constitution[20] designated sets of categories and created dichotomies of human and non-human. However, all entities achieve their significance by their relations to other entities. Therefore, categories should be dissolved and each entity should be investigated by their ability to generate networks within daily contacts and connections in everyday engagement.

These arguments aim to construct an understanding of mobility as an instrument in the investigation of social formations, specifically the constitution of distinctive urban cultures. What the discourse raises is the consideration of different forms of mobilities in the understanding of urban space, which are neither only social nor physical, but temporal processes operating in diverse space-time dimensions.

Then the question can be asked as to how we can investigate and translate these mobilities into spatial instruments in order to comprehend cultural processes on the back of materiality of the urban space. What is the city itself doing with respect to our social, economic, cultural lives? Is it a static perceiver or alternatively a generator of these dynamic processes? What is the role of public space as a space of interactions?

The City as generator of Cultural Processes Read argues these questions in his article 'Intelligent body'[21] where he proposes a spatial model of the city. According to him, the city is a productive space, which is not passively receiving social, economical or cultural practises; instead, it is a generator of these processes. Further, for him, the city is a product of path making by means of daily operations in which it becomes intelligible for us. In other words, intelligibility is realized through daily mobilities. The article further says that paths constitute stratified layers of horizontal connections between speeded and scaled movement patterns of the city. These constitutions form the urban environment.

Read describes several types of movement patterns, which he designates as 'global, metropolitan, middle ground and backstreets'. This stratification is based on differences in intensity and speed of movement patterns. Within this hierarchical modelling of the city, the middle ground, which he also calles 'supergrid', is the most intelligible spatial pattern. Supergrid, he argues in another paper[22], reveals different intensities than the regular grid by constituting a continuous network facilitating the longer distance movement. For example, a busy shopping street might operate as a supergrid.

According to Read, what makes urban space productive is the relationship between these different stratifications, which are in fact constructed on the local level. In many diverse and creative ways, what the city offers is appropriated creatively by hybrid entities in everyday social existence. Connectivity between these movement patterns promotes connection, exchange and interchange. It is where productivity and spatial appropriation occurs. What might be questioned here is the differences and similarities between different cities, in terms of relations between these stratified movement layers. This question can only be answered by testing the model in different case studies, in order to address the various forms of public space.

Healy, in his paper 'There are many ways to say Polis'[23] discusses the connotations of the word 'city' by examining the Greek agora. According to him, the word 'agora' as a place of exchange, recognition, communication and improvisation is a key concept in order to understand mechanisms of urban space. Further, he argues that community in the Aristotelian sense, which is termed 'koinonia' also refers to the city, including all 'societies within societies' represented in the public sphere where active participation is prominent. He argues that the city does not provide an 'internal coherence' for community formation; rather social networks are emergences of self-organization.

How can we investigate public space as a relational space? How can we develop instruments for this investigation? What Healy proposes is the investigation of the city as an 'event space' or fields of temporal reconfigurations and forces, by 'seeing' it in participant observations. As he argues in another work[24], seeing is an 'event of appropriation' or 'lived experience' in which we, as experimental subjects involve with endless constitutions of urban space. This experimental way of engaging with our environment (*Umwelt*[25]) which drives the process of intelligibility, is not to see something and interpret it, but rather a 'meaningful given without any mental detours across thing-oriented apprehension'.[26]

18 **ibid.,** p. 15.
19 Latour (1993) p. 30.
20 **ibid.,** pp. 59-62.
21 Read (2005).
22 **ibid.**
23 Healy (2006).
24 Healy (2005) p. 22.
25 The concept of **'Umwelt'** was introduced by Jacob von Uexkull who is founder of the fields of ethology and semiotics, in his work **Stroll through the Worlds of Animals and Man** in 1934. With this concept he refers to a 'lived environment' which is constituted by perceptual and effector worlds together. See in Ingold (2000).
26 This also goes with the notion of 'affordances' in the theory of ecological psychology which deals with perception of an object or event through what it affords. See J.J.Gibson in Ingolf (2000) pp. 166-168.

Further, Healy refers to Latour's concepts of the 'oligopticon' in which he proposes a microscopic investigation of places in order to make the whole city visible. As he argues, 'oligopticon' understanding of the city (seeing little), which is set against the 'panopticon'[27] (seeing whole), deals with an analysis of point conditions which construct relations through different times and spaces, and can provide an understanding of spatial operations in urban space.

Healy's argument raises the question as to how we can translate the information we get from the city through this 'experimental way of seeing' into spatial instruments with which we can analyze the mechanisms of cultural processes? As an answer, I would like to propose an investigation of the city at street level through the practice of 'walking'. Here what I mean by 'walking', has the sense that De Certeau argues for in his book *The Practise of Everyday Life*,[28] as a way of dwelling-engaging with the city, producing a kind of cognitive mapping in order to observe (and note) daily practices which are in fact invisible to us in a totalizing view of the city. For me, the practice of walking will localize the notion of an experimental way of seeing the city.

A framework for analytical tools: Level Analysis Following this theoretical framework, I want to introduce as an analytical tool 'Level Analysis' in order to explore appropriation spaces in the scaled movement patterns of the city. The aim of this tool is to reconstruct new maps of relations out of the reduced information in the production of 'existential mapping'.[29] I developed this approach during a short-term of fieldwork in one of the migrant districts in Istanbul, analysing the economical and social engagement of migrant groups in the city.

Therefore, Level Analysis refers to a process of mapping the information obtained through daily-life perception on the street scale – represented by photographs taken instantaneously – and projecting to the city scale in order to construct a new comprehension of the city. This way of understanding suggests that urban context is a set of intermingled connections between different layers in the city. These layers refer to different street intensities, which are represented by the term 'level'. This also suggests the presence of a kind of hierarchic structure in the urban environment. This hierarchical abstraction provides possibilities for mappings between levels and produces opportunities for multiple interpretations. [see figure 4]

Demonstration of tool: Istanbul case study During my walking through the study area in Istanbul, as a first step of investigation, I took photos of places where I found differences in terms of street vitality, shopping streets, backstreets, highways and so forth. Here, the most interesting thing was similarities discovered from these snapshots taken in different parts of the district. This situation provided a categorization according to their strongest attributes such as crowdedness, density, etc, by using different sections of the same frame. Following this idea, my case study allowed for five distinctive categories. [see figure 5]

Using these categories, I diagrammatized the existing situation in the following steps: Firstly, I chose a sample photo from each grouping. Secondly, I noted dominant elements in the chosen photos such as build environment, pedestrians, cars, cars in parkings, etc. As the third step, I eliminated the background source (photographic image) and as the fourth step, to be able to obtain further information through abstraction, I signed a legend naming the different components of the current situation that each photo reveals, such as moving cars, parked cars, or pedestrians in movement. As the final step, I reduced the actual condition in order to examine and explore the possibilities rising from the existing situation. [see figure 6]
The analysis of various movement patterns provided me with an awareness of a dominant character in each category: Differences in continuity of the flows. Here 'continuity' refers not only to flows of observable impacts of visible elements such as cars/pedestrian mobilities, but non-visible elements like time-related aspects, rhythms generated by rituals/ festivals as well. However, I only considered observable elements in my analysis that can influence and add further aspects to the continuity of flows by stopping and slowing down their complementary factors which I called 'breaks'.
Based on this continuity aspect, which is related to street flows, and the participants of this street motion, I set up a hierarchical definition of movement patterns from the strongest line until the weakest line, which I named Level 1, Level 2, Level 3, Level 4 and Level 5. Following that, I remapped the study area in these five distinctive levels. [see figure 7]

In order to explore the qualities that each category reveals, I did additional analyses such as locating different scales of economic, and social activities in each level. Further, I located where some specific spatial appropriations occurred in order to construct informal activities such as street vendors, informal workshops with children workers, gathering places such as teahouses or mosques. As a final step, through individual case studies, I analysed trajectories of daily life mobilities within clock time (24 hours), which generate different levels of movement patterns (I chose various case studies on the basis of gender differences and participation in economic activities). By doing so, I aimed to analyse how daily mobilities operate constitutive relations between different movement patterns of the city. [see figure 8]

27 The **panopticon** (concept of Foucault) provides a model which encapsulates the characteristics of a society founded on discipline. It embodies a system in which surveillance plays a crucial role, and in which knowledge is inseparably bound to power.' See in Foucault's definition in Leach (1997) pp. 356-367.
28 See De Certeau (1984).
29 Here, what I mean by 'existential mapping' is producing relational maps-diagrams out of existing condition from street level, projecting it upon a whole city in order to represent a new way of understanding the urban.

Outcomes of the Level Analysis This analysis showed me that in the categorical definition of movement patterns each level constructs regional, middle and local scale relations. However, there were some dominant qualities within the same level and that is the basis of the definition of their hierarchic build-up. In this sense, Level 1 connected to high scale operation and Level 5 was generating more local scale activities. Consequently, while a high level (L1) suggests inflexible administration of a collective space such as the highway, lower levels were suggesting locally realised conditions which open up possibilities for flexible social and economical appropriations. Probably, this might be a reason why I found many hidden informal workshops (with children workers) in the basements of some residential areas.

Another important aspect that I noted as outcome of level analysis is that there is a tendency to make linkages (jumps) from lower level operations to the upper levels. Linking between levels occurs through real and visual mobilities of agents. I observed two distinct ways of linking that I named 'Gradual' and 'Instant' transition.

Gradual transition operates each level one by one, through corporeal travelling for social and economic purposes. As an example, we can imagine a factory worker who is travelling everyday from his house to the work by using different transportation. The second mode, the instant transition occurs when a lower level activity bypasses the difference between operations and situates itself in the highest level through spatial appropriation. As an example, the Muslim sacrifice ceremony I discussed in the very beginning, which is a local scale activity, situated itself in the highest scale ignoring all administrative regulations regarding to the highway. Obviously, these examples can be varied in different urban contexts. In this sense, my definitions are limited to my case studies.

Conclusion In this paper, I have tried to discuss various spatial dimensions of urban space in order to explore the constitution of distinctive urban cultures. To summarize: (1) The city as a movement space generates constitution of distinctive urban cultures; (2) The conventional categorical analysis of urban space is insufficient to understand the urban social, rather there is a need to understand 'networks'; (3) Networks can be investigated through various dimensions of daily life mobilities; (4) Public space as a space of interface between different mobility patterns needs a further elaboration in understanding urban cultural processes.

The discussion in this paper is still preliminary and further elaboration is clearly needed. I need to further discuss in what way I can translate various dimensions of the 'mobility' concept into spatial tools. How can these tools be utilized in an urban spatial intervention? How do mechanisms of urban cultural processes differ in different urban contexts? These questions remain to be explored in further theoretical as well as empirical work.

Bibliography

Burgess, E.W. 1967. 'The Growth of the City: An introduction to a Research Project,' in: **The City**, edited by R.E. Park, E.W. Burgess, R.D. McKenzie. Chicago, London: The University of Chicago Press, 1967. pp. 47-63.

Catalogue exhibition in Las Palmas: **Between the Waterfronts Istanbul-Rotterdam**, Rotterdam: Stichting Trafik, 2002, pp. 98-99.

De Certeau, M. **The Practise of Everyday Life**, translated by Steve Rendall. Berkeley, Los Angeles, London: University of California Press, 1984. pp. 91-111.

Deurloo, M., C. & Mustard, S. 'Ethnic Clusters in Amsterdam, 1994-96: A micro-area Analysis'. **Urban Studies,** (35), 1998: pp. 385-396.

Erder, S. 'Nerelisin Hemserim?' in**: Istanbul, Kuresel ile Yerel Arasinda,** edited by C. Keyder**.** Istanbul: Metis Yayinlari, 1999, pp 192-206. English version is avaible: Erder, S. 'Nerelisin Hemserim?' in: **Istanbul, Between the Global and the Local,** 1999, edited by C. Keyder**.** Rowman & Littlefield Publishers, Inc, 2000.

Foucault, M., 'Panopticism [1977]' in: **Rethinking Architecture,** edited by Neil Leach. London,New York: Routledge, 1997. pp. 356-367.

Healy, P. **Images of Knowledge: An Introduction to Contemporary Philosophy of Science**. Amsterdam: SUN Publishers, 2005.

Healy, P. 'Pollachos Polis Legetai (There are many ways to say polis),' in: **Visualising the Invisible**, edited by C. Panilla & S.A. Read, Amsterdam: Techne Press, 2006.

Ingold, T. **The Perception of the Environment: Essays on Livelihood, Dwelling and Skill.** USA, Canada: Routledge, 2000.

Isik, O. & Pinarcioglu, M.M. **Nobetlese Yoksulluk: Sultanbeyli Ornegi**. Istanbul, Turkey: Iletisim Yayinlari, 2001.

Keyder, C. 'Arka Plan,' in: C.Keyder, ed. **Istanbul, Kuresel ile Yerel Arasinda.** Istanbul: Metis Yayinlari, 1999. pp. 9-40. English version is available at: Keyder, C. 'Introduction' in: **Istanbul, Between the Global and the Local**, edited by C.Keyder. Rowman & Littlefield Publishers, Inc. 1999.

Latour, B. **We Have Never Been Modern**. Trans.Catherine Porter. Hertfordshire: Harvester Wheatsheaf, 1993.

Mellor, J.R. **Urban Sociology in an Urbanized Society**. London, Henley & Boston: Routledge & Kegan Paul, 1977. p. 206.

Ozbek, M. 'Arabesk Culture: A Case of Modernization and Popular Identity', in: **Rethinking Modernity and National Identity in Turkey,** edited by S. Bozdogan & R. Kasaba. Seattle & London: University of Washington Press, 1997. pp. 192-211.

Read, S. A. **Attractor of the Ground**. Presented at Dennis Kingsley, Bob Jessop and John Urry's Complexity and Social Theory Session, Complexity, Science And Society Conference, Liverpool 2005. Available online at: www.spacelab.tudelft.nl/publications/researchpapers.html. [Accessed on February 2006].

Simon, P. **Ghettos, immigrants and integration: The French dilemma**. Neth.J.of Housing and the Built environment, (13), 1998. pp. 41-61, 1.

Urry, J. **Sociology Beyond Societies: Mobilities for the twenty-first century**. USA, Canada: Routledge, 2000.

Urry, J. **Global Complexity**. UK, USA: Blackwell Publishing Ltd, 2003.

van Kempen,R. & Ozuekren, A.,S. 'Ethnic Minorities Housing in the European Union: A case study of Turks.' **Tijdschrift voor Econ. en Soc. Geografie,** (89), 1998. pp. 459-466, 4.

van Kempen, E.,T. 'The dual city and the poor: social polarization, social segregation and life chances.' **Urban Studies,** (31), 1994. pp. 995-1015, 7.

[1]

ɜANGAR, B. Exposition: 9 November – December 2002. Colour Photograph. ırce: Exhibition Catalogue – Las Palmas: **tween the Waterfronts Istanbul-tterdam**, Rotterdam: Stichting Trafik,)2, pp 98-99.

.eft: A tea house in **Umraniye-anbul**. Source: Author.

ht: A mosque in **Delft** – The herlands. Source: Author.

ıformal activities within public space in nbul. The 'informal' provides flexibility allows for a variety of opportunities such [a] jogging near the highway, [b] grazing ıs in the garden of an apartment block, [c] king opportunities for child labour, selling wing gum on the pedestrian bridge, and a perfect business location for a snack near a national highway. Source: Author.

[2]

[3]

Sultanbeyli DISTRICT
Sultanbeyli CENTRU
centre
centre
centre
centre
centre
airport
marmara sea
[4]

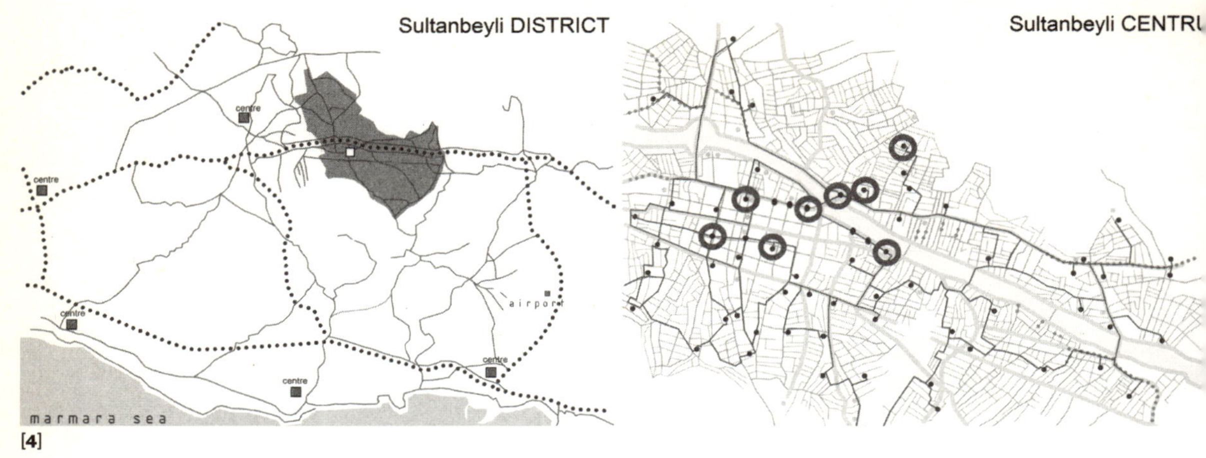

[5]

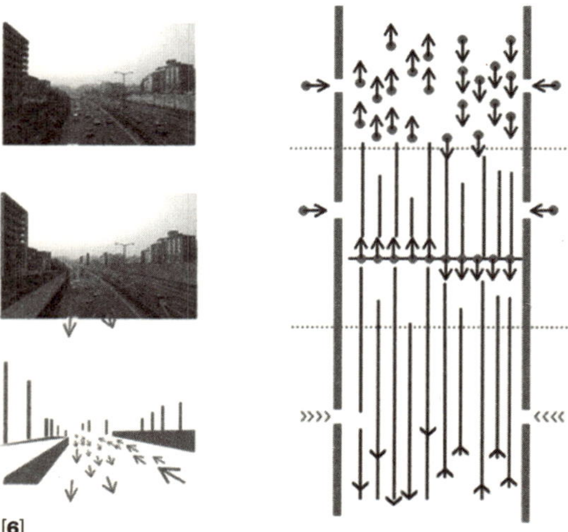

[6]

A case study: **Sultanbeyli**, known for its
n migrant-populated district in the Asian
rict. The national highway divides the dis-
into two parts which are connected by
and pedestrian bridges. **Left:** locates the
rict in the city scale, with its movement
vorks, whilst **right:** represents the pedes-
n route I took to survey public space and
vities. The red circle represents the spe-
empirical cases I noted, as illustrated in
previously noted images of activities.
rce: Author.
Figures 5-8 represent one analytical
hod for a particular case study of **Sul-**
beyli. This figure highlights the categori-
on of urban setting and urban places.
rce: Author.
solation of each category of activities as
nd in public space. Source: Author.
n depth analysis of five distinct urban
ls of activities.
Reflection of analysis upon the geography,
rder to re-map the social scenario as
d in the case studies.

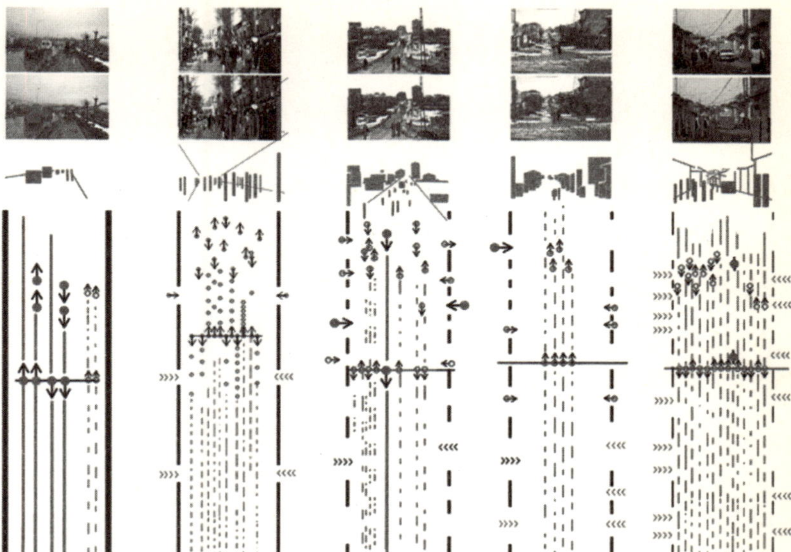

[7]

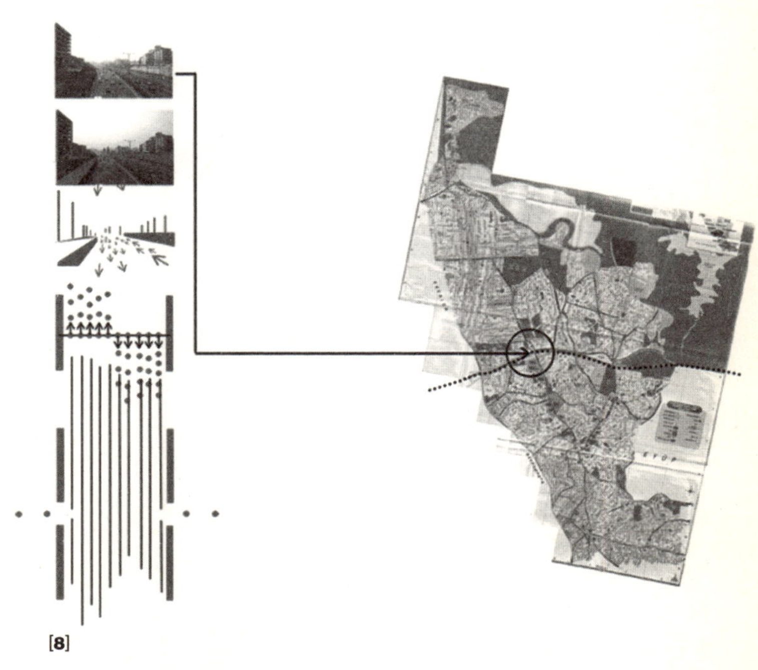

[8]

Tying the Subjective to the Objective: The Agencies Determining Cultural Choices and Taste

Tahl Kaminer

> There are two motives behind the search for [...] the reasons one likes what one does, despite the conviction that the reasons may not be found, and perhaps cannot be found. The first is the virtually transcendental need to understand why one likes those things. The second is the desire to find coherence and congruence within one's own aesthetic personality.[1]

Understanding the manner in which taste is construed is far more significant than the quote above suggests. Taste determines the assessment of quality in the arts, and is therefore responsible also for the economy which, in turn, determines them: government grants, competition prizes and other awards; it is responsible for creative choices by artists and designers, determining the actual artistic production, and it is the basis for communication on which entire discourses rest. It is the reason for the architect drawing a line in a specific place on a paper, creating a certain form or selecting a specific cladding material. These choices and decisions need an explanation which is more accountable than the ones supplied by the architects themselves. This task is general, therefore not architectural-specific, and comprises all arts.

The interest of the investigation is the relationship between the subjective realm of the designer and the objective world around him and the manner in which they influence and manipulate the designer's decisions. The extent to which a human being is the construct of biology and genetics or of social conditioning could shatter politics, ideologies and self-perception. The model which is necessary to form in order to conclude this study is the scheme of *the constitution of the subject.*

Ted Cohen attempts to expose, in his essay 'On Consistency in One's Personal Aesthetics', the reasons for specific aesthetic choices and decisions. His argumentation oscillates from the specific to the general. Cohen's reliance on logic and reason fails to produce the result for which he is searching:

> Explaining the coherence –the total sense- in a work of art is like explaining the coherent style of another person, and both are like explaining one's own aesthetical self. None of these explanations, in the end, is possible, and all must be attempted.[2]

Cohen's search cannot identify the reason and logic of taste because reason is the least relevant factor in the construction of taste. Arnold Isenberg has pointed this out already in his 1949 essay, 'Critical Communication':

> There is not in all the world's criticism a single purely descriptive statement concerning which one is prepared to say beforehand, 'If it is true, I shall like that work so much the better' [...] *The truth of R* [the reason] *never adds up the slightest weight to V* [the verdict] because R does not designate any quality the perception of which might induce us to assent to V.[3]

1 Ted Cohen, 'On Consistency in One's Personal Aesthetics', Jerrold Levinson (ed.), **Aesthetics and Ethics: Essays at the Intersection** (Cambridge, New York: Cambridge University Press, 1998) p. 113.
2 Ted Cohen, 'On Consistency in One's Personal Aesthetics', Jerrold Levinson (ed.), **Aesthetics and Ethics: Essays at the Intersection** (Cambridge; New York: Cambridge University Press, 1998) p. 122.
3 Arnold Isenberg, 'Critical Communication', in Susan Feagin & Patrick Maynard (eds),

In order to proceed in the study of 'the reasons one likes what one does', it is necessary to identify the agency primarily responsible for the creation of 'taste'. There are three possible agencies, related to biology, sociology and psychoanalysis. While it is quite reasonable to expect a complex involvement of all three in determining taste and choices, the manner in which each is involved and the leverage each has, need to be outlined. The biological agency – the determination of identity and taste by DNA, genes and hormones – has been almost completely discredited. It stands in sharp contrast to the two other agencies, and, at its extreme, posits a person constructed by his genes, predestined to be violent or obedient, adventurous or petty, in opposition to the social agency, which, in its extreme, depicts the human as a blank document: a person as a container of ideas and tendencies forced upon him by society.

Both views have problematic baggage: the first is the source of racist doctrines; the second manifests itself in religion – the myth of the Garden of Eden – and in the desire to escape humanity. The belief in a *true*, *authentic* self that could be regained once the social constructs are removed is paramount in numerous cultures and religions; certain strains of psychology as well as conservative politics and eastern religions and philosophies adhere to this principle. The impression that social pressures produce an inauthentic, *masked* man is not a modern idea, yet the transformations and changes in society, the accelerating pace of culture and technology and growth in communication and media have enhanced this view, as exemplified by Simmel's *blasé individual*. This idea is often linked to a belief in the existence of a place liberated from these social constraints, whether in some 'simple' society or in the distant past.

A typical example of such sentiment can be found in the writings of the 18th century philosopher Jean Jacques Rousseau, who expressed disgust with modern civilization, warned of culture and education perverting natural innocence and sought to rediscover the authentic human being in the less-advanced cultures of 'the south'. He proposed an educational model drawn from nature as an alternative. Derrida has criticised Rousseau, arguing that all human societies need to educate their young in order to survive[4]; even the most 'primitive' cultures have conventions, norms and regulations, and rely on conditioning and education. The desire for an existence that precedes social conditioning is the desire for a pure natural origin, the mother's womb, the lost Garden of Eden: an unattainable desire, a utopian dream.

The manipulations of ideology and indoctrination – society's traces – are easier to identify in others rather than in oneself. Nietzsche's blunt criticism of his peers echoes this:

They all pose as though their real opinions had been discovered and attained

> through the self-evolving of a cold, pure, divinely indifferent dialectic [...] whereas, in fact, a prejudiced proposition, idea, or 'suggestion', which is generally their heart's desire abstracted and refined, is defined by them with arguments sought out after the event. They are all advocates who do not wish to be regarded as such, generally astute defenders, also, of their prejudices, which they dub 'truths'. [5]

Ideology and social indoctrination, in their wider sense, are everywhere, including language, and prove impossible to avoid or escape: the subject is *within* it:

> [W]hen we speak of ideology we should know that ideology slides into all human activity, that it is identical with the lived experience of human existence itself. [6]

The self has difficulty identifying the constructs it accepts and takes for granted, hence the ease of identifying them in others who adhere to different ideals. It is necessary to be 'outside' an ideology in order to observe it, yet one can never be completely 'outside' ideology in general.

The decisions regarding creativity are no different than any choice which reflects one's identity. The choices vary from politics to clothes, from taste in art to furniture. These choices reflect one's self-identity and the perception of this identity. In the case of designers and artists these choices have to be taken regularly: regarding the methodology of work, the content, preference of material, colour or form. The process of making choices remains most of the time a non-conscious operation. Only when a choice proves to be difficult does it require full attention, becoming a conscious operation. Artists and designers may offer explanations for some decisions, yet these would always be the particular decisions which *need* explanation, the decisions which may be otherwise questionable by the norm or the dominant understanding. The explanation will be communicative, attempting to resonate with the audience's preferences or to provoke the audience, rather than supply the actual motive for the decision. It will use logic and reason as a justification method. The actual motivation may remain obscure to the designer himself. The model this text will propose will avoid the over-determinacy and reductionism which are the danger of such constructions. It does not amount to a definition of artistic quality, and is not an aesthetic theory: 'It unlocks phenomena, but falls short of the phenomenon of art'.[7]

A prevailing belief is that the human being has free choice. This perception is essential for legitimising the moral castigation of people who have opted for the 'wrong' choice. It legitimises state law, social-judgement and, in religion, God's moral judgement of mankind for its bad decisions and misbehaviour. Nowadays, it is common to differentiate between the western civilization and third world civilization or between the 'sophisticated' urban person and the 'simple' rural person,

Aesthetics (Oxford; New York: Oxford University Press, 1997) p. 370.

4 See Jacques Derrida, **Of Grammatology** (Baltimore, London: Johns Hopkins University Press, 1976).

5 Friedrich Nietzsche, **Beyond Good and Evil** (Mineola, N.Y.: Dover Publications, 1997) pp. 3-4.

6 Louis Althusser, in Steve Burniston, Chris Weedon, 'Ideology, Subjectivity and the Artistic Text', Centre for Contemporary Cultural Studies [University of Birmingham], **On Ideology** (London: Hutchinson, 1977) p. 203.

7 Theodor Adorno, **Aesthetic Theory** (London; New York: Continuum, 2002) p. 9.

believing the 'sophisticated' makes a choice whereas the less-sophisticated has little or no choice. The distinction is not based on economic differences between the two groups, but on different levels of awareness. The lower class person choosing to wear imitation gold ornaments and the middle class, sophisticated person making the same choice are seen as different: the former is unaware of his choice of *kitsch*, the latter is aware, and therefore selects *camp*. The latter is seen as having a choice due to his awareness.

This view leads to a further conclusion: that authenticity exists in unawareness, whereas *the aware* are not authentic- they adorn masks to satisfy their social interests. Thus, simplicity is perceived to be a synonym of authenticity. In architecture this view has led to a great interest in minimalism and in vernacular forms of architecture – the Arab or Greek village, the African village, or Venturi's interest in the Las Vegas strip; in fine art – *Surrealism*, *outsider art*, *Art Brut* and *Cobra*. The view is misleading. Awareness does not necessarily infer *choice*. Those who are aware have only limited choice and their preference is predetermined by their identity just as is that of the unaware.

The key to the process of making choices lies in the social agency, the psychoanalytical agency and the relationship between the two. The most evident influence on choices is the social sphere: peer pressure and pressure by a group in a dominant social position. Evident, because it operates relatively visibly, in society, in relations between groups and individuals. In order to belong to a certain group in society, it is necessary to obey not only the group's explicit rules but also the implicit ones. The 'correct' choices earn a place in the group and the possibility to identify with it. The group, in this case, can be as large as a social-class or as small as a musical ensemble.

The sociologist Pierre Bourdieu has argued that '[t]he definition of cultural nobility is the stake in the struggle which has gone on unceasingly, from the seventeenth century to the present day, between groups differing in their ideas of culture and of the legitimate relation to culture and to works of art'.[8] In this struggle, the diverse cultural groups exercise social pressures and exclusion in order to maintain their identity and to prevent members transgressing the norms of the group.

The educational progress of a student who enters architecture school without a preconceived idea of his taste or preferences in the discipline can serve as an example of the process of acquiring a taste, a necessary process on the route to becoming a designer. The student, in this new environment, searches for some identifiable ideas, images or reasons he can distinguish and grasp easily. He may be able to identify architecture which corresponds to a preconceived taste in another discipline, such as fine-art or cinema. In the meantime, the student needs his teacher to be the arbiter of right and wrong, to compensate for his own lack of confidence and knowledge. Therefore, at this early stage of professional education, the teacher exercises great influence over the student. Once the student establishes his taste – the mechanism of the acquisition of taste will be mapped in the following paragraphs – he can proceed in greater self-confidence, as he has acquired his tools to differentiate between good and bad. The role the educators have in manipulating the choices and emerging taste of the student is, no doubt, substantial, yet there are other agencies in operation. The history of architecture – as well as the history of art and culture – is testimony to this, demonstrating changes and progress in taste: students do not necessarily have the same taste as their tutors. Peer pressure, which may be no more than the social pressure to adhere to the socio-cultural norms established by the peerage group, has certain influence as well. It defines the guidelines and the boundaries of the acceptable interests and practices, forcing individuals to submit to the authority of the group. Yet not everyone submits to his peers, and, moreover, any inspection of the work produced by individuals who seem to form a peerage group would reveal differences and discrepancies. The peerage group itself often has a limited lifespan, with the individual's reference group changing according to institute, location or time-period.

Bourdieu's work outlines taste and the decisions that are determined by taste as a social construct, demonstrating how educational level, social and economic background as well as the place of residence – urban or rural, centre or suburb – determine both taste and the legitimacy of taste. Bourdieu's social categories are primarily social-class groups. This infers that the role of the family is fundamental in the social construction of taste and the choices related to it. The family and upbringing must be added, therefore, to the role of the teacher and the peerage group in the establishment of taste and determination of creative choices. The early years of life of an infant, the years in which it is taught to differentiate between right and wrong and develops its own identity, become the major force in this process. Here, the social becomes interwoven with the psychoanalytical, an issue Bourdieu acknowledges[9] but refrains from investigating, stopping at the level of *family*.

Early attempts to use psychoanalysis to interpret art were based on the notion of the artist as an outcast, *mad* genius; a cultural myth based on figures such as van Gogh[10], Pollock and Bacon. This myth is largely based on 19th century artists moving to the margins of society, becoming transgressors of social norms, a position which they relished as an expression of their autonomy. Thus, the artist became estranged from society, whether seen as genius or delinquent, roles which appear implicitly counter-dependent. The idea of the artist as a genius can be traced back to the writings of Immanuel Kant:

8 Pierre Bourdieu, **Distinction: A Social Critique of the Judgement of Taste** (London: Routledge, 2003) p. 2.
9 'Sociology is rarely more akin to social psychoanalysis than when it confronts an object like taste [...]' Pierre Bourdieu, **Distinction: A Social Critique of the Judgement of Taste** (London: Routledge, 2003) p. 11.
10 Van Gogh, in fact, created his masterpieces during his moments of sanity rather than lunacy.

> *Genius* is the talent (natural endowment) which gives the rule to art. Since talent, as an innate productive faculty of the artist, belongs itself to nature, we may put it this way: *Genius* is the innate mental aptitude (*ingenium*) *through which* nature gives the rule to art. [...] fine arts must necessarily be regarded as arts of *genius*.[11]

The myth has become culturally accepted thanks to the media's need for colourful, outrageous figures and artists' dependence on the media. As a result, psychoanalysts and art critics searched for evidence of neurosis in the biographies of artists. René Laforgue, for example, extended Freud's analysis of da Vinci and popular fiction to an analysis of the artist, of Baudelaire in this case, claiming that the poet's obsessive interest in the negative was a result of a mother complex:[12]

> Would not the general problem of artistic creation, whether it concerns Baudelaire or another, be that of the manner in which this creative power has been set to work in the realm of thought, independently of *normal* sexuality, of its paths, and of its laws?[13]

Laforgue's approach embodies two fundamental errors: the belief in an easily discernible cause-and-effect *index* of neurosis and result, and the belief in the need to search for the centre of creativity in neurosis and trauma, in the abnormal.

This study assumes that a majority of artists' decisions and taste evolve not as a result of a neurosis but in a more common manner. Neurosis and trauma are an exception in the arts, just as they are in society. Freud's topological model of the id and the ego will be the basis for explaining the constitution of the subject. The model was an addition to his earlier conscious-preconscious-subconscious model. Although Freud's writings on the ego and the id were published more than eighty years ago, they have maintained their credence in the canon of psychoanalysis.

The id is, according to Freud, the agency responsible for the basic, instinctive desires. It exists in a new born baby and is not acquired. The super-ego is the agency responsible for differentiating right and wrong, a conscience. It is an acquired agency, the product of education on the most basic level – that of the family, the level in which psychoanalysis completes Bourdieu's sociological insights – and is part of the ego:

> [H]ere we have that higher nature, in this ego ideal or super-ego, the representative of our relation to our parents. When we were little children we knew these higher natures, we admired them and feared them; and later on we took them into ourselves.[14]

The super-ego, once established, remains relatively stable:

> Although it is accessible to all later influences, it nevertheless preserves throughout life the character given to it [...] namely, the capacity to stand apart from the ego and to master it.[15]

The ego develops throughout the life-span; it is the agency responsible for mediating between the id, the super-ego and the outside world:

> For the ego, perception plays the part which in the id falls to instinct. The ego represents what may be called reason and common sense, in contrast to the id, which contains the passions.[16]

The architecture student identifies in the new discipline some aspects he can relate to his previous experiences, creating a link between the new profession and preconceived opinions and tastes. This process can be associated with the operations of the super-ego and involves also the ego, in the form of reality-testing.

The super-ego guides the ego by positive reactions and, when its ideals are transgressed, guilt feelings. Therefore, in a situation in which the student will be taught to think, act or practice in a certain manner which the super-ego identifies as opposing its own ideals and identity, the student will encounter a feeling of guilt which would drive him to oppose or transform the ideas enforced on him. Only extreme pressure by the teacher will force the student to overcome the edict of his super-ego. The example of the student can be projected on practicing artists and designers: the *uncompromising artist*, almost a mythical figure in culture, is motivated by his super-ego and its edicts, a guilt-feeling responsible for his inability to compromise. Therefore the super-ego plays a significant role in the establishment of taste and the control of creative choices.

On this premise a model can be created, in which the super-ego is responsible for what can be called *the core of creativity*, the most abstract and essential ideas and ideals that motivate creativity, dictate choices and are at the heart of taste. The ideas and ideals contained in the super-ego are not part of aesthetics; they are general, and also take part – with the id and the ego – in decisions the student may make which are not related to the arts or architecture. In addition to this uncompromising core, social influences and pressures define the less abstract aspects of taste and creativity; they can be seen as an elaboration of the ideas and ideals existing in the core, and they are more easily compromised.

The ideas and ideals concentrated in the core of creativity are, as mentioned above, directly linked to the ideals of the super-ego. Until the student can identify something in the new profession which corresponds to an ideal in the super-ego, he remains at a loss and depends solely

11 Immanuel Kant, 'Art and Genius', in Susan Feagin & Patrick Maynard (eds), **Aesthetics** (Oxford; New York: Oxford University Press, 1997) pp. 182-183.
12 In René Laforgue, **The Defeat of Baudelaire** (London: The Hogarth Press, 1932).
13 René Laforgue, **The Defeat of Baudelaire** (London: The Hogarth Press, 1932) p. 167. My emphasis.
14 Sigmund Freud, 'The Ego and the Id', **On Metapsychology: The Theory of Psychoanalysis** (London: Penguin Books, 1991) pp. 375-276.
15 Sigmund Freud, 'The Ego and the Id', **On Metapsychology: The Theory of Psychoanalysis** (London: Penguin Books, 1991) p. 389.
16 Sigmund Freud, 'The Ego and the Id', **On Metapsychology: The Theory of Psychoanalysis** (London: Penguin Books, 1991) p. 364.

on his tutors and peers. The ideals of the super-ego are themselves a result of family influence, as Freud pointed out in the quote above. Hence, it is possible to claim that the core of creativity *is* the super-ego, holding together the individual and the social in an iron grip.

It must be understood that the ideals existing in the core are more of an abstract feeling than a precise definition; the core's interests vary significantly from one person to another. Whereas in spoken language we may refer to ideals such as nationalism or humanism, they would appear in the super-ego in a vague, rather obscure manner, as an emotional reaction to something with which one identifies. The super-ego does not, however, reflect the ideals of the parents directly. This is not only the result of a certain obscurity of the ideas' existence in the super-ego, but also the result of a 'filter' through which the child perceives his parents and environment. The filter is emotional, and often distorts the ideals of the parents. It may cause the ideal to appear in the child's super-ego in a stronger or weaker manner, in a certain distorted sense etc. The emotional filter 'colours' the reception of the ideal, manipulating it according to the child's specific emotional condition at the time and the manner in which he perceives his parents. Thus the 'filter' is central to transformations in human perception and ideology: it is by distorting the edict of the parents that the child's super-ego is never identical to that of the parents, and parental conditioning remains partial rather than total.

It is possible to use the idea of *identification*, a theme prominent in Lacan's writing, as an alternative system of describing the same scheme. Identification means the identification of the child with his mirror image in the Mirror stage, and the creation of an idea of otherness as a means of establishing an imaginary 'I'. According to Lacan, the ego, the 'I', is an ideal construct, an imaginary and symbolic idea which represents a person's mistaken self-image, such as the perception of the mirror-image as the 'self'. The mirror image is the 'ideal ego', the concept of the self; although it is based on a misidentification, the person strives towards the completeness and wholeness of this 'ideal ego'. By constantly comparing everything to its self-perception, the 'ideal ego' directs the person, guides him towards the unachievable goal of uniting with it. Lacan's mirror image may be constituted differently from Freud's super-ego, but its function, as far as taste and decisions are concerned, is similar. Here, the student needs to be able to differentiate between issues which belong to *the other* and issues which are incorporated in the mirror image, in the 'ideal ego'. He would be drawn to those aspects of the profession with which he can associate, aspects which are also part of his own perceived identity.

As a result of peer pressure, the student may find himself in a context with which he does not identify, and will slowly strive to reposition himself in a new, more congenial context. Thus, the student strives to find in the new profession an identity which relates to his own. This identity – to which the core of creativity relates – may be expressed in an explicit manner, such as in a specific style, but may also be implicit, undefinable in its emphasis of less visible aspects of the profession. Without the creation of the linkage between the discipline and the super-ego the student is unable to practice, as he is at a loss when he needs to decide and to assess. Such a situation would often cause the student to drop out of the profession. The core of creativity is not a determination of quality; rather, it is a necessity.

The model of creativity presented here attempts to outline a common process of the development of taste and of decision-making, of the constitution of the subject. The family – represented by the super-ego – the tutor and peer-pressure, are not the only agencies involved. Trauma or neurosis may take part in the formation of taste, though only in a marginal number of artists or designers, reflecting their distribution in society in general. Therefore, the complete model contains (1) the super-ego as *the core of creativity*, (2) social influences and pressures as an added force and, in some cases, (3) trauma or neurosis as an additional or alternative influence.

The core is responsible for coherence in the work produced by the practitioner, yet even this coherence often remains cryptic: while the expressionist forms of Frank Gehry are immediately discernable, the line running through the work of Rem Koolhaas is veiled by the diversity of forms and styles his designs express. Even the attempt to 'explain' Gehry's forms would prove to be a guessing game. The ambiguous, murky manner in which the core of creativity and the super-ego function – the super-ego itself being a psychoanalytical construct rather than a tangible 'thing' – prevent any possibility of producing a precise description of a specific process of a decision being made rather than the general model explained above. [see figures 1 and 2]

When inspecting the process of decision-making, all three factors may be responsible or any combination of them. The social agency may often be responsible for the most visible elements of a choice – such as style – as they are often articulated on a much less obscure level than the ideals of the super-ego. Yet the inevitable conclusion is that all the fundamental, significant choices – significant to the architect or artist, not necessarily significant to his environment – will not be determined by the social element but rather by the super-ego or neurosis. This means that the result of the decision is pre-inscribed; the choice is never free, but dictated by the person's *identity*, which, in turn, is constructed by the environment.

Absurdly, free choice exists exactly when it matters the least: in the incidents in which none of the possibilities in question can be identified with an ideal existing in the super-ego, when the result has the least significance. This is precisely the moment in which the artist is at a loss. In case of a conflict between the super-ego and the demands of the social milieu, the ego can decide by appraising the strength of the super-ego edicts against the social pressure. When there is no clear motivation, no pressure by the ego or super-ego, a decision is the most difficult to make.

The loss of free choice may be a bitter pill to swallow. The model of creativity suggests, however, some positive conclusions as well. The debate regarding the authenticity of artists' decisions, deriding what may seem a surrender to the dictates of a social group, becomes obsolete once it is clear that without identifying with his major decisions the artist cannot produce work. This does not mean that artists never 'betray' their super-ego or that they never modify their work in order to achieve social acceptance. They may adopt a position that contrasts with the super-ego as a result of social pressure, yet their guilt feeling will direct them away from this position. They may also need to overcome their guilt and objections and compromise their ideal in order to make a living. The architect or artist may compromise many of the visible qualities of his work in order to gain acceptance or praise, without compromising any of the aspects of the work which may be related to the core of creativity.

The explanations for decisions given within the discourse by architects and artists do not relate to the model suggested above. They resort to reason, reason being a communicative instrument and enabling discussion. The model demonstrates that reason is involved in decisions mostly in situations in which the super-ego cannot identify with any of the possibilities. Therefore the debate that takes place regarding creative work is always at a distance from the agencies that control and determine the decision-making; the debate can take into account the social aspects but not reach as far as the super-ego or any neurosis or trauma.

The model can be described as a core with additional layers. The core is the super-ego; the layers, added throughout a lifespan, are determined socially but selected by the super-ego to 'fit' the core; together, the core and the layers form 'taste'. A layer which does not 'fit' is rejected or causes contradictions, uncomfortable feelings and guilt. The layers tend to be the result of the social agency. The model functions as the bridge between psychoanalysis and sociology and between the subjective and the objective. The objective becomes part of the subjective through the creation of the super-ego, hence the attempts to separate these two worlds are futile; the subjective and the objective are immersed in each other and inseparable. The objective takes part in the constitution of the subject.

Bibliography

Pierre Bourdieu, **Distinction: A Social Critique of the Judgement of Taste.** London: Routledge, 2003.

Roy Boyne, **Foucault and Derrida: The Other Side of Reason**. London: Unwin Hyman, 1990.

Ted Cohen, 'On Consistency in One's Personal Aesthetics', Jerrold Levinson (ed.), **Aesthetics and Ethics: Essays at the Intersection**. Cambridge; New York: Cambridge University Press, 1998.

Sigmund Freud, 'The Ego and the Id', **On Metapsychology: The Theory of Psychoanalysis**. London: Penguin Books, 1991.

Arnold Isenberg, 'Critical Communication', in Susan Feagin & Patrick Maynard (eds), **Aesthetics**. Oxford; New York: Oxford University Press, 1997.

[2]

1 Guggenheim Bilbao. Source: Thomas Mayer.
2 The Dutch Embassy in Berlin. Source: Helge Kühnel.

The instrumental use of representations of space in the practices of production of space in a postcommunist city

Łukasz Stanek

The paper investigates the instrumental roles played by representations of urban space in the practices of production of space of Nowa Huta, an industrial city in Poland. The investigation is focused on representations of Nowa Huta which were present in the local printed mass media after the fall of Communism in Central Europe.

This research perspective is based on the theory of the production of space by Henri Lefebvre. According to Lefebvre, space is produced by three types of practice: spatial practices of physical transformation of the environment; practices of representation of space; and everyday practices of appropriation of space. The first practice produces spaces as perceived, the second produces representations of space which allow space to be conceived, and the third transforms space into what is called 'representational spaces', i.e. space considered as lived.[1] Lefebvre's characteristic of representations of space as institutionalized conceptualizations of space produced by intellectual practices applies fully to mass media representations of space[2] thus justifying the choice of Lefebvre's theory as the basis for the envisaged investigation.

The representations of space have played a crucial role in the production of space of Nowa Huta since its foundation by the Communist regime in 1949. The construction and development of the city was a constant process of catching up with the most influential representation of Nowa Huta in the state-controlled media: that of 'the first socialist city in Poland'. Located near Kraków, the Polish historical capital, as an independent industrial city for the workers of the future steelworks,[3] Nowa Huta became a district of Kraków in 1951.[4] The reasons of this localization are still a controversial issue in the public debates, but today most historians agree, that the motives were both economical and political, aiming at a change of the social structure of the conservative city of Kraków.[5] During the postwar years many young people, mostly of rural origin, came from all over the country to Nowa Huta attracted by the possibility of a professional training, work and accommodation. The ensembles in the center of the city and the administrative buildings of the steelworks were built in the style of socialist realism, translating the representation of a 'socialist city' into forms reflecting Polish historical architecture; this style was abandoned already in the 1960s for an impoverished version of modernism.[6] The city witnessed much political unrest and

1 Compare the interpretation of Lefebvre's theory of production of space in: Stanek: 2004.

2 To 'representations of space' (referred to also as 'mental space') Lefebvre counts representations produced by planners and urbanists (Lefebvre 1991:38) as well as philosophical (compare Lefebvre 1991:1-7) and scientific (Lefebvre 1991:107,8) theories on space. Lefebvre stresses the danger of the reductionist (compare Lefebvre 1991:38) and ideological (Lefebvre 1991:44) application of representations of space and their dependency on the social and economic relations (Lefebvre 1991:3). Representations of space are institutional since they are 'tied to the relations of production and to the "order" which those relations impose' (Lefebvre 1991:33). They are systematic, since they 'subordinate' the relations between 'objects and people in represented space' to a 'logic' (Lefebvre 1991:41) and thus need to be consistent, although their consistency may be challenged (ibid.).

3 The name of the city – Nowa Huta – means in Polish 'new steelworks'.

4 After the administrative reform in 1991, Nowa Huta was divided into five smaller districts (XIV, XV, XVI, XVII and XVIII). Within Kraków, Nowa Huta remained a unique and specific place, and therefore I refer to it in this paper as to a 'city'.

5 Compare Salwiński: 1999, 77–94.

6 For a discussion on the urbanistic concept of Nowa Huta, compare Juchnowicz: 2002 or in the 1980s Nowa Huta became famous as one of the most important centers of anticommunist opposition in Poland. After the political transition in the year 1989, the steelworks faced serious economic problems, and the district came to be widely associated in the Kraków local media with criminality and unemployment. Since the official statistics do not support this association, sociologists diagnose a 'striking difference between (the statistics) and the consciousness of the inhabitants' (03.03,[7] compare Bukowski: 2003). [see figure 1]

The examination of articles from the local press can contribute to a better understanding of the reasons for this 'striking difference'. After the fall of Communism (and thus of censorship), the former subversive representations of the city gained access to the mass media, without, however, replacing the former official ones. The investigation (Stanek: 2005) reveals that the representations of Nowa Huta may be grouped into five pairs of oppositions, which originate in the dichotomous language, imposed during the Communist period on the discussion about the city by the state-controlled press.

• The representation of Nowa Huta as a '**socialist city**' has remained central for the discussion after 1989; at the same time this representation is opposed by a widespread representation of the city as the **center of antisocialist opposition**.

• Nowa Huta, planned without churches, was claimed to be an '**atheistic city**'; but after 1989 this representation is usually evoked in order to introduce a dramatic contrast between the intentions of the authorities and the reality of Nowa Huta as a '**religious city**'.

• An important reason for this energetic religiosity is the rural origin of the workers employed by the steelworks; that is why Nowa Huta is called both an '**industrial city**' and a '**big village**'.

• Even the least politicized representations do not evade the dichotomous language: the representation of Nowa Huta as a '**green city**', a 'garden city' (01.8) and a 'city of parks' (03.08) which is widely supported by the inhabitants, is often contrasted by the image of an area of **ecological catastrophe**.

• The discussion, held in the local media in the early 1990s, on the pollution caused by the steelworks renewed the old **conflict between Nowa Huta and Kraków**. The representation of Nowa Huta as 'foreign' and 'hostile' to Kraków clashed with voices which stressed the inherent attachment of the district to Kraków's economy, culture and politics.[8]

This analysis reveals Nowa Huta to be a contested city. All of these opposing representations can be supported by a sufficient number of arguments, data, private histories, emotions, and there is no unifying narrative which would link the opposing representations to a relatively consistent whole. The inability of dealing with these opposing representations leads to the rhetorical acceptance of the impasse by a shortcut diagnosis of Nowa Huta as 'the town of paradoxes' (89.19; 99.60, Stenning: 2001,10).[9] As 'the town of paradoxes', Nowa Huta is something uncanny: an *aporia*, a curiosum, a failed experiment. This association seems to contribute to the previously mentioned pessimistic view of the inhabitants on their city: an opinion which cannot be supported with economic statistics. [see figure 2]

Analyzing Nowa Huta with Lefebvre's theory opens up the question about the impact of the discussed representations, considered as produced by practices of representing space, on other practices of the production of space. The understanding of this impact, however, requires a theoretical concept of the relationship between different practices of production of space. Lefebvre gives only a sketchy description of this relationship which he calls 'dialectical' but at the same time distinguishes it from the classical dialectics of Hegel and Marx. Most of Lefebvre's interpreters try to explain this relationship by a reconstruction of the principles of Lefebvre's dialectics, but these attempts are neither philosophically convincing nor directly applicable to urban reality.[10] Instead of speculating on the principles of dialectics, the paper suggests an alternative interpretation, based on the concept of practice, which is fundamental for Lefebvre's philosophy.[11] According to this perspective, products of a particular practice of the production of space are used as tools by other practices of the production of space. In the case discussed in this paper, the representations of space produced by the printed mass media gain various instrumental roles in other practices of representing space as well as in practices of the physical transformation of space and in the quotidian practices of appropriation of spaces. The paper is neither a didactic demonstration nor a secure application of the suggested interpretation of Lefebvre's theory, which provides a general framework for collecting and examining data; this framework allows revealing dependencies between various aspects of the urban reality which were unnoticed or unexplained in available analyses of Nowa Huta. At the same time, the discovery of these dependencies might be seen as an argument in favor of the proposed interpretation of Lefebvre's theory, showing its productivity for urban analysis.

The investigation about Nowa Huta's recent history reveals a variety of roles played by the mass media representations of this city in the practices of the production of space. These representa-

Irion, Sieverts: 1991. For a discussion of socialist realism in architecture, or 'architecture socialist in content and national in form', compare Leach (1999).

7 This type of reference refers to articles listed at the end of this paper.

8 An extensive discussion of these representations, based on the investigation of ca. 700 articles from the local press, may be found in: Stanek: 2005.

9 When the expression 'city of paradoxes' is typed into Google, it returns ca. 250 links to web pages on cities, including Vienna, Washington and Mumbai. The success of this shortcut expression clearly indicates how closely the contemporary theorizing of the urban problematic is connected to the contemporary philosophical project of deconstruction of traditional (logical and dialectical) ways of dealing with contradictions. For a critical discussion on the relationship between the urban problematic and the postmodern discourse, compare Boyer:1996 (particularly the end of chapter I); for a discussion on the artistic ways of dealing with contradictions in Nowa Huta compare Stanek, Winskowski.

10 Compare Soja (1989), Dimendberg (1998), Shields (1999), Schmid (2003), Elden (2004); for a discussion on these interpretations, compare Stanek (2004). Soja's contribution in (1996) is a development (or modification) of Lefebvre's theory rather than an interpretation.

11 David Harvey (1990) was among the first who recognized the fact that the three aspects of space in Lefebvre's theory can be related only in social practice. For the discussion and critique of Harvey's reading of Lefebvre compare Schmid: 2003 and Stanek: 2004.

tions are instrumental in the decision-making processes which lead to the physical transformation of space (the political representations were referred to as arguments in the discussion on municipal credit guarantees for the steelworks[12] and on the investments in the districts[13]). The mass media representations of Nowa Huta were applied to other practices of representing space: they were reservoirs of new street names[14] and shaped the way architectural and urbanistic themes in Nowa Huta were set.[15] They constitute an important part of the architectural context and thus influence the way spaces are used.[16] An investigation dealing with all these issues separately would explode this paper. Instead, I would like to focus on the role the representations of space play in the perceived, conceived and lived aspects of one iconic site in Nowa Huta. This site – a broadening in the Aleja Róż (or Alley of Roses) where before 1989 the Lenin monument was standing – is clearly a representational space in Lefebvre's sense and his concept of representational spaces will be very useful for the analysis. [see figure 3]

In 'The Production of Space', Lefebvre provides the following description of representational spaces: 'Representational spaces: space as directly *lived* through its associated images and symbols, and hence the space of "inhabitants" and "users", but also of some artists, (…) writers and philosophers, who *describe* and aspire to do no more than describe' (Lefebvre 1991:39; Lefebvre 1986:49).[17] In the analysis of the site in the Alley of Roses two issues will be of particular importance:

• Lefebvre writes that representations of space 'coexist, concord or interfere' with representational spaces (Lefebvre 1991:41). The examination of the chosen site in the Alley of Roses will aim at finding out more about this relationship. It will be argued that the representational spaces, about which Lefebvre writes that they are 'lived through (…) images and symbols' are also 'lived through' representations of space.[18]

• Lefebvre describes representational spaces as spaces of 'inhabitants' and 'users'; by putting these words in quotation marks, Lefebvre demonstrates his distance from the functionalist discourse and in particular to the functionalist concept of use. The examination of the site in Nowa Huta will reveal the shortcomings of this concept which can be overcome with Lefebvre's concept of use. An important feature of this alternative concept is that it allows registering the impact of representations of space on the use of urban spaces.

The site I would like to focus on is left without an official name, but it is currently called colloquially 'the square after Lenin'. It is a broadening in the Alley of Roses: a pathway which connects the Plac Centralny (Central Square) with the Plac Ratuszowy (City Hall Square).

It is important to notice that this site was not designed as an urban square and according to typological criteria it is not a square. The buildings surrounding the site are exclusively blocks of flats; the only entrances accessible from the site lead to the staircases of the blocks of flats. Following the original masterplan, in front of them a rose garden was created. A photograph published in the year 1959 (Ptaszycki: 1959) shows the newly realized design. The arrangement is symmetrical with the main axis of the ensemble, but the routing of paths and the placement of seats stresses the direction perpendicular to the axis. These transversal paths aimed at the entrances to the houses make the rose garden easily accessible for the inhabitants. Thus, the rose garden was designed to be a calm spot between two official spaces: the Central Square (foreseen as closed by an unrealized theatre) and, on the other side, the City Hall Square (designed as closed by the also unbuilt city hall). [see figures 4, 5, 6]

Since the authorities lacked a symbolic place suitable for political celebrations in the city, in the year 1973 the site was redecorated and the monument of Lenin was built on the axis of the whole

12 The opponents to such help argued, that Nowa Huta was founded as 'hostile to Kraków' being a 'revenge of Stalin' (93.30, 99.57) and that its interests are profoundly divergent to those of Kraków (compare in particular the official 'Statement of the Council of the 7th District in Kraków' from 13.08.1993 in: 93.44). This proved to be a successful argument: the first decision on the financial guarantees for the steelworks was negative (91.22; 91.30). The leaders of the community of Nowa Huta opposed this representation with the image of an anticommunist city which 'resisted the Communist indoctrination' (92.43, compare 92.44, 92.48). For an analysis of the ways of dealing with representations in the postcommunist politics, compare Staniszkis: 2001.

13 Compare 99.1, 99.58, 91.8; 92.31, 99.55; 00.18.

14 The old names referring to communist heroes, institutions and events were exchanged for names connected to the anticommunist history, or to these parts of Polish history which were banned during the Communist regime (compare 90.34; 90.36; 94.45; 04.21; compare also Stenning 2000, 107nn). Another source of names was the pre-socialist history of this area (compare 89.01; 90.45, 90.46, 90.49, 97.39).

15 The representation of Nowa Huta as a city which 'expressed' the socialist ideology (Kozłowski: 2002, 23) was fundamental for the 2002 Kraków IX International Biennale of Architecture, held under the slogan: 'Less Ideology – More Geometry'. The introductory text claimed that: 'the city was built as the entity uniting "ideology" and "geometry". The ideology has passed away whereas the geometry has not been completed' (Ibid:5). These claims established the conceptual framework for the majority of the designs submitted to the competition.

16 The representations of space clearly constituted an important part of the architectural context both for public buildings (first of all the churches, like the 'Arka Pana' – 'The Ark of the Lord') and residential complexes (like the postmodern residential complex 'Na Skarpie' which was claimed by the designer to be a 'protest against the architecture of socialist realism' (94.10)).

17 The French original avoids the controversial description of representational spaces as lived 'directly' yet 'though' something else (i.e. in a mediated way): '**Les espaces de représentation**, c'est-à-dire l'espace **vécu** à travers les images et symboles qui l'accompagnent (...)' (Lefebvre 1986:49).

18 One should be careful in distinguishing symbols and images from representations in Lefebvre's writings. Lefebvre introduces two main meanings of the concept of 'representation': a wide and a narrow one. The latter (according to which representations are conventional, institutionalized conceptualization) is particularly distinguished from symbols (Lefebvre 1977c:120nn), which are connected to nature and rudimentary human needs thus being neither arbitrary nor conventional. On the other hand, Lefebvre's most impressive analyses of representational spaces (the analyses of housing (Lefebvre 1991:232nn), leisure spaces (Lefebvre 1991:309nn) and monuments (Lefebvre 1991:220nn)) deal precisely with the issue of influence of representations of space on representational spaces. These analyses show that representations of space may simulate symbols; the issue of nature is here of particular importance.

ensemble.[19] The roses were removed and the whole square covered with stone slabs. The pace of the site changed radically: the slow pace of the rose garden was replaced by the supervised emptiness (a police box was built nearby) interrupted by official mass manifestations and by violent anticommunist riots. By removing the transversal paths and placing the monument on the axis, the site was given a clearly axial direction. Since the theatre and the city hall remained unbuilt, this site was the only place in the center of the city which was finished and urbanistically defined. [see figure 7]

The monument was attacked several times and once even with a bomb which knocked off one foot of the leader of the October Revolution. Shortly after the first non-Communist government was formed (1989), the monument was defaced by paint by young people, who demanded its removal. Under this pressure, the municipal authorities reluctantly[20] decided to remove the monument and sell it to the highest bidder (it was sold to a theme park in Sweden). The Lenin monument, however, dominated the popular imagination about Nowa Huta; the poet and musician Marcin Świetlicki wrote in 1997: 'when I think about Nowa Huta I see the monument of Lenin, although it is no longer there' (97.12). With the removal of the monument, the site was deprived of an element which branded it; thus for the first time it needed a name and was called colloquially 'the square after Lenin', or the 'emptiness after Lenin'. This name not only shows the branding power of the monument, but also, what is more interesting, the fact that the site was accepted as a 'square' in spite of the lack of commercial, cultural or administrative functions which could generate urban activity.[21] The inhabitants and the local press called for a redecoration of this site (96.13). The discussion was clearly influenced by the representations of space, mainly those of antagonism between Kraków and Nowa Huta, which were used as arguments.[22] Following the claims, a new design was provided and realized in the year 2001.[23] The inner part of the square was lowered by three steps. The lowered area was flanked by two rows of stone pedestals. Inside this area, in the place where the Lenin monument had been standing, an elevated flower-bed for roses was built, continuing to preserve this geometrically privileged spot as inaccessible for people. Opposite the flower-bed, a podium for 'artistic performances' (as the designers put it (compare 00.30, 00.37)) was erected. Thus, the gaze of the spectators was redirected: they were supposed to look in the opposite direction to that of the participants at official ceremonies held in front of the Lenin monument. This was the only potentially critical intervention in the design, which – in a clear prefiguration of the IX Biennale slogan 'Less Ideology, More Geometry'[24] – closely followed the geometry set by the 1950s design. The designers called this place a 'forum' and have seen it as an attractor for the whole district (00.30). They seem to have taken for granted what was suggested by the nickname of the site: that it is a square, a place where people gathered. What was, however, omitted was the fact that during Communism the people gathered on this site because of administrative restraints or because of their will to protests against these restraints; this was not longer the case after 1989. [see figures 8, 9]

The new design did not prove to be successful. Apart from the members of the district council (01.39) the inhabitants of Nowa Huta were very critical.[25] Most of the people claimed that more greenery (and in particular – more roses) were necessary.[26] Some state that the best solution would be a return to the square as it had been before the erection of the Lenin monument (01.37).

The particularly strong and unanimous wish for greenery cannot be explained by a lack of the greenery felt by the inhabitants living nearby. On the contrary, the blocks of flats flanking the 'square' have generous park-like courtyards. What is more, in their immediate neighborhood, on the other side of the Przyjaźni (or 'Friendship') street, there are two parks, and the Centralny Square faces the Vistula meadow with a unique and legally protected ecosystem. Thus, the longing for greenery in the only potentially urban place in the whole city and the disagreement with the design cannot be explained by a functionalist model of use, according to which use is a saturation of an isolated need which stems from a (mainly physiological) lack. It is clear that in order to grasp this demand for greenery, an alternative concept of use is necessary. Lefebvre's writings on representational spaces suggest such an alternative concept, which was formulated explicitly in opposition to the functionalist one. [see figure 10]

Use, according to Lefebvre, is a practice of the appropriation of space in which the bodily experience goes hand in hand with its interpretation. This concept of interpreting bodily experiences is clearly inspired by a statement of Nietzsche, quoted in German by Lefebvre at the end of the 6th chapter of *The Production of Space*: 'Eure eignen Sinne sollt ihr zu Ende denken' ('You should think your senses to the end') (Lefebvre 1991:399, compare Nietzsche: 1972, 618). Lefebvre's

19 A design was chosen by a competition, won by Marian Konieczny (compare Miezian: 2004, 85nn).
20 It is a historical irony that the former leaders of the anticommunist opposition defended the Lenin monument, trying to avoid one more irritation of the Russian authorities whose troops were still deployed in Poland (89.05).
21 For a period of time at least one of the staircases in the adjacent blocks of flats was used as a temporary shop.
22 The context of this demand was a broader discussion in the late 1990s in Nowa Huta. The local press registered the rapid degradation of the district (compare 97.50; 99.56; 99.58; 01.38; 02.6; 02.23; 02.33; 02.34; 03.3; 03.16; 03.17; 04.12) to which contributed the policy of uneven investment in the city (according to an article from 1999 (99.1) the district provides 35% of the municipal income while the city invests only 10% of the available money in the district). Thus, the feeling of being discriminated is widely present in the local press (compare 95.13; 97.46; 99.14; 99.57; 00.35) and the discussion was dominated by the old antagonism between Nowa Huta and Kraków (compare 99.1, 99.58, 91.8; 92.31, 99.55; 00.18).
23 The designers were a Kraków-based office Aarcada.
24 In fact, the leader of the designers team joined the program board of the IX Biennale.
25 Compare 01.37; 02.16; 02.25; 02.28; 02.34; 02.36. The opinions were confirmed in the author's interview with Jan Franczyk.
26 Compare 01.37; 02.25; 02.28.

understanding of use and its ties to the concept of representational spaces are revealed in his description of a prominent example of representational space: the space of a cathedral. Lefebvre writes about the medieval visitor to the cathedral: 'The use of the cathedral's monumental space necessarily entails its supplying answers to all the questions that assail anyone who crosses the threshold. For visitors are bound to become aware of their own footsteps, and listen to the noises, the singing; they must breathe the incense-laden air, and plunge into a particular world, that of sin and redemption; they will partake of an ideology; they will contemplate and decipher the symbols around them; and they will thus, on the basis of their own bodies, experience a total being in space' (Lefebvre 1991:220,1; Lefebvre 1986:254). In this description, the use of the cathedral's space is seen as 'necessarily' involving its meaning (i.e. 'answers' to 'questions' which 'assail' every visitor). It is through the awareness of the bodily experiences (of breathing and walking) and their interpretation that the visitor 'plunges' into the world of Christian beliefs (about 'sin and redemption'). In this experience both 'symbols' ('contemplated and deciphered') and 'ideology' (of which the visitor 'partakes'[27]) are involved.[28] Since Lefebvre constantly stresses in *The Production of Space* that representations combine ideology and knowledge,[29] it can be concluded, that both symbols (as stated in the quoted definition (compare Lefebvre 1986:39)) and representations of space play a crucial role in this experience: not only 'through symbols', but also 'through' representations space is 'lived'.[30]

The claim that the visitors to the cathedral are experiencing a 'total being in space' can be explained by Lefebvre's other statement about monumental spaces: 'for millennia, *monumentality* took in all the aspects of *spatiality* that we have identified above: the perceived, the conceived, and the lived; representations of space and representational spaces;' (Lefebvre 1991:220). In the use of the cathedral's space all three aspects of space come together; this representational space is experienced (or 'lived') through its perceived form and its conceived meaning. Lefebvre constantly stresses that none of the three components involved in the experience of space has any ultimate dominance over others; all three combine a relative dependence with a relative autonomy.

For the analysis of the site in the Alley of Roses, one more aspect of Lefebvre's description of the cathedral's visitor is relevant. Lefebvre claims to describe the situation of '*anyone* who crosses the threshold (of the cathedral)' (Lefebvre 1991:221; my emphasis). This is, however, a description of a historical situation: Lefebvre adds that such a universality is possible 'under the conditions of a generally accepted Power and a generally accepted Wisdom' (Lefebvre 1991:220) which mean in the case of the cathedral the political and cultural domination of the Catholic Church during the Middle Ages. The fact that a particular experience of a representational space was shared by everybody (or, more specifically, that this space was lived through a particular set of symbols and representations of space) is called by Lefebvre a 'practical and concrete consensus' (Lefebvre 1991:220). Similarly, *any* visitor to the Alley of Roses during the political and cultural dominance of the Communist regime was forced to obey an analogous consensus. Regardless of his beliefs, the visitor entering this place confronted his being in this space with the ruling representation of Nowa Huta – that of a socialist city. This conceived representation (repeated again and again in the official mass media) and the perceived empty space in front of the monument (offering a location for mass demonstrations of support for this representation) were necessarily involved in the experience of this space; through them the site was 'lived'. The only choice a visitor to the square had was to contest (by taking part in riots) or to support the ruling representation (by participating in mass demonstrations or by restraining from protest). Neutrality was impossible, since the mere presence of the visitor on the square contributed to an image of a lively socialist city; this is why, perhaps, the emptiness showed by the photographs of the square from the 1980s should be interpreted as subversive. Like Lefebvre's visitor to the cathedral, who could yield to the representation or commit a blasphemy, for the user of the square it was impossible either to ignore the ruling interpretation, or to be neutral. Thus, the 'practical and concrete consensus' was not so much focused on a particular way of use of the site, but rather on a particular representation which was a necessary context for *any* way of use.

Besides the removal of the statue from the pedestal, the site was not subjected immediately to major changes following the political transition of 1989. A radical change, however, was the end of a domination of one representation of space and the unleashing of a competition between various mass media representations of Nowa Huta. Thus, the 'practical and concrete consensus' was superceded by a pluralism of representations. This is a rather usual situation for representational spaces which, as described by Lefebvre, have not 'a signified' but 'a *horizon of meaning*: a specific or indefinite multiplicity of meanings, a shifting hierarchy in which now one, now another meaning comes momentarily to the fore, by means of – and for the sake of – a particular action' (Lefebvre 1991:222). This *action* might be understood not only in the situationist sense, but also as a role of an architectural design. It is the architectural design which negotiates between various competing representations of space. And such an understanding of an architectural design is surprisingly, but clearly, present in the statements of the inhabitants about the site (both before the new design was presented, and afterwards, as a critique of the realized project). Their protest

27 '(...) celui qui franchit le seuil (...) reçoit une idéologie' (Lefebvre 1986:254).
28 Being highly critical of the concept of ideology as developed in orthodox Marxism, in 'The Production of Space' Lefebvre adds the classical Marxist concept of ideology (as false consciousness and as a set of false or improperly applied justifications of a certain practice) the Althusserian understanding of ideology as permeating everyday life. A prominent example for Lefebvre is the Catholic Church which managed to dominate everyday life by imposing on people certain ways of speaking permeated with religious meaning (Lefebvre 1977a:227).
29 'The area where ideology and knowledge are barely distinguishable is subsumed under the broader notion of **representation**, which thus supplants the concept of ideology and becomes a serviceable (operational) tool for analysis of spaces' (Lefebvre 1991:45).
30 Lefebvre's concept, according to which the visitor of a cathedral is not a distant reader of coded messages contrasts with the positions on architectural semantics widespread (under the influence of linguistics) in architectural theory in the 1970s and 1980s.

against the design should be understood as a demand for an evasion of a particular representation of Nowa Huta (that of city caught in the opposition between Communism and anticommunism) by means of 'putting to the fore' another influential representation, that of a 'green city'. The latter is able to replace the former since it is both widespread and seen as the least politicized of any representations of Nowa Huta.[31] It is the political neutrality which is so desperately desired by the inhabitants (who wished to avoid any monument (96.13) and criticized the design as a 'parade square' (02.25)).[32] There is no doubt about the fact that the demands for greenery should be understood as a wish for a particular configuration of the perceived, conceived and lived aspects of space: this was not only a demand for a particular function of the site or its particular physical form, but also a support for one of the competing representations and an opposition to others. How crucial for the formulation of these demands the mass media representations of Nowa Huta were, can be exemplified by the fact that one of the articles which criticized the new design was illustrated by a reproduction of a picture of the rose garden, taken in the 1960s, i.e. before the erection of the monument (02.33).[33] It would be a mistake to regard the choice for a particular representation as a rhetorical strategy applied in order to introduce a desired use; the opposite is rather the case: a particular use is chosen in order to support a desired representation and introduce it into everyday life.[34] [see figure 11]

In his analysis of urban space, Lefebvre claims that the most general feature of space[35] is 'centrality', which means the possibility of gathering 'everything' in, or

31 A historical investigation on the concept of a 'green city' would, however, reveal a considerable partiality for this concept by the Nazi and Stalinist regimes; the reasons were both military and ideological (compare Reinborn:1996,157).
32 This sensitivity was revealed during a happening organized by a commercial radio station in Kraków. During the happening a foam 1:1 copy of the monument was placed in its old location; the copy was soon overthrown by angry passers-by and the organizers were sued by one member of the district council for 'propagation of totalitarianism' (compare 01.09, 01.10, 01.11, 01.30).
33 This photograph reveals that the square itself is subject to a distinct set of representations which are, however, closely tied to other representations of Nowa Huta.
34 It should be stressed that this argument does not justify a claim for a greater participation of users in the design process; in fact this argument is indifferent towards the participation debate. In this specific case, it is questionable whether the replacement of the representation of Nowa Huta as a socialist city by a putatively neutral representation of a 'green city' could be a successful solution; instead of forgetting by repressing bad memories, another concept of forgetting should be aimed at by architectural interventions, perhaps inspired by the Nietzschean concept of 'active forgetting'.
35 Lefebvre calls this feature 'the form of space' and investigates it in analogy to Marx's analysis of the form of commodity (the possibility of exchange) in 'Kapital' (compare Lefebvre 1991:101).
36 The first version of this paper has been presented at the conference 'The Work of Stories', Massachusetts Institute of Technology, 6-8 May 2005. I am grateful to Brent Batstra (TU Delft), Christine Boyer (Princeton University), Arie Graafland (TU Delft) and Patrick Healy (TU Delft) for their careful readings and comments on this paper. My understanding of Henri Lefebvre's theory of production of space, applied in this article, is based on a research fellowship at the ETH Zurich supervised by Ákos Moravánszky and intensively consulted with Christian Schmid.

around, one point (Lefebvre 1991:331). The discussed site in the Alley of Roses is such a central space, which, throughout its history, gathered people, objects, ways of use, interpretations, emotions and memories. The site was 'worked on': it was physically transformed, represented and used, thus gathering practices of production of space and their products. The above analysis allows a precise understanding of centrality not as an ontological category (like the category of 'extension' in the Cartesian concept of space) but as a practical and historical category. Centralities are produced by gathering objects, representations and practices: the centrality of the Alley of Roses was potentially present in the initial design, but it has actually been produced by the placement of the Lenin monument, by continuous organization of political ceremonies and by forcing the inhabitants to attend them. But the producer of centrality never controls the product fully: the Alley of Roses with its centrality produced by the Communist regime, gathered subversive representations and practices along with the official ones.

Thus, centrality necessarily involves unity and contradiction between the objects gathered as well as collaboration and competition between the practices of the production of space. The above analysis suggested that the means of this collaboration or competition between the practices are their products, instrumentally used by other practices. Every single practice is dependent on other practices, since it necessarily needs to instrumentalize their products. But instrumentalization subjugates the tools to aims which are other then those of their producers (an obvious example might be the application of historical representations of Nowa Huta to political aims); at the same time the tools utilized always influence the aim they are applied for (only a few projects submitted to the 2002 Biennale were able to break free from the representations of Nowa Huta introduced by the program of the competition (compare IX MBA)). This necessity of collaboration, conflict and mutual influence between various practices of the production of space was studied as one empirical example in this paper. This analysis should be seen in a broader context, as supporting, interpreting and developing Lefebvre's conviction on the dialectical relationship (simultaneous unity and contradiction (Lefebvre 1991:392)) between the practices of the production of space and between space as conceived, perceived and lived. Lefebvre always underscored this conviction, without, however, providing its definite theoretical elaboration and thus opening it to subsequent investigation.[36]

Primary sources

I have used the following referencing system:

Table 1a: Left column: abbreviation of the title of the newspaper or magazine, right column: the full title of the newspaper or magazine. Table 1b: Left column: the number of the article as used in the paper. the first two digits of this number are the two last digits of the publication year. Right column: the title of the article, followed by the abbreviation of the title of the newspaper or magazine (according to table 1a), the number of the issue from the particular year and the page number. For example: 04.21 'Stare nazwy w Nowej Hucie', DP (80), p. 6 refers to the article 'Stare nazwy w Nowej Hucie', published in the issue No. 80 of Dziennik Polski from the year 2004 on page 6.

A Investigated mass media

CK	Czas Krakowski
DP	Dziennik Polski
DP[KK]	Kronika Krakowska/Dziennik Polski
CCP	Czas Przeszły Przyszły/Echo Krakowa
GK	Gazeta Krakowska
GK[EK]	Echo Krakowa/Gazeta Krakowska
GM	Magazyn Gazety Wyborczej
GN	Gość Niedzielny
GNH/GTN	Głos Nowej Huty/Głos Tygodnik Nowohucki
GW	Gazeta Wyborcza
GwK	Gazeta w Krakowie/Gazeta Wyborcza
P	Polityka
R	Rzeczpospolita
Z	Zwierciadło

B List of articles referred to in the paper. The complete list of articles investigated may be found in: Stanek: 2005.

04.21 'Stare nazwy w Nowej Hucie', DP (80), p. 6.
04.12 'O Nowej to Hucie piosenka', DP (25), p. 36.
03.17 'Co się stało z Nową Hutą?', GTN (659), p. 1,14.
03.16 'Szary patos pod rękę z tandetą?', GTN (6), p. 1,8.
03.08 'Nowa Huta – miasto parków', GTN (618), p. 1,8.
03.03 'Nowa Huta za zakręcie', GN (8.06), p. 21.
02.36 'Komisja specjalna', GTN (596), p. 9.
02.34 'Ginący (?) zabytek socrealizmu', GTN (595), p. 1,9.
02.33 'Plac czy klepisko?', GTN (594), p. 1,9.
02.28 'Czego chcą mieszkańcy Nowej Huty', GTN (587).
02.25 'Plac zabaw czy defilad', GTN (584), p. 16.
02.23 'Odchodzi 'Świt', nadcióga zachód', GTN (581), p. 16.
02.16 'Wokół Placu Centralnego', GTN (570), p. 3.
02.06 'Nadal nie potrafimy chronić', GW (174), p. 6.
01.39 'Nowa Aleja Róż', GTN (550), p. 12.
01.38 'Szpetnie i nachalnie', GTN (551).
01.37 'Krajobraz po remoncie Alei Róż', GTN (550), p. 12.
01.30 'Lenin (na chwilę) wrócił', GTN (538).
01.11 'Zakazane żarty', DP (172), p. III.
01.10 'Lenin w prokuraturze', DP (171), p. II.
01.09 'Powrócił bez zezwolenia', DP[KK] (170), p. I.
01.08 'Stara Nowa Huta', GK (29), p. 13.
00.35 'Mieszkańcy się boją', GTN (505), p. 1,9.
00.30 'Forum w Alei Róż', GTN (491), p. 1,9.
00.18 'Nowa Huta w budżecie Krakowa', GTN (457), p. 1,9.
99.58 'Zapomniane obietnice', GTN (449).
99.57 'Niechciana Nowa Huta', GTN (448).
99.56 'Szczur z ogryzkiem w zębach', GTN (447).
99.55 'Huta nie zginie', GTN (442).
99.14 'Krakowska sypialnia', GK[EK] (261), p. IV.
99.60 'Róg Marksa i Obrońców Krzyża', GTN (452), p. 1,9.
99.01 '1/3 miasta', GwK (13), p. 2.
97.50 'Problem z fontanną', GTN (350), p. 8.
97.46 'Co prezydent proponuje mieszkań'com Nowej Huty', GTN (348), p. 9.
97.39 'Nowe ulice w Grębałowie', GTN (343), p. 3.
97.12 'Pocałunek tysiąca dygnitarzy', GW (307), p. 20,1.
96.13 'O Nowej to Hucie są słowa: historia z perspektywy 'Stylowej'', P (18), p. 30,1.
95.13 'Dyskryminacja Nowej Huty', CK (255), p. 5.
94.45 'Plac Centralny placem Dmowskiego?', GTN (144), p. 2.
94.10 'Nowa Huta, Azory, Berlin'. GM (292), p. 16,7,8.
93.45 'Uchwała dzielnicy Bieńczyce', GTN (123), p. 3.
93.44 'Stanowisko Rady Dzielnicy VII', GTN (123), p. 3.
93.30 'Zemsta Stalina', GTN (124), p. 1,4.
92.48 'Czy uratujemy Nową Hutę?', GTN (50), p. 3.
92.44 'Czy zdążymy uratować Nową Hutę?', GTN (46), p. 3.
92.43 'Czy zdążymy uratować Nową Hutę?', GTN (45), p. 3.
92.31 'Zakaz inwestycji w Nowej Hucie? ', GTN (73), p. 1,2.
91.30 'Huta – co dalej?', GNH (1768), p. 3.
91.22 'Racjonalizm czy brak wyobraźni', GNH (1766), p. 6,7.
91.08 'Problem Pana Boga?', GK (15.11), p. 10.
90.49 'Huta 'Kraków' czy Huta 'Mogiła'?', GK (12.01), p. 4.
90.46 'Oświadczenie', GK (6,7.01), p. 2.
90.45 'Huta to też Kraków', GK (9.01), p. 2.
90.36 'Nowohuckie objawienie św. Franciszka', GNH (1747), p. 6,7.
90.34 'Uliczna lekcja historii', GNH (1743), p. 6,7.
89.19 'Symbol, sukces, porażka?', GNH (1693), p. 6,7,8.
89.05 'Zamachy na Lenina', P (50), p. 7.
89.01 'Były tu podkrakowskie pola', CCP (158), p. 3.

Secondary sources

Anon. **Narodziny Nowej Huty: materiały sesji naukowej odbytej 25 kwietnia 1998 roku**. 1999. Kraków: Towarzystwo Miłośników Historii i Zabytków Krakowa.

Anon. IX MBA (IX International Biennale of Architecture). 2002. Kraków.

Boyer, M. C. **CyberCities. Visual Perception in the Age of Electronic Communication.** New York: Princeton Architectural Press, 1996.

Bukowski, A. **The Diagnosis of Social Situation in Nowa Huta in the context of socio-therapy centers establishing** – paper presented at the **5th transnational Meeting; Demos – improving local democracy** (Kraków, 15-17.05.2003).

Dimenberg, E. Henri Lefebvre on Abstract Space. **In:** LIGHT, A., Smith, J., eds. **The production of public space.** Lanham [etc.]: Rowman & Littlefield, 1998.

Elden, S. **Understanding Henri Lefebvre. Theory and the Possible**. London: Continuum, 2004.

Harvey, D. **The Condition of Postmodernity.** Oxford [etc.]: Blackwell, 1990.

Irion, I., Sieverts, T. **Neue Städte. Experimentierfelder der Moderne**, Stuttgart: Deutsche Verlags-Anstalt, 1991.

Juchnowicz, S. 'Nowa Huta, a Relict of the Past or a Chance for Cracow', in: Anon., **IX MBA (IX International Biennale of Architecture),** Kraków, 2002.

Karnasiewicz, J. **Nowa Huta: Okruchyżycia i Meandry Historii**, Kraków: Towarzystwo Słowaków w Polsce, 2003.

Karsznia, N.**Życie rodzinne w Nowej Hucie. Obserwacje i rozważania**, Kraków: Sponsor, 1997.

Kozłowski, D. Less Ideology – More Geometry **In:** ANON., **IX MBA (IX International Biennale of Architecture),** Kraków, 2002.

Leach, N., ed. **Architecture and Revolution. Contemporary perspectives on Central and Eastern Europe**. London: Routledge, 1999.

Lefebvre, H., 1977a, **Kritik des Alltagslebens**. Vol 1, Kronberg/Ts: Athenäum Verlag, 1977.

Lefebvre, H., 1977b, **Kritik des Alltagslebens**. Vol 2, Kronberg/Ts: Athenäum Verlag, 1977.

Lefebvre, H., 1977c, **Kritik des Alltagslebens**. Vol 2, Kronberg/Ts: Athenäum Verlag, 1997.

Lefebvre, H. **La production de l'espace**. Paris: Anthropos, 1986.

Lefebvre, H. **The Production of Space**. Oxford [etc]: Blackwell, 1991.

Light, A., Smith, J., eds. **The production of public space.** Lanham [etc.]: Rowman & Littlefield, 1998.

Miezian, M. **Nowa Huta. Socjalistyczna w formie, fascynująca w treści.** Kraków: Bezdroża, 2004.

Ptaszycki, T., et al., eds. **Nowa Huta**. Kraków: Miastoprojekt, 1959.

Salwinski J. Decyzja o lokalizacji Nowej Huty pod Krakowem. Stan wiedzy. **In:** ANON., **Narodziny Nowej Huty: materiały sesji naukowej odbytej 25 kwietnia 1998 roku**. Kraków: Towarzystwo Miłośników Historii i Zabytków Krakowa. 1999.

Schmid, C. **Stadt, Raum und Gesellschaft. Henri Lefebvre und die Theorie der Produktion des Raumes** (manuscript), 2003.

Shields, R. **Lefebvre, Love and Struggle**. London [etc.]: Routledge, 1999.

Siemienska, R. **Nowe życie w nowym mieście**. Warszawa: Wiedza Powszechna, 1969.

Soja, E. **Postmodern Geographies.** London [etc.]: Verso, 1989.

Soja, E. **Thirdspace. Journeys to Los Angeles and Other Real-and-Imagined Places**. Cambridge, Massachusetts [etc.]: Blackwell, 1996.

Stanek, Ł. **The theory of production of space by Henri Lefebvre.** Paper worked out at the Department Architecture Theory ETH Zurich (manuscript), 2004

Stanek, Ł. **The production of urban space by mass media storytelling practices: Nowa Huta as a case study**. Paper presented at the conference 'The Work of Stories', Massachusetts Institute of Technology, 6-8 May 2005. http://web.mit.edu/comm-forum/mit4/papers/stanek.pdf

Stanek, Ł., Winskowski, P. Ponowoczesne strategie w poprzemysłowym mieście. **In:** Kraków i Norymberga w kulturze europejskiej. Międzynarodowe Centrum Kultury, forthcoming.

Staniszkis, J. **Postkomunizm. Próba opisu**. Gdańsk: Idee – Słowo/Obraz Terytoria, 2001.

Stenning, A. Placing (post)socialism: the making and remaking of Nowa Huta, Poland. **European Urban and Regional Studies**, 7/2, 2000. pp. 99-118.

Stenning, A. **Representing Transformations/ Transforming Representations: Remaking Life and Work in Nowa Huta, Poland**. Paper presented to WES 2001: 'Winning and Losing in the New Economy, University of Nottingham (11-13.09.2001). Available from: http://www.nowahuta.info/papers/wes2001.shtml [Accessed April 2005].

Stenning, A., 2003a, Shaping the economic landscapes of post-socialism? Labour, workplace and community in Nowa Huta, Poland. **Antipode** 35/4, 2003a. pp. 761-780.

Stenning, A., 2003b,Życie w przestrzeniach (post)socjalizmu: przypadek Nowej Huty. **In:** J. Karnasiewicz, **Nowa Huta: Okruchy życia i Meandry Historii**, Kraków: Towarzystwo Słowaków w Polsce, 2003b, pp. 66-75.

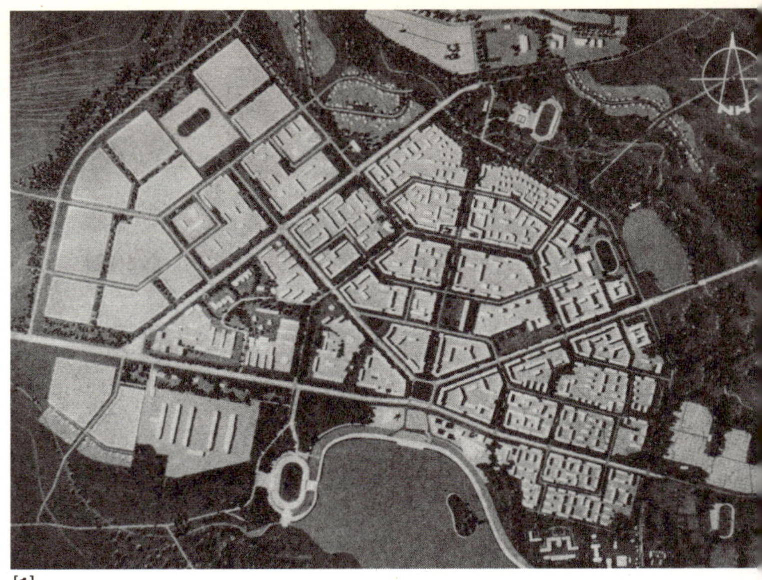

[1]

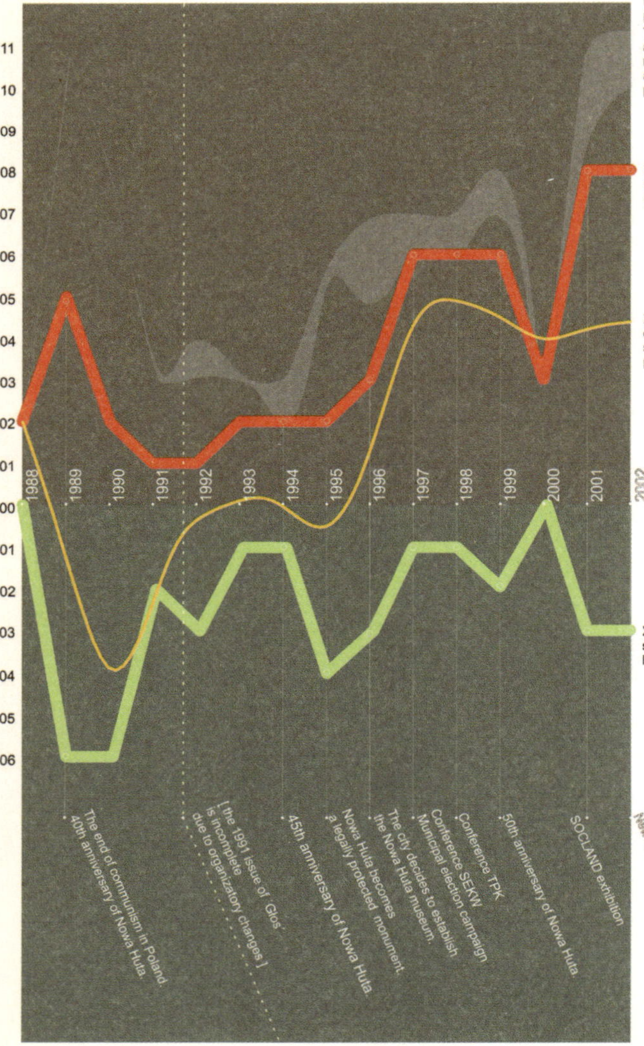

Upper curve: $\Sigma S + \Sigma A$

Lower curve: $[\Sigma S + \Sigma A] - \Sigma[S \cap A]$

The distance between the lower and the upper curve shows the number of articles which provide arguments for both oppository positions.

ΣS : the number of articles supporting the representation of Nowa Huta as a ´socialist city´.

$\Sigma S - \Sigma A$: the curve shows the difference between the articles supporting the oppository positions.

ΣA : the number of articles supporting the representation of Nowa Huta an ´antisocialist city´.

[2]

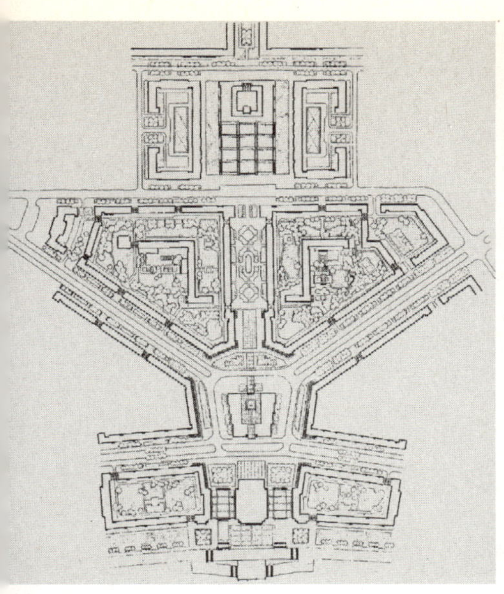

[4]

[6]

[7]

Project of Nowa Huta, 1949-1959
aszycki:1959].
The diagram shows the number of articles
he local weekly magazine of Nowa Huta
os Nowej Huty'/ 'Glos Tygodnik
wohucki' between 1988 and 2002 which
port the representation of Nowa Huta as
ocialist or antisocialist city. If one article
vides arguments for both of these repre-
tations, it is included to both of these col-
tions.
The plan of the centre of Nowa Huta.
urce: Garlinski:1953.

4 The design of the centre of Nowa Huta, only partially realized. Source: Garlinski:1953.
5 Aleja Róż at the beginning of the 1950s. Source: Garlinski:1953.
6 Aleja Róż in the 1960s. Source: picture by Henryk Hermanowicz, property of the Muzeum Historyczne Miasta Krakowa/ Historical Museum of Kraków.
7 The Lenin monument. Source: picture by Henryk Hermanowicz, property of the Muzeum Historyczne Miasta Krakowa/ Historical Museum of Kraków.

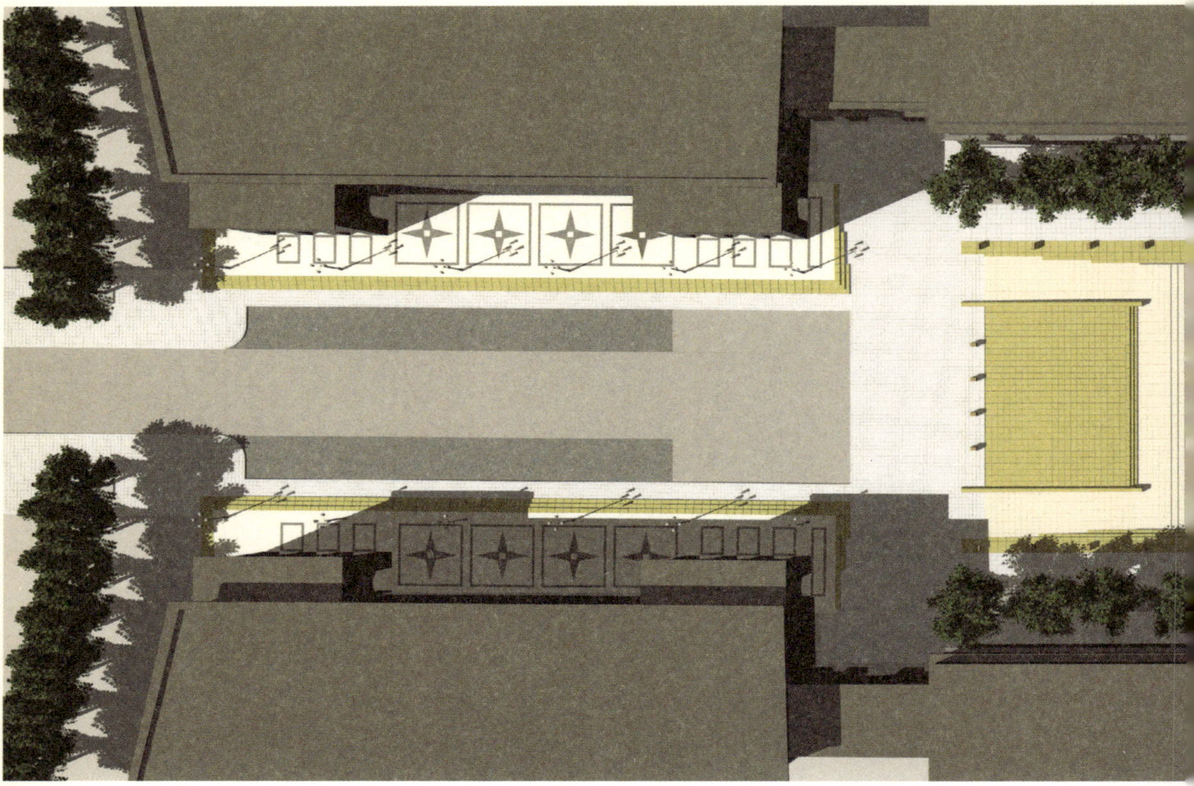

[8]

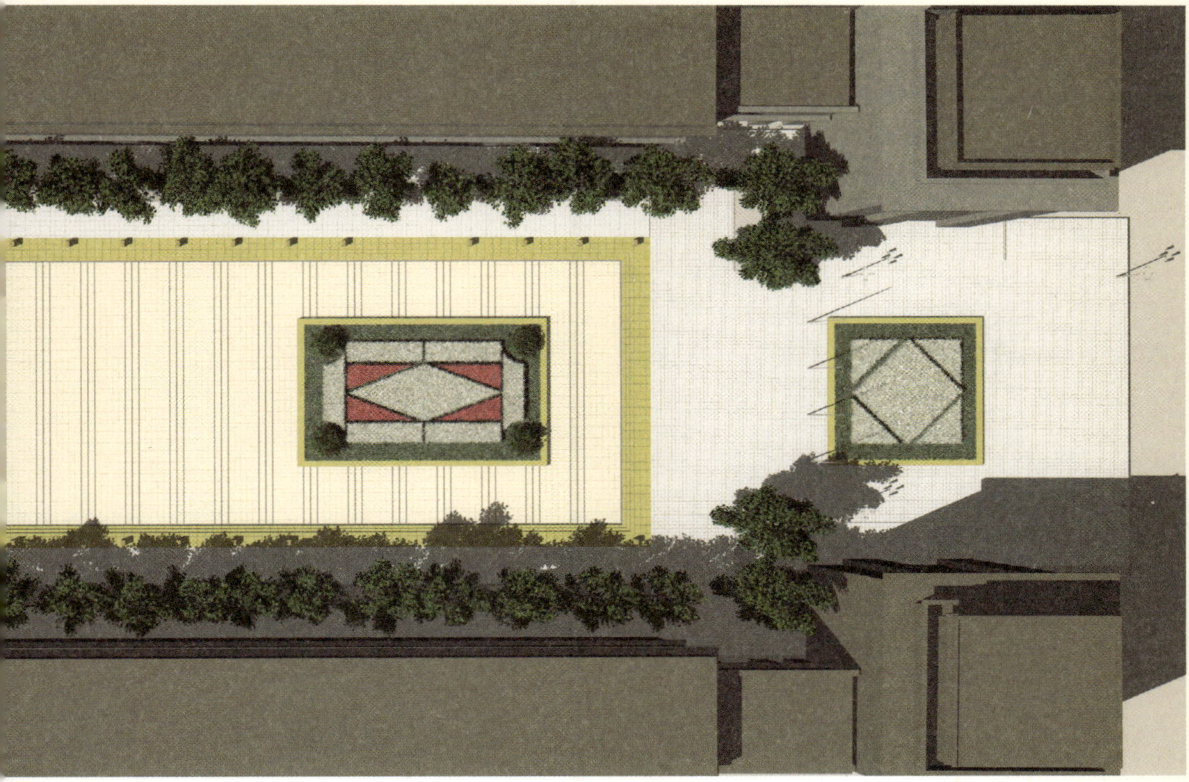

[11]

8 The design of Aleja Róż (2002). Source: drawing by Piotr Gajewski Architects, Kraków.
9 The design of Aleja Róż (2002). Source: rendering by Piotr Gajewski Architects, Kraków.
10 Nowa Huta as a 'green city'. Source: GwK 1997 (3.07).
11 The picture of Aleja Róż from the 1960s as a critique of the realized design. Source: GTN 2002 (no.35).

The Politics of Spatial Difference in the Monument and the Model – The Affective Versus the Useful in Architecture

Alta Steenkamp

Background This paper is related to an ongoing doctoral study of the politics of apartheid space in South Africa, directed by the thesis that architecture can be investigated by studying how power is represented in space. It is well known that the relationship between space and power in apartheid South Africa deliberately included some and excluded the 'other' through its nature, location, ordering and limits. I am specifically interested in the relationship between conceptualisations of space and power and their practical applications in architecture: How power worked through space within the political period of apartheid, and how space was made an object of the exercise of power.

The doctoral study focuses on this process as it pertains to two projects of the apartheid built environment: the Voortrekker Monument and the Native Township Model. The Voortrekker Monument (Pretoria), designed by Gerard Moerdijk, was conceived in 1938 at the centenary of the Great Trek and inaugurated on 16 December 1949. Built to remind coming generations of the history and significance of the Great Trek, it became 'the' representation of the Afrikaner nation. A year later, in 1950, the Group Areas Act became the decisive law to govern the spatial separation of the white population from the 'other' races. The Native Township Model, which created separate areas for blacks that were (ironically) modelled on a 'European' lifestyle and presented as a civilising space for urban blacks, was developed and implemented during the 1950s. By comparing these two projects, I propose to investigate the politics of spatial difference. In this way, the doctoral study will endeavour to contribute to the post apartheid discourse on apartheid architecture and planning in the South African public domain.

This paper explores one facet of the study referred to above by comparing the relationship between space and power, as articulated by Henri Lefebvre and Michel Foucault, respectively, in the monument and the model. *Monument* is understood as a singular and commemorative project and *model* as a project that aims to regulate behaviour in space to a chosen standard (for example the panopticon). The monument is a unique object with a specific interest, whereas the model can be replicated along general principles with a norm as goal (for example a successful prison or school system). The paper is not concerned with a description or analysis of the specific projects of the Voortrekker Monument and Native Township Model referred to above, but rather with a generic condition where the monument and the model have a connection when generated by a common political focus – as projects of a single ideology. Firstly, the concept of difference in relation to politics and its projects will be defined by way of Foucault's concepts of ascending and descending individualisations. An argument, based on a postulation in which these conditions exist simultaneously, will be formulated to illustrate how a common political focus sets up a connection between the two projects. Secondly, the approaches proposed by Lefebvre and Foucault for investigating these projects will be explored. It will be shown that their work necessitates a consideration of the body as subject of the relationship between space and power. It will be argued that this concern with the body is *embodied* in architecture by way of its distinction between the affective and the useful: the emotional and the functional. Finally, I will argue that the modernist view of the *active body* as an element in space guided by *vital forces* (originating from Gottfried Semper) is transposed by the introduction of the *political body* as a product of power relations to the theory of architecture concerned with space. This facilitates, in fact necessitates, a re-conceptualisation of space in architecture.

Politics and projects of difference In *Discipline and Punish*, Michel Foucault[1] describes a political axis of individualisation that reverses at specific moments marked by the disciplines. This reversal is related to the degree of power an individual possesses. Individualisation is greatest or *ascending* when one is privileged and acknowledged as an individual, when one is knowledgeable of and included in rituals and ceremonies, and when one benefits from economic and social networks. Individualisation is weakest or *descending* in a disciplinary regime when a more anonymous and more functional power is exercised by surveillance, observation and comparative measures that have the norm as reference.

> The moment that saw the transition from historico-ritual mechanisms for the formation of individuality to the scientifico-disciplinary mechanisms, when the normal took over from the ancestral, and measurement from status, thus substituting for the memorable man that of the calculable man, that moment when the sciences of man became possible is the moment when a new technology of power and a new political anatomy of the body were implemented.[2]

Foucault does not elaborate on the nature of 'the moment' and, as with the 'paradigm shift' articulated by Thomas Kuhn (1970) one is left to ponder the characteristics, temporality and duration of these changes.

Furthermore, if an individual either has or lacks power, that individual most likely finds him/herself in a group or society that, too, either has or lacks a comparable level of power. Therefore one should also be able to refer to and examine ascending or descending *socialisations*. Foucault did not consider a scenario where these levels of individualisation/socialisation exist simultaneously. I would argue that this is true of power that deals with or dealt with an 'other', such as colonial and apartheid South Africa. At the same time as power was implemented to define and refine the history and kinship of the dominant group, it was also applied to suppress the dominated group. In this scenario of the domineering/dominated, individuals are either privileged or disadvantaged, either superior or inferior, either 'in' or 'out', as Jennifer Bloomer explains:

> Or is the second term of the conjunctival pair either/or. It is a categorizing

designator of exclusion based on difference. If a person, place, or idea appears under the aegis of 'either', that person, place or idea may not appear with 'or'. Or, a contraction of 'other' is conventionally the marker of the inferior category.[3]

The politics of difference, I put forward, can be seen when ascending and descending socialisation exist *at the same time* – when one group uses its power not only to construct and affirm its own identity but at the same time to suppress the identity and liberty of another. This further proposes that, when scientifico-disciplinary mechanisms and historico-ritual mechanisms are conceived as spatial projects of the same power, they might be described and compared as projects of political difference. Foucault referred to the monument as a good example of a historico-ritual mechanism, and the model, as an example of a scientifico-disciplinary mechanism. As an architect, I am specifically interested in the spatiality of this distinction, the articulation of the relationship between space in the theory of culture (with specific reference to the philosophies of Foucault and Lefebvre) and the opportunities offered by its intersection with the investigation and interrogation of architectural spaces.

The monument In *The Urban Revolution*, Lefebvre[4] presents an argument for and against the monument in order to illustrate the urban problematic. The fact that the monument is potentially repressive, institutional and formal, and that it is a coloniser and oppressor of surrounding space, is presented as counting *against the monument*. The misfortune of architecture, according to Lefebvre, is that it wants to construct monuments but lacks an idea of *habiting* them.

> And although the monument is always laden with symbols, it presents them to social awareness and contemplation (passive) just when those symbols, already outdated, are beginning to lose their meaning…[5]

This criticism of the monument is poignantly illustrated in the short story *The City Coat of Arms*, in which Franz Kafka contemplates the complexities of building a monument: the Tower of Babel. As is still the case today, the project needed 'buy-in', especially as many nations were to be involved in its construction:

> People argued in this way: The essential thing in the whole business is the idea of building a tower that will reach to heaven. In comparison with that idea everything else is secondary.[6]

The planning of the project was perfectly ordered – every detail concerning the design and building of the tower was contemplated, the necessary infrastructure was considered, and building could commence. By this time it had become clear that it was beyond all hope for the tower to be completed in one generation. As it was assumed that knowledge would increase and that

1 Foucault (1977) pp. 192-4.
2 **ibid.,** p. 193.
3 Bloomer (1992) p. 167.
4 Lefebvre (2003) pp. 21-2.
5 Lefebvre (2003) p. 21.
6 Kafka (2005) p. 433.

the art of building would develop, it was understood that the next generation would be able to build better and faster than the present. The next generation might, indeed, find it necessary to demolish the present generation's efforts. This knowledge paralysed people's ability to build the tower and, consequently, they focused instead on constructing the city for workers. The different nationalities were housed separately, and constant conflicts and disputes erupted, as each group perceived that its housing was worse than that of the others. This lack of universal peace among the nationalities further impeded commitment to the building of the tower.

> In this fashion the age of the first generation went past, but none of the succeeding ones showed any difference; except that technical skill improved and with it occasion for conflict. To this must be added that the second or third generation had already recognised the senselessness of building a heaven-reaching tower; but by that time everybody was too deeply involved to leave the city.[7]

This parable illustrates the temporality of the monument and the transience of the ideological powers that produce it. The realisation of this fact could lead to stasis (the inability to build an idea), or 'a loss of meaning' (the inability to maintain an idea). 'Meaning' and an ability to communicate or 'lose' it are central to Lefebvre's investigation of the monument. As a counter argument *in favour of* the monument, he mentions its beauty, its ability to bring people together and to project a conception of the world as a complement to the way in which the city projects social life. The monument possesses an ethical and aesthetic power, and it is 'the only conceivable or imaginable site of collective (social) life.'[8] This dialectical relationship is expanded on in *The Production of Space*, where Lefebvre[9] develops a unitary theory concerned with the physical, mental, and social fields as a hypothesis that can account for the 'schism' between 'ideal' and 'real' space. The theory is developed from the universal notion of production, not to produce a (or the) discourse on space, but rather to '*expose the actual production of space…*' [Own emphasis].[10]

How, then, can the production of space be 'exposed'?
An already produced space with a particular spatial/social practice can be decoded; it can be *read* through a spatial code produced along with space.[11] The decoding of space helps us to understand the transition from representational space to representations of space, 'showing up correspondences, analogies and a certain unity in spatial practice and in the theory of space.'[12] The spatial code encompasses the unitary theory, as it does not merely facilitate a reading or interpretation of space; rather, it is a means of addressing living in that space (the physical), of understanding it (the mental), and of producing it (the social). It brings together verbal signs (words and sentences, along with the meaning

invested in them by a signifying process) and non-verbal signs (the sensorial and architectural).[13] Lefebvre[14] identifies the 'reader' as a subject who deciphers or decodes, and the 'speaker' as the subject who expresses himself 'by translating his progression into a discourse':

> Words are in space, yet not in space. They speak of space, and enclose it. A discourse on space implies a truth of space, and this must derive not from a location within space, but rather from a place imaginary and real – and hence 'surreal', yet concrete. And, yes – conceptual also.[15]

Concerning the 'reading' of space, social space cannot be viewed as 'a blank page upon which a specific message has been inscribed'; rather, it (as space) is 'over-inscribed': 'everything therein resembles a rough draft, jumbled and self-contradictory.'[16] In social space, the reader encounters not signs, but rather 'directions' – multifarious and overlapping instructions. The text, inscriptions and writings of social space relates to its conventions, intentions and order. Thus the 'reading' of space follows the production of space; moreover, the space of the monument is unique in that it is produced *especially* to be read. In the monument, then, the signs and 'graphic impressions of readability' become a *trompe-l'oeil*: Although the message may be clearly embodied and intelligible, it also 'hides a great deal more'.[17] In reading the monument, it is therefore important to also uncover what it hides – to explore all its *horizons of meaning*. A monument offers an individual in society an image of their membership to that society, i.e. 'a collective mirror more faithful than any personal one.'[18]

What, then, is the relationship between space and power? Hegemony makes manifest the connections between knowledge and power: the exercise of power cannot leave space untouched, as space is more than just a passive locus of social relationships.[19] Spatial practice, according to Lefebvre, regulates life – it does not create it. 'Space has no power in itself...'[20] Similarly, political power cannot *produce* space; rather, space is the locus and context of the reproduction of social relationships – relationships governed by political power.[21] The power of space can be described as one of its properties, in that it benefits some, excludes some, deprives some. Monumental space, according to Lefebvre,[22] is determined by what may or may not take place in it, the 'prescribed/proscribed' and 'scene/obscene'.

7 **ibid.,** p. 434.
8 Lefebvre (2003) p. 21.
9 Lefebvre (1991) pp. 11-14.
10 Lefebvre (1991) p. 16.
11 **ibid.,** p. 17.
12 **ibid.,** p. 163.
13 **ibid.,** p. 47.
14 **ibid.,** p. 142.
15 **ibid.,** p. 251.
16 **ibid.,** p. 142.
17 **ibid.,** p. 143.
18 **ibid.,** p. 220.
19 Lefebvre (1991) pp. 10-11.
20 **ibid.,** p. 358.
21 **ibid.,** p. 321.
22 **ibid.,** p. 224.

> A spatial work (monument or architectural project) attains a complexity fundamentally different from the complexity of a text, whether prose or poetry[23]

How should an analysis proceed? What is needed, according to Lefebvre[24] is a *critique of space*, an approach that analyses space itself, not things in space. The aim of such a critique would be to uncover the social relationship embedded in space. Lefebvre[25] repeatedly calls for distinctions between thought and discourse *in* space (i.e. in one particular space, dated and located), thought and discourse *about* space (i.e. restricted to words and signs, images and symbols), and thought *adequate to the understanding of* space (i.e. grounded in developed concepts). These differences, for him, rest on the 'fundamental distinction' and 'careful critical attention' to, on the one hand, the materials used (words, images, symbols, concepts), and, on the other hand, to the *matériel* used (collection procedures, tools for cutting-up and reassembling, i.e. building). Furthermore, the productive process of space locates it within history, but it also requires a reconsideration of how 'history' is viewed.[26] This calls for, beyond the history of space, the history of representations and relationships (with space, practice and ideology). The history of space includes the genesis, interconnections, distortions, displacements, mutual interactions, and is linked with the spatial practice of the particular society or the mode of production under consideration.[27] We are in space; we cannot absent ourselves from it. This is, according to Lefebvre, the 'truth of space'.[28]

The model The subject of Foucault's *Discipline and Punish* is the epistemic shift that occurred when punishment as a spectacle disappeared at the beginning of the 19th century. Foucault shows how, since then, discipline has developed into an instrument that deprives the body of liberties by way of a system of constraints and privations, obligations and prohibitions. This form of punishment acts in the depths of the heart, the thoughts, the will, and the inclinations: even within the soul:

> ...a correlative history of the modern soul and of a new power to judge; a genealogy of the present scientifico-legal complex from which the power to punish derives its bases, justifications and rules, from which it extends its effects and by which its masks its exorbitant singularity.[29]

How, then, can the genealogy of space be studied?
A genealogy is the study of the historical transformations within the relationship of power and the body, thus a political 'anatomy': it is not a study of the state as 'body' (with elements, resources and forces), nor a study of body and its surroundings, but rather a study of the 'body politic'. A genealogy traces a shift in this 'body politic', as:

> ...a set of material elements and techniques that serve as weapons, relays,

> communication routes and supports for the power and knowledge relations that invest human bodies and subjugate them by turning them into objects of knowledge.[30]

Within the social body, a new economy gives rise to a new technology of power with its own object, scale, tactic, target, technique, principle of regularization, refinement, and effectiveness located in the reduction of economic and political cost.[31] When investigating and constructing a genealogy, four general rules should be followed:

1 One should not focus on 'repressive' effects alone, but find positive effects too, and regard the subject as a complex social function;

2 One should analyse social functions, not simply as a consequence of legislation or indicators of social structures, but as techniques possessing their own specificity, and regard the working of power as a political tactic;

3 Instead of separating histories (e.g. of penal law and social sciences) and then searching for overlaps, one should search for the common matrix and the single process of 'epistemologico-juridicial' formation;

4 One should study the metamorphosis of methods on the basis of a 'political technology of the body' in which might be read a common history of power and object relations.[32]

Foucault stresses the complex nature of social systems and phenomena constructed through complex powers that operate in space.

What, then, is the relationship between space and power?
Power is exercised rather than possessed. Furthermore, it is not exercised simply as an obligation by those who have it or as a prohibition on those who do not have it; it is invested in the social body as a whole and is transmitted by and through it. All pressure generated by power is countered by resistance. Lastly, power produces knowledge, and the two directly imply one another. There is no power relation without the correlative constitution of a field of knowledge, nor any knowledge that does not presuppose and constitute power relations.[33]

> [P]ower produces; it produces reality; it produces domains of objects and rituals of truth. The individual and the knowledge that may be gained of him belong to this production.[34]

The individual is a reality fabricated by a specific technology of power that Foucault[35] calls a

23 ibid., p. 222.
24 ibid., p. 89.
25 ibid., p. 16, pp. 104-5, p. 132.
26 ibid., p. 46.
27 ibid., p. 42.
28 ibid., p. 132.
29 Foucault (1977) p. 23.
30 ibid., p. 28.
31 ibid., p. 89.
32 ibid., pp. 23-4.
33 Foucault (1977) p. 27.
34 ibid., p. 194.
35 ibid., p. 211.

discipline. Disciplines function as techniques for making useful individuals. Apparatuses and institutions operate a micro-physics of power, and the study of this power presupposes that 'the power exercised on the body is conceived not as a property, but as a strategy.'[36] Effects of domination are attributed not to 'appropriation' of power by the dominant group but to a complex set of dispositions, manœuvres, tactics, techniques, functioning, with a network of relations that can be deciphered. Although institution or apparatus may define its type or modality, a discipline is a complex relationship 'comprising a whole set of instruments, techniques, procedures, levels of application, targets; it is a *physics* or an *anatomy* of power, a technology.'[37] Its task is to adjust (i.e. behaviour) by reducing inefficiency, reducing unmanageability of multiplicity, and reducing that which opposes it. Finally, it must also:

> [M]aster all the forces that are formed from the very constitution of an organized multiplicity; it must neutralize the effects of counter-power that spring from them and which form a resistance to the power that wishes to dominate it; agitations, revolts, spontaneous organizations, coalitions – anything that may establish horizontal conjunctions.[38]

Subjection is not only obtained by instruments of violence or ideology; it may also be calculated, organised, technically thought out. It may be 'knowledge' of the body and mastery of its forces: a political technology of the body.[39] This technology is diffuse; it does not have a continuous, systematic discourse, but it implements a disparate set of tools and uses many different methods. In spite of a coherence of results, it is generally no more than a multiform instrumentation and it can be localised in a particular type of institution or state apparatus. Foucault presents panopticism as a general principle of a new 'political anatomy', its object being the relations and spatial manifestations of discipline. The panopticon, a prison model developed by Jeremy Bentham in the late 18th century, according to Foucault, introduced a new carceral technique by its focus on surveillance and submission to the gaze. Disciplinary institutions define a certain mode of detailed political investment of the body, a 'micro-physics' of power that covers the whole social body.[40] It operates in and through 'functional sites' with coded space: disciplinary space – a space and architecture that transforms individuals.[41] In the model, the norm becomes imperative to space.

> It is easy to understand how the power of the norm functions within a system of formal equality, since within a homogeneity that is the rule, the norm introduces, as a useful imperative and as a result of measurement, all the shading of individual differences [42]

If a space in which the norm can function is 'produced', and this is a social space, how does this 'process' differ from that described by Lefebvre? What is the implication of this difference in a reading/history of the architectural projects of the monument and model?

The body of the monument and model compared – the living body versus the docile body

> Architecture produces living bodies, each with its own distinctive traits. The animating principle of such a body, its presence, is neither visible nor legible as such, nor is it the object of any discourse, for it reproduces itself within those who *use* the space in question, within their lived experience.[43]

> ...discipline produces subjected and practiced bodies, 'docile' bodies.[44]

The differences in the embodied spatiality of the monument and the model are central to the differences in their production and the strategies and tactics of power that distinguish the two projects. *Embodied* refers both to space 'made material' and space experienced 'in the flesh'. For Levebvre,[45] architectural genius is realised in spaces of meaning and immortality: 'enduring, radiant, yet also inhabited by a specific local temporality'. Society, as a space, is described as made up of the abstract (an architecture of concepts, forms and laws with an 'abstract truth') that imposes itself on the reality of the senses, the body and its wishes and desires. The *spatial body* becomes social not by being 'inserted' into a 'pre-existing 'world', rather it produces and reproduces itself and/in its space, and it perceives (and contemplates!) what it reproduces or produces.[46]

> Inasmuch as the poet through the poem gives voice to a way of living (loving, feeling, thinking, taking pleasure or suffering), the experience of monumental space may be said to have some similarity to entering and sojourning in the poetic world[47]

The affective level of the body is transformed into a property of monumental space in which the body's level of spatial awareness is heightened, as can be seen in Lefebvre's[48] description of the cathedral space: visitors become aware of their own footsteps and of other noises and smells; they 'plunge into a particular world, that of sin and redemption; they will contemplate and decipher the symbols around them; and they will thus, on the basis of their own bodies, experience a total being in total space'.

36 **ibid.,** p. 26.
37 **ibid.,** p. 215.
38 **ibid.,** p. 219.
39 **ibid.,** p. 26.
40 Foucault (1977) p. 139.
41 **ibid.,** p. 172.
42 **ibid.,** p. 184.
43 Lefebvre (1991) p. 137.
44 Foucault (1977) p. 38.
45 Lefebvre (1991) pp. 137-8.
46 Lefebvre (1991) pp. 195-9.
47 Lefebvre (1991) p. 224.
48 **ibid.,** pp. 221-4.

For Foucault,[49] the systems of society are reflected in its systems of production and situated in a history of the *political body*. The Classical Age discovered the real/physical body as an object and target of power. Subsequently, the biology of this body was extensively studied, but its involvement in the political field had not been studied until the 20th century: this became Foucault's field of interest. However, it is not the power of the monument to create a heightened awareness of the senses, but rather a power that, like disease, works on the body to:

> [I]nvest it; mark it, train it, torture it, force it to carry out tasks, to perform ceremonies, to emit signs. This political investment of the body is bound up, in accordance with complex reciprocal relations, with its economic use; it is largely as a force of production that the body is invested with relations of power and domination; but, on the other hand, its constitution as labour power is possible only if it is caught up in a system of subjection (in which need is also a political instrument meticulously prepared, calculated and used); *the body becomes a useful force only if it is both a productive body and a subjected body* [Own emphasis].[50]

The power that works through the disciplines, as defined by Foucault [51] and described earlier, is subtle and supported by a calculated technology of subjection, thus the disciplines cross the 'technological' threshold and its technicians elaborate 'procedures for the individual and collective coercion of bodies'. Its aim is to achieve docility, for the technology produces itself in and through the body that can be analysed and manipulated – a docile body that may be subjected, used, transformed and improved.[52]

> [I]t is always the body that is at issue – the body and its forces, their utility and their docility, their distribution and their submission.[53]

Clearly the distinction between the affective body and the disciplined body is embodied in architectural space that serves a specific power. Diverse projects require diverse responses, ranging from emotional engagement to docile submission. It is not assumed that architectural space is singular in its embodied qualities but that power *has the power* to express its wish to affirm itself and subjugate its 'other' in space. The two images selected for this paper succinctly illustrate the distinctly different *embodied* spaces: *The Room* by Louis I. Kahn showing the affective body in monumental space, and *Plan for a Penitentiary* by N. Harou-

49 Foucault (1977) p. 136.
50 **ibid.,** pp. 25-6.
51 **ibid.,** p. 221, p. 224, p. 169)
52 **ibid.,** p. 136.
53 **ibid.,** p. 25.
54 (1978: 239-246).

Romain (one of the ten illustrations in *Discipline and Punish*), of the docile body in disciplinary space. [see figures 1 and 2]

Conclusion: The monument and the model compared – the affective versus the functional In *Space in Architecture* Cornelis van de Ven[54] proposes that architecture finds meaning in its visions of space, and that all architectural innovations are related to new concepts of space. He shows how developments related to new materials and technologies led to the production of new conceptions of space. Thus, the late 19th century idea of space as expression of new techniques abolished eclecticism and evolved into a prevailing functional principle of the early 20th century. The late 20th century introduced an interest in corporeal mass, meanings and messages, and the concept of space became secondary in architectural ideas to sign and form. Concurrently, the relationship between space and power became the focus of cultural studies, and this interest was extended to a concern with the body and space as sites of interaction and confrontation in social theory. This concern has found its way into architectural studies of space that deal with the politics of difference. Lefebvre and Foucault both stress the complex nature of power and its relationships to multifaceted processes in society. Both view power as a dynamic component in the production of society's projects and spaces. Both show how strategies and tactics of power create resultant spaces that aim to manipulate the body into participation or submission. Architecture is no longer a neutral object, defined by its architectural elements, composition and style. Likewise, the user is not a neutral independent subject or object in/of space. Instead, and with acknowledgement to Beatriz Colomina (1992), architecture must be thought of as a system of representation and the body must be understood as a political construct, a product of such systems of representation and complex powers, rather than the means by which we encounter them. The politics of difference is inscribed in the spatiality of the monument and model by way of its embodied characteristics: its tactic and strategy to achieve an emotional or functional response.

Bibliography

Bloomer, J. 'D'Or,' in **Sexuality and Space**. Edited by B. Colomina. New York: Princeton Architectural Press, 1992.

Colomina, B. (ed.). **Sexuality and Space**. New York: Princeton Architectural Press, 1992.

Foucault, M. **Discipline and Punish: The Birth of the Prison**. London: Penguin Books, 1977.

Kafka, F. **The Complete Short Stories**. Edited by N. Glatzer. London: Vintage, 2005.

Kuhn, T. **The Structure of Scientific Revolutions**. 2nd Edition. Chicago: The University of Chicago Press, 1970.

Lefebvre, H. **The Production of Space [1974]**. Translated by Donald Nicholson-Smith. Oxford: Blackwell Publishing, 1991.

Lefebvre, H. **The Urban Revolution [1970]**. Translated by Robert Bononno. Minneapolis: University of Minnesota Press, 2003.

Van de Ven, C. **Space in Architecture**. Amsterdam: Van Gorcum Assen, 1978.

Architecture comes from The Making of a Room

The Plan A society of rooms is a place good to live work learn

A great American Poet once asked The Architect 'What slice of the sun does your building have, what light enters your Room' as if to say the sun never knew how great it is until it struck the side of a building.

The Room

s The place of the mind. In a small room one does
not say what one would in a large room. In a room with
nly one other person could be generative. The vectors of each meet.
A room is not a room without natural light. "natural light gives the time of day and the mood of the seasons to enter."

[2]

The Room, sketch by Louis I. Khan,
strating the space of the effective body.
urce: Van de Ven (1979) p. 19.
Penitentiary by N. Harou-Romain,
strating the docile body.
urce: Foucault (1977).

Crossing the times of urban space – manipulating temporal characteristics of relations in the network city

Jeroen van Schaick

Introduction The paper will explore the field of *urbanism of the network city* problematizing the approach of Gabriel Dupuy as developed in his *book; L'urbanisme des réseaux: Théories et* méthodes (Collection U. Géographie) *(Unknown Binding)* (1991). The paper will focus on the dynamic character of relations in the network city which is regarded as a hybrid socio-physical system. The 'network city' here is not regarded primarily as a poly-nuclear spatial constellation – as it is often used in urban design discourses -, but as a conceptualization of the urban system through theories of networks. The main question raised in this paper is how dynamic relations, and relations between dynamics, in a complex urban system can be addressed in urban design and planning. The concept of operators of urban networks as introduced by Dupuy – (a) the services, operators and structure of technical networks, (b) functional networks of common-interest users and (c) the network of the urban household/company – will be used to develop an understanding of different types of dynamics in cities on a theoretical level. Furthermore this paper attempts to make the relations between these types of dynamics explicit, where Dupuy has left these implicit, through ideas developed in network theory and chronogeography. This exercise delivers building blocks for a further exploration of time-oriented urban design approaches.

Times of the Network City The concept of the Network City, advanced by Gabriel Dupuy (1991) and elaborated on by Paul Drewe (2005), represents an approach to urban design, which falls under what Trancik calls *linkage theory.*[1] The layered character of this model must be understood from bottom to top as a set of levels, on every layer focussing on the urban system seen from a different perspective defined by what Dupuy calls operators – *la ville des opérateurs des réseaux*. Thus the urban model Dupuy puts forward, the Network City, can actually be regarded as a set of perspectives to understand the workings of the social-technical, temporo-spatial, urban system as a whole. [See figure 1]

Interpretation of the Ville de Reseaux (Network City) by Dupuy

> Level one involves the suppliers of technical networks such as water and sewerage, energy, transport and ICT; level one covers the infrastructure, the services offered and the operators. [...] On level two we find functional networks of common-interest users centering on consumption, production, distribution and social contacts; specific location factors apply to each of the networks. It is on level three that the users of functional networks make actual, selective use of technical networks and services for their special purposes.[2]

Every level implies different conceptions of time for an 'urbanisme des reséaux'.

From the natural sciences (e.g. Barabasi) and philosophy (e.g. Latour) we can learn that a number of different processes with their own dynamics interact, meanwhile forming an evolving

1 Cited by Ina Klaasen (2004) p. 80.
2 Drewe (2003) pp. 29-30.
3 See Stalder (1997).

network. Looking at the model developed by Gabriel Dupuy this could be applied to the practice of urbanism. Latour distinguishes largely two categories of dynamics – actor dynamics and network dynamics – coming together in the emergence, development and stabilization of actor-networks[3] – an approach similar to the topological, kinetic and adaptive dynamics of operator-networks.[4] Barabasi shows, from his studies on the Internet as '*scale free*' network – i.e. answering to the 'power law' with regard to internal relations – a comparable basic distinction: local events – i.e. attachment or detachment – and growth of the network itself. Moreover Barabasi hints at other types of processes that have to do with relational dynamics. 'Most networks offer support for various dynamical processes, and often the topology plays a crucial role in determining the system's dynamical features.'[5] The range of possible dynamical processes is wide according to Albert & Barabasi: (1) the impact of clustering and topology on several processes, including games, cooperation, the Prisoner's Dilemma, cellular automata, and synchronization (2) search and random walks in complex networks, (3) spreading and diffusion (e.g. ideas).

Times of physical networks: first level network operators Dupuy distinguishes three basic dimensions for all networks through which he implicitly defines the dynamic characteristics of physical, urban networks: the topology of networks, the kinetics of networks, and the adaptive capabilities of networks.[6]

Topology: the making of physical networks The making of physical networks implies basically two topological dynamics. On the one hand we can distinguish dynamics on the level of a node or a relation, on the other hand we can distinguish dynamics on the level of the 'whole' network.

Dynamics on the level of a node or a relation function binary: switching 'on' or switching 'off', including or excluding a node, relating two nodes or not. Due to what Dupuy calls the 'ubiquity-ideal'[7] the topological dimension of networks further means that the continuous growth and/or decline of networks is an inclusive concept to networks. Static networks do not exist, as Barabasi, mathematician and theoretician on networks, shows as well through his modeling work on networks. The development and growth of a physical network is a process with a large temporal grain relative to the processes that 'inhabit' a network (e.g. transporting goods using a rail network in development). This is the reason that physical networks often are regarded as static or fixed in socio-spatial models. The effort and time required to make significant changes means that physical networks in social or spatial analysis regarding smaller time scales is often regarded a given.[8] In network theory this is explained thus: 'Modeling dynamics on a fixed topology is legitimate when the time scales describing the network topology and the dynamical process superposed to the network differ widely. A good example is Internet traffic, whose modeling requires time resolutions from milliseconds up to a day compared with the months required for significant topological changes.'[9]

However, this static approach is not sufficient for urbanism, because urbanism explicitly tries to intervene in and change the physical urban system including physical networks. The topological dynamics on both scales need to be incorporated in our thinking.

Kinetics: circulation and communication In addition to the above described type of dynamics, mainly regarding time in the sense of 'change', we can distinguish a different type of dynamics associated with physical networks. One can say that physical networks are *inscribed* with a specific understanding of time. 'The network defines simultaneously space and time. It establishes amongst those a new relation based on the circulation, the flux, the speed, tending towards instantaneous, "real-time".... This notion of a network time, different from the rest of the world, measured differently, imposed wherever the network exists, is progressing amongst urbanists ...'[10]

New types of physical (communication and transportation) networks are thus said to have effected a speeding up of societal processes[11] and play an important role in the phenomenon 'time-space compression.'[12] To speak simply of acceleration in the context of the 'kinetics-dimension', however, does not suffice to describe the impact of physical networks. Different physical networks coexist and co-evolve in the urban system and they facilitate different speeds and processes simultaneously and in relation. Drewe sees in current temporal trends three overall effects on temporal development: acceleration, expansion and flexibilization.[13]

Adaptation Physical networks do not *prescribe* behaviour, but in addition to a supposedly inscribed nature of the relation between use and physical network, the main role of physical networks is facilitating specific use of time and space. This means that the physical network is continuously adapting to the faster changes of demand or potential. Dupuy distinguishes short term adaptation and long term adaptation:

4 A discussion on the relevance of using the concept 'operators' instead of **'actors'** is not taken on here, for it has no direct relevance to the exploration of the notions of time in networks. For the issue of intervening in urban networks, however, it does have implications not addressed here, requiring an additional discussion on the notion 'collectivity', which would require a more extensive study.
5 Albert & Barabasi (2002) p. 91.
6 Dupuy (1991) pp. 81-106.
7 Dupuy (1991) p. 82.
8 See also Klaasen (2005).
9 Albert & Barabasi (2002) refer to Crovella and Bestavros (1997); Willinger **et al.** (1997); Sole and Valverde (2001).
10 **op. cit.,** (Dupuy) p. 88.
11 Virilio (1998).
12 Harvey (1990).
13 Drewe (2004).

> The adaptive dimension of the network appears to come down do the possibilities of modifying the nature or the structure of the offered connections. On the short term the network must try to provide the use of a maximum of possible relations at every moment ... On the long term the network must also be able to tolerate major morphological adaptations, to create new support for new relations by inscripting in space new points, accessible for new linkages.[14]

Thus we can distinguish adaptation in capacity, relational adaptation and nodal adaptation.

Times of functional networks: second level network operators The spatial logics of production, consumption and social networks govern this second level of the model developed by Dupuy. Again Dupuy speaks only of spatial logics, where for the purpose of this paper the exploration is broadened to temporo-spatial logics. It is shown that implicitly these networks depend as much on space as on time. This level of Dupuy's model offers us the possibility to develop a more specific understanding of a notion of time in relation to space than the first level offered us. The existence of extensive bodies of knowledge on production, on consumption and on social networks in their own right is acknowledged here, but for the purpose of this paper an exploration of these individual fields is not taken up. The concepts are worked here from the perspective of Dupuy, who bases a lot of his thinking in this respect on the work of Fishman.[15]

Production The temporo-spatial logics of production are generally thought of in terms of logistics, and specifically logistical chains.[16] In this context Dupuy mentions the relation of production processes to the labour market and to the availability of the necessary information for specific companies. More recent network-based approaches of temporo-spatial production logics are being developed due to processes of globalization in relation to processes of outsourcing.[17] In this context Drewe (2005) has proposed to develop the concept of time-space budgets, as we know it for individuals, as well for companies. The temporo-spatial logics of production thus have not only a spatial component, but concern the match between temporal regimes where the 'producer', generally a company, acts at the center of, as mediator between or is balancing with both times and spaces. These temporo-spatial logics come for example to ground in locational choice of companies, specialized chains of infrastructures and interface type locations. This means for the relation between space and time that these logics are governed by, respectively, general accessibility for multiple actors, the spatial and temporal interdependence of production phases (e.g. Just-In-Time planning), possibly the *splintering* of infrastructures and the possibilities for simultaneous (spatially and temporally) use of networks or places.[18]

Consumption The temporo-spatial logics of consumption seem to come to ground for example in the location and accessibility of shopping centers, distribution networks of brands and franchises. Dupuy regards the logics of leisure to be an integral part of the concept of consumption. Consumption times and spaces are slightly elusive in their spatial or temporal logic, because they are based in the consumer instead of the producer, which is much more difficult to visualize or grasp in the context of urban design or planning without losing a lot of information about the dynamics that regard consumption. To grasp this, consumption could be regarded more in terms of specific flows of and relations between both objects and subjects. These flows and relations offer then the possibility to develop general principles regarding the temporo-spatial configurations of consumption. For this we should include notions such as appropriation,[19] inscription and domestication as processes of everyday life.[20] Consumption thus typically links different logics, e.g. that of production with that of the domestic networks.

Domestic networks In a way, the notion of domestic networks on this second level is less elusive than the notion of consumption, because we know from our own daily lives what their temporo-spatial logics are. However, for urban design it is still difficult to grasp because of the inherent complexity of accumulation of all domestic networks in an urban system. To get a grip, a twofold orientation is necessary. One belongs on this second level of the network city, the other orientation is developed on the third level (see below). The orientation of the temporo-spatial logics of domestic networks on this level strongly depends on the distinction of specific aspects of personal lives, such as children, which brings with it a specific infrastructure (e.g. that of education). But also the role (and logics) of family, friendships or other collective notions bring specific orientations to a domestically networked logic. Domestic networks looked upon this way give people strong external spatial and temporal markers to move through cities, to the extent where a consistent social network can superimpose strong temporo-spatial regimes on our lives. Regimes can be institutionalized in spatial or temporal rules or laws or can be informal and more culturally established. These regimes make it necessary for urban design to think of synchronization of actions (e.g. in the relations institute-individual, or individual-individual). On the other hand the notion of social networks can be viewed upon in terms of production of social space and time through perception, conception, and direct living.[21]

The three temporo-spatial logics, described on this level, act together in the urban system as an

14 **op. cit.** (Dupuy) p. 92.
15 Fishman (1990).
16 Hesse & Rodrigue (2004).
17 Boelens (2005).
18 See for elaboration Graham & Marvin (2001), Hesse (2002).
19 See Lefebvre (1974).
20 See De Certeau (1984).
21 Lefebvre (1974).

ensemble des points – collection of points[22] and are thus in a sense without direction. They function within their own sectoralized logics and thus give rise to conflicts of time and space in the urban system. How physical urban systems – or, according to Dupuy, the operators of the physical urban system – deal with these sectoralized logics, was the subject of the first level of thinking in his model. How urban households deal with these conflicts in daily life is the subject of the third level of thinking.

Times of the urban household: third level operators

'The urban household, using all means of communication put at its disposal by the first level operators, has to make its own necessary connections between the three types of networks (of the second level) in fact designing the complex scheme of multidirectional relations that constitutes its own city. Fishman stated that the new city has neither centre nor periphery, nor a final frontier, nor a clear distinction between residential zones, industrial zones end commercial zones. The city has no more a characteristic structure that distinguishes it from the chaos that some want to see in it: it is a network structure that we can qualify as third level.'[23]

One could indeed easily suggest that, devoid of traditional structure, these network structures do not answer to spatial or temporal logics. The work of Martin Dijst (1995, 2005) shows clearly otherwise, although in his study the number of temporo-spatial logics vary greatly. He distinguishes 17 actual action spaces, which can be regarded as temporo-spatial configurations on this third level of thinking. These typologies are based on two dimensions: the shape of a specific action space (temporo-spatial relation between base, destination and other action spaces: line, circle or ellipse) and spatial scale (based on maximal distance). [See figure 2]

Relations between temporo-spatial logics An urban system consists of an accumulation of action spaces (individual temporo-spatial logics), of an accumulation of collective, sectoral temporo-spatial logics, and of an accumulation of the temporo-spatial logics of the physical urban system. How then can we grasp the emergent complexity of these related temporo-spatial logics?

To make sense of this large range of times brought up by an 'urbanism of networks' we go back to a categorization developed in the field of chronogeography.[24] Where our exploration up till now taught us about the spatio-temporal logics of urban systems, the complex concept 'time' in the context of socio-spatial structure can be understood through the following set of temporal components of functional social-geographic structure: Circadian rhythms – biological and psychological time, time scale – e.g. hour, day, year, life, duration – compare Jong

(1992), sequence, time surplus or deficit, elasticity of time – relating different activities within a time or a space, pressured by e.g. obligatory activities, time perspectives / images – mediated by individual experience and culture, creating particular 'life spaces',[25] and monochronic or polychronic times – referring to the degree of synchronization of rhythms.
[See figure 3]

In our exploration of new possibilities for a time-oriented urbanism, this gives a comprehensive overview of the temporal aspects we should include in our discussion. Figure 3 shows us the complexity of this approach through the interweaving of 'space', 'time', 'place' and 'location' in social-geographic structure, bringing together formal structures and functional structures. 'Physical space, social space, and time together act in concert as structural factors in the ecology of the city.'[26] Time in this view should be regarded as time-space, a relative and relational concept as a product of social interactions, just as can be concluded from the analysis of the levels of the network city. The conception of time in relation to space as a conceptual complex of different temporo-spatial scales, temporo-spatial types, and temporo-spatial perspectives is inherent to time-oriented urban design.[27] Coupling these two approaches – the network city and the complex of time-space – we can come on the one hand to the definition of specific relations between times (or 'temporo-spatial constructs'). On the other hand we will be able to distinguish a 'moment of intervention', as attempted in the last part of this paper.

Crossing times: the moment of intervention

Categories of temporo-spatial limitations and possibilities Each level of the network city offers limitations and possibilities for temporo-spatial behaviour – actions or projects – on other levels. Interacting projects and actions in time and space show different types of relations through their specific temporo-spatial characteristics. We can distinguish for example crucial relations, (un)expected relations, (dis)harmonized relations, possible relations. Together relations between different projects and actions make up the complex socio-spatial system. From matching the network city model by Dupuy (see figure 1) with the principles from social-geographic structure (see figure 3) we can distinguish determinants, regimes and balances: the logics of a networked time-space configuration such as an urban (sub)system.

Determinants and constraints: time-space and place Looking at both social-geographic structure and a network-based model one can distinguish the constraints *capability, coupling and authority* in the relation between time, space and place – a terminology borrowed from Hagerstrand.[28] These constraints function as specific determinants of temporo-spatial configurations.

22 **op. cit.,** (Dupuy) p. 116.
23 **ibid.,** p. 117.
24 For elaboration see also Schaick (2005).
25 Parkes & Thrift (1980) p. 65.
26 **ibid.,** p. 359.
27 See for elaboration Schaick (2005).
28 Hagerstrand (1969).

The notion of capability (to move, to choose, etc.), both biological and instrumental, can be characterized by – in the terminology of Dupuy – 'kinetic' determinants such as the possibility to communicate and circulate, the possibility to make sequences of actions, to match speed and action, to change direction, etc. 'Capability' in this sense addresses the capability to match the logics of a time-space and a place. The notion of 'coupling', based on the need for activities, for interaction with others and thus some sort of temporo-spatial synchronization, is linked to 'topological' determinants such as distance (time-space), on/off-status (of activity places), and clustering.[29] The notion of authority, mainly addressing the control of access, but in my interpretation broadened to the control of change, is strongly linked to 'adaptive' determinants, i.e. the power to change or appropriate the physical nature of a network. These determinants are strongly based on the characteristics of what is in the model by Dupuy the first level.

Regimes: the formal and the functional Between the urban-design-based model as developed by Dupuy and social-geographic model of Parkes and Thrift we can, on top of the specific temporo-spatial determinants, distinguish another mechanism through which time-space is configured. Three notions, here called regimes, are apparent throughout the literature. First of all we can note the social context or social space, according to Parkes and Thrift determined by ethnic status, social status and family status. This brings together a number of temporo-spatial regimes we know from daily life such as the rhythms and sequences of events we associate with living (bringing together different members of a family or company), working (the relation between internal network and external network), free time (the way we deal with leisure and non-allocated time) and our 'circadian rhythm', i.e. the biological need for a sleep-wake rhythm.

A second type of temporo-spatial regime is also made explicit by Dupuy – that of consumption and production. The institutionalization of spaces and times of consumption and production determine for a large part the way people deal with space and time. From the opening hours of shops, to the degree in which we can monetarize time and/or space, to the number of hours we are not 'free' to choose what to do and where to be, consumption and production are strong mechanisms to configure the urban system.

The last type of regime I want to clarify here is the degree of interrelatedness of times and spaces. In chains of events or simultaneous happenings a clear temporo-spatial interdependence can be noticed in urban systems. Whether the dependence is one of need or one of incompatibility, the complexity of the relations between different actors and their time-spaces seem to increase.[30] This 'networked' regime, where not some sort of top-down regime, but rather an emergence of complex dependence configures times and spaces is difficult to grasp and holds the biggest challenge for urban and regional design and planning (see for example the work of Luuk Boelens). It can be clear that these regimes mainly function from the second level of the model by Dupuy and bring into relation the formal and functional spheres distinguished by Parkes and Thrift (1980).

Balances: strategies and tactics In addition to the determinants and regimes, such as described above, I would like to emphasize one last category of limitations and possibilities of the configuration of time-spaces. Authors, such as Henri Lefebvre, Nigel Thrift, Ash Amin and Michel de Certeau, show a line of thinking, which comes mainly into play on the third level of thinking, such as proposed by Dupuy. I will limit myself here by merely drawing attention to three issues directly relevant to the field of urban and regional design and planning: strategies and tactics of collectives[31] in the social production of space-time and place, strategies and tactics of daily life by multitasking and network-tasking, and strategies and tactics of commercial stakeholders breaking out of sectoralization fusing social, consumption and production networks. A time-oriented urban or regional design or plan should be able to develop these strategies and tactics and explicitly translate them into temporo-spatial designs. An urban design would then rather become a design of a proces than a design of an object or composition.

Types of temporo-spatial interventions: design tasks

The issue of type To come to building blocks for a time-oriented urban design, a good starting point would be to look at the issue of types and typologies of time or rather time-space, just as we generally use types and typologies of two-dimensional and three-dimensional space in urban design. From the exploration in this paper one could assume that to develop types or typologies of time-space it is necessary to look at types of relations in time and space. The shift towards typologies is one still to make, but goes beyond the scope of this paper. Four types of building blocks could be distinguished, giving us four types of time-space relations: (1) Harmony – relating time-space configuration of similar (e.g. stations to stations, neighborhoods to neighborhoods) and different (stations to neighborhoods) order or nature, (2) Structurization – the realization of place through reoccurrence, (3) Synergy effects – stimulation of parallel time-space use for safety, economic or socio-cultural motives, and (4) Legibility – realizing manifestations of time and time structures in space to increase the experiential and user value of the urban environment

The issue of scale An important issue to deal with to come to a time-oriented urban design is the issue of scale. When we shift from a purely spatial approach towards a time-oriented or relational approach, new notions of scale come into play. It becomes apparent when looking at

29 See also Dijst (1995) p. 46.
30 E.g. studies by Hesse (2002) and SCP (2001).
31 See Amin & Thrift (2002).

the exploration in this paper that it is important to relate different temporal scales and thus include some kind of temporal scale system in our urban designs. As to the scale of relations a network approach suggests a further focus on a relational scale system in which intensity of nodes and links is reflected in relation to time-space. A number of building blocks follow from this line of thinking, although they are highly abstracted here: Relations between different time scales through spatial configurations – e.g. daily life in relation to life (of objects, people, urban space, etc.), relations between temporal and spatial scales through network configurations of time-space – e.g. dealing with the disassociation of scales (footloose time-spaces) through globalization effects, relations between different spatial scales through temporal configurations – e.g. sustainability of urban (regional) structure through flexible facilitation of a broad range of time-space utilizations on lower spatial scales.

The issue of place The significance of place in relation to time-space and as specific time-space configuration becomes apparent in both network thinking and social geographical (chronographical) thinking. Places are simultaneously the instigator and the result of various relations between various networks. The production of place through a combination of persistence, mobility, specific time-space budgets, and dependent chains of activity could for example be aimed at optimal urban structures for multiple time-space on different scale levels.

The issue of variation in mobility Mobility cannot be seen as a straightforward, value-free notion. Network thinking and social-geographic studies working from the same premises as this paper show the significance of variation of/in time and space.[32] The variation in friction of time, the hierarchy of space-time, and dominant time-space structures are issues from which spring the tasks of the urban and regional designer. One such task could be the realization of optimal specialized time-space paths for specific (groups of) actors on specific scale levels, but also the inclusion of diverse groups in the accessibility of mobility networks comes forth as an important task.

Conclusion

Starting from a specific way of thinking about urban and regional design and planning – *l'urbanisme des réseaux*, urbanism of networks – this paper has explored the ways different time-space configurations in urban

32 See e.g. Harvey (1990) and Graham & Marvin (2001).

systems can be related. The concept of networks seems to be relevant in relation to the conceptualizations used in 'chronogeography'. This paper shows that the action of relating and configuring times and spaces goes beyond analytical approaches in a geographical manner. The idea has been developed that it is a 'designerly' action and thus defines a possible new direction for urbanism as science and practice. Concluding with specific building blocks for intervening in the urban system, a first glimpse of new time-oriented spatial manners of design can be distinguished. This paper has shown, through the conceptualization of the urban system as a complex of networks, that the issue of time is complex to handle in urban designs, since it is not a singular time, but a complex – or structure – of related times which for urban design cannot be seen apart from space. The multiscalar, networked urban designing of place and variation is at the fore of this new type of urban design. We can conclude that urban and regional design as both science and field of practice require a time-oriented, but also an integral temporo-spatial design-research agenda, with both a fundamental character as a practical concrete character to deal with new structural and ethical questions in design and planning.

Bibliography

Albert. R. and Barabasi. A.L. Statistical Mechanics of Complex Networks. **Reviews of Modern Physics**, Vol. 74, No. 1, January 2002: pp. 48-94.

Amin, A. & Thrift, N. **Cities – Reimagining the Urban**. Cambridge: Blackwell Publishers, 2002.

Boelens, L. **Inaugural lecture for the University of Utrecht.** Available from http://www.urbanunlimited.nl. [Accessed 21 January 2005].

Boelens, L., Sanders, W., Schwanen, T., Dijst, M., and Verburg, T. **Milieudifferentiatie langs de Stedenbaan – Mobiliteitsstijlen en Ketenprogramma's voor Milieu's die Sporen**. Rotterdam, Utrecht: Urban Unlimited, Universiteit van Utrecht, Provincie Zuid-Holland,2005. Available from http://www.urbanunlimited.nl [Accessed 18 August 2005].

De Certeau, M. **The Practice of Everyday Life**. Los Angeles: University of California Press, 1984.

Dijst, M. Het **elliptisch leven, actieruimte als integrale maat voor bereik en mobiliteit**, PhD. thesis, Faculty of Architecture, Delft University of Technology. Utrecht: Nederlandse Geografische Studies,1995.

Dijst, M., Zandvliet, R., and Bertolini, L. Examining Space-time sustainability: Economic, Environmental and Social Impacts of Temporary Populations. In: AESOP 2005 Conference, Vienna 13-17 june 2005. Available from http://aesop2005.scix.net/data/papers/att/283.fullTextPrint.pdf [Accessed 18 November 2005].

Drewe, P. **ICT and Urban Form – Old Dogma, New Tricks**, Delft: Technische Universiteit Delft, 2003. Available from http://www.networkcity.bk.tudelft.nl [Accessed 18 November 2005].

Drewe, P. 'Time in Urban Planning and Design in the ICT Age,' in: **Shifting Sense – Looking Back to the Future in Spatial Planning,** edited by E.D.Hulsbergen, I.T.Klassen, and Kriens, I. Amsterdam: Techne Press, 2005. pp 197-212.

Dupuy, G. **L'Urbanisme des Réseaux – Théories et Méthodes.** Paris: Armand Colin Éditeurs, 1991.

Fishman, R. 'Metropolis Unbound: The New City of the Twentieth Century.' in: **Flux**, no.1, spring 1990.

Graham, S. and Marvin, S., 2001. **Splintering Urbanism: Networked Infrastructures, Technological Mobilities and the Urban Condition.** London: Routledge.

Hagerstrand, T. 1969. 'What about People in Regional Science?' **in: Papers, Regional Science Association, European Vol. 1970**.

Harvey, D. **The Condition of Post-Modernity.** Oxford: Blackwell, 1990.

Hesse, M. 'Zeitkoordination im Rahmen der modernen Logistik – mehr als nur ein Impulsgeber für die räumliche Entwicklung,' in: **Raumzeitpolitik,** edited by D. Henckel and M. Eberling. Opladen: Leske + Budrich, 2002. pp. 107-126.

Hesse, M., Rodrigue, J.-P. **TheTransport Geography of Logistics and Freight Distribution**; **In: Journal of Transport Geography 2004**. Available from http://www.geog.fu-Berlin.de/~teas/publika/pub_sele.htm#hesse [Accessed 16 March 2005].

Jong, T.M. de. **Kleine Methodologie voor Ontwerpend Onderzoek.** Amsterdam, Meppel: Boom, 1992.

Klaasen, I.T. **Knowledge-based Design: Developing Urban & Regional Design into a Science**. Delft: Delft University Press, 2004.

Klaasen, I.T. 'Putting Time in the Picture – The Relation between Space and Time in Urban Design and Planning,' in**: Shifting Sense – Looking Back to the Future in Spatial Planning,** edited by E.D.Hulsbergen, I.T.Klassen, and Kriens, I. Amsterdam: Techne Press, 2005. pp. 181-196.

Lefebvre, H. **The Production of Space (1974)**. Oxford: Blackwell Publishing,1991.

Parkes, D.N., Thrift, N. **Times, Spaces and Places – A Chronogeographic Perspective**. Chichester: John Wiley & Sons, 1980.

Schaick, J. van. 'Multiplicity of temporal grains in the city as research subject in urbanism,' in: **Proceedings Urbanism and Urbanization,** Barcelona, Spain, June 27-29 2005. Barcelona: Universitat Politècnica de Catalunya, 2005.

SCP, Sociaal en Cultureel Planbureau, 2001 **Trends in Time – The Use and Organization of Time in the Netherlands, 1975-2000**. Den Haag: Sociaal en Cultureel Planbureau.

Stalder, F. **Actor-Network-Theory and Communication Networks: Toward Convergence**. 1997. Available from http://felix.openflows.org/html/Network_Theory.html [Accessed 15 April 2005].

Virilio, P. **The Virilio Reader**. Edited by J. Der Derian. Oxford: Blackwell Publishers, 1998.

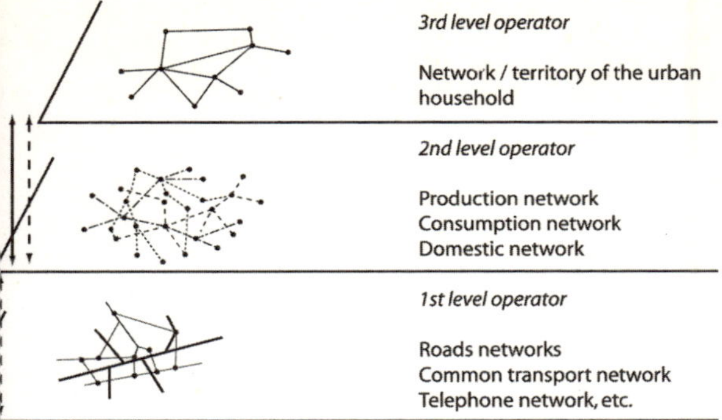

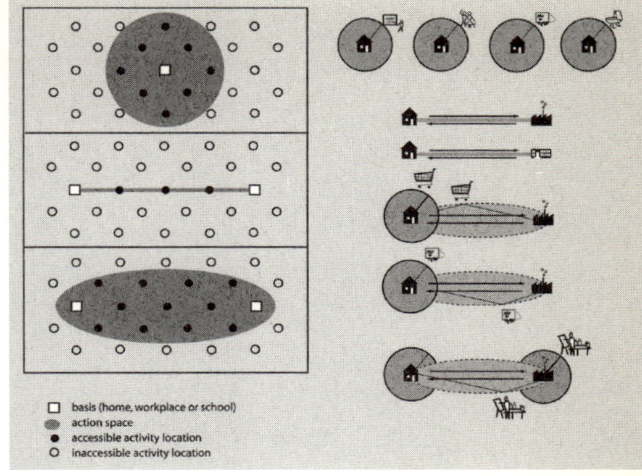

[2]

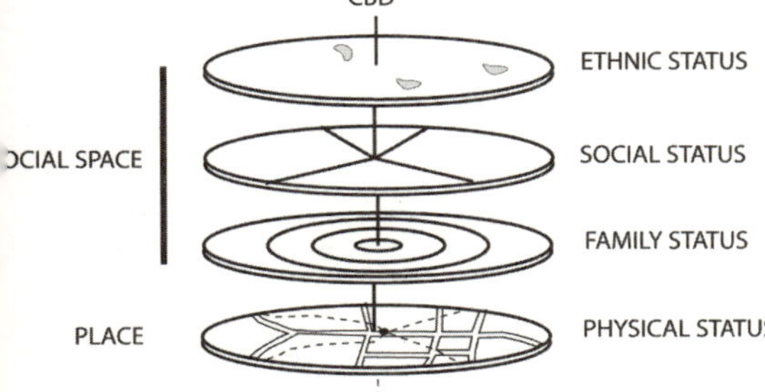

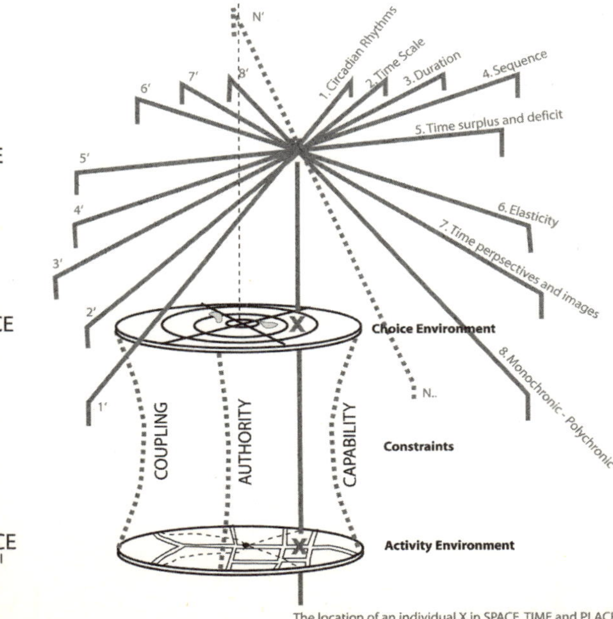

1 In an **urbanism of networks** operators of the Network City function on three levels: (1) operators of technical networks, (2) operators of functional networks, and (3) operators of household networks. Source: Dupuy (1991).

2 Dijst (1995) distinguishes between three different, basic shapes of action space. This definition is dependant on the relation between: the 'home base' position and the place where all the activity occurs, therefore the term; **action space.** A circular action space consists of one 'home base' from which different actions are being undertaken, each time coming back to this base before undertaking a new action. A linear action space consists of two bases (e.g. work and home) between which no other actions are undertaken. A third action space is an elliptical action space that consists of two bases in between which other actions are undertaken outside of the direct trajectory of movement. Source: Boelens, L., Sanders, W., Schwanen, T., Dijst, M., and Verburg, T., (2005).

3 'Social space, physical space and time in the ecology of the city.' Source: Parkes & Thrift (1980) p. 361.

Negotiation and connectivity: a boundary approach to multi-layered landscapes

Isabelle Doucet

Introduction The increasing complexity and fragmentation of contemporary cities can be considered as both the result of the superimposition of economic, social, cultural, geographical, political, etc., layers as well as a consequence of the emerging network society.
The superimposition of layers has resulted in tangible as well as intangible boundaries that today often generate tensions between entities: administrative entities, activities, population groups.... Although those tensions have been generated by historical boundary processes and successive urban strategies, they also derive from contemporary discrepancies between a multitude of urban ambitions – and stakeholders – and the often conflicting urban conditions. Contemporary cities are proof of urban planning's difficulty in dealing with those tensions and taking into account the *entirety* of urban conditions. Therefore the enhancement of complexity and multi-layeredness as a constructive tension seems to be an unavoidable planning issue.
In addition, the emerging network society, itself characterised by spatial fragmentation and decentralisation of economic and urban activities, seems to encourage and intensify the further spatial fragmentation of cities.

A significant gap arises in contemporary planning and architectural theory in developing strategies for dealing with the multi-layered and fragmented character of cities. The emerging network society, in which dynamic networks generate both the centralisation and decentralisation of activities, seems to intensify especially the further *fragmentation* of activities and communities. Nevertheless, an important re-clustering and re-concentration of meeting, power, production, etc. also takes place.[1] Due to new socio-cultural, economic and political bindings, the meanings of connectivity, of boundaries and of place and time have drastically changed. Nevertheless, contemporary studies mainly *detect* rather than *deal with* fragmentation, multiplicity and complexity. Moreover, new methodologies prioritise layers within complexity rather than take into account the multitude of conditions. To fill this gap, and to consequently develop spatial approaches based on connectivity and re-clustering, one should therefore be able to enhance multi-layeredness and boundary tensions in a constructive rather than destructive way, enriching rather than reductive.

The research project that lies at the base of this paper focuses on this multi-layeredness by analysing boundary tensions [2] and by exploring how boundary shapes and conditions will change in a context that is increasingly characterised by connectivity – as is obviously the case in the emerging network society. This paper aims to address the city's complexity and fragmentation in relation to boundaries, multiplicity and connectivity. Therefore I will focus on both traditional and contemporary boundary interpretations and how those do or could contribute to the development of appropriate boundary strategies.[3] Further contemporary methodologies are analysed for their

1 Regarding the potential of re-clustering in the emerging network society: Luuk Boelens (2004). pp. 48-53 and Luuk Boelens (2005).

2 The research report on the Brussels context (I. Doucet 2004 p. 32-60) provides a more detailed analysis of boundary interpretations and mechanisms.

3 Urban strategies often tend to start from a reduced reality as a – necessary? – way to deal with complexity. Boundary strategies can offer an alternative approach in the sense that they start from the **acceptance** rather than **avoidance** of complexity and conflict. Moreover they do not effectiveness in dealing with boundaries. In addition, origins of fragmentation – multi-layered landscapes and the emerging network society – are investigated, partly within the context of the Brussels Capital Region, serving as a major case study for this research project. Particularly the relationship between multi-layeredness and urban development strategies is addressed.

Boundary interpretations

> a space is something that has been made room for, something that is cleared and free, namely within a boundary, Greek Peras. A boundary is not that at which something stops but, as the Greeks recognised, the boundary is that from which something begins its presencing. That is why the concept is that of horismos, that is, the horizon, the boundary.[4]

Boundaries are by definition '*that which serves to indicate the bounds or limits of anything whether material or immaterial; also the limit itself.*'[5] A boundary thus may be physical, social, conceptual and/or symbolic. It may be permeable and negotiable; created, maintained, elaborated and dismantled; it may be separating and unifying, divisive and inclusive.[6]
Notwithstanding this versatile – anthropological – interpretation of a boundary, urban spatial development seems to practice a much more limited definition, generally considering boundaries as lines, fractures, divisions and to a significant extent related to conflict. Such a narrow definition of a boundary is problematic for dealing with multi-layeredness. Furthermore its association with conflict complicates the enhancement of boundary tensions as usable dynamics. By reconsidering basic boundary characteristics, problematic interpretations can be converted into qualities.

Mental – physical Though all boundaries are basically mental they are to a certain extent translated into a physical form. Boundaries are indeed formed by class, race, gender and language, and notwithstanding the power of physical forms, those mental boundaries are strongly experienced during the act of crossing.[7] Boundaries are historically related to the notion of *city* and its division from the rural, traditionally expressed by the city wall. '*The traditional Chinese words for "city" and "wall" are identical; the character ch'eng expresses both of them. The English word 'town' comes from a Teutonic word that means hedge or enclosure*'.[8]

The physicality of boundaries gained historical importance due to its association with *efficiency* whereas non-physicality stands generally for *flexibility*. This is clearly illustrated in the constructive difference between medieval defensive walls – solid, physical, efficient – and the toll boundaries – non-physical, adaptable to urban fabric's growth and shrinkage, flexible. Nevertheless, explosive city expansions took place only after the abolition of the toll boundary, not after the earlier demolition of the city walls. Eighteenth-century Paris' smuggling problem was not solved by materialising the toll boundary, but rather by transforming the toll *gates* into fortress monuments, serving more as a mental deterrent than as a real physical defence. This is illustrated through the engraving of the Barrière du Trône, built by Ledoux in Paris in 1784-87.[9] [see figure 1] Also more recent examples – the mental survival of the Berlin Wall after its fall, the political drawing of boundaries in Israel-Palestine and the rise of electronic gates in airports, residential settings, and shopping areas – are proof of the fact that today, non-physical boundaries are no longer underestimated in terms of power and efficiency.[10]

Division – distinction The common physical consideration of boundaries makes them function as divisions whereas their mental character nevertheless allocates distinctive qualities enabling boundaries to make – 2D or 3D – space readable: '*we make spaces by drawing lines … although a line distinguishes space(s), it has qualities of its own. That is, it is what it is, in its own right*'.[11] Underlying this is the Aristotelian tradition that associates boundaries with the notion of *place*. Since an object's place is defined by its first unmoved neighbouring boundary, and since this first *distinction* of space according to Aristotle can merely take place by an *unmoved* boundary, mobile boundaries cannot give identity to a place: a statement that in contemporary cities no longer holds.[12]

Line – space for negotiation When considering boundaries as distinctions rather than physical divisions, they cease to function as pure lines and obtain spatial qualities. As the scientific reaction towards the Aristotelian 'Either-Or' logic already indicated, boundaries are multi-dimensional spaces consisting of particles that move somewhere between the ones and zeros of bivalent thinking[13]. This *in-between* value of boundaries has been explored by, amongst others Aldo van Eyck, who enhanced boundaries as spatial mediators in the shape of a *threshold* between different scale levels and as a means to achieve a better functioning of space.[14] The functioning of the spatial threshold is illustrated in the film *Rear Window* (Hitchcock, 1954). [See figure 2]

approach space from a centre-versus-margin hierarchy, but consider boundaries as a significant and often crucial part of space.

4 Martin Heidegger in **Building, Dwelling, Thinking** cited by Kenneth Frampton (1992).

5 Pellow (1996).

6 Deborah Pellow (1996) **introduction**.

7 Insights into margins as mental boundaries and thoughts on marginality are explored by bell hooks (1989) pp. 203-209.

8 Kostof (1992) p. 11.

9 Mercier © 1991, A. S. Maclean.

10 The effect of Palestine's territorial division, for example, became more obvious as soon as strategic-political lines were gradually transformed into a concrete wall. Nevertheless an ongoing, less visual war continues on paper, in the battle for the West Bank and Gaza strip (Eyal Weizman, 2003)

11 Ranulph Glanville (2000) pp. 1-2.

12 Interpreted from Van De Ven (1980) p. 17.

13 In sciences, the principle of the Fuzzy Logic explores multivalent values as alternatives for the 'either-or' bivalent values. An analysis and overview is provided by Bart Kosko (1994).

14 To Aldo van Eyck (K. Frampton, 1992), the threshold forms the transition between universal double-phenomena as interior versus exterior and house versus city. Van Eyck seeks to find the relation between the physical form and the socio-psychological needs that are translated in the

The spatiality of boundaries has been articulated at several moments in time and in different cultures. During the fifteenth and sixteenth century, the space between the double city wall was – for military reasons – significantly enlarged into an *intra-muros* space. Centuries later, those spaces, having become redundant, were transformed into bourgeois promenades and leisure fields. Also the Roman *Pomerium* – the vacant zone on both sides of the holy trenches demarcating the city's draft boundaries – formed a boundary space.[15] The Mayans intentionally built non-necessary and non-functionally spatial boundaries or *zero spaces* that kept the inside and outside space ('+' and '–') in balance: '*... in their spatial definition of the interior and exterior spaces (+ and -) and the thick wall that they called 0 (zero) ... the space of the line ... was a space in its own right.*'[16]
Even linear, two-dimensional boundaries – such as the traditional façade – can mediate a world-on-the-other-side. Nevertheless their lack of spatiality makes them function more as a representation than as a real spatial mediator. Even the modernist glass façade does not generate more mediation but, on the contrary, enables a better observation of the world without the need to actually take part in it.[17]

Space for In(ter)vention When considering boundaries as both mental and physical distinctions that behave like spaces rather than lines, a boundary's negotiating qualities allow it to function as an active space where interaction takes place. The boundary becomes a space for in(ter)vention.

The historical city's boundary restrictions – the defensive wall and toll boundary – were often bypassed by the invention of *extra-muros* activities close to the city gates – inns, *fanti portes*, trade settlements[18] – which were often triggers for expansion. Although boundary activities were creative in(ter)ventions in dealing with restrictions, they were also a downright necessity. For marginal groups, creativity is crucial. '*Survival depends on their ability to invent alternatives and to find spaces of resistance and radical openness – to invent margins. Understanding marginality as a state and place of creativity is crucial. Those groups staying in the margin develop a special way of observing reality – by focussing on both centre and margin – which results in the awareness that boundary communities are, despite the clear distinction between centre and margin, a vital part of the whole.*'[19] Boundary creativity's traditional association with marginality derives from a spatial approach that is strongly based on centrality in which the margins of centres are considered as residual space, of minor importance and grounds for conflict. Consequently boundaries seem to comprise neither quality nor identity: a belief that was repeatedly confirmed by all sorts of outsider and abusive activities that felt particularly attracted by the boundary's lack of attention and control. Is it surprising that early squatter communities occupied the residual space that was abandoned by the city centre, was adjacent to and even inside the medieval city walls – as illustrated through the image of the nineteenth-century Paris slums? The fourteenth-century tax penalties on those prohibited dwellings demonstrate the rather averse approach to residual activities. More empathically, residual and out-of-scale activities – such as cattle-markets, leper houses and religious centres – were simply expelled into outcast zones or the so-called 'Urban Fringe Belt'.[20] [See figures 3 and 4]

Boundaries between polarities Problematic and conflicting boundaries are related to a centre-versus-margin approach and to the non-recognition of boundary creativity as a space for in(ter)vention. A dividing and defensive rather than distinctive and negotiating approach to boundaries has led to polarities such as inside/outside, public/private, inclusive/exclusive. The problematic nature of those polarities is highly influenced by socio-cultural shifts in the understanding of the opposing notions.

As such, the contrast between private and public only became problematic in the eighteenth-century bourgeois society, where major shifts took place on the level of social life as well as in dwelling typologies. As soon as the private life was divided into a *social* sphere and a newly introduced *intimate* sphere, the latter was increasingly domesticated, while the former no longer coincided with public space but took place in intermediate spaces as the salons and coffee houses. Both the disappearance of those intermediate spaces in the nineteenth century as well as the flourishing of the intimate sphere took the social sphere out of the public space in favour of private life. Due to this intensified private-public boundary, public space not only became increasingly silent but, moreover, became a space against which private life was supposed to be protected.[21]

Similar transformations took place within dwelling typologies. As soon as eighteenth-century rooms acquired specific functions within the house and were connected by a corridor that replaced the room-through-room connection, the notion *privacy* was introduced. '*Although we take this for granted, rooms had no fixed functions in European houses until the 18th century.*'[22] The cultivation of privacy resulted in the cocooning of the dwelling and the increased role of the façade as an expression of the inhabitants' identity.

relation between the levels house, street, quarter and city. Van Eyck treated the boundary as a spatial threshold and negotiator between different scale levels.

15 Interpreted from Kostof (1992).

16 Ranulph Glanville (2000) p 3.

17 See within this context Richard Sennett (1977) and René Boomkens (1998).

18 Several activities rose adjacent to the city gates. Trade settlements were set up in order to avoid paying toll when passing through the gates. Hence those early wholesalers could shift the tax payment to local traders who were forced to leave the city to buy their goods. Also loose gate communities or **fanti portes** gained identity from their adjacency to the city gates, for whose defence they were responsible. Temporary whereabouts or **inns** also rose at the city gates, as a sort of sleeping place for spending the night after the gates had closed (interpreted from Kostof, 1992).

19 To be in the margin is to be part of the whole but outside the main body. It means entering a world but not living there... always having to go back to the margin (Bell Hooks, 1989. pp. 203-209).

20 Interpreted from Kostof (1992).

21 Interpreted from René Boomkens (1998) and Richard Sennett (1977).

22 P. Aries, 'Centuries of Childhood', in Edward T. Hall (1982).

Today's challenge is to re-allocate active qualities to highly polarised boundaries – such as between public and private life – and to explore overlaps and connections between intimate, social and public domain.[23]

Boundary tensions – conflicts Boundary conflicts are obviously related to marginality, centre-versus-periphery and polarisation. Furthermore, the act of crossing is itself considered a conflict. Territorial boundaries are therefore highly sensitive to political strategies. In the Israel-Palestine conflict on the West Bank '*the region is no longer seen as a two-dimensional surface ... but as a large three-dimensional volume*' subject to '*politics of verticality*'.[24] Territorial war is no longer limited to the division of the land but is expanded to the fight for water, oil, sacred places and other vital elements present in the vertical territory. The Israel-Palestine conflict as described by Eyal Weizman, gives an insight into the simultaneous appropriation by warfare of horizontal and vertical as well as physical and mental landscapes.
Boundaries in the sense of territorial divisions to be defended and sanctioned when violated, will easily lead to conflicts. Outside the context of warfare, however, boundaries are likewise stressed by human and animal tensions towards critical densities. When treating such boundaries as simple territorial *demarcations* of our personal *bubble*[25], they do not necessarily lead to conflict, though relate to tension when avoiding critical density. As soon as conflict is seen as a constructive tension and boundaries are constantly negotiated, they become possible places for dynamics.[26]

Boundaries and urbanity – identity As discussed, boundaries are historically related to the notion of *city* and its division from a rural area. This relation is traditionally described by the city wall and toll boundary, but changed completely after the abolition of city boundaries during the eighteenth century. Moreover nineteenth-century industrialised cities' economical boundaries shifted from a regional to a national level, which influenced the notion of urbanity even more drastically. From then on, cities exploded by annexing or transforming adjacent rural areas into urban agglomeration. The fast growth of those metropolitan areas generated an urban colonisation varnished by rational city planning; an approach that would be further reinforced by, amongst others, CIAM.

The perception of the city boundary as the *demarcation of a place* has today largely disappeared. The explosion of peripheral suburbs or *edge cities*[27] has generated an urbanity that derives from a city that today can be functionally everywhere. Thanks to our ability to cover distances, everything is everywhere and at all times available: an evolution that in the emerging network society has expanded to all sorts of urban and economic activities. As a result, the notion of urbanity is increasingly associated with fragmentation as well as with an unlimited availability of, and connectivity between activities.[28] With a view to dealing with contemporary cities' complexity and fragmentation, a thorough understanding of this altering urbanity and changing shapes and conditions for boundaries are of central and mutual importance.

Boundaries as spaces for negotiation, tension and in(ter)vention

> To intervene on *[sic]* a territory is not merely an act of planning but an act of creation, an attempt to assemble contradictions and transform them into poetic relationships: ultimately one is more attentive to modifying how space is perceived than the way space itself exists.[29]

The exploration of traditional and contemporary boundary interpretations – as set out in the first part of this paper – aimed to re-consider boundaries in order to develop appropriate boundary strategies for multi-layered cases. Instead of physical lines of division, characterised by fracture and conflict, boundaries become a space with allocated qualities: they can negotiate and regulate communication between entities. Moreover boundaries generate tensions leading towards dynamics rather than conflict. The recognition of marginality and non-centrality generates spaces for creation and in(ter)vention. Exactly this re-visioning of boundaries – as spaces for negotiation, tension and in(ter)vention – can be the start towards strategies for dealing with complex, fragmented and multi-layered cases.

How do contemporary methodologies deal with boundaries and multi-layeredness?
Planning instruments are demonstrably inappropriate and out-of-date for dealing with multi-layered landscapes. Even more visionary and strategic planning instruments – as the Brussels Regional Development Plan[30] still start from a highly functional division of the city. And although the intentions of those development plans demonstrate – in comparison to traditional Area Destination Plans[31] – already a step forward to a more diverse and surpassing approach to the city, their execution demonstrates the inability to effectively deal with a multitude of actors and ambitions. Instead they still express a one-sided version of urbanity. Boundaries – where tensions occur – are still used as lines for division, not as spaces of overlap with intrinsic charac-

23 Richard Sennett (1977).

24 The 'politics of verticality' is the **process that split a single territory into a series of territories**: Eyal Weizman (2003) p. 65.

25 According to Edward T. Hall (1982) a territory can be defined as one's individual space: a sort of **bubble** that surrounds us and is crucial to hold one's own in space. This **bubble** regulates both privacy and communication and thus functions as a spatial negotiator.

26 Related to the enhancement of conflict as part of a design strategy, Fucklecorbusier (FLC, 2003. p. 4) considers **the opportunity of conflict as a recurring attitude.**

27 Garreau (1992). Contrary to sociologists who claimed that the middle-class abandoned the concept of the city, they simply built a new kind of city with well-protected open space and identity (C. Steenbergen a.o., 2000. p. 95).

28 Luuk Boelens (2004) pp. 48-53.

29 Stalker (2003) p. 240.

30 The Regional Development Plan is officially called the 'GEWOP' Gewestelijk Ontwikkelings Plan, 2001.

31 The Area Destination Plan is officially called the 'GBP' Gewestelijk Bestemmingsplan, 1998.

teristics and qualities. Strategies are developed for functional zones that are fragmented over the city, not for the way those fragments are interconnected. On the contrary, theoretical studies demonstrate an increasing interest in boundaries. Particularly the qualities of the margins, voids and residual spaces of the urban fabric gain a renewed attention. The opportunity to enhance marginal space as qualified public space where spontaneous interventions can lead to more interpretative forms of identity, has been explored by several studies, amongst others *Spaces of Uncertainty* and *Urban Catalyst*.[32] The Italian collective Stalker engages in research and action within the (boundary) landscape. In Stalker's *'Actual Territories'* – the negative of the built city – the physical experience is more important than pure representation while border crossing is a creative act. This *archive of experiences* allows an *input* into *the actual territories in cognitive maps and hence deal with the territory including its margins, in a more comprehensive and perceptive way*.[33] The Multiplicity team around Stefano Boeri investigates phenomena of territorial transformation that are not immediately readable in the landscape and seeks for the mechanisms that lay behind those phenomena. *'An investigative project on borders should not search for the effects of processes and policies already observed and codified in the territory; rather, it should inquire into the physical and spatial signs of social and cultural changes in progress.'*[34] The almost literal translation of spatial interpretations into methodologies for reading landscapes, detecting boundaries and discovering the hidden mechanisms behind territorial mutations – as in *Border Devices* and *Uncertain States of Europe* – leads to classification systems directly applicable for design.

The first series of studies contribute mainly to the discourse on boundaries, either theoretically – as Spaces of Uncertainty and Urban Catalyst – or by actual interventions – such as Stalker. Despite the interesting contribution of those first examples to the detection and registration of boundaries and territorial complexities, they do not always offer ways for concretely dealing with urban space. They interestingly detect rather than employ the potential of the margin. On the contrary, studies like those from Multiplicity/S. Boeri seem to aim at classifying territorial complexity in a rather narrow and reductive way. When analysing fragmentation and transformation mechanisms, the question arises if complexity can be reduced to a methodology and classification system. The projects discussed briefly here are but a fraction of contemporary boundary research. Nevertheless they are illustrative of the difficulties of effectively dealing with boundaries and developing boundary strategies without slipping into reductive planning instruments and strategies.
The research project that lies at the base of this paper therefore focuses on the investigation of boundary dynamics with a view to developing working methods and strategic scenarios for defining conditions and developing shapes for boundaries. Consequently it is more crucial to develop guidelines than strict methodologies.

Complexity and fragmentation In the first part of this paper, boundary definitions have been re-interpreted as spaces for negotiation, tension and in(ter)vention. With a view to further developing *strategies* for dealing with multi-layeredness and fragmentation, the origins of both the superimposition of layers as well as the emerging network society are set out below.

The superimposition of layers has resulted in both tangible and intangible boundaries generating tensions between entities. Those tensions derived from historical boundary processes, from the contemporary discrepancy between a multitude of urban ambitions and often conflicting conditions[35] as well as the social and spatial consequences of a drastically changed society.

In the Brussels Capital Region – the major case study for this research project – **successive urban strategies** were historically based on either zoning or mixture. This resulted in a functional planning that – in the case of *zoning* – derived from ambitions superimposed on the existing context, often by demolition, and that – in the case of *mixture* – derived from an ideal, conservative image of the existing situation. Urban politics' alternating conservation and demolition strategies resulted in Brussels' multi-layered fabric requiring today a comprehensive rather than functional approach. Through Brussels' history, boundaries have been considered as lines of division, mainly associated with fractures and conflicts. Before the Enlightenment and the modernisation of society, boundaries came into existence and transformed rather organically. After Enlightenment and especially during the Industrial Revolution of the nineteenth century, boundaries increasingly became subject to planning and politics. Positioned as problems-to- solve, boundaries unwillingly whitewashed demolition strategies, as the large-scale re-furnishing of Brussels by the King-Urbanist Leopold II. This *conflict strategy,*[36] based on demolition and rational zoning, was reintroduced by the CIAM planning conferences and intensively applied during the 1960s. A pragmatic technical-rational approach to the city was believed to achieve a better functioning of that city.[37] Nevertheless, boundaries were also enhanced for achieving more mixture and liveability. At the turn of the twentieth century, the Garden Cities as well as Charles Buls' *organic-conservatism*[38] were attempts towards a planning that was based on conservation rather than renewal. Obviously those reactions to the conflict strategy's denial of the organic city could not restrain planning's ambition to create organised cities by means of functional zoning and rationality. Although the planning of the 1970s strongly contested the destructive consequences of rational planning, its conservative approach to the city was quickly absorbed by the pragmatic-technical urbanism at the end of the 1980s.

32 Kenny Cupers and Markus Miessen (2002), and Urban Catalyst (2003).

33 Stalker (2003) pp. 238-240.

34 Stefano Boeri (2003) p. 53. For additional information on Multiplicity's territorial analysis, see Rem Koolhaas and Stefano Boeri (2003); www.multiplicity.it; and Multiplicity (2003).

35 Within the context of the Brussels Capital Region, see Isabelle Doucet (2004) pp. 32-54.

36 The conflict model in comparison with a reconciliation and potential model: Isabelle Doucet (2004) pp. 58-64.

37 As illustrated in the 1968 Voorontwerp Gewestplan Alpha.

38 Charles Buls, Major of Brussels from 1881 to 1899 and reacting to the demolition politics of his predecessor Anspach, who worked closely with King Leopold II.

39 Tracy Metz (2002) p. 105.

Due to the economic crisis as well as a changing society in which more ambitions started to meet in increasingly conflicting contexts, the planning of the last two decades has found itself confronted with ambitions deriving from a multitude of stakeholders such as dwellers, consumers, politicians and economic growth partners. As a result, alternating zoning and mixture strategies became far from appropriate in realising those ambitions within existing contexts. And even though certain stakeholders such as visitors and residents have become interchangeable in our *consumption of the city as a pleasure dome* – since they feel attracted by the same things – there remains *'the essential difference that ... at the end of the day or of the city trip, the city leaves while the resident is left – probably with the peels and empty boxes as well.'* [39]

Apart from historical urban strategies and a multitude of ambitions, contemporary cities have been during recent decades increasingly confronted with the social and spatial consequences of a drastically changed society. Those shifts in society had far-reaching consequences for architectural and urban practices. *'Modern architecture, according to Charles Jencks, died in St. Louis Missouri on July 15 1972 at 3.32 pm (or thereabouts). That was when Yamasaki's Pruitt-Igoe was blown up, some 20 years after its construction, on the grounds that the extraordinary amount of vandalism proved its total unsuitability...'*.[40] According to the post-modernists, modernism had failed in its ambition to optimise the living circumstances of inhabitants without blocking economical development. The rationalisation, individualisation and differentiation processes that characterised modernisation did not provide the promised better life. On the contrary, they suggested a controlling organism that neglected the individual needs of inhabitants and allowed little identification or expression of popular taste. The shift from modern to post-modern society hence implicated for architecture the rise of popular aesthetics for mass culture and for planning the belief that urban development was more linked to the free market and private initiatives than to collective goals. Planning's emphasis on economies paid central attention to the consumer, conflating needs for dwelling with city marketing. Not only did the shift from a supply economy towards a demand and mass-consumption economy generate a whole range of new urban questions and identities – as expressed by suburban dwelling, shopping malls and leisure centres – the shift from an economy of scale towards an economy of scope with adaptability as its main characteristic, expects urban structures to be increasingly flexible: *urban structures are required to be flexible to absorb a continuous spatial reformulation without loosing specificity and centrality.*[41] The fall of the welfare state had far-reaching spatial and social consequences, which became increasingly readable in the social dualisation and segregation of contemporary cities in homogenised groups, which resulted in gentrification and in the sometimes physical separation of some of those groups. In the Brussels Capital Region this polarisation is literally readable in the socioeconomic boundary between the more peripheral south-east and the more central north-west areas.

The awareness that the rationalisation process has had a destructive effect on man, society and the natural environment, and that a more flexible economy did not necessarily bring more freedom or authenticity to all levels of society, does not implicate the denial of the modern heritage. Rather than dropping rationality – as Lyotard's '*to free ourselves from the compulsive, rational, modern thinking, we must work outside sciences and its institutionalised applications*'[42] – rationality could be completed. Jürgen Habermas considers rationality as to be re-considered as a tool for analysis and control, but in the first place as an element of justification that focuses on the happiness and righteousness of mankind.[43] Those shifts in rationality imply that the traditional planning based on control, makeability and rationality, should, rather than being replaced, be completed with an alternative planning that also takes into account the spontaneous, intangible aspects of urban society and landscapes. Policy makers are increasingly aware of the consequences of a reductive planning based on zoning and its inappropriateness for dealing with multiplicity. The strategy for mixture on the other hand is irrelevant when enhanced in a purely functional way. Planning strategies that focus on urban fragments not only fail to deal with the multi-layered character of contemporary cities, they also leave significant gaps between the institutionalised planning entities. The need for a planning approach that deals with those gaps and takes into account the multitude of layers has therefore become unavoidable. A planning approach that '*leads to a new relational management and to the use of urban spaces in dynamic clusters of changing activities, starts from the study of boundaryless flows and approaches the city as a Civitas: as a socio-cultural and economic-political practice of a multiplicity of actors*'[44]. Following contributions towards the analysis of fragmentation and decentralisation – as Splintering Urbanism (Graham and Marvin 2001), Cybercities (Boyer 1996) and City of Bits (Mitchell 1996) – it is crucial to investigate the possibility of re-clustering urban fragments as a way towards new bindings and identities.[45]

More particularly within the emerging network society, and according to Manuel Castells' *Space of Flows*, the key features of the city are instability and flow.[46] Hence a rational approach in terms of control is no longer relevant when *the techno-economic development behind this network process gets more and more dissociated from the corresponding mechanisms of the social control of such a development* (Castells, 1989).[47] In a society that is built upon individual flows and nodes of a net-

40 Broadbent (1977).
41 Zaera-Polo quoted by Arie Graafland (2001).
42 Van Reijden (1987).
43 Interpreted from Van Reijden (1987).
44 Luuk Boelens (2005, pp. 12-13) speaks in this context about 'Fluviology' where reclustering can take place around new patterns of interaction.
45 The reclustering of activities can be seen as a mechanism that opposes – and possibly compensates, counters… – the further spatial fragmentation of space. Also see Luuk Boelens (2004) pp. 48-53.
46 Manuel Castells (1989).
47 in C. Steenbergen et al. (2000) pp. 94-95.

work, where flows gather and disperse, the fragments and margins as consequences of the rationalised society, not only become more frequent but also more crucial for analysing their collective and structuring qualities. Traditional planning's functional fragmentation of the city into dwelling, work, mobility and services is indeed no longer relevant in a society where both local and global network connections lead to new types of *communities.* Those communities are linked in a totally different way as in their relation dwelling-working, dwelling-recreation and work-recreation.[48] The re-clustering of traditional fragments, steered by new types of local, regional and supra-regional network connections, will not only generate new community types, but also new shapes and conditions for the *boundaries* of communities and entities. When communities and their activities constitute on some levels homogeneous entities and on other levels heterogeneous wholes, then this has implications for the way those entities are bordered and the way those borders are shaped. As a consequence, urban planning's focus on activities and competence areas should shift to the *connections* between those activities and to the possible new formations that occur.

In the emerging network society – where the space of *flows* exists parallel to the space of *places* – particularly the '*Genius Loci*' seems to have become increasingly relevant within architecture, urbanism and planning.[49] However, the Space of *Flows* – with its own reality, laws and potential – also requires a proper spatiality. The changing conceptualisation of space and time indeed not only implicates the continuing compression of both, but, moreover *'arises a picture of a layered urbanism, in which some parts are close to one another and others are not, and where personified temporalities of distinct lifestyles emerge, along with introverted activities in continual contact with the rest of the world'.* [50] According to Luuk Boelens, '*this multiplicity of times and of all kinds of spatial realities requires an urbanism as a system of separate activities in open, meaningful global and local connectivity*'. One should question the new meaning or relevance of – both architectural and planning – boundaries in a context that is not only characterised by *spatial* fragmentation but also increasingly by *virtual* connectivity. Moreover, particular attention should be paid to society's socio-cultural changes. With the rise of the network society, *bindings such as family and local neighbourhood are being lost while*

48 Interpreted from Luuk Boelens (2004) p. 50.
49 According to Luuk Boelens (2003) the term 'genius loci' has been reintroduced by C. Norberg-Schultz (1979) in **Genius Loci; Paesaggio ambiente architettura**, Electa: Milan, but leads back to the antique Romans, the phenomenology of E. Husserl and the existentialism of M. Heidegger. More details were found in the digital version of the article at www.urbanunlimited.nl.
50 Luuk Boelens (2005) p. 6.
51 Luuk Boelens (2005) p. 8.
52 Luuk Boelens (2005) p. 9.

other personal networks are occurring amongst friends, soul mates and colleagues[51]. Those new socio-cultural networks are not only becoming increasingly complex when simultaneously deriving from dwelling, work and leisure. They also appear today as *a multiplicity of lifestyles overlapping with each other or even joining simultaneously or successively within one individual.*[52] The re-interpretation of spatial settings and typologies as nodes on the network rather than unique geographical places does not only require radically new spatial settings, but has consequences for the boundary conditions of those settings.

Conclusion With a view to developing guidelines for dealing with the increasing urban fragmentation and complexity, this paper started with the re-interpretation of traditional boundary definitions as *spaces for negotiation, tension and in(ter)vention.* With a view to further developing *strategies* for multi-layeredness and strategic scenarios for defining conditions and developing shapes for boundaries, origins of fragmentation and complexity have been set out: a superimposition of layers as well as the consequences of the emerging network society.

The emerging network society, apart from being itself characterised by spatial fragmentation, also demonstrates a potential for virtually and mentally *re-clustering* fragments and activities. This re-clustering can reinforce the enhancement of boundaries as dynamic spaces for negotiation and communication. By using the intrinsic strengths of today's complex landscapes – virtually re-clustering and negotiating boundaries – complexity and fragmentation will no longer be considered a *problem* to be *solved.* On the contrary, they will be positively enhanced in order to discover new bindings, whether or not physical. Hence the development of boundary conditions within a context that is increasingly characterised by connectivity, might lead towards urban strategies that both theoretically and practically start from the *qualities* rather than merely the *problems* of contemporary cities.

Bibliography

Boelens, L. 'La Città Muovere: Towards a Phenomenology of the Space of Flows,' in: **Urban Development in Rotterdam**, P. Meus, M. Verheijn (eds). Rotterdam: NAi Publishers, 2003.

Boelens, L. 'Sturen door netwerken: voor reclustering van ruimtelijk beleid.' S&RO 2 (2004): pp. 48-53.

Boelens, L. **Inaugural Lecture** 13 January 2005. Available from: http://www.urbanunlimited.nl/uu/urbanltd.nsf/12/cv%20luuk%20boelens [Accessed 30 May 2005]

Boeri, S. 'Multiplicity, 2003 Border-Syndrome: Notes for a Research Program,' in: **Territories: Islands, Camps and Other States of Utopia**, edited by A. Franke, R. Segal, E. Weizman. Berlin: KW, 2003. p. 53.

Boomkens, R. **Een drempelwereld: moderne ervaring en stedelijke openbaarheid**. Rotterdam: NAi, 1998. pp. 272-300.

Broadbent, G. 'The Language of Post-Modern Architecture: A Summary.' **Architectural Design**, Volume 47 No 4, 1977. p. 261.

Castells, M. **The Informational City, information technology, economic restructuring and the urban regional process**. London: Blackwell Publishers, 1989.

Cupers, K.,Miessen, M. **Spaces of Uncertainty**. Wuppertal: Müller + Busmann Publishers, 2002.

Doucet, I. **Renewed conditions and shapes for boundaries in multi-layered contexts** (Research Report) IWOIB, Prospective Research for Brussels, 2004. pp. 32-64.

Frampton, K. **Modern architecture: a critical history (3rd edition)**. London: Thames & Hudson, 1992. pp. 280-340.

FLC. **Future Conflicts**. **Young Architects in Flanders series**. Antwerp: VAI, 2003. p. 4.

Garreau, J. **Edge Cities: Life on the New Frontier**. New York: Anchor, 1992.

Glanville, R. **Living in Lines.** source: http://homepage.mac.com/ranulph/FileSharing1.html. p 1-3; and published in Glanville, R. 'Living in Lines,' in: **Interior Cities**, edited by R.M.C. Leod. Melbourne: RMIT Press, 2000.

Graafland, A., ed. **Cities in Transition**. Rotterdam: 010 Publishers, 2001. Introduction.

Hall, E.T. **The Hidden Dimension**. New York: Double Day Garden City, 1982.

hooks, b. 'Choosing the margin as a space of radical openness.' In: **Gender, Space, Architecture: An Interdisciplinary Introduction**, edited by J. Rendell, B., Penner, I. Borden. London/New York: Routledge, 2000. pp. 203-209.

Koolhaas, R., Boeri, S. **Mutations**. Spain: Actar, 2003.

Kosko, B. **Fuzzy Thinking**: **The New Science of Fuzzy Logic**. London/New York: Flamingo, 1994.

Kostof, S., 1992. **The City Assembled: The Elements of Urban Form Through History**. London: Thames & Hudson Ltd, 1992. p. 11.

Metz, T. **FUN! Leisure and landscape**. Rotterdam: NAi Publishers, 2002. p. 105.

Multiplicity. **USE, Uncertain States of Europe, a Trip through a changing Europe**. Milan: Skira Editore. 2003.

Pellow, D., ed. **Setting Boundaries: The Anthropology of Spatial and Social Organisation**. Westport, Connecticut: Bergin & Garvey, 1996.

Sennett, R. **The Fall of Public Man**. New York: Alfred A. Knopf, 1977.

Stalker. 'Through the Actual Territories,' in: **Territories: Islands, Camps and Other States of Utopia**, edited by A. Franke, R. Segal, E. Weizman. Berlin: KW, 2003. pp. 238-240.

Steenbergen, C., ed, et al. **Architectural Design and Research: Composition, Education, Analysis**. Bussum, the Netherlands: THOTH Publishers, 2000. pp. 94-95.

Urban Catalyst, 2001-2003 EU project (www.urbancatalyst.de). [Accessed 30 January 2006].

Van de Ven, C. **Space in Architecture**. Assen: Van Gorcum, 1980. p. 17.

Van Reijden, W. **De onvoltooide rede: modern en post-modern**. Kampen: Kok Agora, 1987.

Weizman, E. 'The Politics of Verticality: The West Bank as an Architectural Construction,' in: **Territories: Islands, Camps and Other States of Utopia,** edited by A. Franke, R. Segal, E. Weizman. Berlin: KW, 2003. pp. 65-118.

[4]

1 Mercier, after Courvoisier. **Barrière du Trône, Paris, by Ledoux, 1784-87**. Engraving. © 1991, Alex S. MacLean. Source: Kostof, S., 1992. **The City Assembled: The Elements of Urban Form through History**. London: Thames & Hudson Ltd. p. 15.
2 James Stewart, Grace Kelly and Alfred Hitchcock on the set of Rear Window, 1954. In: Source: www.cinestills.com – Stills Collection: Rear Window – director: Hitchcock, A. Paramount Pictures.
3 Marville, C. 1856-1865, **A shanty-town on the eastern edge of Paris, near the present Rue Champlain, just outside the Boulevard de Belleville.** Source: Photograph. In: Kostof, S., 1992. **The City Assembled: The Elements of Urban Form through History**. London: Thames & Hudson Ltd. p. 53.
4 Konrad, A. 2000. Shanghai. Source: Konrad, A., 2000. **Elasticity**. Rotterdam: NAi Publishers.

Leisure coast city. Waterfront leisure areas as an instrument of social transformation at the turn of the 20th century

Agustina Martire

Introduction At this moment of inflection in the planning and development of urban leisure waterfronts, it becomes essential to have an insight as to what these developments can offer to the user. It is relevant to ask the purpose of these areas, the way they relate to the rest of the city and how they affect urban behaviour. The historical, recent and ongoing re-functionalising of harbour areas into leisure spaces gives meaning to the choice of focusing the study on urban waterfronts.

Urban waterfronts have developed into attractors and have been an active part of urban life since our overcoming of the fear of water. The process of the reshaping of waterfronts in the last 150 years is a complex one. The combination of technical, political, social and economical transformations provoked significant changes in the spatial configuration of the city in general and of their waterfronts in particular.
The processes that have affected the transformation of urban waterfronts have had a similar logic to the general growth of cities. However, certain urban issues have been particularly present in the waterfronts. This problem has been addressed consistently in the last decade, but some knowledge gaps have been found. The main phenomena observed by architects and urbanists[1] has been either the conflict between the development of technical facilities and the need for open space, or the search for a typology within this problem. An issue that has not been properly analysed is the evolution of the theories and practices of leisure behind these spatial transformations. This is the reason why this paper intends to explore the impact of leisure concepts acting as a key element in the transformation of the urban waterfront.

Urban projects for waterfronts have responded to certain leisure concepts, related to their location and to the international network of professionals dedicated to urban design and planning. From the picturesque approach of isolated nature, to the beaux-arts movement of organic relation between the built and the natural, through the modern rational use of landscape, to the commercialisation of the leisure coast in recent decades of the 20th century, waterfronts have been key elements in urban design.

This paper is based on the research project 'Leisure Coast City. A comparative history of the urban leisure waterfront'. This project is analysing the discourse of the professionals and authorities in charge of these urban transformations, relating them to leisure concepts and practices at the turn of the 20th century. On the other hand there is an analysis of the perceptual systems that received these projects, studied through the corresponding literature and periodicals. In

1 Among others Meyer, H; **City and port: urban planning as a cultural venture in London, Barcelona, New York, and Rotterdam: changing relations between public urban space and large-scale infrastructure,** (Utrecht: International Books, 1999);
Fava, N; **Progetti e processi in conflitto: il fronte maritimo de Barcelona,** PhD thesis, (Barcelona: UPC, 2004);
Breen, A. and Rigby, D; **Waterfronts; Cities Reclaim Their Edge** (New York: McGraw-Hill, 1994);
Bruttomesso, R; **Waterfronts: a new frontier for cities on water** (Venice: International Centre Cities on Water, 1993).

order to study the evolution of concepts of leisure and water in the city throughout the last century, three particular case studies are being used: Buenos Aires, Chicago and Barcelona. However, this particular paper will refer to a more specific section of the study. It will only begin to explore the discourse of the professionals intervening in urban waterfronts at the turn of the 20th century in Buenos Aires. The paper will be divided into three sections. The first one will give an insight into the development of the appeal of the waterfront and the urban situations related to it. The second section will briefly describe the *rational recreation* and the *park movements* of the 19th century and their will of social transformation through leisure. Finally, the third section will explore the influence of these movements in the design of waterfront parks in Buenos Aires.

The appeal of the waterfront In order to introduce this paper and address the above mentioned discursive element to be analysed it seems necessary to introduce the previous ideas referring to water and the birth of its appeal. The study of Alain Corbin[2] can serve here for the wider understanding of the processes that lead to the appeal of the waterfront. His analysis of variables that may have provoked this phenomenon, such as the emotional relation of the user to the water, from fear and respect to lure and attraction, is valuable for the present study.

The purpose of this first section is to present some of the ideas about the waterfront that will later be crucial to the discourse of the architects on the case studies. The use of the waterfront as leisure space was gradual, and the categories of leisure practice diverge from case to case. It is intended here to give a partial observation of this phenomenon, which will be influential on the case later analysed.

Precedents and change in perception The approach to the seaside as a leisure source is a relatively modern social practice. In both the Classical and the Judeo-Christian cultures, oceans and rivers had always been looked at as dangerous and menacing, home of creatures and monsters. In all kinds of myths water was depicted as a vibrating extension of chaos, which symbolised the disorder that preceded civilisation.

The waterfronts were mainly a source of nourishment, transportation and commerce, and were reserved for the fishermen and sailors, whose towns were built regularly with their 'backs against the water'. *'Polis',* or cities, such as Athens or Carthage were separated from the port by walls or other barriers, not providing the average citizen with a distinct relationship between city and coast. The myth of the seas can be found in authors such as Dante, St. Augustine or Shakespeare. There it is possible to perceive this fear and respect for troubled waters.

Until the 18th century, river or sea bathing was considered an immoral pastime

better left to the 'ill-mannered' lower classes. These ideas began to change, and the causes of this change are described by Corbin as being the result of three phenomena: the idyllic vision of the prophets of natural theology; an exaltation of the fruitful shores of Holland, a land blessed by God; and the fashion for the classical voyage along the luminous shores of the bay of Naples.
In this context, the beginning of change in the appreciation of the sea is the birth of natural theology in France and England, which starts to analyse man in a different way. From considering the relation between man and the universe in terms of analogies it switches to considering the external world as a spectacle. Another issue that made the sea become a source of appeal was the spreading of the idea that it was a source of health provision. It became increasingly popular to believe that salt water was beneficial to health, and drinking it even an effective method for losing weight. By the mid-18th century another health issue came to be related with the seashore, that of the relief of melancholy. Patients would go to the seashore, accompanied by their doctors, convinced that the sea air would soothe the patient's psyche.
According to Bollerey, the main causes for the birth of the appeal to the waterfront were the ideas of Enlightenment and Romanticism[3]. With the Enlightenment the scientific approach to nature brought the recognition of the seaside as a source of health. The Romantic view provided an idealistic image of the coast that increased its appeal. These causes brought with them the moving of urban social practises to the shores.
I have to add that even though all these causes are plausible, the story that follows changes then substantially, the appropriation of the waterfront takes the role of a civilising tool and leisure practices and theories are very influential in the shaping of the turn of the 20th century's urban coasts.

Travel and the sea resort A popular centre for the appreciation of the sea was the Mediterranean coast, which was in the 17th and 18th century a great attraction. Among English and French elites it was increasingly fashionable to go to the coast of Italy, to be in contact with what was becoming an ideal, the classical Greco-Roman culture. The *Grand Tour* practised by the English elite was at first a strong influence in the approach to the waterfront as spectator, but later it turned into a tool for the development of sea resorts on the Continent. In this period of industrial development and the intense crowding of the urban centres, the seaside holiday became an escape from the crowded and polluted cities.
The first bath resorts began to appear in the first quarter of the 19th century; those of Dieppe and Boulogne intended to order their entire social life by the organisation of space. The spatial layout and buildings would reflect the rules that were implicit in society, such as the division of space by gender, class and age. Sea resorts in North America were also becoming popular, such as Rockaway Point and Coney Island near New York.

2 Corbin, A.; **The Lure of the Sea: The Discovery of the Seaside in the Western World 1750–1840** (London: Penguin Books, 1988).
3 Bollerey, F.; 'The Urbanization of the Shore. From Fishing Village to Seaside Resort,' in **Daidalos 20, On the Waterfront: Town and Harbour,** 15 June 1986.

When they began to be used as sea resorts, places like Brighton, Blackpool and Scarborough were first reserved for the elite. With the development of railroads and mass transportation these resorts became accessible to the less affluent classes, which allowed the railroad companies to build hotels and transform the whole resort facility into a fully urbanised area.

The harbour In the city of the 18th century the difference between social classes in the use of the waterfront areas was not very evident. The port area was an extension of the working class street. However, the upper-class visitor would also be an active member of everyday harbour life. The merchant would control his business from there. 'The harbour was a public space in which the theatricality of social positions was played out.'[4]

The harbour in the second half of the 18th century was a nest of diversity, of international relations and active exchange. This was a place for tourists as well as for locals, the morning or evening visit to the harbour became part of the classical sea-side holiday, even a part of the education of aristocratic youth. Thus, the harbour became an important meeting and mingling place for all social levels and gave rise to the creation of new institutions for leisure time activities and culture.

But this didn't last long. During the wars of the Revolution and the Empire the ports closed and some of them were even abandoned. After these wars a short period of enjoyment of the spectacle of the city harbour took place, but it was soon replaced by the idea that the harbour had nothing to do with the lure of the sea. According to Corbin, there was a return to the appreciation of the coast as a part of nature, not of the urban. Meanwhile what turned out to be the attractions of the city were now monuments and the classical picture of the city, which had little to do with the industrial port.

This was the case by mid-19th century. However, it is at the turn of the 20th century that the urban waterfront stops being considered as a harbour facility in communion with the city, and instead it becomes a leisure space in need of intervention for the civilisation of the masses.

Rational Recreation and the Park Movement

Rational Recreation In the second half of the 19th century a new wave of reformers took charge of the issue of leisure and how to use it. These new ideas depicted leisure as being the best area in which to inculcate self-control, familiarism and respectability. These ideas were practised by the middle and working classes in an environment of competition, urban life and bureaucracy. Both the working- and middle-class reformers embraced an ethic of self-control, individualism and respectability.

As Cunningham[5] described it, *Rational Recreation* was a movement to restrain and control leisure, stressing the improvement of the individual, although

some reformers sought not to suppress or moralise popular leisure but to transform it.
This movement was not only represented in the new norms and behaviour but also in works of literature such as Defoe's *Robinson Crusoe*. In this book the taming of the sea as well as the new rational recreation ideas are shown. The island provided a potential for happiness, as long as the protagonist did not 'spare his sweat, organised his time and ordered his labour.'[6] This is a reflection of the puritan and the *rational recreation* movement in England, which sheds light on their concept of the relation between work and leisure.

Rational recreation also had a deep influence on the urban built environment as well as on park design. New urban services such as libraries and museums became a leitmotif as the cities grew. But mainly parks were crucial in the new concept of leisure and the capacity of the natural environment to civilise urban behaviour. This movement was not exclusive to the Anglo-American environment, it also spread to different parts of Europe, even having a mirrored movement in the catholic communities of southern Europe and South America.
Eventually, the result of reform brought a sort of leisure that would more deeply reflect the social class differences and a more privatised, sedate and universal leisure would arise.

Olmsted and the Park Movement

In the 1850s it was Frederick Law Olmsted, within the *Park Movement*, who focuses on parks as a main fragment of urban development. He produced parks intended to inspire the urban man to 'new standards of courtesy, self control and temperance.'[7] We can see here the will to be able to experience nature, even within the city. Apparently, one of the main influences on Olmsted was the work of Henry Thoreau, who considered idleness a means of feeding and developing the spirit, and nature the ideal environment for this.
Olmsted believed that it was the purpose of his art to affect the emotions. This was evident in his park design, where he created passages of scenery in which the visitor would become immersed, experiencing the restorative action of the landscape by what he termed an 'unconscious' process. To achieve this result, he subordinated all elements of the design to the single purpose of making the landscape experience itself, a profound experience. Olmsted always sought to look beyond current taste and fashion and to base his designs on fundamental principles of human psychology. In particular, he drew from the analysis of earlier British theorists of naturalistic landscape and their emphasis on the special qualities of 'pastoral' and 'picturesque' scenery.
Olmsted is considered a precursor of the picturesque. The definition of it given by Corbin seems suitable for this case: 'The picturesque journey is an endless pursuit of spectacle and the pleasure

4 Corbin, A.; **The Lure of the Sea: The Discovery of the Seaside in the Western World 1750–1840** (London: Penguin Books, 1988) p. 191.
5 Cunningham, H.; **Leisure in the Industrial Revolution** (New York: Palgrave Macmillan, 1980) p. 78.
6 Defoe, D.; 1719. **Robinson Crusoe** (Penguin Books, 2003).
7 Olmsted, F. L. jr., Kimball, T. (eds); **Frederick Law Olmsted, Landscape Architect, 1822–1903** (New York: Benjamin Blom, 1970) volume 2.

it provides'[8] and according to Corbin it allowed the focus on a complex network of sensations, memories and knowledge.
Even though Olmsted's descriptions and recommendations about landscape design were mainly directed to the emotional development of individuals there is a very strong implicit drive towards the civilisation of the masses and the capacity of urban and landscape design to achieve these objectives. Overall, one of the main aims of his landscape architecture was to civilise the city, and to provide an environment in which the spiritual progress of man could take place. '... one of the more important elements of value in a park, never to be lost sight of in a study of its economies, lies in its power to divert men from unwholesome, vicious, and destructive methods and habits of seeking recreation, and inducing them to educate themselves ...'[9]

In *Justifying the Value of the Public Park* Olmsted qualifies the park movement as evolving by public demand and that this movement would save man from corruption, artificiality, materialism, and vices of commerce and cities. He describes it as 'a common, spontaneous movement of that sort which we conveniently refer to as the Genius of Civilisation.'[10]
In his texts about the design and development of first South Park (1871) and then Jackson Park (1893) for the World Columbian Exposition in Chicago it is possible to see the picturesque quality given to the water and its boundaries.
'There is but one object of *scenery* near Chicago of special grandeur or sublimity, and that, the lake, can be made by artificial means no more grand or sublime. By no practical elevation of artificial hills, that is to say, would the impression of the observer in overlooking it be made greatly more profound'.[11] 'The lake, as an element of the scenery, must be considered to be not merely the water of the lake but the margins.'[12]
One of the ideas that ruled most of Olmsted's landscape design was that 'simplicity and reserve will be practised and petty effects and frippery avoided.'[13] This contrasts with what he had observed in the gardens of Paris, which he found gaudy and childish and not pleasant for the eye or foot.
Still thinking of the waterfront and its influence on the landscape design of the turn of the century it is necessary to mention Burnham and his Plan for Chicago, to understand the profound and long lasting influence of the *Park Movement*.

> The lake has been singing to us many years, until we have been responsive. We see the broad water, ruffled by the gentle breeze; upon its breast the glint of oars, the gleam of rosy sails, the outlines of swift gliding launches. We see racing shells go by, urged onward by bronzed athletes. We hear the rippling of the waves, commingled with youthful laughter, and music swelling over the Lagoon dies away under the low branches of the trees...[14]

It is interesting to point out the remark that Cross makes about the *Park Movement*: 'Park commissioners also believed it their duty to reform leisure time as well as space.'[15]
This caused the first cultural centres to become the hallmark of rational recreational movement. The reciprocal influence between spatial design of parks and leisure concepts and activities is shown in the following quote: 'these trends contributed to cultural uniformity and reduced the disorder associated with both rural popular leisure and the degrading pleasures of the new industrial cities.'[16]

Buenos Aires waterfront 1870-1925 The turn of the 20th century was a prolific period for landscape design, especially in the urban context and more so in the waterfronts. The coast of cities in an international network of commerce and transportation were subject to technical transformations regarding the building and moving of harbour areas. But this was not the only reason for these transformations. Waterfront areas were being used as a platform for new leisure practices. Parks and gardens, promenades and avenues, baths and beaches were being incorporated in the city plans. These projects were developed by architects who had different positions towards the physical qualities of these spaces. However, they had one aim in common: the ambition of providing a 'better' environment for city dwellers, therefore restructuring the space for changes in behaviour.
In this section, the discourse of the protagonists of one case study will be addressed, that of Buenos Aires at the turn of the 20th century. The city underwent modifications to its waterfront, which were deeply related to the *rational recreation* and the *park movements*. This was the case of the projects of Sarmiento. The discourse of social transformation was embedded in the projects for the waterfronts. Later on, as the city grew and social interest for the civilisation of the people wore off, the discourse was more concentrated in the provision of leisure spaces, mainly for the rich, but still giving attention to the common city dweller. This is the case of Carrasco and Forestier.
As projects evolved, with the influence of foreign ideas, waterfront and leisure became one system of development that had seen few precedents in the past.

8 Corbin, A.; **The Lure of the Sea: The Discovery of the Seaside in the Western World 1750–1840** (London: Penguin Books, 1988) p. 143.
9 Frederick Law Olmsted's 1883 vision for Belle Isle.
10 Olmsted, F.L.; 'The Justifying Value of a Public Park,' in: **Journal of Social Science**, No.12, pt.1, 1880 (Boston, A.Williams & Co. For the American Social Science Association).
11 Sutton, S.B. (ed.) 1871; **A selection of Frederick Law Olmsted's writings on City Landscapes** (The Massachussets Institute of Technology. 1971)p.162; Olmsted, Vaux & Co. 'Report Accompanying Plan for laying out the South Park', (Chicago South Park Commission).
12 Olmsted, F. L. jr. Kimball, T. (eds); **Frederick Law Olmsted, Landscape Architect, 1822–1903** (New York: Benjamin Blom, 1970) volume 2.
13 Olmsted, F.L. 1892. Letter to Burnham, May 15, Olmsted's papers, reel 22.
14 Burnham, D. H. 1897. **Letter to the Merchant's Club**. 13th April .
15 Cross, G.; **A Social History of Leisure since 1600** (Venture Publishing Inc, PA, 1990) p. 98.
16 **ibid.,** p. 101.

Waterfront parks – a tool for social transformation

Buenos Aires in the 1850s was nothing but a small town on the banks of the Rio de la Plata. Trade was not yet institutionalised but the population was already a mixture of a majority of Spanish and minorities of European immigrants. This situation would soon change as Buenos Aires turned into an international harbour and became the gateway to the rest of South America. Cattle rearing and agriculture boosted the potential of the city for becoming a powerful economy by the end of the 19th century. During the last decades of the century, immigration from Europe escalated intensely, showing a need for the city's re-organising its spatial and urban qualities.

Politicians saw themselves in the position of shaping a new and diverse society, and for this purpose they relied on either help and influence from both urban professionals or practitioners aboard as well as locals that had gained some expertise elsewhere.

This process of growth was accompanied by the development of industry, railroads and harbour facilities that were mainly provided by the British. What was relevant for this study was not only that techniques were imported from the Anglo culture, but also social reform. The *rational recreation* movement in the Anglo-American environment had a very strong influence on urban planning and especially the park planning of the earliest parks in Buenos Aires. This movement and its main ideas of civilisation were brought to Buenos Aires by Domingo Faustino Sarmiento.

Sarmiento was president of Argentina from 1870 to 1874. Despite his short administration, he was extremely influential in the development of the city and its inclusion in an international network of cities. Before his position as president, Sarmiento was appointed ambassador to the United States, where he was a thorough observer of the tools of organisation and administration that were displayed in new urban strategies. Even though he was not an architect or designer he was the brain behind the birth of park development in Buenos Aires which set a precedent for the park system for the following decades. The *Park Movement* was for him a great influence and an example of the civilising powers of urban development.

The Parks of Palermo, then on the northern riverside of the city, intended to imitate the civilising intentions of the parks of North America, borrowing their image and landscape architecture. Central Park was the main referent for the design of the Parks of Palermo: the organised but wild looking vegetation, the undulating greensward and the scattered growth of trees, the pathways and reflecting lagoons were all implemented in the Buenos Aires park. Palermo, in contrast to Central Park, was placed on the fringes of the city (a location more comparable to the South Park of Chicago) but the waterfront condition was not treated or mentioned in the park project.

This would not be the case in Sarmiento's general idea of the potential civilisation qualities of the waterfront. Sarmiento was deeply interested in the waterfront condition of the city, which is shown in the book he wrote about a utopian Capital for Argentina. He called it '*Argiropolis*', and would have situated it on an island in the Rio de la Plata. In his book he states the virtues of a waterfront society.

> Returning to the advantages that the creation of a capital city on that island would assure to the States of el Plata, we will point to one that is, at least for us, of an incalculable importance. Such is the influence that this society thrown in the water would necessarily exert on the national habits, if it is possible to say, and surrounded by all the means of power that the civilisation gives. It is not hidden from anybody the defects that the sort of life carried out in the continent has inoculated us, the farm, the horse, the cattle, the lack of utensils, like the facility to replace them by old means. What change in the ideas and the customs! If instead of horses they were boats needed for the young people to take a stroll; if instead of taming the colts, people had to tame excited waves with the oar; if instead of straw and earth to improvise a cabin one were forced to cut the granite to square! The town educated in this school would be a cradle of intrepid navigators, laborious industrialists, eloquent men familiarised with all the uses and means of action that the North American peoples so superior to those of South America.[17]

Sarmiento was one of the most important producers of the enlightenment premise that underlines the didactic qualities of urban space. In his discourse for the inauguration of the Parks of Palermo he pronounced: '*Only in a vast, artistic and accessible park, the people will be people; only there will there be neither foreigners, nor nationals nor plebeians.*'[18] The spectacle of the park is considered, for the first time in Buenos Aires, as a tool to give balance to the social differences, to erase the old habits and provide a new social order. The morphology of the Park is definitely reminiscent of that of Olmsted, the integration of nature and a few scattered buildings would be the essence of Palermo.
Sarmiento had three ideas for his civilising plan in the choosing of the location of the park. First of all, it would be placed in the land that used to be the home of the dictator Rosas, a political barbarian in the eyes of Sarmiento. Second, the park would be a representation of the taming of the pampas, vast lands on the fringes of the city. Finally, the park would be an alternative to the traditional city, which was filled with mistakes and obstacles left by the colonial system.

After the intervention of Sarmiento in Palermo in 1885, engineer Maraini, working for mayor Alvear, presents a project for public baths in the waterfront, which are still in the tradition of

17 Sarmiento, D.F; 'Discurso Inaugural del parque', en Obras Completas (Buenos Aires: Editorial Luz del Dia, 1953) tomo XXII. p. 73.
18 **ibid.,** p. 11.

civil social transformation, as a tool for social equality. This time the park is placed closer to the city, more accessible for the working classes that could not approach Palermo by coach.
'This project will contribute to the conquest, for the city, of a great stretch of land, destined to an object of vital importance to the neighbourhood, as public baths. It will be transformed as a whole into a promenade that we hope will have its rank of preference among those of South America.'[19]
This is the last example of the use of these waterfront developments as a tool for social integration. Since then, these ideas would gradually change and the need of a representative prestigious promenade would become the essence of the new projects.

Waterfront promenades – a search for international recognition Ten years later, approaching the turn of the century and the celebrations of the centenary of independence, there is a shift in aesthetics parallel to a shift in ideas backing up the projects. As much as Sarmiento's and Alvear's civilising and democratising intentions were materialised in the picturesque landscape, the new ideas of a prestigious waterfront avenue were materialised in the Beaux Arts style. This does not mean that the parks become exclusively privatised space, but that priorities are changing compared to previous projects. The influence of French principles was not only brought from abroad in ideas, but also in the hiring of French urban designers such as Bouvard or Forestier, coming to intervene in the urban design of the city.
The Coast Boulevard or Promenade replaces the picturesque paths of the Anglo-American parks. New perspectives are open and the waterfront projects become part of a general urban plan for the city, an interconnected, related and hierarchical system of parks and avenues. The projects designed by Morales (1896), Carrasco (1914) and Forestier (1925) share these characteristics. These three professionals were very clear in the recovery of the river as spectacle and in their interest in having a prestigious avenue, which could be comparable to those of Europe.
Carlos Maria Morales, engineer in charge of the waterfront design in the context of the Plan of Bouvard 1909, was the first to propose a waterfront avenue that would not only be a source of international prestige for the city. It would also be a source of needed leisure space, as well as part of a network of avenues that would give the needed limits to the city.
'Few cities, in fact, will have the possibility, for its placing in front of a river like ours, of being able to build a promenade of this extension, which magnificence can be previewed without effort. On one side the river, whose display will be always a main attraction. On the other side beautiful country houses, modern constructions, a site preferred by people of good taste and fortune, big hotels, bath houses, etc. And in the promenade, with its grand perspective, the wide

attendance this city already has, in some years will have assumed proportions that escape any estimate.'[20]

Carrasco was in fact the first landscape designer to finally conceive a park system for the waterfront across the harbour, which is finally realised and built in its entirety.

> [T]he day [the coast avenue] is built, the province will be able to be proud of carrying out one of the greatest works of embellishment done in the world, (...) superior to the works done in Europe, where there has been no river with the characteristics of ours, wide, picturesque in great part of its waterfront and close to important populated centres that with time shall acquire an extraordinary development.[21]

The idea of prestige becomes evident in taking over the social importance of these projects. Nonetheless it is relevant to say that this project, especially its pier, fulfilled its needs of leisure space close to the city. This can be read in the articles of the inauguration day. The result of the design and building of the avenue and baths was stunning. The city dwellers were evidently welcoming the recovery of the shore.

'The river was very low, giving a more outstanding role to the old beach of the resort, with the beautiful perspective of the workshops of Riachuelo and the crossing of some ships in the canals of the harbour. Numerous persons dived into the river. The circles of children that would defy the imminent tides were numerous. More than one severe person, in the enthusiasm of the pleasure of bathing, would take off their shoes and walked ceremoniously, with their top hat well on their heads.'[22]

'Today the south zone of the capital receives, in equal proportion to that of the north, the benefits of municipal action. This new baths zone, built on the sand banks that until recently were deserted, is a clear demonstration of the new order of things opening for the neighbourhoods of the south. The proud promenade shows its elegant silhouette to the horizon of the Rio de la Plata. (...) What a great spectacle the waterfront promenade will give, with its thousands of souls strolling in the wide avenue that borders the estuary!'[23]

Carrasco's strongest competitor in the landscape design of the waterfront of the city was J.C.N. Forestier. Within the urban plan for Buenos Aires of Noel in 1925 they opted for Forestier, instead of hiring the local designer. The French designer Forestier was commended for his work

19 Alvear, T. 1885. **Letter to Concejo Deliberante**. Beccar Varela (1925) **Torcuato de Alvear**, primer Intendente Municipal de la Ciudad de Buenos Aires. Su acción edilicia.

20 Morales, C.M. 1896. Memoria presentada al Concejo Deliberante por el Intendente Municipal Sr.Emilio.V.Bunge. Año 1895. Buenos Aires. Establecimiento de Impresiones G. Kraft.

21 Carrasco, B. J. 1914. **Plano y memoria descriptiva de las obras de embellecimiento de la costa** (elevada al señor ministro de Obras Publicas de la Provincia de Buenos Aires por la Comisión nombrada por Decreto de fecha abril 22 de 1912) Buenos Aires , Compañia Sudamericana de Billetes de Banco, in: Berjman, S; **Benito Javier Carrasco, sus textos,** (**UBA:** Facultad de agronomía, 1997).

22 'Balneario Municipal. Inauguración Oficial' 1918. **La Prensa**. Jueves 12 de Diciembre.

23 'Balneario Municipal' 1926. **La Razon**, 24 de Diciembre, p. 8.

on the coast project. In his short description of his project it is clear that his main attention is driven to the strength of the river and the aesthetic qualities of the waterfront.
'The natural conditions of the capital and its own tradition suggested a way to find the recovery its most beautiful quality, to return its physiognomy of city situated on the border of a great estuary.'[24]

> [T]he realisation of a great avenue that would be a real work of aesthetic beautifying, as the similar cases of Nice, Rio de Janeiro, as the promenade of Coney Island and the beautiful Maritime avenue of Posilipo in the Bay of Naples.[25]

The discourse of Morales, Carrasco and Forestier is very much directed towards the outstanding qualities of the waterfront and to the necessary recognition of Buenos Aires as an international city.
Forestier's discourse is not literally concerned with the social aims of his projects but his drawings show his attitude clearly. There is a strong beaux-arts image permeating the drawing. The relation between the built and nature, be it parks, squares or water, is one of contrast. His design can probably be related to that of Burnham's White City or to Haussman's project for Paris. Nonetheless, in contrast with Burnham's position of developing an exclusively public waterfront, Forestier proposes a wide area reserved for high rate private building.

Conclusions It is difficult to draw conclusions out of such a particular study but a couple of remarks can be noted out of this research. There seems to be a pattern of intervention in social behaviour through the design of these waterfront spaces. Leisure concepts are consistently reflected in the built environment. By the end of the 19th century, at the peak of growth of social diversity, the projects for the waterfronts are being designed as spaces of social reform, spaces to breach the gap between different social conditions. This position is reflected in a romantic and picturesque image of the park and the waterfront, where nature is seen as a taming tool of urban behaviour. Later on, the ambitions of the designers and authorities go further, and the need of social equality is made redundant, so the designs are decisively directed to a specific section of society and to the attraction of the city as an international metropolis. This is represented by the beaux-arts order and urban organisation.
It is not intended to provide a universalising view or position towards the subject, but further research on the case studies should shed light on this phenomenon more extensively.

24 Forestier, JCN. Comisión de Estetica Edilicia, **Proyecto Orgánico para la Urbanización del Municipio, El Plano Regulador y de Reforma de la Capital federal.** Intendencia de Buenos Aires, (Buenos Aires: Talleres Peuser, 1925) p. 203.
25 ibid., p. 205.

[2]

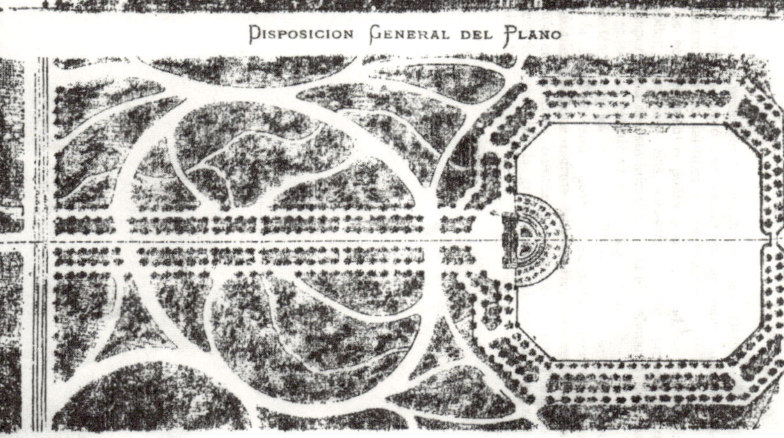

1 Southern waterfront promenade. Buenos Aires – Jean Claude Nicolas Forestier. 1925. Source: Forestier, JCN Comisión de Estetica Edilicia (1925), Proyecto Orgánico para la Urbanización del Municipio. El Plano Regulador y de Reforma de la Capital Federal, Intendencia de Buenos Aires, Buenos Aires, Talleres Peuser.

2 Southern waterfront promenade . Buenos Aires – Project of Carrasco. 1914. Photo 1938. Source: Archivo General de la Nacion. Departamento Documentos Fotograficos Argentina. Caja 70 sobre 7.

3 Project for public baths in the riverfront in front of the Paseo de la Recoleta – Project Commended by Torcuato de Alvear. 1885. Source: Beccar Varela, Torcuato de Alvear, primer Intendente Municipal de la Ciudad de Buenos Aires. Su acción edilicia, Publicación oficial, biblioteca Municipal E. Echeverria. 1925.

4 Waterfront park and passenger pier – photo circa 1900. Source: Archivo General de la Nacion. Departamento Documentos Fotograficos Argentina. Inventario 216762. Caja 865. Sobre 4.

Virtual, emergence and resilience of contemporary urban place

Qiang Sheng

Introduction Against the conventional view on the city as an artefact or architecture, this paper starts from the understanding of place (and the social relationships it supports) as an emerging product out of the everyday movement scaffolded by the configuration of urban space. Moreover, I will try to explore the detailed mechanism of this production, and the problem of emergence or self-organization through DeLanda's terminology of 'virtual.'[1] Although I will mention 'Space Syntax' as a successful model, or, new agent-based modeling approach in the paper, at the beginning I have to claim that the term 'virtual' here is less related to any digitally based virtual reality. The total structure of this paper contains three issues regarding the concept of 'virtual': firstly, the modality problem, I will mention 'virtual' as 'real' instead of merely 'possible' conditions for the emergence of our urban place; secondly, which is also the main part of this paper, I will focus on the regulating function of virtual singularity on the self-organized behavior to avoid total indeterminism when thinking of emergence, and determinism when thinking of structure. Two claims will be made within this part: 1, The emergence is divergent actualization of singularity. 2, Both space and process or history matter for the production of urban place. Last but not least, the understanding of 'virtual' as 'quasi-causality' will serve as a background of certain 'natural logic' of the urban organism. As an example, I shall make reference to one case study in Beijing throughout this paper. As a conclusive remark, I will propose the necessity of studying those city areas of high 'virtualities' to examine the 'natural tendencies' of urban systems. It will help us to look at the urban as a living system which has the capacity to adjust itself to the border of chaos, the complexity to obtain high adaptability confronting external shocks.

Modality, virtual as real concrete conditions Ironically, my initial interest in the concept of the 'virtual' came from a typical Darwinist example: the resemblance between *ichthyosaur* (one kind of extinct dinosaurs living in the ocean) and the modern dolphin. Although these two species lived in completely different times and evolved through different evolutional trajectories, they occupied the same 'niche' which resulted in their similar appearances. This concept of 'niche', like an invisible locality defined by logistic condition of the ecosystem, leads to my first understanding of the 'virtual' as a parallel world to the actual ecosystem with real species. However, we must abandon the fallacy that there exists a realm of possibility while our actual world is nothing more than a copy of one trajectory out of this virtual reservoir filled with infinite possibilities. On the contrary, our active world 'will follow the dynamic and uncertain processes that characterize the schema that links a virtual component to an actual one.'[2] A 'niche' can be occupied accidentally by certain species or eradicated by the changing of its supporting conditions. It is like the adventure in a labyrinth where the configuration of the path and wall will change depending on each step moving forward. This inter-affected relationship of 'niche' and 'species' gives us a wonderful metaphor for understanding the relationship between 'virtual'

1 DeLanda (2002).
2 See Sanford Kwinter (2001).

and 'actual'. Deleuze writes: 'The virtual is not opposed to the real but to the actual [...] The reality of the virtual is structure. We must avoid giving the elements and relations that form a structure an actuality which they don't have, and withdrawing from them a reality which they have.'[3] The first part of the quotation challenged our common understanding of 'virtual' as 'unreal'. 'Niches' are fully real as 'species'; they are even more real than 'species' for their descriptive 'concreteness', for their power to capture the attributes of real entity. The extinction of 'species' seems a lesser catastrophe to the ecosystem than that of 'niches'. It is multiple conditions, urban logistics, no matter whether physical or non-physical, visible or invisible, which build our urban everyday life and lead to the emergence of varied levels of 'places', programs or activities, all of them are fully 'real' and functional. However, our conventional urban study somehow limits itself to fetishism, which looks at the city and a certain type of urban place as industrial products, the urban space as negative background, which only plays a constructive role as certain typologies, or archetypes that can produce a certain urban atmosphere. This fetishistic point of view blinds us to the changed conditions behind the seeming stabilities, especially in some renewal projects driven by nostalgia-cultural industries. [See figure 1]

One example in Beijing is the declining Longfusi traditional shopping street during the last decades after the fire accident in 1993. Both government and developers have made huge investments in some big projects to revitalize this commercial area but the output is still depressing. The street is occupied by the emerging micro-economies selling fashion. If the physical condition remains the same, the program itself is also attractive, and the input of investment is sufficient; what are the missing ingredients, on what conditions our urban places constitute themselves and how those conditions are interrelated, these are the urban questions this paper tries to address within the framework of 'virtual'.

Virtual and structure In the preface of *The Order of Things*, Michel Foucault cites one passage written by Borges, it was from a certain Chinese encyclopedia about the taxonomy of animals: *(a) belonging to the emperor, (b) embalmed, (c) tame, (d) sucking pigs, (e) sirens, (f) fabulous, (g) stray dogs, (h) included in the present classification, (i) frenzied, (j) innumerable, (k) drawn with a very fine camelhair brush, (l) et cetera, (m) having just broken the water pitcher, (n) that from a long way off look like flies.*'[4] This obscure taxonomy inspired him to the idea of the 'rupture of episteme.'[5] Similarly, from the quotation from Deleuze in the last chapter, if there exist certain 'structures' which became relevant and important in a certain period, what should be the proper way of classification in a paradigm of complexity? How to categorize things without crystallizing their dynamic relationships?

Combinatorial constraints, emergence and self-organization In *One-Thousand Years of Non-linear History*, DeLanda quotes linguist Zellig Harris's study as opposition to Chomsky's theory. By defining the combinatorial constraints Harris offers us a model which can capture the language as a learning and evolving process without taking the classification of words (such as noun, verb or adjective, etc.) and structure of sentences as given.[6] From this example we can see the importance of 'local rules' as 'combinatorial constraints' for the behavior of the self-organizing system.

As most contemporary urbanists realise the top-down planning approach is often compromised by the contingent emergence as hidden forces affecting our cities. As a consequence of both this problem and the development of the complexity and chaos theory, a paradigm of emergence, self-organized or bottom-up approach is prevailing in our urban studies and models. There are two main advantages this bottom-up/agent-based model can offer us. Firstly, the attributes are given to the individual agents. Even this decision is somehow an arbitrary idea from programmers, but since we are interested in the collective results instead of singular cases, and the rule is given to the local individuals, the uncertainty of this arbitrary action (naming attributes) will be effectively decentralized.[7] Secondly, it can prevent the dependence on the complexity as global abstraction or grand-narratives such as cultural differences or any other artificial boundary-defining actions, but still have the power to grasp the diversity in terms of the different attributes individuals have. This diversity or difference will be illustrated as a continuous changing landscape instead of closed classifications. However, as I have mentioned before, this paper will be sceptical to any claims that the urban condition makes as a product of agent-based modeling. Due to the different scale or the power of individual agents, our urban environment is never a neutral environment affording all the movement, but in most cases produced by a centralized decision-making (top-down) process. The creativity or resistance of the individual agents is on how to appropriate this given urban space rather than how to create it. Many urban problems are caused by these conflicts between the ideas from designers concerning the benefit of certain groups or activities while neglecting certain natural tendencies of the city. These 'natural tendencies' are not the deviation of the planning system, but follow their own immanent logics. And it is just the coexistence and interaction between these systems, which constitute the urban complexity I described. It is necessary both to understand better the multiple needs/tendencies/

3 See Deleuze's: **Difference and Repetition.**

4 See Michel Foucault (1970).

5 In the **Order of Things**, Foucault describes the evolution of human knowledge as a process of rapture instead of continuity. For instance, in the 17th and 18th centuries, the organization of knowledge was based on 'resemblance', while in the 19th century, it was based on 'difference'.

6 DeLanda (2000). Harris proposes three combinatorial constraints: Likely-hood constraint (the linkage between world), argument-operator constraint (the linkage of 'kinds of words') and reduction constraint (the birth of new words). See Manuel DeLanda, (2002), Intensive science and virtual philosophies. For DeLanda, this model is both concrete, that can capture the real dynamic in the formation process, and abstract that can be used to explain the formation of other systems, such as music, which have the pressure of being repeated and convey certain meaning. Similarly, the topological connectivity has this value as well, it can reveal certain aspect of space (like Space Syntax model did) and the social relationships (friendship circle).

logics and to conceptualize them in a 'structure' which can make these differences visible, comparable and modelable. Therefore, what we should focus on is the reacting behavior of individual agents rather than on how the environment can be formed in a merely bottom-up, autopoetic process.

Structure and the 'natural tendency' of space System Engineering offers us tools to analyze the regulating role of those 'virtual structures', such as hierarchy or meshwork and their effect on the dynamics of geographical, biological and cultural entities.[8] These ways of 'classification' re-open the question of 'form' or 'space' as 'formation' or 'organization' instead of typology, prototype or pattern language.

These 'abstract machines',[9] or 'virtual structures' as I call them, can relate our professional scope in three layers: the functional relationship (economy of agglomeration or economy of scale), social organization (network or institution) and spatial configuration (grid or tree-like structure), while classification of those layers is based on the interaction between them. The most obvious relationship could be the grid structure which is both the product and the facilitator of the interdependency between different functions, and the tree-like structure will result in a distribution of functions and programs of different scales. The latter example will illustrate the regulating or scaffolding power of urban space on the emerging centralities.

The research starts from the spatial analysis in Beijing. The main emphasis at first is to examine the urban space as main generator of activity instead of neutral container. Based on the understanding of urban fabric as a sorting device for the emergence of programs of different scales, most modern cities shared the common figure that the open grid system is the proper form to support centrality. Beijing's urban fabric also is affected by this long-term tendency to achieve certain 'openness' or 'gridness', but due to the inequality of development or historical reasons, the spatial pattern remains the same in the local sense in the inner city.

Beijing used to be regarded as an ideal grid city.[10] From this research of Beijing's traditional urban fabric we can see it actually formed by serials of spatial hierarchies and this phenomenon has a 'bottom-up' explanation with two 'combinatorial constraints' based on the traditional housing typology. The first constraint: each courtyard house prefers to have an entrance to the south, this leads to form the ordered fabrics. Whereas the second constraint, as a kind of noise factor, breaks this order by inserting big 'tree structures' into the system. The higher the social/ economical level is, the more courtyards one house has, and it will extend in a north-south direction as well. One extreme example is the Forbidden City in the middle of Beijing, which became a big barrier to east-west direction. The later development solved this problem by superimposing the 'XL' scale on the existing. [See figure 2]

The outcome of this historical analysis to a certain extent manifests in the production of urban places, what matters is urban space instead of history itself. The old urban fabric gives to the fact that most traditional high streets are south-north oriented because these 'X' scale streets are topologically better integrated than others. Therefore it tended to be occupied by flow with higher intensity and scale. The second constraint described before became relevant in this part of the story because some of these 'important' buildings are temples which behave like a catalyst for commercial activities. So it produced some 'events-based' high streets, the Longfusi high street is one example. Of course, these events can be consolidated if they are strong enough for historical reasons. But they are also fragile when facing external shocks. As we can easily see, the individual movement actualizes the functioning of this spatial logic, the role played by agents and environment cannot be divided. Furthermore, this mechanism doesn't have to depend on specific history or culture, it is always present and drives the urban development to actualize its tendency in one way or the other. Obviously, this is good news for urban planners and designers, because if it is only the history that matters in our 'place' production, we can do nothing more than preserving them or waiting for them to emerge by chance. However, the real city is a 'dynamic' system which evolves in real time rather than purely a 'computational' system.[11] Therefore, we have to dig out how history or process matters in this context as a complementary argument.

Virtual singularity and divergent actualization Up to now I have mentioned the combinatorial constraints of agents and the structure which is formed by, but more importantly can regulate individual agents' collective behavior. Another virtual entity which needs to be highlighted here is the 'singularity' as 'long-term tendency of the system'. For instance, in urban systems, we can conceptualize the 'sorting mechanism' of urban fabric as one singularity, it means given enough time, certain scaled programs or activities will sediment on corresponding scaled urban space. As an example, in *Urban Machine*, Stephen Read and Gerhard Bruyns[12] propose layered networks of different scales of movement (interface of intensive productive differences) as an alternative model opposing the old 'center-periphery' model, which is

7 See DeLanda, **War in The Age of Intelligence Machine** (1991). Manuel DeLanda conceptualized the evolution of the 'War machine' from 'clockwork' army, 'motor' army and 'network army', each of them have their own organizing principles based on the available social and technical background. However, one clear line within this evolution is the tendency of 'decentralization of control'. The uncertainty can be classified and give for each level of decision makers instead of concentrated on top level. See **War in the Age of Intelligent Machines.**

8 DeLanda (2000).

9 DeLanda mentions this term as equivalent to what Deleuze and Guattari called 'engineering diagrams'. In **One Thousand Years of Nonlinear History**, DeLanda particularly focuses on 'hierarchy' and 'meshwork' as emerging products out of a historical structure-generating process.

10 Most of these writings mentioned the ideal form of city in an ancient Chinese book **Kao Gong Ji** (around 1000 B.C.). The plan of Beijing, as a capital city, is considered as one of the examples which follows this paradigm.

11 Robert F. Port and Timothy van Gelder (1995).

12 See Gerhard Bruyns and Stephen Read **The Urban Machine** (Amsterdam: Techne Press, 2006).

a 'horizontal classification' without losing the interactive behavior by fixing the border and naming the things. In this case, one model can explain both contemporary cities and historical cities, the spatial logic is always present, while history, in this sense, is not something given but a product of this spatial logic. [See figure 3]

The singularity as a virtual entity is very relevant in this context because of its similar characteristic: the actualization process of singularity doesn't depend on a specific mechanism: one example used by DeLanda is: guided by singularity like minimizing the bonding energy, the formation process and also the final form of babble and salt crystal are very different. For Deleuze or DeLanda, the divergent actualization is the real innovation.[13] This understanding is crucial because it on the one hand can prevent the trap of indeterminism when facing the problem of emergence while on the other still keep the world open-ended. As for the urban study, this understanding became extremely useful when facing the contingency of reality and other social/cultural differences as given. Again let me take the 'sorting mechanism' as an example. The layered homogeneity as a result can only be understood through the different intensity of uses and scales of users: The sedimentation of main streets (large scale flow) can be shops, banks or even a nice housing area for different cultures and social contexts, but they are all 'divergent actualizations' of one singularity. This understanding can open the gate of looking at the city not only as a man-made object, as a product to feed different social or economical needs, but an organism with its own 'natural tendencies' independent on human intervention or interpretation, those 'natural tendencies' defined by certain singularities have to be actualized while the human being is 'nothing more than' a catalyst for this process.[14] This, as it seems, is such a strange or machinic hypothesis that is not convincing for most of us as intelligent beings on this planet. Of course, the city at its very beginning was made by and for us, and based on different cultural and social backgrounds constructed as worlds with diversities. However, looking at these diversities as a kind of guided 'openness' will be a more productive and operative theory for our profession today when facing more and more uncertainties. Therefore, my objectives are: firstly to try to understand how guidance produces different 'solutions' based on different initial conditions; secondly to explore how this open-ended process (locally linear) can make the system open by its interaction with the environment. A crucial claim this paper tries to make is that looking at the issue of emergence or self-organization as divergent actualization of singularities which stands in-between the determinism and indeterminism.[15]

Now, it is the time to pick up our question about how history or process matters in the production of contemporary urban place. First I will continue the spatial story of Beijing's inner city. As a consequence of modernization described before, today's Beijing on the large scale is transformed to a grid city with super blocks (about 700m by 700m each). But on the local scale the opposite story is happening. 1, the downgrading of the courtyard housing formed a small-scale labyrinthic condition. 2, the insertion of the 'unit system' (as a kind of institution), which is a socialist organization prevailed combining working, recreation and housing in one gated area after the foundation of the People's Republic of China, enlarged the effect of the second principle to form a complex fabric inside the super block. The latter cases focused on the effect of this complex spatiality on modern urban life. [See figure 4]

Taking spatial analysis as a starting point, the sorting mechanism will lead to a final stable state (equilibrium) when all programs or activities of different scales are coherent with their spatial hierarchies. However, this research focuses on the alternatives for 'stable states' within attempts to reach 'equilibrium' for two extremes: [See figure 5]

1 When the spatial condition is good but the social condition can only support the emergence of low economy, those micro-economies start to organize themselves to behave like an attraction of high scale. This organization is what I refer to as the 'quasi-unit system'. [See figure 6]

In the first example, that small courtyard area located at the corner of super-block has a superb connectivity to the super-grid outside. The emerging micro-economies reveal high system resilience by combining the production part with retail business of fashion. It is such a hidden community within the courtyard, and yet a small restaurant is located inside the block. This small area, normally occupied by immigrants coming from other cities, is a typical example of urban village. Despite its importance to the vitality within a whole urban ecology, the spatial quality of these villages always reveals double characters: as a relatively closed (either gated or labyrinthic) area, it is normally located at a very open or accessible site, giving the image of the city as a shallow skin of lively commercial atmosphere.

2 When the social conditions can support the large-scale activity (and there is a shortage of those facilities) while the spatial condition is inferior, the 'unit system' will half release the inner program to outside. Therefore, it can hold certain higher scale programs like hidden places inside the super block. [See figure 7]

The second example is a dance center inside the super block which is intensively used by Beijing's local inhabitants (most of them coming from long distances outside the block). It was formerly a meeting hall or club of the largest government unit nearby: the National Mineral Institute.

13 DeLanda (2000).
14 In **War in the Age of Intelligent Machines** by Manuel DeLanda, he mentions the original intention of the book is writing a history for the **machinic phylum**.
15 DeLanda (2000).

Comparing two examples, we can conceptualise both of them as 'divergent actualization' of the singularity defined by the 'sorting mechanism'. The critical difference here is about the time approaching this singularity ('relaxation time' in technical terms); in the second case, it seems the system is temporarily 'locked-on' to certain alternative stable states defined by the initial conditions. In Comparison with the claim that the urban complexity is 'computational', here we can re-conceptualize it as 'dynamical' which the process unfolds in real time. This complex situation formed by the multiple alternative stable states, offered our living environment not only the chaotic fragmentation but also diversity of urban ecology with different niches for individual agents to act on. Therefore, rather than looking at this phenomenon as a consequence of the different relaxation time of the system, the alternative assumption is to claim that the city, as a living organism, has to constantly adjust itself on the edge of chaos, the statue of complexity to achieve certain adaptability.

The first example strongly facilitated the emerging micro-economies on the Longfusi high street, although, for government and developers, it is a symptom of decline, but in terms of vitality, at least being something is better than being nothing. The niche for a 'city-scaled high street' vanished, but the local condition is still there, holding its 'placeness' as a district centrality. The second example has its generic value as well. After the Reformation in 1978, the former 'unit system' which used to take care of the people's everyday life is declining. However, during this process, it can release many internal programs to the outside, offering people the middle-scaled facilities which is hard to come by from purely market driven emergence. This complex situation composed of multiple alternative stable states rather than best stable states can be conceptualized as a non-linear system with multiple attractors.

The easiest way to understand those attractors could be the urban functions: a city or an area with diversified functions or programs is normally considered more sustainable. Taking those functions as emerging products out of urban space or social relationships instead of something artificially inserted, we can examine how the complexity of urban fabric or its inhabitants can give affordance to a certain urban 'place'. Manuel DeLanda pointed out: '*A nonlinear system with multiple attractors continues to display its virtuality even once the system has settled into one of its alternative stable states. Other alternatives are there all the time, coexisting with the one that happens to be actualized.*'[16] Thus this high virtuality brings greater system resilience confronting the external shocks. However, our conventional design approach, either influenced by market forces, or holding the prejudice that there must be a 'best solution' or 'perfect form', used to consider one layer of relationships by reducing or simplifying the urban complexity.

Quasi-causality Before I finish, I'd like to extend the topic to the causality understanding of the virtual, as a 'quasi-causal system' which puts the reason and its effect in an inter-affected relationship. It is also called circular causality or advanced causality. Brian Massumi points out that: every society creates a quasi-causal system (Example: In capitalist society the ultimate quasi-cause is capital itself) and they function 'realer than real'. In urbanism, this quasi-causality is reflected in: First, the most direct link is urban, as a system of images, signs or slogans which produced by our conventions and daily life, later affect emergence of places like the actual 'reasons'. Zoning or branding certain areas can also be regarded as these 'quasi-causes'. However, their effectiveness will depend on how they fit the 'natural tendency' of the city, or the 'concreteness' of this actualization process. Second, one specific issue that will be involved in this understanding is the social/spatial relationship, the discussion of social-produced space versus social relationship as an emerging product of everyday spatial practice. Obviously, the urban space is built by and for its inhabitants as a product of their social relationships, but the space also plays an active role on consolidating the social relationships. What is relevant here will be the interactive process between these two actors, whether they strengthen or weaken each other, instead of trying to find out who holds the initiative in this interaction.

Conclusive remarks: cities of virtuality Much has been written before about the partly modernized situation (both in a Spatial sense and a Social sense) in Beijing. The city of virtualities refers to those city areas transforming rapidly, with high intensity/tension and of multiple tenses/tendencies.

Due to a lack of investment or attention to certain areas, certain social groups or public realms in the rapid development, the spatial or social inertia provisionally occupied the intermediate niches between the global and local and reached certain alternative stabilities. Therefore, other than the linear evolution, these city areas followed the complex trajectory of divergent actualization with multiple attractors. Other alternatives are there all the time, coexisting with the one that 'happens to be actualized'. Thus these urban areas have better capacity to reveal the 'virtual' by obtaining the multiple conditions which have their own stable states/tendencies. Obviously, the negative sides should never be neglected, such as the inefficiency of the infrastructure, social segregation and polarization, economical or ecological instability, etc. But this paper tries to point out that the richness of economical activity or social vitality somehow built on a basis far from equilibrium, which on the one hand can be regarded as living organism but vulnerable to external shock and crisis. There is a necessity to study those urban areas with high 'virtuality' to decode the 'natural logic' of the city. Therefore, important questions left are how to make use of these conditions and alternative stabilities, that can lead the way in transition from the 'productive' to the 'positive', as well as questioning how the high 'virtuality' contributes to system resilience within urban areas.

16 DeLanda (2002).

Bibliography

Bruyns, G. and Read, S.A. 'Urban machine', in **Visualising the Invisible**, edited by Panilla C. and Read S.A. Amsterdam: Techne Press, 2006.

Intensive Science and Virtual Philosophies. London: Continuum Press, 2002.

DeLanda, M. **One Thousand Years of Nonlinear History**. New York: Zone Books, 2000.

DeLanda, M. **War in the Age of Intelligent Machines**. New York: Swerve Editions, 1991.

Deleuze, G. **Difference and Repetition**. London: Continuum International Publishing group, 2004.

Foucault, M. **The Order of Things: An Archaeology of Human Sciences [1970]. London: Routledge, 2002.**

Kwinter, S. **Architectures of Time: Towards a Theory of the Event in Modernist Culture**. Cambridge, Massachusetts, London: MIT Press, 2001.

Massumi, B. **Realer than real, the simulacrum according to Deleuze and Guattari. 1987.** Available on website: http://www.anu.edu.au/HRC/first_and_last/works/realer.htm. [Access date: 10/06/2005].

Robert F. Port and Van Gelder, T. 'It is about time: An overview of the Dynamical Approach to Cognition,' in: **Mind as Motion: Explorations in the Dynamics of Cognition**. Cambridge, Massachusetts, London: MIT Press, 1995.

Read, S.A. 'Neighborhood spatial process: notes on public space, "thick space" scale and centrality,' in: **Globalization, urban form and governance 5,** edited by Carmona, M. Delft: Delft University Press, 2000.

Read, S. 'A question of form,' in: **Proceeding of 5th international Space Syntax Symposium**, edited by Nes, A.v. Delft, Delft University Press, 2004.

Waldrop, M. **Complexity**, translated by Ling Chen.1995. Available on webiste: http://www.shuku.net:8080/novels/zatan/tjzatvsfu/fuz.html. [Access date: 10/06/2005].

Urry, J. **Global Complexity**. Cambridge: Polity Press, 2003.

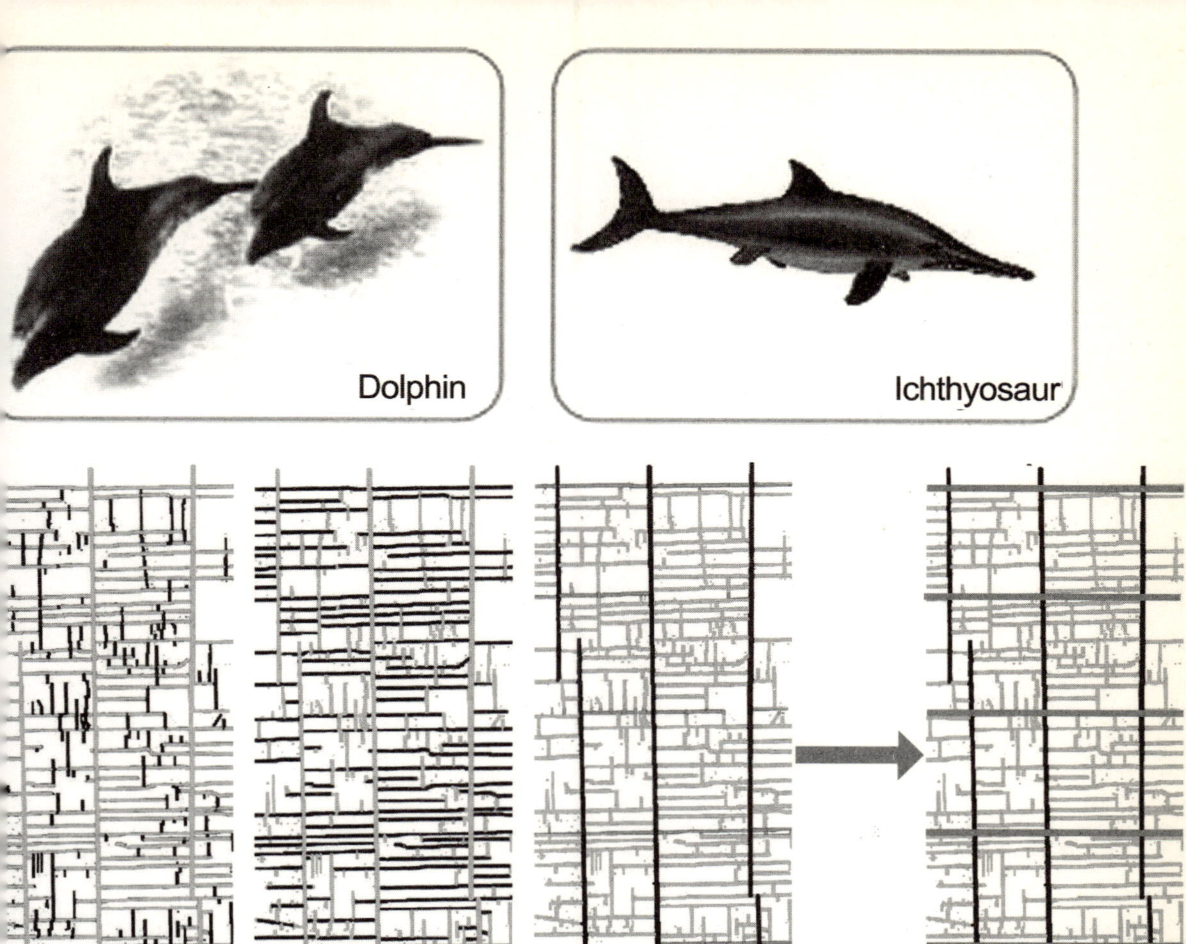

1 The resemblance between dolphin and ichthyosaur. Source: Author (2005).
2 The spatial structure of Beijing's inner city, expressed in different scales. Source: Author (2004).

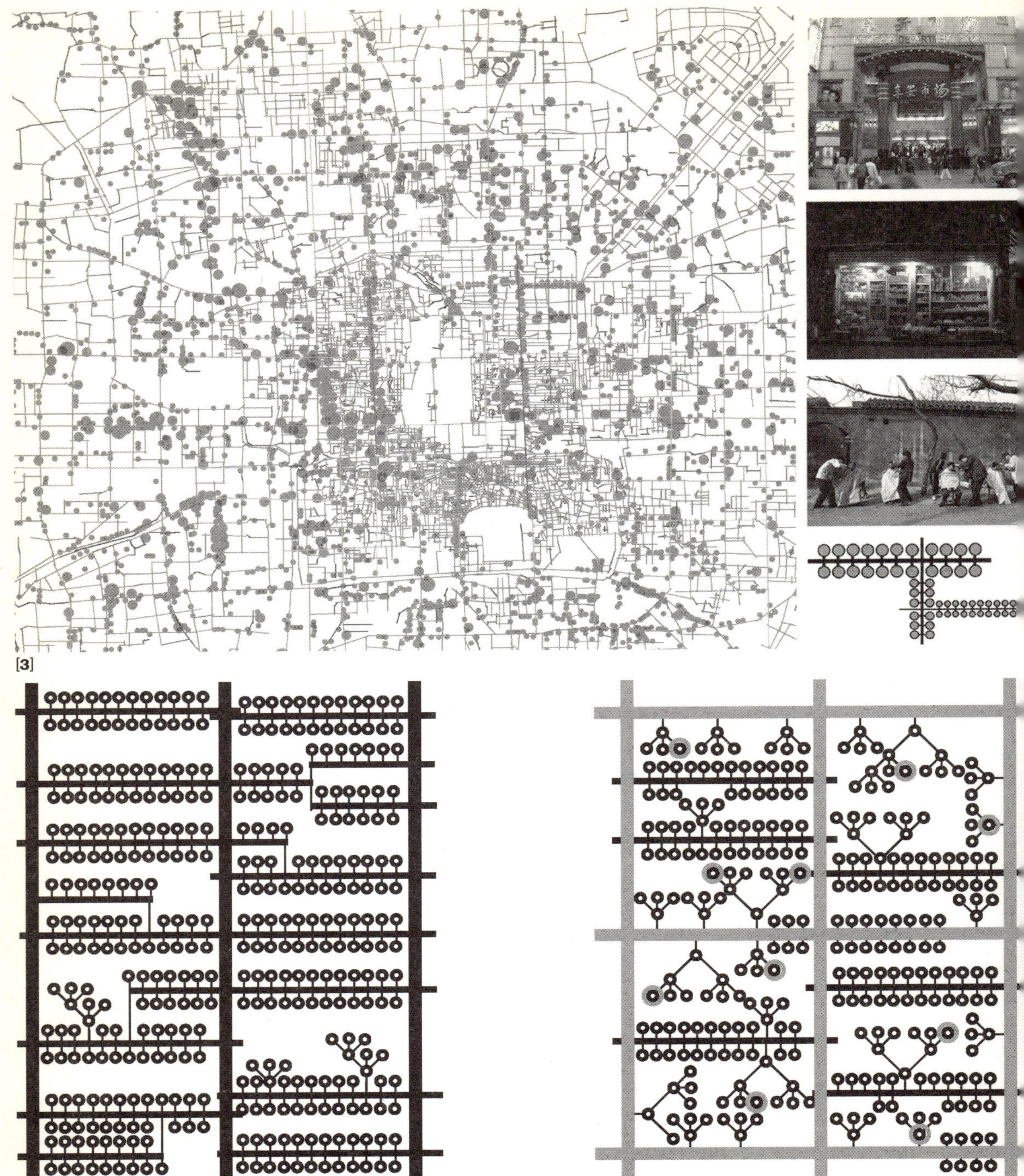

3 Sorting mechanism and its working diagram. The map on left is based on the local integration analysis in Space Syntax. Source: Author (2005).
4 The spatial effect of 'Unit systems'. Source: Author (2004).
5 The spatial and social/functional analysis of the **Longfusi** area in Beijing. Source: Author.
6 Left: the Longfusi high street; right: the hidden community behind the street. Source: Author (2004).
7 Left: the Poster of the dance center on the main street; right: the entrance of the dance center. Source: Author (2004).

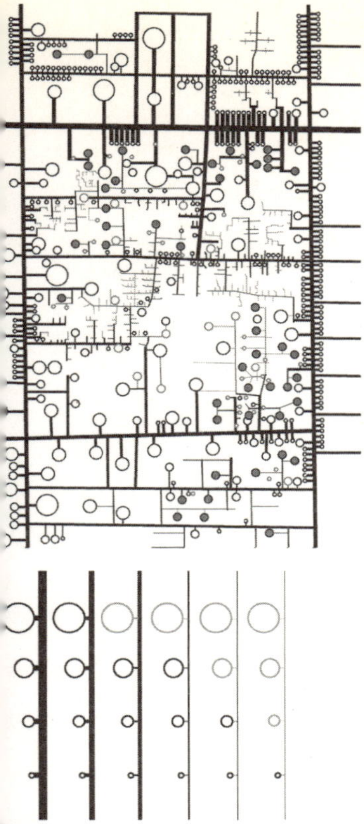

Spatial hierachy and affordance

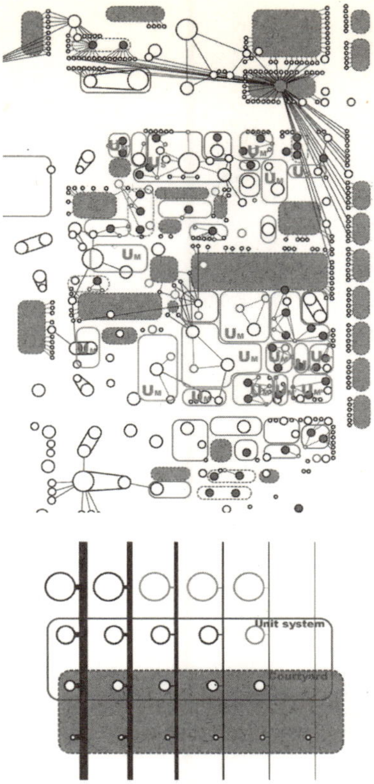
Unit system
Courtyard

Social background

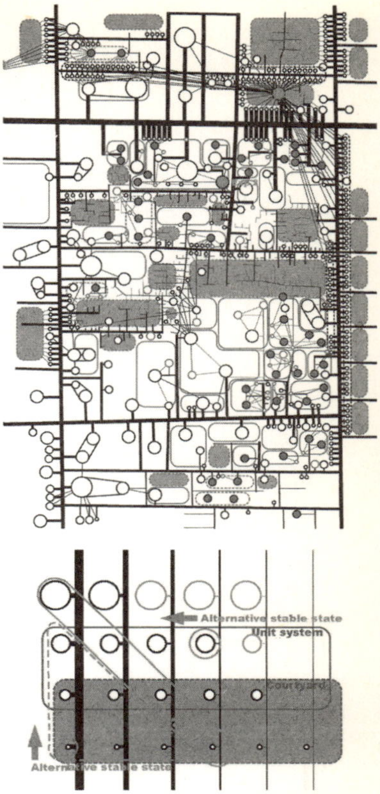
Alternative stable state
Unit system
Courtyard
Alternative stable state

Condition of Emergence

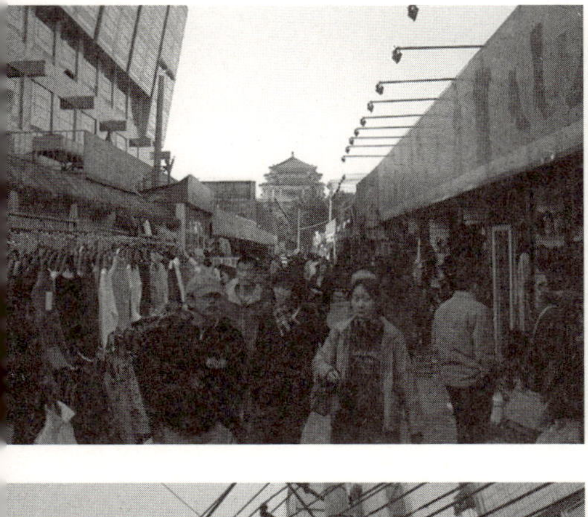

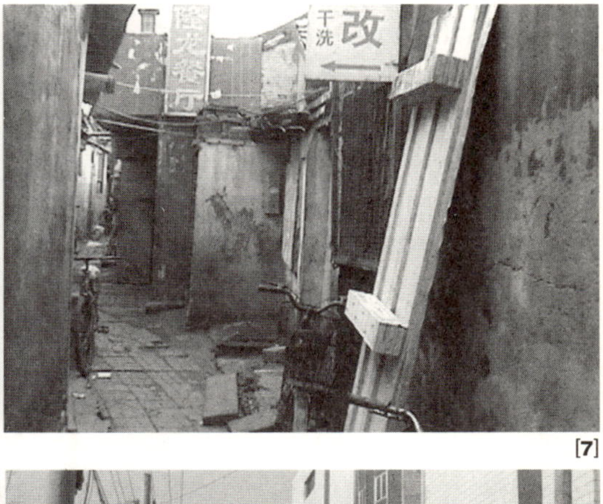
干洗
改

[7]

舞厅

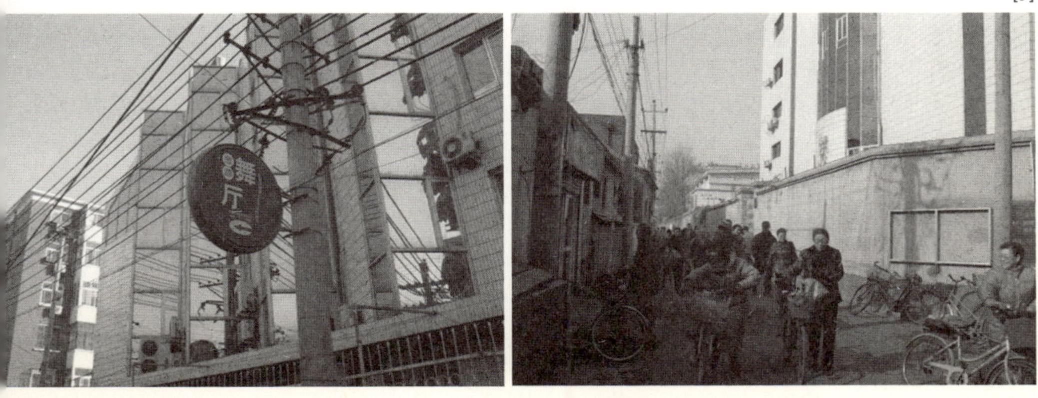

The Politics of Design: Designers as Transparent Mediators

Camilo Pinilla

Complexity drawn from a systems way of thinking

> But regardless of how you define them, each agent finds itself in an environment produced by its interactions with other agents in the system. It is constantly acting and reacting to what the other agents are doing. And because of that, essentially nothing in its environment is fixed.[1]

Much has been said about the increasing complexity of processes of all kinds and the role of emergence in change and creation. The 'systems approach' introduces important arguments engaging notions on change by studying organisation not in terms of parts or composing elements, but by observing the relations and behaviour patterns emerging from their interactions.

A systems way of thinking A 'systems way of thinking' came into use as a response to the increasing needs of modern man. Thus, to achieve better technological solutions for war, spaceships or computer production, processes involving the agglomeration of heterogeneous specialisations were developed. This issue lead to the need of dealing with complexes, 'wholes', or 'systems', in varied fields. Given the necessity for comprehensiveness, and as an attempt to unify modern scientific tendencies, Von Bertalanffy introduced General System Theory. The idea was to use 'parallelism' in different scientific fields, where 'order and organisation appear whether the question was the structure of atoms, the architecture of proteins, or interaction phenomena in thermodynamics.'[2]

As a result, and based on mathematical equations, principles can be applied to generalised systems irrespectively of their particular kind or nature. Von Bertalanffy cites the following example: an exponential law of growth applies to certain bacteria cells, to populations of bacteria, to animals or to humans. Here, the entities in question and the causal mechanisms are different; yet, the mathematical law is the same. The correspondence between such mechanisms is due to the fact that entities can be considered as systems.[3]

Systems can be defined by (a) the number of participating elements, (b) the element types, or (c) the elements' relations. In cases (a) and (b) systems are understood as the addition of elements in isolation. In case (c), not only the quantity and types of elements should be known, but also their relations. Definitions (a) and (b) are summative, while (c) is the constitutive feature of the system. Therefore, System Theory studies relations between elements forming wholes; it defines systems not by the properties of constituent parts, but by their organisation. On this perspective, systems are 'constructs' of interacting and functionally related elements, forming a complex whole.[4] [See figure 1]

1 J. H. Holland cited in Waldrop (1992).
2 Von Bertalanffy (1968) p. 4.
3 Von Bertalanffy (1968) p. 32.
4 **ibid.,** p. 54.

Equilibrium, open and closed systems In order to organise, systems must use energy. Particular qualities appear in accordance with the way energy is acquired to attain organisation. According to science, systems can be observed because differences exist, thus, to characterise a system is to establish the differences distinguishing it from its environment. A system's boundary is real or fictitious, yet in principle open or closed to the exchange of energy with its corresponding environment.[5]

In life energy disperses or dissipates. According to thermodynamics, the produced work of a system is not equal to the energy it consumes. This means there is a portion of non-useful energy escaping the work-energy equation: entropy is introduced as a function of this quantity. Because energy is lost in all transactions entropy always increases with time, reaching a maximum value of equilibrium where no other process can alter it.[6]

Entropy yields to ideas on probability, known as 'the arrow of time'. Accordingly, entropy's tendency to increase signifies change is irreversible, making systems forget initial order and evolve towards states of disorder and equilibrium. This explains why the past is remembered and not the future; the higher probability of seeing coffee cups breaking into pieces, rather than visualising pieces gathering to become cups. Furthermore, the fact that a group of elements can be organised in many different ways, but what is called 'an organised structure' or 'beauty', such as a cell, a living tissue, a painting, a building, or a city, is largely less probable than the total number of configurations of its participating elements.[7]

Now, how do systems acquire energy and produce work? How do we cope with the fact that life is full of improbable and unstable organisations? If an augmentation on the level of organisation is associated with a lowering of entropy, then to re-organise, systems must restore the lost portion of non-useful energy. Accordingly, systems must either possess internal sources of energy, or 'borrow' it from the environment. A system is named *'closed'* when no exchange with the environment is produced, and *'open'* if imports and exports occur. Examples of open systems are living organisms; for them to survive, which is to maintain far-from-equilibrium, means to exchange energy with the environment.[8]

Complexity and complex adaptive systems Open systems introduced a first notion of complex-systems, as the battle against reductionism defended the holistic perspective by postulating 'the whole is more than the sum of its parts'. Further developments followed spin-offs from System Theory and Cybernetics, concentrating on feedback, self-regulation and control. Current approaches study mechanisms sustaining complexity, focusing on adaptive systems, chaos, genetic algorithms and cellular automata.[9]

As presented by Weaver, complexity begins with simple systems. Those described by two or three elements where calculations can be easily solved. Further, there is 'disorganised complexity', where the amount of elements increases, but because there are no (observable) relations among them, recognisable patterns are not generated. Finally there is 'organised complexity' where the number of elements is large and multiple relations generate patterns. Complex systems are therefore defined as composed of many elements interacting with each other, producing varied patterns of behaviour at different levels.[10]

Complex adaptive systems (CAS) are of particular interest because their elements, denominated 'agents', are active. This means they change behaviour in accordance with past experience, necessity or will. Such adaptation produces feedback loops at micro levels, which simultaneously generate organisation patterns at other levels. Accordingly, CAS progress on the basis of their participant's agency, represented in their adaptive capacity; therefore, their control is not exerted from external sources, let's say from a manager or a pre-defined action plan, but from the aggregation of individual needs. Bird flocks, crowds, traffic, cities and markets are examples of CAS, as composing agents adapt to the actions of neighbours, generating higher levels of organisation in the form of recognisable patterns.[11] It could be argued then, that for CAS, the division system-environment is vague, as the openness of the organisation of composing parts and sub-systems, constantly re-generates dynamic environments. Although a definition of the environment is possible, its constitution changes in time, as agents' actions are part of other agents' environments. [See figure 2]

Urban transformation as a complex adaptive system Taking into account the increasing necessity of exchange and competition across territories, urban transformation can be firstly understood as an *open* system. By exchange it is meant that as a requirement to progress, people, goods and information are in constant movement from one place to another. Accordingly, common activities of daily urban life are carried on with the movement of commuters, immigration or tourism, the trading of materials and merchandises, or the use of virtual commerce, businesses and non face-to-face contacts. To support these activities, transport infrastructures, such as air, sea, road or train networks, and information and communication technologies, such as Internet, digital or wireless communication become the usual aspects to constantly update in the improvement of the functioning of urban landscapes. [See figure 3]

Parallel to the need for exchange, competition between cities and regions plays an ever-increasing role. Thus, with the augmentation in communication, territories follow a double process of

5 Wagensberg (1985) p. 29.
6 Wagensberg (1985) p. 46; Prigogine and Stengers (1984) p. 111.
7 Prigogine and Stengers (1984) p. 122; Wagensberg (1985) p. 30.
8 Wagensberg (1985) p. 46; Prigogine and Stengers (1984) p.127; Von Bertalanffy (1968) p. 39, p. 121, p. 141.
9 Simon (1996) p. 169.
10 Waldrop (1992) p. 11; Simon (1996) p. 183; Johnson (2000) p. 47.
11 Holland (1995) p. 3; Waldorp (1992) p. 10, p. 145; Johnson (2000) p. 39.

homogenisation, because it is easier to 'copy and paste' aspects from one place to another, and differentiation, because with the increment in similarities and correspondences across territories, competition and diversity become alternative strategies to improve performance.[12] Competition is exerted with strategies of branding – through events, fairs, promotion of architectonic features or city centres – ; plans to attract global, national and regional investment – such as new centralities, logistic platforms or the implementation of the so-called 'key' projects – ; the creation of new kinds of coalitions to improve performance – among governments and companies, nations and regions, etc. – ; and the appearance of new monitoring systems to observe and rank spatio-economic development. Both exchange and competition enlarge the performative capacity of towns, cities, regions and nations. They imply an increase in the extent of relations and territorial openness. [See figure 4]

Furthermore, the open scenario becomes *complex*, as urban transformation is influenced by social fragmentation and spatial connectivity, both introducing new sources for participants' agency. Accordingly, current conditions of uncertainty and disbelief in progress and institutions enhance individualisation, and particular and diverging forms of action and legitimation appear.[13] In the meantime, new spatial situations of connectivity permit countless relations among this fragmented variety of participants, bringing additional conditions of immediacy and interaction.[14] The result is the complexification of the process of transformation by the involvement of larger amounts of participants and the facilitation of their interactions. This scenario affects transformation both in social and spatial terms. Socially, with the appearance of non-public institutions, private and public associations and the increasing participation of independent groups in the intervention and transformation process; and spatially, with the blurring of territorial and political boundaries, and in consequence, the rising of all sorts of local, regional, national and transnational territorial organisations. Spatial configuration under these conditions is subject to the emerging logics of location and organisation recurring on everyday urban discourse: new centralities, suburbanisation, agglomerations, logistic platforms, hubs, teleports, mainports, enclosed or segregated communities, networks, regions and so on.

Finally, openness and complexity imply a notion of *adaptability*, as transformation depends on the capacity to adjust to contextual conditions: 'Adaptation in biological usage, is the process whereby an organism fit itself to its environment.'[15] Since the social and spatial contexts permit interactions at several levels of scale, local territories and foreign influences adjust to the effects of each other. Territories no longer operate on their own, but respond to the actions of others. Municipalities, regions, nations and international groups participate or detach from associations on varied levels of scale; conflicts and differences mean adaptations must occur. For this reason, it is not strange to see cities adapting to global economies, regions to population change and populations to new urban conditions. All of these systems and subsystems are dynamically interrelated, adapting and affecting the structure and constitution of each other.

In conclusion, in the complex-adaptive-system of urban transformation, both spatial and social conditions trigger the transformation potential of each other. From this point of view, urban transformation assembles the unfinished and changing pattern emerging from the dynamic interactions among participants and territories: individual faculties, collective institutions, social trends, spatial capacities, economic ability, chance and opportunities mix; the outcome of this combination is the city at a specific time.

Urban intervention: the taming of the beast and the politics of design A big question in this complex adaptive scenario is how can intervention occur within the dynamic settings of urban transformation? What are intervention's power, role of action, position and attitude? And what are the means to be utilised to face these intricate conditions?

The first notions on urban intervention as a discipline or practice appeared in modern times when techniques of design tackled the problem from the adaptation perspective. Thus, circumstances originated at the Industrial Revolution lead to the birth of what we know today as urban or town planning: the idea was to adapt urban milieus to new social and technical conditions.[16] A modern approach to intervention is therefore based on the 'know-ability' of factors affecting outcomes; to each input a defined response, so to speak. Prediction and calculation were based on this essential loop.

Yet, the acknowledgment of these new technical and social conditions yielded to standardisation, repetition, and the well-known division of labour. Production skills were arranged in accordance to hierarchical needs and organisation transferred power from key workers to less-important employees and finally to machines. Routines, repetition and time management over assembly lines intended overall control of processes; starting from the causes (means), which on an outcome-oriented production (aims), could not generate anything different than predefined results. These processes, usually referred to as 'Fordism' – because of its association with mass production- or 'Taylorism' – because of the introduction of new management paradigms – radically changed conceptions of organisation at the time. Among these concepts, the introduction of hierarchy, control, mastery, and the abstraction of qualities into quantities developed a scenario of power and command: the 'makeability' or the 'engineering of society'.

12 Ascher (2004).
13 Beck (1993); Giddens (1990); Lyotard (1984).
14 Ascher (2004); Lash (2001); Urry (2003).
15 Holland (1995) p. 7.
16 Bruton (1974) p. 9; Ascher (2004) p. 25; Hall (2000).

In the urbanisation arena, science, technology and production contributed to the creation of adverse spatial qualities, but in the meantime offered the means to control life and the environment in an unprecedented manner. Thus, as industrialisation and urbanisation seemed to endanger quality of life, modern urban intervention followed the organisational trends of the time, and proceeded with an attitude towards rational order, authority and coordination.[17] Accordingly, if there is anything in common among the forerunners of modern urban intervention – Howard, Wright and Le Corbusier – and their dreams – Garden City, Broadacre City and Contemporary City, respectively – it is the fact of visualising humankind capable of directing and controlling its own development.[18] In this manner, their models, nevertheless constructs of outstanding qualities and revelation, exalted the belief people had in the capacity to recognise and organise constraints to rationally 'put in order' spatial and social matters.

Now, to these circumstances the demands for fast and productive solutions inherited from the wars must be added. The result is the reinforcement of a legacy towards production by means of recognition, domestication and organisation of the variables affecting outcomes. In accordance with these logics, urban areas grew initially under the demands of industrialisation and the impact of the extension of transport systems, which generated patterns of decentralised housing settlements and industrial states; and subsequently, under the demands of the 'post war planning machine' and the redistribution of population and employment offer, which generated modern types of housing and new towns after World War II.[19] [See figure 5]

However, modern techniques for intervention are distant from the complex-adaptive transformation scenario described earlier in this paper, as the legacy on command, knowledge and controlled organisation suppose designers, planners or social workers sitting behind their drawing boards regulating the outcome of the transformation. According with this visualisation, the 'matter' with which such designers work is submissive and passive, comprehensively known, and characterised as possessing no agency. While what is currently known about transformation processes, leads towards an understanding of the impossibility of acquiring full-knowledge and the increasingly active involvement of interested and affected participants. Accordingly, architects and planners operate with little information, fragmented reasoning, diverging needs and several constraints. Hence, under what seems to be a collection of 'hidden logics' intervention cannot concentrate on planned results, but take into account the collective actions and decisions of an ever-increasing multitude of related parts and participants.[20] It is no accident that architecture has been presented as a 'chaotic adventure', and control as the main pitfall of urbanism.[21]

But it is Manuel DeLanda [2002] who clearly distinguishes between these two traditions, namely those working with the passive or active role of matter in design as two different philosophies of design. Thus, drawing from Deleuze's notions on the immanence of matter, and to introduce materials as active participants in the design process, he explains the materials' ability to organise as a condition capable to introduce their participation in the design procedure. Accordingly, what science has denominated phase transitions, 'those critical points in which materials change structure, such as the condensation of steam into liquid droplets, or the crystallisation of water into ice', are key moments in understanding matter's active role in the design process.

The effects of this organisational ability are exemplified with the way metallurgy has developed in history. Accordingly, in the past, blacksmiths worked with active matter, as materials came from different sources and were characterised as possessing heterogeneous qualities. This fact would demand extra creativity from them, as they were obliged to have notions on the materials' mixtures, impurities and differences in melting points, and work with these variations in order to produce required consistencies; for example, cooling them off more rapidly or slowly to achieve different levels of resistance and flexibility. With the advent of modern techniques of metallurgy and the need for speed and productivity, actions were routinised and standardised, and the process obliged to conceive matter as a passive element. Averaging and regularising these differences meant materials were made obedient and homogenised, excluding all possible variations in the outcome by fixing the elements and conditions to generate it.

De Landa makes the distinction between these two philosophies with the fact that in working with active matter, the designer cannot impose a pre-established or pre-conceived idea into the design. Thus, as materials are not unresponsive containers of mental ideas imposed from the outside, they become operative participants in the accomplishment of the design process. In this sense, the designer works with the material idiosyncrasies and particular behaviours respecting their influence in the process and allowing their agencies to affect possible outcomes. In his view, designers, as much as craftsmen in the past, should act more as triggers or facilitators for natural or emergent behaviour, than commanders imposing desires from outside the process. The designer's ability lies therefore in the competence to work with heterogeneous components and in the mediation between them to generate new modes of articulation.

Now, let us summarise the standpoints throughout this paper. On the one hand, there is urban transformation as an open, complex, and adaptive system. In this system, urban transformation is the result of the open interaction and adaptation between diverse participating elements.

17 Cherry (1980); Sutcliffe (1980).
18 Fishman (1977).
19 Hall (1975) p. 99.
20 DeLanda (1997) p. 17; Boyer (2003); Forester (1989) p. 48.
21 Koolhaas (1998).

Accordingly, spatial and social conditions interact with each other, and the transformation equation is solved every time there is adaptation between them: territorial potentialities mix with needs and desires, and the outcome is the city at a specific time. The consequence of seeing transformation in this manner is the fact that intervention is conditioned to take into account the active role of the (spatial and social) matter it deals with. On the other hand, there is the legacy of modern techniques of production and organisation, which made traditional approaches to design and intervention operate against the active-matter-notion. Thus, the use of command, hierarchy and power utilised matter as an inert container or passive receptacle. For the urban intervention arena this meant space and society were seen as inactive and mouldable, their capacity to act disqualified.

Now, it is not difficult to challenge modern techniques for design and intervention by considering the active role of space and society, as on an open, complex and adaptive perspective is hard to conceive of anything without agency or devoid of being in action. As we also know from DeLanda, urban dynamics arise from the flow of matter and energy though different territories generating landscapes of possibilities and constraints. However, 'urban dynamics also include an analysis of the institutions that inhabit cities, whether the bureaucracies that run them or the markets that animate them.'[22] Transformation is therefore better described as the result of continuous action and reaction processes, adaptations between the spatial (flows of matter and energy) and the social (of markets and bureaucratic organisations). Influences, different rationales, levels, orders, permissions and resistance are therefore the forces within the process. Is anybody or anything not inflicting, not affecting, or being inactive?

If DeLanda's notions on active matter and design are correct, then the politics behind design processes can be changed. Accordingly, the agency and disobedience of the participating elements in the procedure would alter hierarchical orders and the uses of power in the course of actions. Notions of control and expertise, traditionally linked to top-down approaches would be drawn against personalisation and new senses of equality oriented towards bottom-up or emergent attitudes. Designers in this perspective would become more transparent and less dominant. Thus, instead of determining the elements and actions to compose a plan, their task would become to mediate and orchestrate wishes and needs alongside potentials and opportunities coming from different participating levels.

Within the contemporary intervention scene, some attitudes towards this mediating way of operation are already present. One of them, pointing at democratising intervention, yields at seeing transformation as the solution of conflicts and differences among interested and affected participants. Accordingly, based on existence of a large variety of cultural and social standpoints and backgrounds, the city is seen as a field for negotiation and discussions where conciliation, total solutions, or overall consensus are difficult to achieve. Here, the politics of design are a case of putting democracy into practice: to collaborate in the joining of individual action in favour of social wealth without giving exclusive benefit to one or the other.[23] Whoever is behind the making of the plan, observes the needs of the different parties and on the basis of knowledge and social justice must arbitrate to find solutions.[24] The main obstacles this approach confronts are firstly related to the fidelity of the communication process, as it presupposes parties know what is necessary and how to communicate their necessities; and secondly, related with the negotiation process, as in making deliberations among groups being neutral is difficult and self-interests and pressures might always be present.

Another approach leads towards intervention as the accomplishment of a sort of infrastructure into which future actions occur. The characteristic of this type of procedure is to arrange a set of conditions, usually in diverse levels of scale and time frames which would in turn, trigger other participants actions. 'Infrastructure works not so much to propose specific buildings on given sites, but to construct the site itself.'[25] The idea is to offer 'some broad frame of reference, which gives guidance to lower level activities.'[26] This kind of intervention operates on a strategic nature, as its procedure concentrates on the implementation of particular actions ranging from projects, regulations or guidelines, which encompass the minimum but most important principles for future operation. During the process, aims and means can be evaluated and improved in accordance with feedback received from related participants.[27] The task for the making of such a plan is to find arguments to set the initial conditions, and to continuously elaborate by means of explorations, a body of knowledge of the possible outcomes and alternatives, and desirable or unwanted results. It can be argued then, that although the process broadens its political realm by allowing participation of varied actors, the initiative, guidance and arbitration are still conceived in hierarchical fashion; let us say the limit on command is diminished and hierarchies are reduced.

Finally, with the advent of computer technology, the intervention process cannot only be accompanied by more action among participants and less guidance or command from the top, but also run in parallel with varied sorts of simulation, diagramming, decision-making, prediction and optimisation models and techniques. In this scenario, models can become an aid to making decisions, as they are explorative tools to produce novel spatial configurations, or machines to process vast amounts of information rapidly.[28] Further, they contribute to the acknowledgment of contextual influences as outcomes can be modelled in relation to other objects, agencies, flows,

22 DeLanda (1997) p. 29.
23 Healey (1997).
24 Friedmann (1987); Sager (1994).
25 Allen (1999).
26 Faludi and van der Valk (1994) p. 2.
27 Rosemann (2000).

etc. defining an active space of force and motion; thus, shifting from a passive space of static coordinates to an active space of interactions.[29] Computer tools are consequently of particular importance because they can rapidly simulate the effects of large chains of nonlinear feedback processes, and because, with the use of algorithms they can bring virtual elements together and simulate the interaction. In certain cases, these combinations can produce emergent and random outcomes, which in turn, can be of enormous aid to the design process.[30]

In all cases, and considering the relational complexity of urban transformation processes, the idea of the designer as an omnipotent creator is fading and moving towards a more 'transparent' role. Even with the increasing competition, which in many cases derives the need to implement focal projects where certain buildings or areas must be designed as 'jewellery', there is always an influencing context in which the architect or the planner is accompanied by technical, economic and social constraints; as De Landa reminds us, even the issue of authorship is at stake. In this scenario, intervention mediates between theory and practice, expertise and everyday life, fixed and variable conditions. The varied perspectives and wishes of participants filter through issues of purpose or intentionality. The task has become to handle and orchestrate the agency of participating elements, factors and actors, and to steer the emergence of situations; thus to consider intervention, and in consequence design, as one of the -many- variables affecting the transformation outcome.

> The macrobehaviour is another matter. You don't control that directly. All you can do is set up the conditions that you think will make that behaviour possible. Then you press play and see what happens. [31]

28 Allen (1998) p. 242.
29 Lynn (1998).
30 DeLanda (1997) p. 17.
31 Steven Johnson (2001).

Bibliography

Allen, S. **Points + Lines, Diagrams and Projects for the city**. New York: Princeton Architectural Press, 1999.

Allen, S. 'Terminal Velocities', in: Beckmann, J. **The Virtual dimension: Architecture, Representation, and Crash Culture**. New York: Princeton Architectural Press, 1998.

Ascher, F. **Los nuevos principios del urbanismo**. Madrid: Alianza, 2004.

Beck, U. **Risk Society; Towards a New Modernity**. London: Sage, 1993.

Boyer, C. 2003. 'Playing with information in the XXI Century,' in: Van Eldijk, Rosemann, Read (Editors) **Future City**. London: Routledge, 2003.

Bruton, M. J. **The Spirit and Purpose of Planning**. London: Hutchinson, 1974.

Cherry, G. 'Aspects of twentieth-century planning,' in: Cherry, G. (Editor) **Shaping an Urban World**. London: Mansell, 1980.

DeLanda, M. **A Thousand Years of Non-linear History**. New York: Zone Books, 1997.

DeLanda, M. 'Philosophies of Design, the case of modelling software,' in; Salazar, J; Ferré, A; Gausa, M; Prat, R., Sakamoto, T. and Tetas, A. (Editors). **Verb Architecture Boogazine No. 1: Authorship and Information**. Madrid: Actar Press, 2002.

Faludi, A. and Van der Valk, A.J. **Rule and order; Dutch planning doctrine in the twentieth century**. Dordrecht: Kluwer Academic Publishers, 1994.

Fishman, R. **Urban Utopias in the Twentieth Century**. New York: Basic Books,1977.

Forester, J. **Planning in the Face of Power**. Berkeley: University of California Press, 1989.

Friedmann, J. **Planning in the Public Domain: From knowledge to action**. Princeton: Princeton University Press, 1987.

Giddens, A. **The Consequences of Modernity**. Cambridge: Polity, 1990.

Hall, P. **Urban and Regional Planning**. London: Newton Abbot – David and Charles, 1975.

Hall, P. 'The Centenary of Modern Planning,' in Freestone, R. (Editor) **Urban Planning in a Changing World**. New York: Routledge, 2000.

Healey, P. **Collaborative planning: Shaping Places in Fragmented Societies**. Vancouver: University of British Columbia Press, 1997.

Holland, J. **Hidden Order: How Adaptation Builds Complexity**. New York: Perseus Books, 1995.

Johnson, S. **Emergence: The Connected Lives of Ants, Brains, Cities, and Software**. New York: Touchstone, 2001.

Koolhaas, R. & Mau, B. **S, M, L, XL**. New York: The Monacelli Press, 1998.

Lash, S. 'Informationcritique,' in: Graafland, et al., **Cities in Transition**. Edited Hauptmann, D. Rotterdam: 010 Publishers, 2001.

Lyotard, J.F. **The Postmodern Condition: A Report on Knowledge**. Minneapolis: University of Minnesota Press. 1984.

Prigogine, I. and Stengers, I. **Order out of Chaos, Man's New Dialogue with Nature**. New York: Bantam Books, 1984.

Rosemann, J. 'The Conditions of Research by Design in Practice'. In **Conference Proceedings A. Research by Design International Conference**. TU Delft, Faculty of Architecture. Delft: DUP Science, 2001.

Sager, T. **Communicative Planning Theory: Rationality versus power**. Aldershot: Avebury, 1994.

Simon, H. **The sciences of the artificial**. Cambridge: MIT Press, 1996.

Sutcliffe, A. 'The debate on nineteenth-century planning,' in: Sutcliffe, A. (Editor). **The Rise of Modern Urban Planning**. London: Mansell, 1980.

Urry, J. **Global Complexity**. Cambridge: Polity Press, 2003.

Von Bertalanffy, L. **General System Theory: Foundations, Development, Applications**. New York: Brazillier, 1968.

Wagensberg, J. **Ideas Sobre la Complejidad del Mundo**. Barcelona: Tusquets Editors, 1985.

Waldrop, M. **Complexity: The Emerging Science at the Edge of Order and Chaos**. London: Viking, 1992.

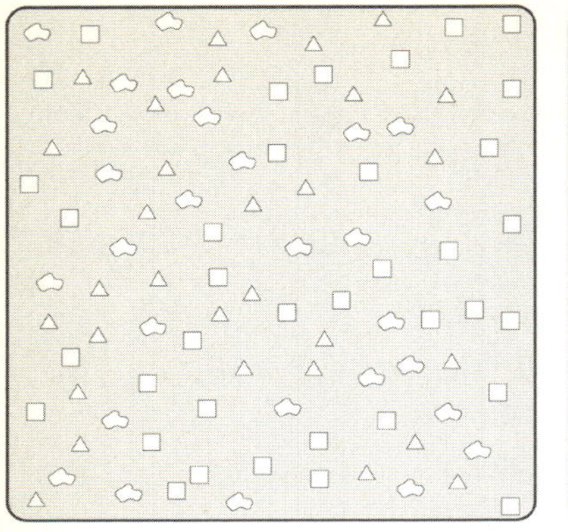

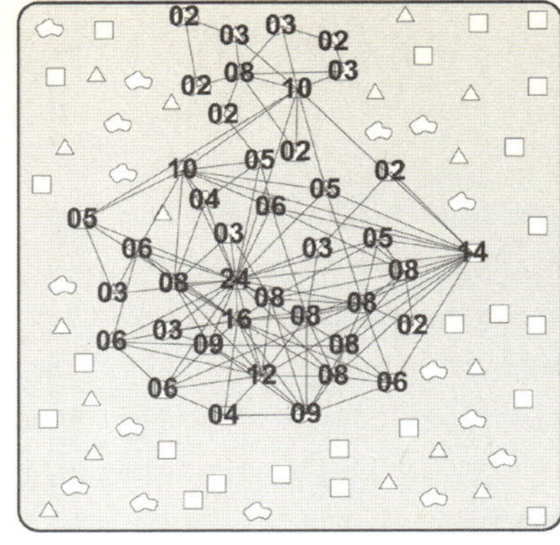

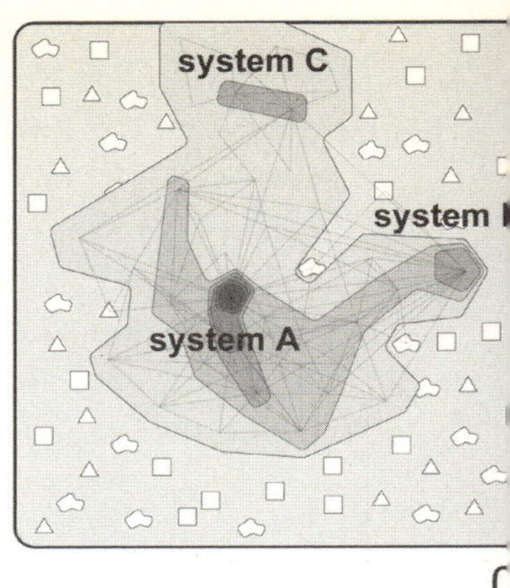

[1] 01 02

Index	Value	Change Net / %	Market Status
NASDAQ Composite Index	2133.67	12.20 ▲ 0.58%	Closed
NASDAQ-100 Index	1556.17	5.12 ▲ 0.33%	Closed
American Stock Exchange Composite Index	1874.94	8.89 ▲ 0.48%	Closed
Dow Jones Industrial Average Index	11045.28	56.19 ▲ 0.51%	Closed
Standard and Poor's 500 Index	1250.56	6.06 ▲ 0.49%	Closed
New York Stock Exchange Composite Index	7966.79	42.17 ▲ 0.53%	Closed
30 year Treasury Bond Index	52.72	0.15 ▲ 0.29%	Closed
13 Week T-Bill Index	48.50	0.15 ▲ 0.31%	Closed
CBOE Gold Index	137.28	1.53 ▲ 1.13%	Closed

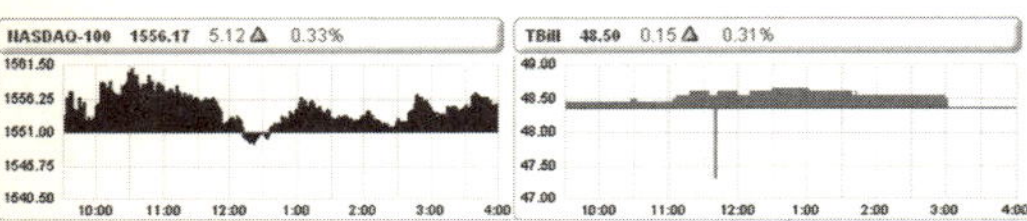

[2]

1 Abstract representation of a system:
1) Elements
2) Relations
3) Perceived systems in accordance to existing relations.
2 Examples of complex adaptive systems.
3 Information and communication technologies:
1) Schiphol International Airport, The Netherlands
2) Freight Traffic by Truck in the US. Retrieved October 2005, From http://ops.fhwa.dot.gov/freight/freight_analysis/state_info/texas/truckflow_tx.htm
3) Tokyo Subway Station
4) Tokyo elevated expressway
5) Global flows.

Next page:
4 Examples of studies or plans as respor
to competition:
1) Economic strategy for the Randstad. F
Randstad Regio association
2) Comet Report of Amsterdam Region. Retrieved October 2005, http://www.comet.ac.at
3) Medicon Valley Plan in Copenhagen. Retrieved October 2005 http://www.mediconvalley.com.
5 Modern urban Utopias:
1) Howard's Garden City
2) Wright's Broadacre City
3) Corbusier's City for Three Million Inhabitants.
6 Some urban transformation variables.

1

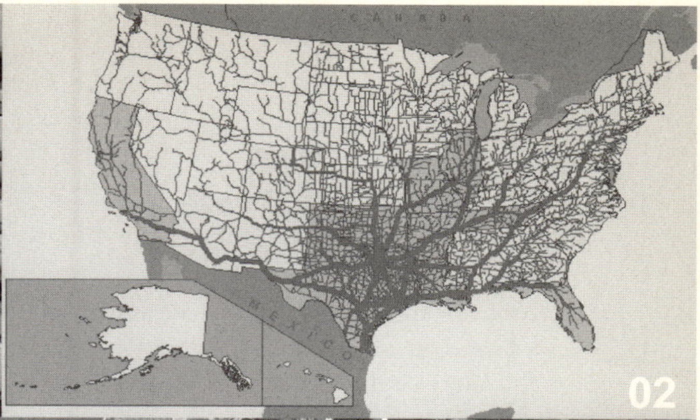

02

3

04

5

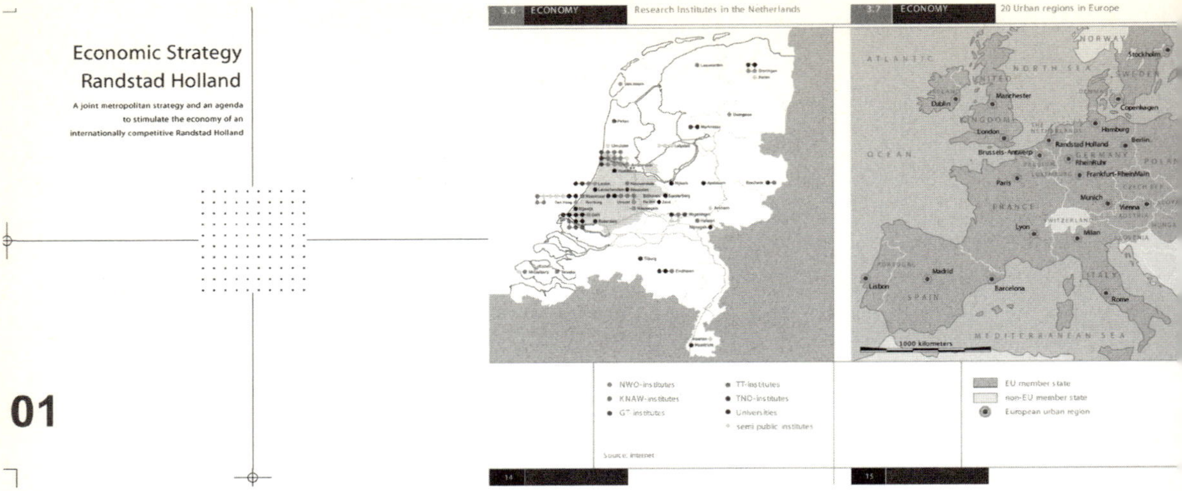

Economic Strategy
Randstad Holland

A joint metropolitan strategy and an agenda to stimulate the economy of an internationally competitive Randstad Holland

3.6 ECONOMY Research Institutes in the Netherlands

- NWO-institutes
- KNAW-institutes
- GT-institutes
- TT-institutes
- TNO-institutes
- Universities
- semi public institutes

Source: internet

14

3.7 ECONOMY 20 Urban regions in Europe

- EU member state
- non-EU member state
- European urban region

1000 kilometers

15

01

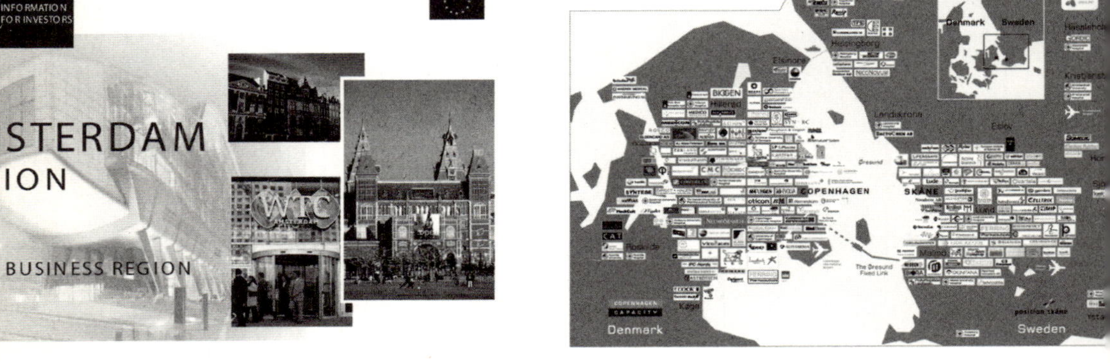

02

[4]

03

[5]

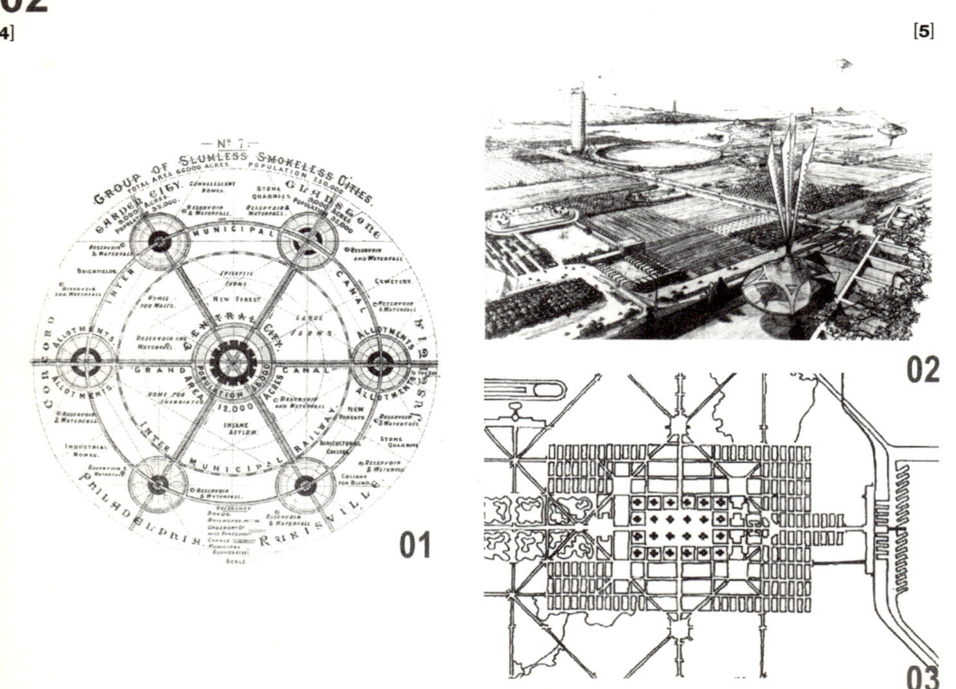

01

02

03

Vertrek 17 33 Stoptrein
MONTHLY SALES
plans
negotiation
time
landscape
culture
nature
politics
light
creativity
mainports
mobility
economy
speed
strategies
lifestyles
business
multitude
accesibility
density
free time
globalisation
capacity
height
conservation
ideas
image

The Body in Digital Architecture – From Representation to (Re)Invention

Henrietta Bier and Douglas Spencer

The morphogenetic concerns of contemporary 'digital architecture' are typically framed in terms of a paradigm shift from Euclidean to non-Euclidean. Whilst non-Euclidean geometry originates in the nineteenth century, its contemporary coalescence with the digital is based in the capability of computers to undertake extensive computations involved in the digital generation and physical materialization of its complex forms, prompting architecture to depart from modernism's standardization of forms and their usage.

The semiotic and linguistic paradigms that informed postmodern, deconstructive and neo-vernacular architectures are replaced with a renewed focus on the generation of form: a morphogenetic shift toward emergent potential and the generative in architecture. But this 'return to form' also risks and invites the easy critique of the 'merely formal', the charge of 'formalist' self-indulgence and social abnegation.

Sanford Kwinter has argued against the terms of this critique by taking issue with its equation of forms with objects. This 'sloppy' and 'untenable' conflation obscures the generative and dynamic character of form and wrongly equates it with the terminal and inert nature of the object. Form, he writes, is 'ordering action, a logic deployed, while the object is merely the latter's sectional image, a manifest variation on an always somewhat distant theme.'[1] So form is better understood as formation, a matter of emergence, organising principles and generative forces. Only when subjected to some degree of arrest, when fixed as a privileged moment in these processes does formation become an architectural object. And even at this juncture the embedded forces continue to resonate and to offer generative possibilities. There is no good reason to suppose that these possibilities preclude engagement with the body, or a social dimension.

In effect, however, the productive potentials of these architectures are typically foreclosed, arrested, and re-cast within the habitual conventions of architecture-as-sign: 'non-standard' architectures readily fall into line with the prevailing spatial politics of late capitalism. A larger cultural and economic formation reduces these novel formations to the 'merely formal' realm of urban objects.

Such politics, as Henri Lefebvre observed, foreground the consumption of space as a purely visual phenomenon in which the urban is reduced to a series of commodified signs of space, deployed as objects for consumption or signifiers of subjection.[2] Of course the pre-eminence of vision has a long precedence in Western metaphysics. From Plato's privileging of sight as the principal instrument of knowledge, through Albertian perspective, Cartesian philosophy and architectural modernism's emphasis on visual purity, the optical has been placed at the centre of our experience and representation of the world. This ocular-centric epistemology necessarily relegates other senses, principally those of touch, in a hierarchical schema that always elevates the visual over the haptic. The implications of this, as Merleau-Ponty indicated, are that perception becomes a disembodied affair where the physical gets subtracted from our experience of the world.[3]

1 Kwinter (2004) p. 96.
2 Lefebvre (1991).

On the back of this long-standing phenomenon, late capitalism invests social space with a spectacular orientation where architecture is mobilised for consumption by the 'tourist gaze.'[4] In this climate corporate and leisure economies support an architectural star system whose products iconically mark existing and emergent tourist destinations, metropolitan museums, department stores and global brand identities.

In this context the full import of emergent and non-standard digital architectures are reduced to the provision of the visually novel and its potential for iconic status. To put this another way, the evolutionary model, with its suggestion of development and change, and the possibilities of experiential and social transformation implicit in non-Cartesian geometries, is negated by this architecture's appropriation as a purely visual style, as the mere addition to a grammar of existing architectural semiotics. Existing spatial relations and the regimes in which these parcel and alienate human experience remain intact because the relationship between the human and the architectural remains one of consumer and 'spectacle' (as Lefebvre and the Situationists would have it). Supposedly non-Cartesian geometries and non-standard architectures are caught in some very Cartesian and very standard ways of operating in the world.

Some of these architectures actively accommodate such operations. Take Gehry's Guggenheim museum in Bilbao. The complexity of this building's form is frequently cited in relation to complexity theory and non-Euclidean geometry.[5] Certainly its shredded, deformed and recomposed architecture suggests the dynamic mobility and becoming of form in opposition to static and essential geometries, and the CATIA-based modeling techniques demonstrate the possibilities for translating the non-standard geometries of digital architectures into real-world iterations. But the proliferation of media images of this architecture transmute its complexity into a mere sign of 'complexity'. Complexity of form is commuted to consumption of architecture-as-sign, a global icon of the Gehry-Guggenheim brand. [See figure 1]

Inside the museum, where the building's non-standard geometries might have engaged the body with some challenging haptic encounters, the mind-body split in perception is maintained. The reassuring conventions of the museum experience are articulated about the visual as a source of fascination, and the haptic as an unremarkable and habitually-coded corporeal function. This is reinforced by the museum's ten traditional 'white cube' galleries, typologies that reproduce a disembodied vision. As Lars Spuybroek remarks of such spaces:

> We should always realise that this architecture is that of the Cartesian body: the part that sees is separated from the part that walks. You either walk or see. Perception and action are completely separated.[6]

Or take the work of Greg Lynn. This architecture employs digital technologies to produce formal structures akin to organic ones. Biological evolution's strategies and formations inspire their analogues in Lynn's formal vocabulary of 'skins', 'branches', 'folds' and 'teeth'. But whereas these are operative formations in biology – skins that shield or camouflage, teeth that bite or chew – inserted into complex fields of interaction, their tectonic analogues only bear witness to their own means of production as an end in itself. Lynn provides extensive accounts of design methods, technologies, and formal devices, but says very little about how people might interact with his architecture, or what uses might evolve from its novel forms. Together with his professed concern for accommodating the requirements of branding and identity this makes clear how his architecture is one of end results, of sign-objects, not formations. The vitalism and non-linearity of the biological world is not carried over into architectures that are content to provide illustrations of the organic in the fashion of a tectonically sophisticated revival of art nouveau symbolism.

Is there any possibility, then, that digitally enabled and non-standard architectures are capable of formation? Once instantiated as built architectures can their embedded generative potentials and resonances carry over into corporeal and social encounters that transcend the act of signification?

To achieve this, some sort of relay between architecture and the body would need to come into play – the type of encounter that visually-centred perception and experience implicitly precludes. And while these conventional techniques of perception are deeply grounded in habitual experience, there is no reason to suppose that the mind-body or optic-haptic split is an essential feature of our experience of the world. In fact, there are good grounds to suggest the opposite.

Cognitive architectures Writing of the necessary reintegration of visual perception with physical action, Henri Bergson argued, in Creative Evolution:

The distinct outlines which we see in an object, and which give it its individuality, are only the design of a certain kind of influence that we might exert on a certain point of space: it is the plan of our eventual actions that is sent back to our eyes, as though by a mirror, when we see the surfaces and edges of things.[7]

What Bergson intuits is given substance in current cognitive neuroscience: '[...]perception is more than just the interpretation of sensory messages', writes Alain Berthoz, 'Perception is constrained by action; it is an internal simulation of action. It is judgment and decision making, and it is anticipation of the consequences of action.'[8]

So the grounds from which to oppose the reduction of experience to the optical are not only political, or social, but go to the heart, mind and body of human cognitive processes. Vision, contra the belief in a disinterested aesthetic perception, prefigures action. Perception is tactical. It makes plans to engage with physical space. More than this, our cognitive architectures are

3 Merleau-Ponty (1962).
4 Urry (1990).
5 Taylor (2001).
6 Spuybroek (2002) p. 94.
7 Bergson (1998) p. 11.
8 Berthoz (2000) p. 9.

created through these engagements:

> 'In adopting what I call an "enactive approach to cognition"', writes Francisco J. Varela, 'two principles are essential: first, perception consists of perceptually guided action; and second, cognitive structures emerge from the recurrent sensorimotor patterns that enable action to be perceptually guided.'[9]

These structures, these 'cognitive architectures', can be standardised, habitually ingrained through our inhabitation of, and repetitive movement through, standardised spaces and architectures, so that they recede to the background of perceptual activity as established sensorimotor schemas. Or they can be non-standard, produced through non-orthogonal, non-Cartesian spaces. In this case the perceptual activity is foregrounded in its stimulation to seek out new sensorimotor schemas on the fly. All this is possible because the bodies we are, are not fully pre-formed, pre-programmed coherent wholes or absolute identities, but composed of 'microidentities',[10] lower level provisional assemblages themselves built up from microscopic responsive neuro-cognitive processes.

So, standardised orthogonal and Cartesian spaces play some part in reproducing standardised identities and experiences of space, and the attendant optic/haptic split with its larger implications for the social experience and politics of space. Conversely, how might non-standard digital architectures challenge these processes?

The oblique, and other functions The pioneering work of Claude Parent and Paul Virilio within the Architecture Principe group is instructive in this respect. In the late 60s Parent and Virilio challenged the dominance of the orthogonal in architecture and urbanism and its neutralising consequences for the human sense of movement and gravity. In its place they proposed a reinvigoration of this proprioceptive capacity through the function of the oblique: a surface for both circulation and inhabitation.

Lars Spuybroek of NOX has taken up this concern with proprioception in his own practice to challenge the sensory-deprivation of orthogonal architecture and its habitual splitting of perception from action and the optic from the haptic. '[...] subject and object', he writes, 'must be deeply intertwined, hardly distinguishable, as are action and perception, the motoric and the sensory. In short [...] a deep critique of the architectural programme, the mechanistic layout of all human behaviour within a built system purely viewed as tasks, routines and habits.'[11]

NOX's renovation within the V2 building in Rotterdam demonstrates these principles. The given orthogonal space of the office is deformed by the introduction of an interior landscape of hills and valleys and the animation of the space through fluctuating surface tensions that form a continuous feedback loop between bodies, furnishings, walls and floors. What NOX challenges here is the mechanisitic functionalism of architecture and its corresponding mechanisation of human spatial experience. [See figure 2]

Foreign Office Architects share a similar concern with the response to human movement and its organisation through haptic and proprioceptive techniques, as opposed to semiotic directions. Their Yokohama Port Terminal project employs a landform structure whose horizontality explicitly refuses the vertically orientated semiotic function typical of iconic architecture. Instead, like similar FOA projects concerned with transportation hubs, its unassuming formation is generated from studies and projections of circulation patterns and their management.
In their projects for urban and suburban parks FOA extend these processes beyond the limitative paradigm of efficiency. Their Downsview Park project in Toronto uses digital modelling techniques to generate artificial topographies that both facilitate traditional sports and offer the sensorimotor challenges sought in their more contemporary 'extreme' versions. The demand for such topographies by this kind of activity and other surfing and board sports indicates a real desire for the mobile haptic experience of non-orthogonal space, a demand that can evidently be served by the capacities of non-standard digital architecture.

SpaceCustomiser Exploring a similar concern with the potentials of the body's encounters with non-Euclidean geometries, SpaceCustomiser, a recent experimental project at Delft School of Design, inverts their relationship in making the moving body the generative source of non-standard formations. Registering the trajectories of the human body and its movements through space and then digitally redeploying this data to develop complex and curvilinear topologies, this project proposes an alternative digital design strategy.
The project draws extensively upon the specific properties of NURBS (Non Uniform Rational B-Splines), which are a mathematical model used to represent free-formed curves and surfaces. NURBS offer the capacity to produce and parametrically manipulate the typically complex curvilinear patterns generated in mapping the body's movements. [See figure 3]

What NURBS, as a means of non-Euclidean mapping and manipulation, offer to an exploration of the body's relationship to digital architecture, has been a significant question for the SpaceCustomiser project. Whilst it is easy to manipulate NURBS surfaces by pulling control points, the question of what this manipulation can do encompasses not only geometrical, but also architectural issues, since it involves axioms different from Euclid's and departs from architecture's long historical engagement with Euclidean geometry. In particular, the questions of what these methods imply for the body's representation and conceptualisation within architectural practice, the opportunities afforded to move beyond a standardising modularity, and the potentials for new and haptically orientated experiences of architectural space are worth exploring in this context.
In terms of the body's representation and conceptualisation, the project departs significantly from the use of the Cartesian spatial grid which plots spaces and bodies alike within a uniform

9 Varela (1992) p. 330.
10 **ibid.,** p. 328.
11 Spuybroek (1999) p. 58.

and static grid, *and* with the classically-based deployment of fixed proportional systems and harmonic values. In opposition to the modular and repetitive architecture of grids and proportions that follow from these conceptions, based on functional and formal rules, the curvilinear architecture of this project is developed and generated by tracking the movement of bodies (real, not ideal), in space and time. The curves abstracted from the body's movement in the project generate three-dimensional curves expressing a spatial and temporal trajectory.

This in turn generates a framework for a new and differentiated architectural space. In this sense SpaceCustomiser can be seen as a contemporary response to the Modulor (Le Corbusier, 1948). Le Corbusier's Modulor used measures of the human body in architecture by partitioning it into modules according to the golden section and two Fibonacci Series. It posited man as the measure of architectural space. But this broadly humanist approach, based upon an ideal and static human form (Corbusier imagined this to be best represented by a six foot tall English policeman),[12] necessarily results in a similarly uniform conceptualisation of built space, and its ideal form, as a logical corollary. In contrasts the representation of the body in the SpaceCustomiser follows a more Bergsonian logic in positing the body not as form but as movement. And it is the unique and durational character of each body's movements, not its static proportions that the project works with. The architecture that flows from this representation and conceptualisation affords the potential for architectures that are similarly differentiated and non-standardised. [See figure 4]

What NURBS offers to this enterprise is an effective means of dealing with the body represented and conceptualised in this fashion. Conventional Euclidean geometry would attempt to represent these patterns as a series of conjoined curves with fixed radial values, but would lose the real quality of the body's movement, which does not operate around discrete points of radial articulation, but within a complex topology of interrelated, parametric shifts. Alternatively, the non-Euclidean operation of NURBS can register and represent the motion of a body which is itself non-Euclidean more adequately: the technique's nodal manipulation of multiple curves operates in the same parametric fashion as the body's.

12 'One day when we were working together, absorbed in the search for a solution, one of us – Py – said: "The values of the "Modulor" in its present form are determined by the body of a man 1.75 m. in height. But isn't that a rather **French** height? Have you ever noticed that in English detective novels, the good-looking men, such as the policeman, are always six feet tall?' We tried to apply this standard: six feet=6 x 30.48=182.88 cm. To our delight, the graduations of a new 'Modulor', based on a man six feet tall, translated themselves before our eyes into round figures in feet and inches!" p56. The Modulor, Le Corbusier, English Edition, 1954.
13 Kolarevic (2003).
14 Slessor (1997).

Of course Le Corbusier's modulor-derived standardisation was intended as modernist architecture's contribution to the then dominant industrial and cultural paradigm of Fordism. Significantly, NURBS geometries, within the broader frame of digital design, suggest the means for architecture to transcend this standardisation not only on screen, but in its fabrication and production. In digital architecture architects no longer produce merely drawings, but *data*, which becomes a single source of design and fabrication,[13] implying that 'uniqueness is now as easy and economic to achieve as repetition.'[14]

The implementation of the physical model from digital data using such methods and techniques has been employed as crucial modelling tool within the SpaceCustomiser project. This method of modelling returns the digital formations to a three-dimensional iteration from which their potentials can be explored in terms of the uses, experiences and qualities that they might offer to the inhabitant or visitor. Rather than seeing in these novel forms a purely semiotic novelty, they are explored in terms of what they might offer to our haptic, embodied experience of built space. In these examples and experiments neither architectures nor bodies are taken as givens, as preinscribed and precoded entities, but through their mutual interaction and engagement, through generative processes, both achieve new modes of being and becoming. They indicate the potential for digital architectures to resonate with the social and cognitive practices of human bodies; to produce new spatial experiences that cut through the separation of perception from action, and point to the possibility of something more than the visual consumption of representational space – the possibility for invention, and reinvention between architectures and bodies.

Bibliography

Bergson, H. **Creative Evolution**. Translated by Arthur Mitchell. Mineola, New York: Dover Publications, 1998.

Berthoz, A. **The Brain's Sense of Movement**. Translated by Giselle Weiss. Cambridge, MA and London: Harvard University Press, 2000.

Kolarevic B. **Architecture in the Digital Age – Design and Manufacturing**, Spon Press, New York, 2003.

Kwinter, S. 'Who's Afraid of Formalism?' in S. Kubo and A. Ferré (eds), in collaboration with FOA, **Phylogenesis: foa's ark**, pp. 96-99. Barcelona: Actar/ICA, 2004.

Slessor C. **Atlantic Star**, Architectural Review: Museums, 1210, Emap, London, 1997, pp. 30-42.

Spuybroek, L. 'Deepsurface: The Univisual Image'. In S. Perella (ed.), **Hypersurface Architecture II** (pp. 58-59). Chichester, UK: Academy Editions, 1999.

Spuybroek, L. 'WET GRID – the soft machine of vision'. In N. Leach (ed.), **Designing for Digital World**, pp. 93-100. Chichester, UK: Wiley-Academy, 2002.

Lefebvre, H. **The Production of Space.** Translated by Donald Nicholson-Smith. Oxford, UK and Cambridge, US: Blackwell, 1991.

Merleau-Ponty, M. **Phenomenology of Pereception**. Translated by Colin Smith. London and New York: Routledge, 1962.

Taylor, M.C. **The Moment of Complexity**: Emerging Network Culture. Chicago: Chicago University Press, 2001.

Urry, J. **The Tourist Gaze: Leisure and Travel in Contemporary Societies**. London: Sage, 1990.

Varela, F. 'The Reenchantment of the Concrete.' In J. Crary and S. Kwinter (eds) **Zone 6: Incorporations**, pp. 320-338. New York: Zone, 1992.

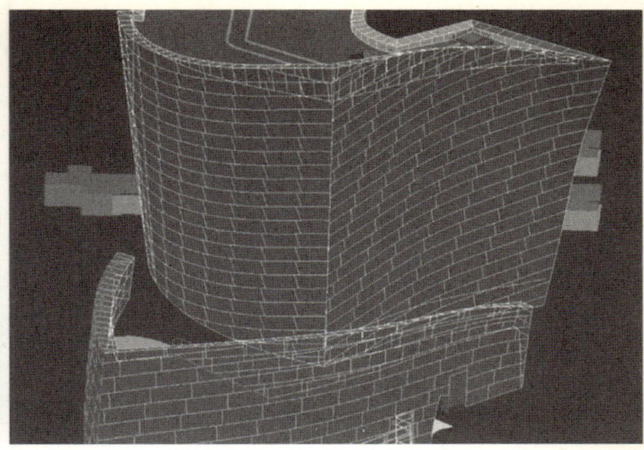

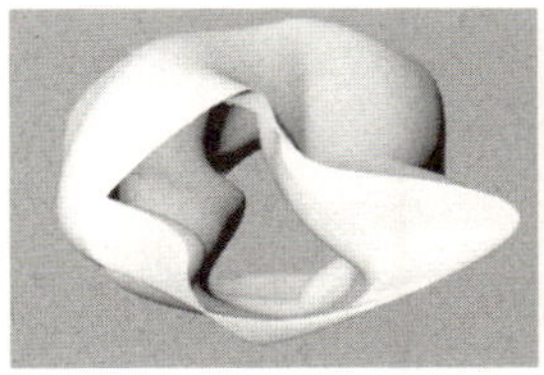

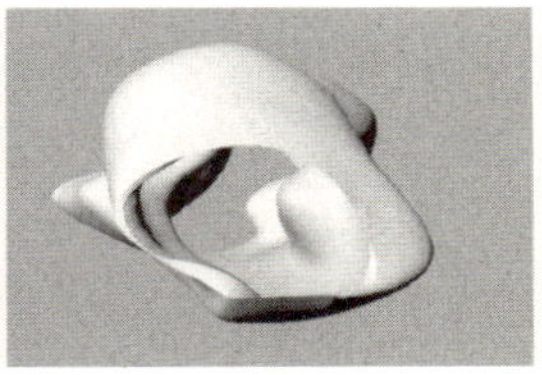

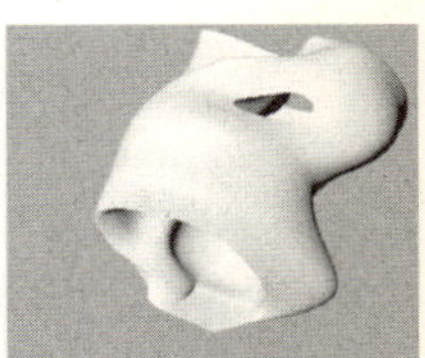

[3]

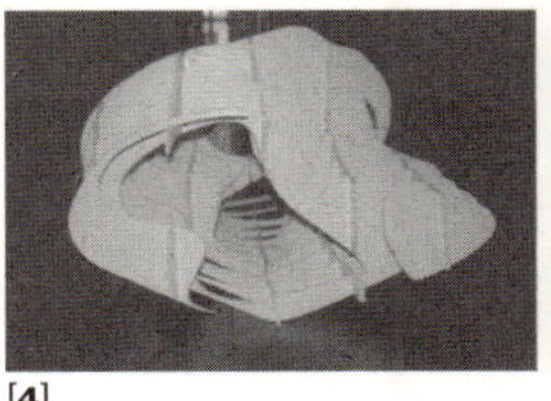

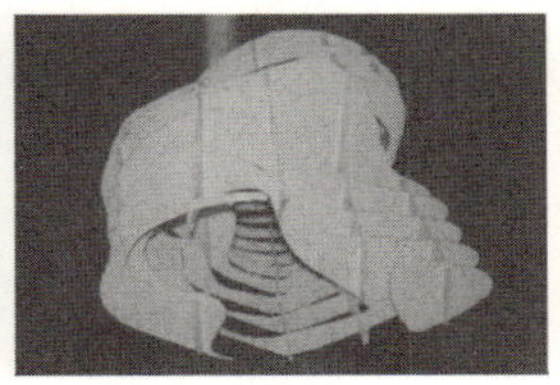

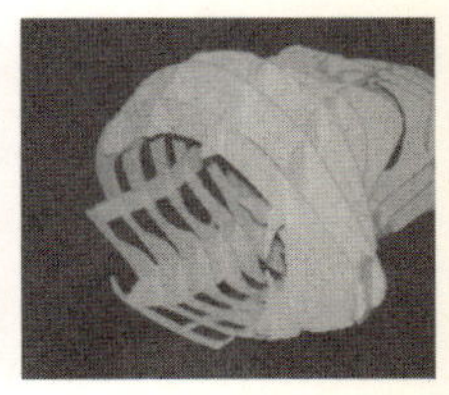

[4]

F. O. Gehry's Architecture – Construction
e and 3D-model. Source: J. Glymph –
olution of the Digital Design Process',
cle published in **Architecture in the**
gital Age, Ed. B. Kolarevic, Spon Press,
03.
FOA's Yokohama Terminal – Overview
l Pathway. Source: F. Moussavi et al. –
e Yokohama Project, Actar, 2002.
SpaceCustomiser – Digital Model.
urce: H. Bier.
SpaceCustomiser – Physical Model.
urce: H. Bier.

Credits

Delft School of Design Series on Architecture and Urbanism
Series Editor Arie Graafland

Also published in this series:
1 **Crossover. Architecture Urbanism Technology**
ISBN 978 90 6450 609 3
2 **The Body in Architecture**
ISBN 978 90 6450 568 3

De-/signing the Urban. Technogenesis and the urban image
Editors Patrick Healy and Gerhard Bruyns
Text editing Gijs van Koningsveld and John Kirkpatrick
Book design by Piet Gerards Ontwerpers (Piet Gerards and Maud van Rossum), Amsterdam
Printed by Snoeck Ducaju, Ghent

Photo credits
MVRDV p. 43
Arie Graafland cover

www.010publishers.nl

ISBN 978 90 6450 611 6